Published Comment on William Dean Howells Through 1920: A Research Bibliography

Clayton L. Eichelberger

G. K. HALL & CO., 70 LINCOLN STREET, BOSTON, MASS.

Library of Congress Cataloging in Publication Data

Eichelberger, Clayton L   1925-
    Published comment on William Dean Howells through 1920.

    Bibliography: p.
    Includes index.
    1. Howells, William Dean, 1837-1920--Bibliography.
I. Title.
Z8420.25.E38   [PS2033]   016.818'4'09   76-2030
ISBN 0-8161-1078-6

This publication is printed on permanent/durable acid-free paper
MANUFACTURED IN THE UNITED STATES OF AMERICA

Contents

Introduction

Henry David Thoreau, retiring from Walden Pond, explained the
reason for his withdrawal. "Perhaps it seemed to me," he wrote,
"that I had several more lives to live, and could not spare any more
time for that one." A similar thought came to my mind one warm afternoon last July when the vibrations of the Westminster chimes in the
university tower marked the hour of five and penetrated deep into the
library stacks. I shuffled the few notes which had resulted from a
full day of work into approximate order, ceased the business of com-
pilation, and walked into daylight where my family waited. Even at
the beginning, three years further back in time, I knew the task
would inevitably conclude in this way. Where William Dean Howells is
concerned, there is no end. Eventually one simply stops. So pervasive was his name in literary circles during the sixty productive
years of his life that there is no way to retrieve all the references
to him and his work, nor, given the minor nature of most of the references, would there be any reason to do so except to establish the
breadth of the Howells impact. After one has exhausted previous
listings and has gone further to search the most likely sources not
yet explored, he is still faced by hundreds of leads to ghostly
printings, minor publications, and dozens of newspapers no longer
readily accessible--many of them, if they still exist somewhere, in
the form of flaking pages that have already disintegrated to the
point that they will never be microfilmed. It is consoling to know
that immortality is rooted in the words of the artist rather than in
the words men speak and write about him.

Had I my way, I might choose to subtitle this listing "Chaff and
Otherwise," for a majority of the items precipitated by the Howells
name and entered on the pages of this volume have no real independent
value and are likely to offer only incidental and minimal advantage
to the dedicated scholar. The major entries are already known and
have been noted selectively in a number of earlier listings. Some of
them, indeed, have been given an extended and more permanent life in
critical anthologies such as Kenneth E. Eble's <u>Howells / A Century of
Criticism</u> and <u>The War of the Critics over William Dean Howells</u> by
Edwin Cady and David Frazier. One might argue that what remains
after such basic winnowing scarcely merits preservation. But all of

the independently insignificant items, assembled chronologically, do, in their variety, suggest the full contours and dimensions of a literary life; they do, in a sense, record the very rhythm and pitch of Howells' common day; and they do expose the manner in which literary information was shaped, distilled, and broadcast during the late-nineteenth and early-twentieth centuries.

This checklist (any greater claim would be pretentious) represents the nature of the coverage given to Howells and his work during his lifetime; quantitative focus, however, reflecting both abundance of comment and relative thoroughness of search, is on the last two decades of the nineteenth century, the most fruitful period in the career of this dean of realistic writers. The materials listed take many forms: interviews (included because Howells' comments are not only structured by the interviewer, but are also framed by and mixed with the interviewer's observations and questions), books, parts of books, critical appraisals, introductory surveys, biographical sketches, reviews, editorials, announcements, literary gossip, news items, tributes, advertisements, notes on serialization in contemporary magazines, poems, portraits, caricatures, cartoons. Although varied, in no way is this listing comprehensive. Checklists never are. For instance, I made no effort to record the widespread copying of a minor paragraph referring to Howells and traced by Noah Brooks in "The Evolution of a Newspaper Paragraph" (Item 663), although the fact that it was picked up by some two dozen newspapers that Brooks was aware of indicates the extensive interest in Howells throughout the American provinces; I have not attempted to find in published form (most of them probably were never published) the fifteen hundred tributes to Howells reportedly phrased by distinguished men and women on the occasion of his eightieth birthday; I have not sought to establish a full listing of the innumerable references to Howells' work appearing in literary gossip columns or in the widely prepared notes on the contents of contemporary magazines; I have not tried to identify and locate the school books in which elementary introductions to Howells undoubtedly appeared; I have not had access to the many lesser British periodicals and serials which must have echoed the national resentment of Howells' critical judgments; I did not even consider locating and listing the countless oblique and glancing references to Howells embedded in letters of the period and in the reviews of untold numbers of contemporaneous novels by other authors; I have mounted no systematic search for critical judgments in foreign languages of Howells and his work. "The material on Howells," one colleague said to me, " is a mountain." This listing is merely a core sample.

It is not, may I quickly add, without reason for being. As a research tool it does offer the scholar certain advantages: it integrates earlier listings of its type, it roughly doubles the number of items about Howells and his work previously recorded for the same period (except, perhaps, in the files of certain scholars), it provides clues about the nature and relative value of individual items difficult to come by, and it silently corrects bibliographic inaccuracies which are abundant in some published sources. That is not to say that this listing is without error. I can only claim that instead of relying on the accuracy of foregoing bibliographers, I have entered here as I found them only those items I have personally investigated or that have been recorded for me by direct request. The errors which remain are my own.

Yet another word about the scope of this particular volume is in order. Although I had originally intended to extend coverage to the present, the vastly proliferated comment on Howells and the Howells canon made some limiting factor imperative, and the temporal restriction to the lifetime of Howells, although arbitrary, seemed reasonable. Because more remained to be done in this earlier period, it was here I felt I could work more productively by both emending and adding bibliographic information. For subsequent years, Stanley P. Anderson's annotated "A Bibliography of Writing About William Dean Howells / Part Two: 1920-Present," American Literary Realism, Special Number (1969), 33-139, updated by standard sources such as American Literary Scholarship, Abstracts of English Studies, the quarterly bibliography in American Literature, and the MLA bibliographies, provides generally satisfactory coverage. Vito J. Brenni's William Dean Howells / A Bibliography, The Scarecrow Author Bibliographies, No. 9 (Metuchen, N. J.: Scarecrow Press, 1973), although unannotated, is also of value in locating materials if it is used cautiously. The bibliographic contribution of William Gibson and George Arms, of course, is both highly reliable and invaluable.

Arrangement of materials in this basically chronological listing is quite simple. Books and parts of books stand at the head of each annual grouping, followed immediately by annual serials and by seasonal quarterlies. Within the subsequent framework of individual months, monthlies are grouped ahead of the weeklies and dailies which are integrated and ordered by specific dates. Whenever two or more items share a single date, subarrangement is alphabetical. The checklist itself is preceded by an alphabetical listing of separately published Howells titles that attracted notice, each title accompanied by date of publication as a guide to the location of pertinent comment; it is followed by an index of identified authors of items included. No subject index is offered, partly because of the inadequacy of the annotations in this regard--the scant comments and quotations that serve as annotations are intended to suggest only the general attitude and focus of the commentator and not to specify the substantive range of his comment--and partly because most substantial pieces on Howells, including reviews, make such free reference to multiple titles that they could not be noted consistently without great redundancy.

Only first printings are given numbered status. Although I made no special effort to trace reprinting sequences, those reprintings of which I am aware are noted in the appropriate first-printing entry; and of those, the ones which occurred through 1920 are separately entered for cross-reference purposes but are not numbered. If specialists detect the absence of items customary in previous bibliographic listings on Howells, their omission can be accounted for in one of several ways: they are ghosts, they are empty citations containing no specific reference to Howells, they are reprintings for which I was unable to locate the first printing, they appeared in publications not accessible to me; or they were, simply and perhaps inexcusably, overlooked.

The modified MLA form of each entry is, I think, self-explanatory, except in regard to pagination. When comment on Howells and his work is embedded in a more general multi-page unit such as an editorial or review or gossip column, I have used the column heading (and subheading when appropriate), but in citing pagination I have directed the reader to the specific pages on which the reference to Howells appears. Although this may sometimes seem to be bibliographically confusing, especially as this listing is compared with previous ones, it seemed to me to be an expedient thing to do. Also potentially confusing is pagination for the multiple references to Laurence Hutton and John Kendrick Bang's "Literary Notes" column published in *Harper's* from 1886 to 1900. The usually four-page column that was placed immediately following the "Editor's Drawer" was separately paginated in each issue and, unfortunately, was rarely retained in the bound volumes. The Hutton and Bangs entries included here do accurately record the separate pagination. The full sequence of "Literary Notes," collected for publication elsewhere, should soon be available.

At the conclusion of exercises such as this one, credit and appreciation must be given, and I warmly do so, to any number of people, many of them nameless members of a dozen and more library staffs who contributed valuable assistance, often without knowing how helpful they were. More specifically I am indebted to all those specialists who have already published bibliographically on Howells, especially to James Woodress for the contribution he made in "A Bibliography of Writing About William Dean Howells / Part One: 1860-1919," *American Literary Realism*, Special Number (1969), 1-31, and to the people who compiled the informal Indiana listing on which his work is based; to Ulrich Halfmann and Don R. Smith for "William Dean Howells: A Revised and Annotated Bibliography of Secondary Comment in Periodicals and Newspapers, 1868-1919," *American Literary Realism*, 5 (Spring 1972), 91-121; and to William Gibson and George Arms for *A Bibliography of William Dean Howells* (New York: New York Public Library, 1948). I am further grateful to Lyle Kendall and George Fortenberry, my colleagues, and to Professors Gibson and Arms, David J. Nordloh, and Rudolf Kirk for their encouragement and advice; to Joseph DeFalco and Susan C. Baldwin, who searched unlikely sources and found little to report; to Professor and Mrs. John W. Nichol, Robert Rowlette, Gary F. Scharnhorst, Don Graham and his entire class at the University of Pennsylvania (Paul Bernard, JoAnn Bomze, Norman Carey, William Christ,

Introduction

Marianne Conod, Sharon Hiltz, George Pitts, and William Wright) for
their contributions as identified throughout the listing; to Mary A.
Price for her major help through the Interlibrary Loan division of
The University of Texas at Arlington library; to The University itself for providing some financial aid in the form of a Liberal Arts
Organized Research grant; to Mrs. Leslie Branyan, who assisted with
manuscript preparation; to a family tolerant of a library-burrowing
husband and father; and to Maggie, Madeline, Millicent, Mandy, Myrtle,
and Matilda, who provided between-the-lines adventure. Indeed so
large and varied were the roles of all these contributors that it is
to them I dedicate this work.

                                                            C.L.E.

Arlington, Texas
1 November 1975

Howells' Titles

Alphabetically arranged, with date of initial book publication

The Albany Depot (1892)
Annie Kilburn (1889)
April Hopes (1888)
Between the Dark and the Day-
    light (1907)
A Boy's Town (1890)
Bride Roses (1900)
Certain Delightful English
    Towns (1906)
A Chance Acquaintance (1873)
Christmas Every Day and Other
    Stories Told for Children
    (1893)
The Coast of Bohemia (1893)
A Counterfeit Presentment (1877)
Criticism and Fiction (1891)
The Daughter of the Storage and
    Other Things in Prose and
    Verse (1916)
The Day of Their Wedding (1896)
A Day's Pleasure and Other
    Sketches (1881)
Dr. Breen's Practice (1881)
The Elevator (1885)
Evening Dress (1893)
Familiar Spanish Travels (1913)
A Fearful Responsibility and
    Other Stories (1881)
Fennel and Rue (1908)
Five O'clock Tea (1894)
The Flight of Pony Baker (1902)
A Foregone Conclusion (1875)
The Garroters (1886)
A Hazard of New Fortunes (1890)
Heroines of Fiction (1901)

Hither and Thither in Germany
    (1920)
Imaginary Interviews (1910)
An Imperative Duty (1892)
Impressions and Experiences (1896)
An Indian Giver (1900)
Indian Summer (1886)
Italian Journeys (1867)
The Kentons (1902)
The Lady of the Aroostook (1879)
The Landlord at Lion's Head (1897)
The Leatherwood God (1916)
A Letter of Introduction (1892)
Letters Home (1903)
A Likely Story (1894)
Literary Friends and Acquaintance
    (1900)
Literature and Life (1902)
A Little Girl Among the Old
    Masters (1884)
A Little Swiss Sojourn (1892)
London Films (1906)
The Minister's Charge (1887)
Miss Bellard's Inspiration (1905)
A Modern Instance (1882)
Modern Italian Poets (1887)
The Mother and the Father (1909)
The Mouse Trap and Other Farces
    (1889)
My Literary Passions (1895)
My Mark Twain (1910)
My Year in a Log Cabin (1893)
New Leaf Mills (1913)
The Niagara Book (1893)
Niagara Revisited (1884)

An Open-Eyed Conspiracy (1897)
Out of the Question (1877)
A Pair of Patient Lovers (1901)
The Parlor Car (1876)
A Parting and a Meeting (1896)
Parting Friends (1911)
Poems (1873)
Poems of Two Friends (1860)
A Previous Engagement (1897)
The Quality of Mercy (1892)
Questionable Shapes (1903)
Ragged Lady (1899)
The Register (1884)
The Rise of Silas Lapham (1885)
Roman Holidays and Others (1908)
Room Forty-five (1900)
A Sea Change (1888)
The Seen and the Unseen at
    Stratford-on-Avon (1914)
Seven English Cities (1909)
The Shadow of a Dream (1890)
Sketch of the Life and Character
    of Rutherford B. Hayes
    (1876)
The Sleeping Car (1883)
The Sleeping Car and Other
    Farces (1889)
The Smoking Car (1900)
The Son of Royal Langbrith (1904)
Stops of Various Quills (1895)
The Story of a Play (1898)
Suburban Sketches (1871)
Their Silver Wedding Journey
    (1899)
Their Wedding Journey (1872)
Three Villages (1884)
Through the Eye of the Needle
    (1907)
A Traveler from Altruria (1894)
Tuscan Cities (1886)
The Undiscovered Country (1880)
The Unexpected Guests (1893)
The Vacation of the Kelwyns
    (1920)
Venetian Life (1866)
The Whole Family (1908)
A Woman's Reason (1883)
The World of Chance (1893)
Years of My Youth (1916)

William Dean Howells

1860

1 REDPATH, JAMES, ed. <u>Echoes of Harper's Ferry</u>. Boston:
   Thayer and Eldridge, 1860. Pp. 314-316. Brief reference.
   Whittier's "The Tree Poem" may be "more appropriate to
   Freedom's martyr, John Brown," than Howells' "Old Brown."
   Both poems are reprinted here.

2 "<u>Poems of Two Friends</u>." New York <u>Saturday Press</u>, 3 (28 Jan
   1860), [1]. Review.
   "Mr. Howells is a man of genius"--not of the highest
   order, but genius nevertheless. A striking indication of
   his genius "is the intense compression of style....
   Knowing that the best clothing for a beautiful thought is
   nudity, he has ordained his <u>thought</u> to be more than its
   <u>expression</u>. This is the imperial stroke of genius."
   Piatt is less gifted, but "the book will live."

3 [CONWAY, MONCURE D.] "<u>Poems of Two Friends</u>." <u>Dial</u> (Cincinnati), 1 (Mar 1860), 198. Review. Rpt. in part, <u>The War of</u>
   <u>the Critics over William Dean Howells</u>, ed. Edwin H. Cady
   and David L. Frazier (Evanston: Row, Peterson, 1962),
   p. 1.
   Although Howells seems to fear himself, and so needs
   time for development, his poems show genius and promise.

4 [LOWELL, JAMES RUSSELL.] "Reviews and Literary Notices."
   <u>Atlantic</u>, 5 (Apr 1860), 510-511. Review of <u>Poems of Two</u>
   <u>Friends</u>.
   Howells' verse shows "instinctive felicity of phrase."

1866

5 "Literature / Books of Travel." <u>Athenaeum</u>, No. 2014 (2 Jun
   1966), 734. Review of <u>Venetian Life</u>.
   "Americans seem especially tormented with a desire to
   discuss [Art], and usually discuss as awkwardly as

1866

("Literature / Books of Travel")
dogmatically." Howells is better when sketching "matters requiring less preparatory study."

6   "Politics, Sociology, Voyages and Travels." Westminster Review, 86 (Jul 1866), 108. Review of Venetian Life.
    Howells' "familiarity with both place and people often suggests to him little domestic dramas attached to the merest trifles that fall in his way, which he treats with a certain delicate humour that is very engaging."

7   "Notices of Books." Contemporary Review, 2 (Aug 1866), 594-596. Review of Venetian Life.
    "It is the very model of what a light book of travels ought to be. The author can instruct without prosing, and describe without boring. But moreover he is a genuine poet, with a loving eye for the beautiful, and the keenest sense of humour. The writing is positively creative."

8   [NORTON, CHARLES ELIOT.] "Venetian Life." Nation, 3 (6 Sep 1866), 189. Review.
    "No better book about Venice has been written since Beckford's sketches of the city, just before the French Revolution." The work of the two men is compared. Howells' "genial humor" is commended: "He knows how to write gaily without levity, and seriously without solemnity."

9   "Venetian Life." Round Table, 4 (8 Sep 1866), 90. Full review.
    This is a genuine book and not a compilation.

10 [CURTIS, GEORGE WILLIAM.] "Editor's Easy Chair." Harper's, 33 (Oct 1866), 668. Full review of Venetian Life. Rpt. in part, The War of the Critics over William Dean Howells, ed. Edwin H. Cady and David L. Frazier (Evanston: Row, Peterson, 1962), pp. 1-2.
    "Indeed, its information is so copious under the gayest and most graceful air of loitering observation, that it is sure to become a gondola companion." Howells' "delicate and airy humor keeps everything in its place."

11 [LOWELL, JAMES RUSSELL.] "Venetian Life." North American Review, 103 (Oct 1866), 610-613. Major review. Rpt. The Function of the Poet, ed. Albert Mordell (Boston: Houghton Mifflin, 1920), pp. 146-152, and in part, The War of the Critics over William Dean Howells, ed. Edwin H. Cady and David L. Frazier (Evanston: Row, Peterson, 1962), pp. 3-4.

1866

([LOWELL, JAMES RUSSELL])
Howells' tone is especially striking: "It is so constant as to bear witness, not only to a real gift, but to
the thoughtful cultivation of it."

1867

12   "Howells's Italian Journeys." Springfield Daily Republican,
11 Dec 1867, p. 2. Review.
"It is the work of a modern man of culture, describing
with charming wit and philosophy the manner in which an-
tiquity strikes his senses." Long illustrative quotation.

1868

13   [JAMES, HENRY.] "Italian Journeys." North American Review,
106 (Jan 1868), 336-339. Major review. Rpt. The War of
the Critics over William Dean Howells, ed. Edwin H. Cady
and David L. Frazier (Evanston: Row, Peterson, 1962),
pp. 4-7.
"Mr. Howells has an eye for the small things of nature,
of art, and of human life, which enables him to extract
sweetness and profit from adventures the most prosaic,
and which prove him a very worthy successor of the author
of the 'Sentimental Journey.'" His two books on Italy
belong to "the centre and core" of literature.

14   "Italian Journeys." Nation, 6 (2 Jan 1868), 11-12. Review.
Howells is contrasted with major English writers. "He
was certainly a sentimentalist before he was a satirical
humorist," and that fact marks both Italian Journeys and
Venetian Life. Howells already exhibits exquisite taste
and refined humor.

15   "Politics, Sociology, Voyages and Travels." Westminster Review, 89 (Apr 1868), 263. Brief review of Italian
Journeys.
Appreciation is registered for Howells' "playful fancy
and light genial humor," his historical allusions, and
his "sympathy with the people." His method reminds one
of Hawthorne.

16   [CURTIS, GEORGE WILLIAM.] "Literary Notices." Harper's, 36
(May 1868), 814-815. Brief review of Italian Journeys.

1868

([CURTIS, GEORGE WILLIAM])
It "shows the same fine perception, the same exquisite humor, the same freshness of feeling, the same refinement and delicacy of treatment" found in Venetian Life.

17 CONWAY, MONCURE D. "Three American Poets." Broadway, n.s. 1 (Oct 1868), 240-248. Essay.
"The Pilot's Story" and "The Poet" suggest that Howells is an emerging American poet (pp. 246-248).

1870

18 "Portrait of a Boston Literary Man." Boston Daily Evening Transcript, 22 Jul 1870, p. [1]. Note.
The concluding chapter of "A Day's Pleasure" in Atlantic "is an admirable working up of such incidents and characters as a sail to Hull would naturally develop." The model for one of Howells' characters is identified as Mr. J. E. Dabson, a Transcript correspondent better known as "Tom Folio."

19 "The Atlantic, for December." Boston Daily Evening Transcript, 18 Nov 1870, p. [2]. Brief reference.
"Flitting," in the December Atlantic, in its "appeal to household sensibilities and echo of housekeepers' experience" is characteristic Howells.

20 "New Publications." Boston Daily Evening Transcript, 23 Dec 1870, p. [1]. Brief announcement of Suburban Sketches.
"For their quiet humor, keen and genial observation, and easy and chaste style, they will be found delicious reading and re-reading."

1871

21 [LOWELL, JAMES RUSSELL.] "Suburban Sketches." North American Review, 112 (Jan 1871), 236-237. Brief review. Rpt. The War of the Critics over William Dean Howells, ed. Edwin H. Cady and David L. Frazier (Evanston: Row, Peterson, 1962), p. 8.
"Yes, truly, these are poems, if the supreme gift of the poet be to rim the trivial things of our ordinary and prosaic experience with an ideal light."

WILLIAM DEAN HOWELLS: A RESEARCH BIBLIOGRAPHY

22   "Minor Book Notices." <u>Literary World</u>, 1 (1 Jan 1871), 123.
     Brief notice of <u>Suburban Sketches</u>.
        "These sketches are the best things of the kind in our
     literature."

23   "New Publications." <u>New York Times</u>, 7 Jan 1871, p. 2. Re-
     view of <u>Suburban Sketches</u>.
        Talents such as Howells' (his style is scarcely inferior
     to Hawthorne's) "ought to produce something of more per-
     manent value than a few fragmentary magazine articles."
     Howells could rival Harriet Beecher Stowe.

24   "Howells's <u>Suburban Sketches</u>." <u>Nation</u>, 12 (19 Jan 1871), 44.
     Review.
        Howells is among "the best humorists who have at any
     time written in our tongue," but his subject matter "can-
     not be said to have great intrinsic interest."

25   "American Literature." <u>Saturday Review</u>, 31 (25 Feb 1871),
     256. Brief mention of <u>Suburban Sketches</u>.
        They qualify as padding for magazines of the lighter
     class.

26   "Current Literature." <u>Overland</u>, 6 (Apr 1871), 386. Review
     of <u>Suburban Sketches</u>.
        "We wonder that so much is disclosed where we had be-
     fore seen so little."

27   "Notes." <u>Nation</u>, 12 (11 May 1871), 320-321.
        "No Love Lost," a poem by Howells, was plagiarized in a
     recent issue of Ouida's <u>Broadway</u>.

28   "The Magazines for July." <u>Nation</u>, 13 (13 Jul 1871), 30.
     Brief mention of serialization of <u>Their Wedding Journey</u>
     in <u>Atlantic</u>.
        Howells is "especially good this month." "In using some
     truthful language concerning New York, he subtly contrives
     the derision of Boston."

29   "Literature." <u>Athenaeum</u>, No. 2281 (15 Jul. 1871), 75-76. Re-
     view of <u>Suburban Sketches</u>.
        In his "fidelity to human nature, subtle pleasantry,
     and power to rouse the gentler sensibilities by pathetic
     hints and droll suggestions," Howells "often displays him-
     self as the affectionate disciple and agreeable imitator
     of Charles Lamb."

1871

30   "The Magazines for August." Nation, 13 (3 Aug 1871), 78.
       Brief mention.
          Their Wedding Journey may be "as good as anything
       [Howells] has ever done."

31   "The Magazines for September." Nation, 13 (31 Aug 1871), 148.
       Brief mention.
          Their Wedding Journey appearing in the Atlantic "should
       be missed by no one who likes, and by no one who wishes
       to learn to like, the most delicate of humor."

32   "The Magazines for October." Nation, 13 (28 Sep 1871), 212.
       Brief mention.
          Current installments of the Howells and James stories
       in Atlantic are neither "so perfectly characteristic" of
       the authors as earlier installments have been.

33   "Notes." Nation, 13 (5 Oct 1871), 228. Brief item.
          Corrects mention of Howells and James in preceding issue.
       Howells lacks originality in his humorous treatment of the
       illogicality of women.

34   "The Magazines for November." Nation, 13 (2 Nov 1871), 295.
       Brief mention.
          Isabel and Basil quarrel.

34a "The Magazines for December." Nation, 14 (30 Nov 1871), 358.
       Brief mention.
          Mr. Osgood considers Howells' story, now appearing in
       the Atlantic, "one of the most attractive ever published
       in America."

1872

35   "Minor Book Notices." Literary World, 2 (1 Jan 1872), 124.
       Review of Their Wedding Journey.
          "Certainly no writer surpasses him in appreciative
       apprehension of human nature in its casual manifestations."

36   "Literary Notes." Appleton's, 7 (13 Jan 1872), 52. Brief
       review of Their Wedding Journey.
          "No sketches of travel and character, since the 'Howadji'
       first gave us his lucubrations, have exhibited observa-
       tions so keen, satire so subtle and felicitous, or style
       so fresh and charming."

37 G., J. H. [Untitled.] Boston Daily Evening Transcript, 24 Jan
    1872, p. [1]. Review of Their Wedding Journey.
        Howells, like Dean Swift, "could write beautifully about
    a broomstick." "He is not so trenchant or sparkling as
    Curtis, to whom he is often compared, but his humor is of
    a more subtle character, and is shown in delicate charac-
    terization." "Little touches, pathetic and profound, re-
    mind one occasionally of Hawthorne."

38 "Current Literature." Galaxy, 13 (Mar 1872), 426-428. Re-
    view of Their Wedding Journey.
        Howells succeeds in his "bold experiment to transport
    the 'Pilgrims of the Rhine' to a land so prosaic as ours
    ...by cleverly turning a stronger light on the scenery
    than on the travellers." He seems to give less care to
    the thought than to the style, "and its finish and ease
    compensate, as far as they can, for slightness of materi-
    al."

39 "Novels of the Week." Athenaeum, No. 2315 (9 Mar 1872), 303-
    304. Review of Their Wedding Journey.
        The narrative contains much humor, "and a complete ab-
    sence of that vulgarity" associated with American books.
    Howells, like other American writers, "asserts" himself
    in altering the Queen's English.

40 "American Literature." Saturday Review, 33 (23 Mar 1872),
    385. Review of Their Wedding Journey.
        "Not very striking, but it is lively, pleasant, and
    sensible."

41 [EGGLESTON, EDWARD.] "William Dean Howells." Hearth and
    Home, 4 (30 Mar 1872), 243. Brief biographical sketch.
    Informal introduction. Portrait (p. 241).

42 [ADAMS, HENRY.] "Their Wedding Journey." North American Re-
    view, 114 (Apr 1872), 444-445. Brief review. Rpt.
    Howells / A Century of Criticism, ed. Kenneth E. Eble
    (Dallas: Southern Methodist University, 1962), pp. 11-12,
    and The War of the Critics over William Dean Howells, ed.
    Edwin H. Cady and David L. Frazier (Evanston: Row, Peter-
    son, 1962), p. 9.
        "The vein which Mr. Howells has struck is hardly a deep
    one," but "his dexterity in following it, and in drawing
    out its slightest resources" seems marvellous. Nowhere
    is to be found "so faithful and so pleasing a picture of
    our American existence."

1872

43   "Editor's Literary Record / Miscellaneous." Harper's, 44
        (Apr 1872), 781. Brief review of Their Wedding Journey.
        Howells' style prevents a commonplace theme from being
        in any sense commonplace.

44   "Current Literature." Overland, 8 (May 1872), 481-482. Re-
        view of Their Wedding Journey.
             The curiosity Howells arouses is "a tribute to the re-
        ality of his sketches."

45   "Literature of the Day." Lippincott's, 9 (Jun 1872), 726.
        Review of Their Wedding Journey.
             This is "a tender trifle" that one is tempted to encase
        in glass. Perhaps the rarest of Howells' faculties is the
        ability to record "those little shreds of remark" one over-
        hears in public places.

                                1873

46   "Literary News." Literary World, 3 (1 May 1873), 192. Brief
        note.
             Criticism of Howells' diction inspired by his use of
        "mistakenness."

47   "Literary Matters / Periodicals." Boston Evening Transcript,
        16 May 1873, p. 6. Mention of A Chance Acquaintance.
             "How did it turn out with Kitty?" will be the first
        question asked about the current Atlantic. "The denouement
        will be unexpected, and yet it is entirely natural and
        highly proper."

48   "Literary Matters / New Publications." Boston Evening Tran-
        script, 19 May 1873, p. 6. Review of A Chance Acquaint-
        ance.
             "Every month, for six months past, we have been moved to
        commend its beauty, chastened brilliancy, exquisitely-
        etched romance, distinctly outlined characterizations, and
        poetic and accurate descriptive pictures." It has an ad-
        vantage over Their Wedding Journey in that it adds a "do-
        mestic drama of young American life."

49   "Minor Notice." Independent, 25 (29 May 1873), 682. Review
        of A Chance Acquaintance.
             Very little in the realistic vein is as good as this
        novel. Here the poetic faculty works "upon matters usually
        lost sight of by the commonplace eye."

50 "Minor Book Notices." Literary World, 4 (1 Jun 1873), 13.
      Brief review of A Chance Acquaintance.
         Howells "is not well equipped for novel-writing; his
      touch is too fine for the exigencies of such dramatic
      action as is essential to the novel; his imagination lacks
      fecundity, beautiful as are its infrequent products; and
      he seems utterly incapable of handling persons and events
      en masse."

51 "Book Reviews." New Orleans Daily Picayune, 8 Jun 1873,
      p. [2]. Brief review of A Chance Acquaintance.
         "In point of style, quiet humor, a keen eye for charac-
      ter and pictorial description, this writer is not very
      inferior to some of the earlier works of Washington
      Irving. This is high praise, but not as we think un-
      merited."

52 "Recent Novels." Nation, 16 (12 Jun 1873), [405]. Review of
      A Chance Acquaintance.
         Kitty is well drawn, but in Miles Arbuton Howells records
      a "distorted version of the hated Bostonian as he appears
      to us outside barbarians, [rather] than an accurate repre-
      sentation of even a very priggish man."

53 "American Literature." Saturday Review, 35 (28 Jun 1873),
      862. Very brief mention of A Chance Acquaintance.
      "A pleasantly written novelette."

54 "Current Literature." Galaxy, 16 (Jul 1873), 139-140. Full
      review of A Chance Acquaintance.
         It is premature to begin talking about Howells' work in
      the context of "the great American novel"; but if Howells
      "will continue to write his charming little stories, half
      love, half travel, and at least another half humor, we
      shall be quite content." Arbuton, "as a type, is over-
      done."

55 "Literary Notices." Eclectic, n.s. 18 (Jul 1873), 122. Re-
      view of A Chance Acquaintance.
         "No writer has ever surpassed Mr. Howells in the subtle
      and delicate indication of character, and he possesses in
      perfection the art of clothing the dryest and prosiest of
      subjects with vivid and poetic interest." The denouement
      is disappointing.

56 "Current Literature." Overland, 11 (Aug 1873), 188-190. Re-
      view of A Chance Acquaintance.

1873

("Current Literature")
"On the trellis-work of this love-story, Mr. Howells has gracefully twined much picturesque description of historic Canada."

57 [CURTIS, GEORGE WILLIAM.] "Editor's Literary Record." Harper's, 47 (Aug 1873), 460-461. Brief review of A Chance Acquaintance.
Howells' "first novel is almost a good novel." Arbuton, though well drawn, "is but a sorry representative of a Boston aristocrat, or, indeed, of an aristocrat of any locality."

58 "Howells's Poems." Literary World, 4 (1 Nov 1873), 85-86. Review of Poems.
Although characterized in general by "verbal felicity," an appropriate sub-title for the volume would be "Variations on the Definite Article."

59 "Literary Matters / New Publications." Boston Evening Transcript, 1 Nov 1873, p. 6. Brief mention in review of Elizabeth Phelps' Trotty's Wedding Tour.
Certain readers will admire it more than they would Howells' "graceful and fascinating" Their Wedding Journey.

60 "Poems." Nation, 17 (6 Nov 1873), 310-311. Review.
Howells' poems exhibit the same "humorous observation" found in his prose, but his poetic style "seems to be not altogether equal to that of his prose."

61 "American Literature." Saturday Review, 36 (29 Nov 1873), 712. Very brief mention of Poems.
They have "a strong flavour of American scenery and character."

62 "Minor Notice." Independent, 25 (4 Dec 1873), 1514. Review of Poems.
Howells' poems are "too delicate for the winning of immediate popularity."

1874

63 "Poems." North American Review, 118 (Jan 1874), 190-191. Brief review.
Howells' poems exhibit much the same qualities as his prose: "there is the more than masculine, almost feminine, touch to be found in some."

10

64   "Minor Poets." Athenaeum, No. 2410 (3 Jan 1874), 18-19.
         Brief review of Poems.
              Howells is not "the founder of any new style of poetry."
         Influence is credited to Browning and Heine.

65   JAMES, HENRY, Jr. "Howells's Poems." Independent, 26 (8 Jan
         1874), 9. Full review of Poems.
              Howells' "double skill"--his "verse is as natural and
         unforced as his prose"--is enviable. Howells "is a master
         of the waning art of saying delicate things in a way that
         does them justice."

66   THOMPSON, MAURICE. "A Western Poet / W. D. Howells' New Vol-
         ume." Indianapolis Journal, 24 Oct 1874, p. 5. Review
         of Poems.
              The poems, which contain "a decided dash of the true
         Western feeling," are commended. Howells may be the best
         writer of lyric verses in America. [Scharnhorst]

67   "Literary Matters / Periodicals." Boston Evening Transcript,
         19 Nov 1874, p. 6. Mention of A Foregone Conclusion upon
         completion of serialization.
              "Above all, its sincere, noble-minded, yet passionate
         and contradictory girl heroine, shows a deeper insight in-
         to human nature--and a larger capacity for producing those
         effects which depend upon its truthful presentation, than
         any previous work by the writer."

68   GILMAN, ARTHUR. "A Foregone Conclusion." Independent, 26
         (26 Nov 1874), 7-8. Review.
              Largely literary biography and summary. This is Howells'
         "first novel." As artist Howells ranks with Hawthorne.

69   "New Publications / Mr. Howells' New Novel." New York Times,
         23 Dec 1874, p. 6. Full review of A Foregone Conclusion.
              At last Howells has "fairly launched himself as a writer
         of fiction." Given his talent, his doing so was a fore-
         gone conclusion. The focus of this favorable review is on
         Florida Verain, not only "one of the most strongly marked
         and yet thoroughly natural women" in imaginative litera-
         ture, but also "a thoroughly American woman." Howells'
         "Americanism" is applauded.

                                   1875

70   [JAMES, HENRY.] "A Foregone Conclusion." North American Re-
         view, 120 (Jan 1875), 207-214. Major review. Rpt. in

1875

([JAMES, HENRY])
part, <u>The War of the Critics over William Dean Howells</u>,
ed. Edwin H. Cady and David L. Frazier (Evanston: Row,
Peterson, 1962), pp. 10-15.
"<u>A Foregone Conclusion</u> will take its place as a singularly perfect production."

71   "Literary." <u>Appleton's</u>, 13 (2 Jan 1875), 21. Review of <u>A</u>
<u>Foregone Conclusion</u>.
Forceful and well-constructed.

72   JAMES, HENRY. "Howells's <u>Foregone Conclusion</u>." <u>Nation</u>, 20
(7 Jan 1875), 12-13. Full review.
Howells, "intensely American in the character of his
talent, is probably never so spontaneous, so much himself,
as when he represents the delicate, nervous, emancipated
young woman begotten of our institutions and our climate,
and equipped with a lovely face and irritable moral consciousness." James mentions "the narrow stage," "the
single situation," and the questionable "felicity of the
episodes" which conclude the novel.

73   "American Literature." <u>Saturday Review</u>, 39 (27 Feb 1875),
296. Very brief mention of <u>A Foregone Conclusion</u>.
"Mr. Howells' name will command a welcome."

74   "Editor's Literary Record." <u>Harper's</u>, 50 (Mar 1875), 598.
Review of <u>A Foregone Conclusion</u>.
The "natural, easy grace" of Howells' style may stand
in the way of thought and passion. The novel "is more
notable for its descriptions of the external life of
Venice than for its expression of the internal life of a
priest in conflict between human love and a mistaken sense
of religious duty."

75   SAINTSBURY, GEORGE. "New Novels." <u>Academy</u>, 7 (13 Mar 1875),
264. Review of <u>A Foregone Conclusion</u>.
"The goodness of <u>A Foregone Conclusion</u> quite surpassed
our most sanguine anticipations. Slight as it is in
apparent composition, the four figures of which it consists are all conceived with unquestionable originality,
and drawn with very great skill."

76   "The History of the Future." <u>Literary World</u>, 6 (Jul 1875),
16. Note.
Calls for a guidebook novel and suggests collaboration
of Howells and Mr. Sweetser (Osgood guidebooks).

1876

77   WHIPPLE, EDWIN P. "The First Century of the Republic."
     Harper's, 52 (Feb 1876), 514-533. Essay (concluding
     portion). Rpt. in part, The War of the Critics over
     William Dean Howells, ed. Edwin H. Cady and David L.
     Frazier (Evanston: Row, Peterson, 1962), pp. 15-16.
        Brief reference to Howells (p. 527). His writings are
     "masterpieces of literary workmanship.... He has humor
     in abundance, but it is thoroughly blended with his obser-
     vation, fancy, imagination, and good sense."

78   GILMAN, ARTHUR. "Mr. Howells's New Novel." Independent, 28
     (18 May 1876), 8-9. Review of Private Theatricals.
        This piece, the best of Howells to date, contains a
     skillful delineation of feminine character.

79   [MATTHEWS, BRANDER.] "Notes." Nation, 23 (31 Aug 1876), 136.
     Notice of The Parlor Car.
        Howells strikes "just the right light-comedy key." The
     lack of a market for one-act plays is unfortunate.

80   "New Publications." New York Times, 25 Sep 1876, p. 2. Re-
     view of Sketch of the Life and Character of Rutherford B.
     Hayes.
        In two detailed columns, Howells' book is compared with
     the parallel studies by Russell H. Conwell and J. Q.
     Howard.

81   "Late Publications." Library Table, 1 (Oct 1876), 128. Re-
     view of Sketch of the Life and Character of Rutherford B.
     Hayes.
        General approval of organization and fluency under the
     pressure of politics and time.

82   "Recent Political Biography." Nation, 23 (26 Oct 1876), 259.
     Review of Sketch of the Life and Character of Rutherford
     B. Hayes.
        Howells' literary effort is favorably contrasted with
     the "specially-sanctioned" life prepared by J. O. Howard.

83   "Current Literature." Galaxy, 22 (Nov 1876), 719. Review of
     Sketch of the Life and Character of Rutherford B. Hayes.
        This is not a common campaign biography because "it
     bears the marks of the culture and ability which are ex-
     pected from this author. But the novelist and poet are
     almost lost in the commonplaces of the story."

1877

84   STODDARD, R[ICHARD] H., and others. "W. D. Howells." Poet's
         Homes. Boston: Lothrop, 1877. Pp. 119-138. Illustrated.
         A description of Howells' house on Concord Avenue in
         Cambridge and of his study is followed by a literary biog-
         raphy incorporating samples of his verse.

85   "American Literature." Saturday Review, 43 (27 Jan 1877), 121.
         Very brief mention of The Parlor Car.
         "A lively little story."

86   [BIDWELL, W. H.] "William Dean Howells." Eclectic, n.s. 25
         (Mar 1877), 376. Note.
         Literary introduction to Howells, "perhaps the leading
         exponent of a school whose principal characteristic is a
         refinement of method and a finish of style surpassing any-
         thing hitherto known in our national literature." Full-
         page engraved portrait (issue front piece).

87   "American Literature." Saturday Review, 43 (28 Apr 1877),
         531.
         Mere mention of a new, illustrated edition of Their
         Wedding Journey.

88   "New Publications." New Orleans Daily Picayune, 13 May 1877,
         p. [5]. Brief mention of Out of the Question.
         This "delightfully written" parlor comedy has "just
         enough of dramatic briskness to give it the semblance of
         a stage picture."

89   "New Publications." New York Times, 15 May 1877, p. 7. Re-
         view of Out of the Question.
         Largely summary. The novel is written much like a play
         for the stage. Howells "is in his happiest vein when
         delicately caricaturing women," but his satire is very
         gentle. He seems to lack "Thackeray's healthy loathing
         for a snob."

90   HOMBERGER, HEINRICH. "William Dean Howells." Deutsche
         Rundschau, 11 (Jun 1877), 510-513. Review of A Foregone
         Conclusion.
         Howells, up to now quite unknown in Germany, is likened
         to Turgenev, Thackeray, and Gottfried Keller. His Italian
         experience provided proper background for the novel.

91   "Recent Fiction." Literary World, 8 (Jun 1877), 8-9. Review
         of Out of the Question.

("Recent Fiction")
Howells is gifted with a "subtle intuition of feminine character," but he should reach higher than "the mere amusement of the fancy."

92. "American Literature," Saturday Review, 43 (30 Jun 1877), 811.
Mere mention of Out of the Question.
"A sort of dramatic novelette."

93 "Literary Notices." Godey's Lady's Book, 95 (Jul 1877), 86.
Brief mention of Out of the Question.
"A bright, sparkling story."

94 "Notes." Nation, 25 (26 Jul 1877), 56.
Howells has no American equal for writing "graceful and delicate comedy." Both Out of the Question and A Counterfeit Presentment are suitable for staging.

95 BARRETT, LAURENCE. "Correspondence / Mr. Howells's Counterfeit Presentment." Nation, 25 (2 Aug 1877), 70. Letter.
Mr. Barrett announces that he has purchased Howells' drama and will himself take the hero's role in its scheduled performance.

96 MATTHEWS, J. BRANDER. "Bret Harte and Mr. Howells as Dramatists." Library Table, 3 (13 Sep 1877), 174-175. Short essay. Rpt. in American Theatre as Seen by Its Critics, 1752-1934, ed. Montrose J. Moses and John Mason Brown (New York: Norton, [1934]), pp. 147-148.
Howells "has never worked with a lighter hand or a firmer touch," and if he essays a new form in Out of the Question and Parlor Car, his success is complete. They may be too slight and too lacking in color to endure footlights.

97 "Current Literature." Galaxy, 24 (Oct 1877), 569. Review of Out of the Question.
"The story is bright and amusing, a trifle to be enjoyed, not criticized." Why is it that the sewing phrase "cut it bias" has "so impressed itself on the masculine mind?"

98 "New Publications." New Orleans Daily Picayune, 28 Oct 1877, p. [9]. Brief review of A Counterfeit Presentment.
"Mr. Howells is among the brightest of the story-makers and play-makers of the decade." He is credited with the adaptation of "Sampson" presented in New Orleans the previous season.

1877

99   "Brief Notices." Literary World, 8 (Nov 1877), 101-102.
         Mention of A Counterfeit Presentment.
         Something "more substantial than dainty 'Valenciennes
      lace'" should be expected of Howells.

100   "American Literature." Saturday Review, 44 (24 Nov 1877),
         664. Mention of A Counterfeit Presentment.
         Howells' name is now sufficiently known in England to
      win favorable reception for any of his work.

101   "Autobiography.--Howells." Literary World, 8 (Dec 1877), 112.
         Review of Choice Autobiographies, edited by Howells.
         His critical introductions are commended.

102   "Notes." Nation, 25 (6 Dec 1877), 350. Announcement of forth-
         coming Choice Autobiographies, edited by Howells.
         Nowhere are Howells' literary qualities "more apparent
      or more delightful than in these prefaces."

1878

103   "Current Literature." Galaxy, 25 (Jan 1878), 138. Brief re-
         view of A Counterfeit Presentment.
         "The great charm of Howells's commediettas are the stage
      directions."

104   "Current Literature." Galaxy, 25 (Jan 1878), 139-140. Re-
         view of Choice Autobiographies, edited by Howells.
         Non-critical.

105   [Review of A Counterfeit Presentment.] Sunday Afternoon
         (Springfield, Mass.), 1 (Jan 1878), 92-93.

106   "Marmontel's Autobiography." Independent, 30 (4 Jul 1878),
         10. Brief reference.
         Comment on the deficiency of "historic sense" in Howells'
      critical essay which accompanies Memoirs of Jean François
      Marmontel (republished 1878).

107   "Minor Notices." Literary World, 9 (Aug 1878), 48. Brief
         notice of memoirs of Marmontel.
         Howells' introductory essay is "an excellent miniature"
      of the whole.

1879

*   HIGGINSON, THOMAS WENTWORTH. "Howells." Short Studies of
    American Authors. Boston: Lee and Shepard, 1879. Pp.
    32-39. Rpt. from Literary World, 10 (2 Aug 1879), 249-
    250. See item 119.

108   "'A New Play.'" Literary World, 10 (15 Feb 1879), 56-57.
    Brief mention.
      Negative response to Howells' version of a Spanish play
    on the basis of its immoral theme.

109   "Recent Fiction." Literary World, 10 (15 Feb 1879), 86-87.
    Brief review of The Lady of the Aroostook.
      Bolstered by patriotism and chivalry, this is an "ele-
    vated" story.

110   "New Publications / Howells' New Novel." New York Times, 15
    Mar 1879, p. 3. Review of The Lady of the Aroostook.
      Howells is more "an exact reporter of the doings and
    sayings of typical people than a creator of ideal or
    delineator of unusual persons." He is "much like Henry
    James, Jr., except that he has more movement, more go."

111   [WOODBERRY, GEORGE E.] "The Lady of the Aroostook." Nation,
    28 (20 Mar 1879), 205. Review.
      The novel has all of the excellences of Howells' work;
    however, "what is valuable in literature is not the minia-
    ture of life, but the illumination of life by the inspira-
    tion; not common things set in the light of common day,
    but the revelation of what is hidden in common things by
    the light that never was on sea or land."

112   "New Books." Penn Monthly, 10 (Apr 1879), 316-317. Review
    of The Lady of the Aroostook.
      "A great deal of the exquisite finish of the best work
    of modern French romantic writers," plus "a delicate re-
    finement." Close representation of New England life and
    character.

113   "Novels of the Week." Athenaeum, No. 2687 (26 Apr 1879), 535.
    Very brief review of The Lady of the Aroostook.
      The plot is well managed, the character of the girl is
    well developed, and Howells uses a "purely American"
    language. The object of the book is partly to point out
    American superiority.

1879

114   [CURTIS, GEORGE WILLIAM.] "Editor's Literary Record."
       Harper's, 58 (May 1879), 941. Review of The Lady of the
       Aroostook.
            The story "is told in a way so genial, and the narrative
       is spun out with so many pleasant confabulations and enter-
       taining incidents, that the voyage seems all too short."

115   [Review of The Lady of the Aroostook.] Sunday Afternoon
       (Springfield, Mass.), 3 (May 1879), 480.

116   "Literature." Independent, 31 (29 May 1879), 10. Brief re-
       view of The Lady of the Aroostook.
            Largely summary. The story, true to New England charac-
       ter, exhibits a "restless self-consciousness."

117   HAZELTINE, MAYO W. "Current Literature." North American Re-
       view, 128 (Jun 1879), 691-694. Full review of The Lady
       of the Aroostook.
            Because Howells has established "through the action of
       this story and by the eloquence of his conviction that the
       imitative attitude is essentially abortive and inane,"
       this novel is "the most virile, healthful and estimable
       achievement in recent American fiction."

118   "Literature of the Day." Lippincott's, 23 (Jun 1879), 776.
       Review of The Lady of the Aroostook.
            Here one finds Howells in "a broader, mellower and less
       realistic manner" than before. "Never perhaps have the
       New England provincialisms been rendered in so attractive
       and truly artistic a manner as in the delineation of the
       heroine...." "Incident Mr. Howells appears to regard as
       a rock to be avoided."

119   HIGGINSON, THOMAS WENTWORTH. "Howells." Literary World, 10
       (2 Aug 1879), 249-250. Short essay. Rpt. Short Studies
       of American Authors (Boston: Lee and Shepard, 1879),
       pp. 32-39, and Howells / A Century of Criticism, ed.
       Kenneth E. Eble (Dallas: Southern Methodist University,
       1962), pp. 13-18.
            Howells' position as editor of the Atlantic has shielded
       him from sharp--and beneficial--criticism. The heroine of
       The Lady of the Aroostook seems "the high-water mark of
       Mr. Howells" to date.

1880

120   BORNMÜLLER, FRANZ. _Biographisches Schriftsteller Lexicon der Gegenwart_. Leipzig: Bibliographischen Instituts, 1880. Pp. 350–351.
        Encyclopedia-type entry lists major works through 1880. Non-critical.

*   HIGGINSON, T. W. "Howells." _Short Studies of American Authors_. Boston: Lee and Shepard; New York: Charles T. Dillingham, 1880. Pp. 32–39. Rpt. from _Literary World_, 10 (2 Aug 1879), 249–250. _See_ item 119.

121   "Literary Matters / Periodicals." _Boston Evening Transcript_, 24 Jan 1880, p. 6. Brief comment on serialization of _The Undiscovered Country_.
        "It will take a good deal of Mr. Howells's best writing to dissipate the feeling of dislike which most readers must feel for the self-appreciative journalist."

122   "Topics of the Day." New Orleans _Daily Picayune_ (Afternoon ed.), 14 Feb 1880, p. [1]. Brief ironic notice.
        Howells has been known to reject his own manuscript. "The virtue of a Roman father is nothing to that of the author who consigns the child of his brain to the waste-basket."

123   [Untitled.] _New York Times_, 24 Feb 1880, p. 4. Brief mention.
        A paragraph profile of Howells' appearance and manner.

124   "Literary Matters / Periodicals." _Boston Evening Transcript_, 19 Mar 1880, p. 6. Brief mention of serialization of _The Undiscovered Country_.
        It gives "an exquisite picture of life among the Quakers" and inspires readers "with an ardent desire to strangle Dr. Boynton before he makes any further attempt to convert the world through the sacrifice of his daughter."

125   "Literary Matters / Periodicals." _Boston Evening Transcript_, 20 Apr 1880, p. 6. Brief mention.
        The Undiscovered Country is "carried a step further, with increasing interest."

126   ORR, A. [MRS. SUTHERLAND]. "The International Novelists and Mr. Howells." _Contemporary Review_, 37 (May 1880), 741–765. Full literary essay. Rpt. in part, _Living Age_, 145 (29 May 1880), 599–615, and _The War of the Critics over William_

1880

(ORR, A. [MRS. SUTHERLAND])
Dean Howells, ed. Edwin H. Cady and David L. Frazier
(Evanston: Row, Peterson, 1962), pp. 16-21.
Mrs. Orr judges the success and failure of Howells from
a generally objective British point of view.

*   ____. "International Novelists and Mr. Howells." Living
Age, 145 (29 May 1880), 599-615. Rpt. in part from Contemporary Review, 37 (May 1880), 741-765. See item 126.

127   "Topics of the Day." New Orleans Daily Picayune (Afternoon
ed.), 9 Jun 1880, p. [1]. Brief mention.
Howells refuses credit for Yorick's Love.

128   "Literary Matters / New Publications." Boston Evening Transcript, 18 Jun 1880, p. 6. Brief announcement of comple-
tion of The Undiscovered Country.
It stands above all of Howells' earlier work in "genuine
power" and is scheduled to appear in book form "next Saturday."

129   "Literary Matters / New Publications." Boston Evening Transcript, 21 Jun 1880, p. 6. Review of The Undiscovered
Country.
The grace and artistry of the story have already been
praised. Howells "has taken for his subject one of the
most puzzling and bewildering problems of the age" and has
attempted "to formulate a theory which shall satisfactorily
account for that which so many thousands have found unac-
countable."

130   "Literature and Science / The Undiscovered Country." Chicago
Daily Tribune, 26 Jun 1880, p. 9. Brief review.
"Mr. Howells has a marvellous faculty for observing and
rare skill in depicting character and describing scenery."

131   WOOLLEY, CELIA P. "Mr. Howells's New Novel." Dial, 1 (Jul
1880), 52-53. Review of The Undiscovered Country.
Howells, in a "new phase," adds "the definite moral purpose of the teacher to the grace and finish of the literary
artist."

132   "New Publications." New York Times, 1 Jul 1880, p. 3. Full
review of The Undiscovered Country.
A general contrast of the American and English novel.
The novels of James, Howells, and Aldrich are bringing a
new subtlety, a keener perception, and a more delicate
suggestiveness to literature. Howells "writes books for

("New Publications")
a highly intelligent public, and shows perfect acquaintance with our people and their intellectual capabilities."
His "tenderness, sweetness, and keen analysis are at about
his best in this romance."

133   "Literary Matters / Items." Boston Evening Transcript, 8 Jul
      1880, p. 6. Brief note.
          Venetian Life and Their Wedding Journey are listed among
      Howells' "six" novels.

134   "Literature." Independent, 32 (8 Jul 1880), 12. Very brief
      notice of The Undiscovered Country.
          Although it recalls Hawthorne, it is "a truly original
      work."

135   [BAXTER, SYLVESTER.] "Howells and Aldrich." Boston Sunday
      Herald, 11 Jul 1880, p. 10. Review of The Undiscovered
      Country.
          A reporter rather than a creator, a microscope rather
      than a telescope, Howells is the master of the type of
      fiction he endorses; but he lacks deep feeling, and his
      knowledge of women is questionable. His current study of
      spiritualism is objective.

136   [BROWNELL, W. C.] "The Novels of Mr. Howells." Nation, 31
      (15 Jul 1880), 49-51. Full review of The Undiscovered
      Country. Rpt. in part, The War of the Critics over William
      Dean Howells, ed. Edwin H. Cady and David L. Frazier
      (Evanston: Row, Peterson, 1962), pp. 21-24.
          "The charm of his novels exists independently of a cer-
      tain slenderness which one perceives in the pith of them.
      We think of no works of the kind, the aroma of which is so
      abiding, whose substance perishes so quickly from the mem-
      ory...."

137   [Untitled.] Saturday Review, 50 (24 Jul 1880), 124. Very
      brief mention of The Undiscovered Country.
          "Its interest turns on what is a complete novelty."

138   ADAMS, BROOKS. "The Undiscovered Country." International
      Review, 9 (Aug 1880), 149-154. Essay review.
          Howells "can do no greater service to American letters
      than by practically demonstrating, as he does, that the
      social soil of the United States is not too arid to yield
      materials for an entertaining book" (p. 150). Howells is
      genuine, and this is the strongest work he has done.

1880

139   "The Undiscovered Country." Literary World, 11 (14 Aug 1880),
      274-275. Review.
          In treating an improbable subject, Howells is "skillful
      as diplomatist no less than as a novelist."

140   [HIGGINSON, THOMAS WENTWORTH.] "Howells's Undiscovered
      Country." Scribner's, 20 (Sep 1880), 793-795. Full re-
      view. Rpt. in part, The War of the Critics over William
      Dean Howells, ed. Edwin H. Cady and David L. Frazier
      (Evanston: Row, Peterson, 1962), p. 25.
          Howells "handles the rappings with as airy and impersonal
      a touch as if he were Hawthorne dealing with a supposed
      birth-mark or a bosom-serpent; his treatment is, as it
      should be, dramatic; he is writing a novel, not a polemic
      treatise." "In delicacy of handling, in fineness and firm-
      ness of touch, in that local coloring to which Mr. James
      is so provokingly indifferent," this book ranks with
      Howells' best.

141   BARKER, ARTHUR. "New Novels." Academy, 18 (18 Sep 1880), 200.
      Brief review of The Undiscovered Country.
          Disappointing subject.

142   "The Undiscovered Country." Saturday Review, 50 (2 Oct 1880),
      433-434. Full review.
          Howells has the advantage of James "in a less dogged
      clinging to European themes, in a greater range and fresh-
      ness of subject, and in the absence of all but a very
      faint flavour of mannerism." This is not Howells at his
      best, but it contains fragments of his best.

143   "Genuine Poetry." Boston Transcript Christmas Supplement,
      24 Dec 1880, p. [2]. Feature article.
          Some of the famous authors invited to submit poems to
      the Christmas Supplement responded. Among the poems sub-
      mitted, "The following verses show that fine insight into
      the character of the lowly for which their writer is fa-
      mous. It is necessary to point out this characteristic,
      or otherwise it might not be obvious."

                          Unnoticed.

                      By W. D. H---lls.

                  And if it only could,
                    A glance should speak my mind;
                  'T were better that it should--
                    But thou art so unkind!

                             22

1880

("Genuine Poetry")

> Thou pretty little witch!
>   Thou bend'st above thy work,
> And sett'st with care each stitch,
>   Forgetting how to shirk.
>
> And so I lift my voice
>   And gently woo thy ear--
> Thy brother doth rejoice
>   My chanted song to hear,
>
> And, bending, louts him low
>   Beneath some phantom bags
> As loud I cry, 'Oh!--oh!
>   Old rags today! old rags!'"

1881

144   "Looker On." "'Literary and Social Boston.'" Boston Evening
       Transcript, 27 Jan 1881, p. 6. Letter to the editor.
          Censures the narrowness of Bostonians and defends the
       right of Howells and Aldrich to literary honor and posi-
       tion in Boston.

145   LATHROP, GEORGE P. "Literary and Social Boston." Harper's,
       62 (Feb 1881), 381-398. Brief description.
          Howells' Belmont home is briefly described (pp. 390-391).
       Portrait (p. 381) and sketch "Cozy Corner in Mr. Howells's
       House, Elmwood" (p. 387).

146   "New Editor for the Atlantic." New York Times, 17 Feb 1881,
       p. 1. News item.
          Thomas B. Aldrich will succeed Howells. Atlantic poli-
       cies will be unchanged.

147   [Untitled.] New York Times, 18 Feb 1881, p. 4. A brief bio-
       graphical sketch on the occasion of Howells' resignation
       from the Atlantic editorship.
          His "character-drawing set in dainty description and
       delicate humor" is considered his forte.

148   "Jottings." Boston Evening Transcript, 25 Feb 1881, p. 4.
       Literary gossip.
          Speculation about Howells as possible editor of a new
       journal rumored to be planned, but denied, by Osgood.

1881

149   [Untitled.] Critic, 1 (26 Feb 1881), 50. Editorial on occa-
       sion of Howells' departure from the Atlantic.
       Expresses hope that he will write for the stage.

150   BOYESEN, HJALMAR HJORTH. "Björnson in the United States."
       Critic, 1 (12 Mar 1881), 58. Brief reference.
       Warmly appreciative of Howells' hospitality and under-
       standing during his visit to the United States, and for
       Howells' having gotten a railroad pass for him, Björnson
       wrote, "'That you are sovereign lord of all hearts--that
       I knew; but of the railroads--dear me!'"

151   "Literary Matters / Items." Boston Evening Transcript, 1 Apr
       1881, p. 6. Repeated 16 May 1881, p. 6. Brief announce-
       ments.
       A Fearful Responsibility will appear in two installments
       in Scribner's.

152   "Literary Matters / Periodicals." Boston Evening Transcript,
       21 May 1881, p. 10. Brief reference.
       The "fearful responsibility" is an American girl.

153   "Literary Matters / Items." Boston Evening Transcript, 16 Jun
       1881, p. 6. Brief announcement.
       Dr. Breen's Practice will begin in the August Atlantic.

154   "Typical Americans." New York Times, 22 Jun 1881, p. 4.
       Literary editorial.
       Howells' "typical American is honest, sincere, and ener-
       getic, and his distinguishing American characteristic is
       coarseness, verging closely upon vulgarity, and frequently
       indistinguishable from it." Hoskins, in A Fearful Respon-
       sibility, is typically American in the Howells and James
       manner.

155   "Literary Matters / Periodicals." Boston Evening Transcript,
       27 Jun 1881, p. 6. Brief mention of concluding install-
       ment of A Fearful Responsibility.
       Grouped with "contents of the light sort."

156   "Literary Matters / New Publications." Boston Evening Tran-
       script, 16 Jul 1881, p. 6. Review of A Fearful Responsi-
       bility.
       This fresh and unconventional "sketch rather than a
       finished story" is "full of those subtle touches which
       make the author and the appreciative reader kin."

157 "Recent Fiction." <u>Critic</u>, 1 (16 Jul 1881), 191. Review of <u>A</u>
<u>Fearful Responsibility</u>.
Howells "excels in depicting the conjugal relationship,
and the conversations between Elmore and his wife are the
more delightful because the literary possibilities of the
married state are commonly neglected."

158 "New Publications / Recent Fiction." <u>New York Times</u>, 17 Jul
1881, p. 10. Review of <u>A Fearful Responsibility</u>.
"Mr. Howells has the art of elaborating a slender plot
so agreeably that one forgets how slender it is." His
best is in "the touches of actuality here and there" and
in the national character, "drawn with a most merciful
hand." Two "mistakes" in the novel—in the portrayal of
the Austrian engineer and in the denouement—are suggested.

159 "Literary Matters / Periodicals." <u>Boston Evening Transcript</u>,
18 Jul 1881, p. 6. Brief reference.
Paragraph summary of the first installment of <u>Dr</u>.
<u>Breen's Practice</u> underscoring prejudice toward lady doc-
tors. The story promises to be one of Howells' best.

160 "Recent Novels." <u>Nation</u>, 33 (21 Jul 1881), 54. Review of <u>A</u>
<u>Fearful Responsibility</u>.
"Tonelli's Marriage" and "At the Sign of the Savage"
are "delicate tracings" rather than stories. The persons
and circumstances in <u>A Fearful Responsibility</u> are "the
perfection of commonplace humanity and of ordinary hap-
penings."

161 "Literature / Current Fiction." <u>Chicago Daily Tribune</u>, 23
Jul 1881, p. 9. Brief review of <u>A Fearful Responsibility</u>.
"It is a pleasant little story, remarkable for nothing
except the grace and ease of its author."

162 "Some New Books." <u>New Orleans Times</u>, 31 Jul 1881, p. [2].
Brief notice of <u>A Fearful Responsibility</u>.
Howells sustains his reputation as "one of the most
original and entertaining of American fiction writers."

163 "Briefs on New Books." <u>Dial</u>, 2 (Aug 1881), 85. Review of <u>A</u>
<u>Fearful Responsibility</u>.
Disappointing. One is left with "a sense of thinness
and insubstantiality."

164 "Literary Matters / Periodicals." <u>Boston Evening Transcript</u>,
22 Aug 1881, p. 6. Brief mention.
<u>Dr. Breen's Practice</u> grows more interesting.

1881

165   "Current Literature." Literary World, 12 (27 Aug 1881), 296.
     Brief review of A Fearful Responsibility.
     "Delightful manner...without much matter."

166   [ALDRICH, THOMAS B.] "Mr. Howells's New Book." Atlantic, 48
     (Sep 1881), 402-405. Full review of A Fearful Responsi-
     bility, including two long quotations. Rpt. in part, The
     War of the Critics over William Dean Howells, ed. Edwin
     H. Cady and David L. Frazier (Evanston: Row, Peterson,
     1962), p. 26.
       Howells has been labeled "a man of 'mere talent,'" but
     he "reconciles us to mere talent; it seems to be a finer
     thing than the more Promethean endowment, for it gives us
     subtile characterizations, consummate workmanship, wit,
     humor, and pathos in abundance...." Howells' work has
     the lightness and high finish found in that of Prosper
     Mérimée.

167   "Our Bookshelf." Cottage Hearth, 7 (Sep 1881), 273. Brief
     review of A Fearful Responsibility.
     Good-natured satire with a not entirely pure style.

168   "Literary Matters / Items." Boston Evening Transcript, 13
     Sep 1881, p. 6. Brief reference.
     Notes contributions by and about Howells scheduled to
     appear in the first volume of Century.

169   "Literary Matters / The October Magazines." Boston Evening
     Transcript, 19 Sep 1881, p. 6. Brief note.
     "The serials, Dr. Breen's Practice, by Mr. Howells, and
     The Portrait of a Lady, by Mr. James, continue their re-
     spective courses."

170   "The American Novel." New Orleans Daily Picayune, 16 Oct 1881,
     p. [2]. Editorial.
     Howells is "passed over" for comment on George Washing-
     ton Cable.

171   "Literary Matters / Periodicals." Boston Evening Transcript,
     19 Oct 1881, p. 10. Brief note.
     A proposal of marriage offered to Dr. Breen foreshadows
     the end of Dr. Breen's Practice.

172   "Literary Matters / Periodicals." Boston Evening Transcript,
     22 Nov 1881, p. 6. Brief notice of the December Atlantic.
     "Full-freighted with good things, the principal features
     being the closing installments" of Dr. Breen's Practice
     and The Portrait of a Lady.

173   "Literary Matters / Periodicals." <u>Boston Evening Transcript</u>,
      25 Nov 1881, p. 6. Brief note.
         A "prominent feature" of the December <u>Century</u> is the be-
      ginning of <u>A Modern Instance</u>, "the opening scene of which
      is laid in Northern New England."

174   "New Publications / Recent Novels / <u>Dr. Breen's Practice</u>."
      <u>New York Daily Tribune</u>, 29 Nov 1881, p. 6. Full review.
         This latest work is "similar in lightness of material
      and delicacy of workmanship to <u>A Fearful Responsibility</u>
      and other minor productions of [Howells'] deft hand which
      hold a unique and ill-defined position between the novel
      and the short story." Its motive, however, "approaches
      the intellectual level of <u>The Undiscovered Country</u>."

175   "Literary Matters / New Publications / <u>Dr. Breen's Practice</u>."
      <u>Boston Evening Transcript</u>, 2 Dec 1881, p. 6. Full review.
         The novel is even more artistically done, showing fewer
      "marks of the brush," than Howells' previous work. "Even
      Mr. Howells could not keep up the interest in a heroine
      who could reject two lovers for the sake of her profession,
      and who could be left standing on the last page as 'Miss,'"
      but he shows "consummate skill." The statement made by
      the novel is ambiguous.

176   "Literature / <u>Dr. Breen's Practice</u>." <u>Critic</u>, 1 (17 Dec 1881),
      350–351. Full review.
         The story is "bright, humorous, entertaining, but thin-
      ner than is usual with Mr. Howells."

177   "Mr. Howells on the Characteristics of Women." <u>Literary</u>
      <u>World</u>, 12 (17 Dec 1881), 484. Review of <u>Dr. Breen's Prac-</u>
      <u>tice</u>.
         Mr. Howells pursues his study of women "with quiet humor"
      and scientific curiosity.

178   "Literary Matters / Periodicals." <u>Boston Evening Transcript</u>,
      21 Dec 1881, p. 6. Brief note.
         Howells gives "a remarkably life-like picture of the
      every-day proceedings in the Police Court" in "Police
      Report," which opens the January <u>Atlantic</u>.

179   "Literature / Mr. Howells's New Novel." <u>Chicago Daily Tribune</u>,
      24 Dec 1881, p. 9. Review of <u>Dr. Breen's Practice</u>.
         Extensive summary. "Mr. Howells's American girls are
      much more pleasing and natural characters than those
      painted by Mr. James. His stories are simpler, the poetic
      vein more pronounced."

1881

180   "Literature / Three Notable Novels." <u>American</u> (Philadelphia),
        3 (31 Dec 1881), 186-187. Review of <u>Dr. Breen's Practice</u>
        (along with James's <u>Portrait of a Lady</u> and Hardy's <u>A
        Laodicean</u>).
            Not a tract, this novel is Howells at his best. "Truer
        humor was never put into an American book than is to be
        found here; it goes straight to the mark."

                            1882

181   HUNTINGTON, H. A. "A Pair of American Novelists." <u>Dial</u>, 2
        (Jan 1882), 214-216. Review of <u>Dr. Breen's Practice</u>
        (along with James's <u>Portrait of a Lady</u>).
            Focus is on James. Reference is made to Howells' ability
        in feminine portrayal.

182   "<u>The Portrait of a Lady</u> and <u>Dr. Breen's Practice</u>." <u>Atlantic</u>,
        49 (Jan 1882), 126-130. Review.
            Howells did not design Grace Breen as a type. Rather,
        "he sees people, and he sets himself the task of discover-
        ing what their real lives are, with the purpose of giving
        his readers just those particulars which seem to be most
        indicative" (p. 129). "The perfection of Mr. James's art
        is in its intellectual order.... The oppositeness of Mr.
        Howells's method intimates the more human power which he
        possesses" (p. 129. Howells exhibits a "thorough kindli-
        ness" and "healthfulness."

183   "New Publications / <u>Dr. Breen's Practice</u>." <u>New York Times</u>,
        1 Jan 1882, p. 10. Review.
            "In his unfortunately too needful care for the popular
        distaste of novels that end unhappily, Mr. Howells appears
        to have erred by landing·his heroine in mediocrity."

184   "Recent Novels." <u>Nation</u>, 34 (5 Jan 1882), 18. Review of <u>Dr.
        Breen's Practice</u>.
            Largely summary. Howells exhibits his usual skill and
        "more than an ordinary amount of ingenuity as well." Dr.
        Grace Breen seems to represent the modern form of Puritan-
        ism in a moral rather than religious sense.

185   LITTLEDALE, RICHARD F. "New Novels." <u>Academy</u>, 21 (14 Jan
        1882), 23. Brief review of <u>Dr. Breen's Practice</u>.
            Howells views women as physicians negatively.

186   "Novels of the Week." Athenaeum, No. 2829 (14 Jan 1882), 55.
      Review of Dr. Breen's Practice.
         "The charm of the book lies in the little glimpses which
      it gives of American ways of thought, expression, and ac-
      tion." American novels differ from the English in being
      more straightforward and childlike.

187   "Literary Matters / Items." Boston Evening Transcript, 16 Jan
      1882, p. 6. Brief note.
         "The next instalment of W. D. Howells's story, A Modern
      Instance, will confirm the general opinion that its author
      is now publishing the best novel he has yet produced."
      [Subsequent monthly installments are quite consistently
      noted but without critical comment.]

188   "Literary Matters / Periodicals." Boston Evening Transcript,
      18 Feb 1882, p. 6. Brief note.
         A poem by Howells appearing in the March Lippincott's
      ("Her Valentine," p. 284) "is sure to be widely copied."

189   [Untitled.] New York Times, 22 Feb 1882, p. 4. Brief, rou-
      tine biographical sketch.

190   [PERRY, THOMAS SARGENT.] "William Dean Howells." Century,
      23 (Mar 1882), 680-685. A biographical literary survey.
         Emphasizes Howells' sense of humor, his attitudes toward
      and portrayal of women, his position on conventionality,
      his basic reverence.

191   "W. D. Howells." Century, 23 (Mar 1882), front piece. Full-
      page portrait.

192   "Literary Matters / Periodicals." Boston Evening Transcript,
      23 Mar 1882, p. 6. Brief reference.
         Recognition of Howells' prefatory note to Elizabeth
      Stuart Phelps's Dr. Zay in the April Atlantic pointing
      out "the undesigned coincidence of motive with his Dr.
      Breen's Practice."

193   "Dr. Breen's Practice." Spectator, 55 (20 May 1882), 665-666.
      Review.
         "It is seldom that we have so pleasant a task as that of
      criticising the book now before us, for it is seldom in-
      deed that we have the luck to come across one at once so
      amusing, so clever, and so absolutely inoffensive." Sum-
      mary and extensive quotation.

1882

194 LANG, LENORA B. "New Novels." Academy, 21 (20 May 1882),
       355. Brief review of A Foregone Conclusion.
       Interesting but dissatisfying. American people seem
       enigmatic.

195 "Migma." Our Continent, 2 (26 Jul 1882), 92. Brief note.
       Anecdote of bride confiding to Howells on train her de-
       sire to meet the author of Their Wedding Journey.

196 "A Modern Instance." New Orleans Daily Picayune, 6 Aug 1882,
       p. [2]. Full review.
       Howells' novel "supplies a desideratum of long standing--
       a novel, genuinely and distinctively American." "'Tis a
       sad tale, and o'er true."

197 "Jottings." Boston Evening Transcript, 26 Aug 1882, p. 4.
       Brief note.
       "The flaunting, genial, characterless Bartley Hubbard's
       decline into blackguardism has been plainly shadowed with
       tragedy" in the last installment of A Modern Instance.

198 "Literary Notes." Critic, 2 (26 Aug 1882), 230. Announcement
       of Howells' forthcoming A Sea Change [eventually to become
       A Woman's Reason].
       "Among other subjects treated is the problem of self-
       help among women, with certain tragic phases of New England
       life."

199 PURCELL, E. "New Novels." Academy, 22 (2 Sep 1882), 164.
       Brief review of A Chance Acquaintance.
       Howells' "moral pathology business is all moonshine."

200 "Howells in Paper Covers." American (Philadelphia), 4 (16
       Sep 1882), 363. Brief mention of "summer editions" of
       Their Wedding Journey and A Chance Acquaintance.
       Both "warmly loved" although later, more serious works
       may "rank higher as literary productions."

201 B., A. "Dr. Breen and Dr. Zay." Boston Evening Transcript,
       19 Sep 1882, p. 6. Note.
       A reader attacks the improbability of Dr. Breen and
       Howells' apparent estimate of women.

202 "Literary Matters / Periodicals." Boston Evening Transcript,
       22 Sep 1882, p. 6. Brief note.
       The principal feature of the October Century is the
       closing of A Modern Instance, "which, though painful, is

("Literary Matters / Periodicals")
satisfactory so far as the disposition of the characters
is regarded."

203   "Jottings." Boston Evening Transcript, 26 Sep 1882, p. 4.
Brief mention.
A Modern Instance "has been pronounced by a leading
critic the most important book in moral consequences on
the American people since Uncle Tom's Cabin."

204   DEAN, CLARENCE L. "Mr. Howells's Female Characters." Dial,
3 (Oct 1822), 106-107. Review of A Modern Instance.
A novel with a moral to convey, in careful workmanship
and character interest it follows Howells' earlier novels.

205   "Topics of the Time / Mr. Howells on Divorce." Century, 24
(Oct 1882), 940-941. Note.
Art and moral are effectively combined in A Modern Instance. "The evolution of the moral purpose is mainly
through the trend of the story, through dramatic situations," but the moral is also directly stated in the
speech of Atherton.

206   "Literary Matters / Items." Boston Evening Transcript, 6 Oct
1882, p. 6. Brief announcement.
A portrait of Henry James and Howells' review of James's
work are forthcoming in the November Century. "The numerous readers of Daisy Miller and The Portrait of a Lady
will have hardly less curiosity to see Mr. James's face
than to know what view of his fiction Mr. Howells will
take."

207   "Literature / Novels of the Week." Athenaeum, No. 2867 (7 Oct
1882), 461. Review of A Modern Instance.
The novel is a study of character. Howells is most
original in establishing the relations of the Hubbards,
in narrating the failure of their marriage, and in tracing
Bartley's fall.

208   "Mr. Howells's Shakespearian Titles." Critic, 2 (7 Oct 1882),
269. Editorial item.
The Critic "enlightens the unilluminated" San Francisco
Argonaut, which challenged the Critic's assertion that
Howells drew his titles from Shakespeare's plays.

209   "News and Notes." Literary World, 13 (7 Oct 1882), 334.
Brief item.

1882

("News and Notes")
Howells was "so overrun by social attention in London"
that he has fled to Switzerland.

210   "Literature / Howells' Last Novel." Chicago Daily Tribune,
14 Oct 1882, p. 9. Review of A Modern Instance.
"There are a great many strong points in the book, and
much clever writing, but it is like many another 'modern
instance'--something not worth reading about." Halleck's
falling in love with a married woman casts a yellow light
on the story.

211   M., G. E. "New Books, Plays and Pictures." Boston Evening
Transcript, 14 Oct 1882, p. 10. Brief comment on Howells
and A Modern Instance.
Howells' new novel is "a mature work," an "aggressively
realistic story." It is fortunate that Howells retired
from the Atlantic. "He was a conventional and timid editor. But he is the most observant, fine and artistic
novelist we have." Even Zola or De Goncourt might envy
him.

212   PURCELL, E. "New Novels." Academy, 22 (14 Oct 1882), 273-
274. Review of A Modern Instance.
"A depressing, dreary book, with all its ability and
good intentions."

213   "New Publications / A Modern Instance." New York Daily Tribune, 15 Oct 1882, p. 8. Full review.
Howells' "precision is not the photographic accuracy
which makes a dull copy of commonplace things; it is
vitalized and refined by that imaginative quality which
belongs to true art." The portrayal of Bartley Hubbard
may be Howells' "master-work." Howells has "nobly" ful-
filled "his purpose."

214   "New Publications / A Modern Instance." New York Times, 15
Oct 1882, p. 6. Review.
"It is true that one catches one's self wondering why
so much care and interest are bestowed on matters that
happen to almost every couple, but there is the art."
The fact that Howells is fulfilling his promise to write
of American life, "without foreign admixture," is cause
for rejoicing.

215   WHITING, LILIAN. "Boston Days /.../ Mr. Howells' Modern Instance /...." New Orleans Times-Democrat, 15 Oct 1882,
p. 14. Literary column.

32

(WHITING, LILIAN)
Advance demand necessitated preparation of a second edition even before the first of five thousand copies was available. Added to "the peculiar charm" of Howells' earlier work is "a current of deep insight brought to bear upon a problem of social life."

216 "Literature / A Modern Instance." Critic, 2 (21 Oct 1882), 278-279. Full review. Rpt. "Howells's Great Novel," Boston Evening Transcript, 26 Oct 1882, p. 6.
"There has been no more rigidly artistic writing done in America since Hawthorne's time," but Howells' work lacks "atmosphere." Marcia is not to be considered typical of New England maidens.

217 "A Modern Instance." Saturday Review, 54 (21 Oct 1882), 548-549. Full review.
To Howells' advantage is the fact that he draws his characters from life; "the result is that his people, whether we like them or not, have always the great merit of absolute reality." Further, he recognizes Necessity and Consequence, and he is true to his characters. A Modern Instance is "about as purely American as a book can well be."

218 [Untitled.] New York Times, 26 Oct 1882, p. 4. Note.
Exception is taken to the Athenaeum's review of A Modern Instance. The "wonderful realism" of the colloquialisms helps to make the novel "so supremely good." "James, Howells, and Aldrich are creating a new method for novelists" not understood by the British reader. [The Times frequently links the three names.]

219 "Our Library Table." Athenaeum, No. 2870 (28 Oct 1882), 561.
Brief reference to Howells' article on Lexington in the current Longman's Magazine.
"The only drawback to a paper excellent in tone and in temper is that the author exaggerates the difference in 'civic and social ideas' between America and England."

220 "Book News." Philadelphia Press, 30 Oct 1882, p. 3. Brief review of A Modern Instance.
"Strong and realistic." [Graham]

221 [SCUDDER, H. E.] "A Modern Instance." Atlantic, 50 (Nov 1882), 709-713. Full review. Rpt. in part, Book News, 1 (Nov 1882), 30, and The War of the Critics over William Dean

33

1882

([SCUDDER, H. E.])
Howells, ed. Edwin H. Cady and David L. Frazier (Evanston:
Row, Peterson, 1962), pp. 26-29.
Had Howells written for book publication alone, the
novel would likely have been given greater "dramatic
vigor." As it is, Howells is lured into unnecessary detail. The book is his "greatest achievement, not in an
artistic, but in an ethical apprehension." The portrayal
of Marcia and Bartley make A Modern Instance "the weighti-
est novel of the day"; but "one may fairly expect" of
Howells not only profundity but also "the joyousness of
hope."

222 "New Publications." New Orleans Times-Democrat, 3 Nov 1882,
p. 12. Review of A Modern Instance.
Howells has "unequalled skill and prowess in the arena
of fictitious literature." Because of his "true and
searching wisdom" and his "far-reaching, analytic knowledge of the world," there is "a realism" about this novel.
It "does not seem to be fiction at all." The story of the
Hubbards is "at least as old as life and love," but never
has it been told "with a more pathetic interest."

223 "The Arabian Nights." Saturday Review, 54 (4 Nov 1882), 609.
Review of Stevenson's New Arabian Nights. Rpt. in part,
"Howells, James, and Stevenson," New York Times, 29 Nov
1882, p. 2.
Howells and James are challenged for their preference
for understanding over story.

224 "Current Fiction." Literary World, 13 (4 Nov 1882), 473.
Review of A Modern Instance.
This is the most disagreeable book Howells has written,
but it demands "an interest enlarged and intensified."

225 "Mr. Howells on Mr. James." Boston Evening Transcript, 7 Nov
1882, p. 6. Full review of Howells' "Henry James, Jr.,"
Century, 25 (Nov 1882), 25-29.
"The subject is beautifully treated, but the intelligent
reader does not find that his knowledge is thereby materi-
ally enlarged." Both Howells and James omit the larger
half of human nature from their work.

226 "Literature / A Modern Instance and Doctor Zay." American
(Philadelphia), 5 (11 Nov 1882), 74-75. Review.
Howells' work shows constant growth, but he will proba-
bly never surpass A Modern Instance. It, unlike James's

("Literature / A Modern Instance and Doctor Zay")
Portrait of a Lady, "touches the high-water mark of American fiction."

227   "Literary Matters / New Publications." Boston Evening Transcript, 16 Nov 1882, p. 6.
Brief mention of Howells' introduction to Living Truths,
extracts from the writings of Charles Kingsley, selected
by Emma E. Brown.

228   "Mr. Howells's Titles." Critic, 2 (18 Nov 1882), 314. Note.
The titles A Woman's Reason (chosen by Howells to re-
place A Sea Change when he discovered it was being used by
Mrs. Burnett for a forthcoming poem) and A Counterfeit
Presentment are traced to Shakespeare by Critic readers.

229   "Literary Gossip." Athenaeum, No. 2874 (25 Nov 1882), 700.
Note. Rpt. "Howells on Dickens and Thackeray," New York
Times, 17 Dec 1882, p. 4.
From Switzerland Howells expresses surprise at the response to his Century article on James and proposes "'to
say my say about the art of Dickens and Thackeray in full.'
Next to a new novel from the pen of Mr. Howells, no contribution of his to literature would be more welcome than
such a study."

  *   "Howells, James, and Stevenson." New York Times, 29 Nov 1882,
p. 2. Rpt. from Saturday Review, 54 (4 Nov 1882), 609.
See item 223.

230   "The Earlier and Later Work of Mr. Howells." Lippincott's,
30 (Dec 1882), 604-608. Review of A Modern Instance.
A contrast of Their Wedding Journey and this work shows
that Howells' transition from essayist to novelist is complete. The transition was gradual, except for A Foregone
Conclusion, which already stands out as a novel. The new
Howells exhibits "a closer and finer diction and a somewhat deeper study of life." But in this latest work, "the
strongest and most thoughtful of Mr. Howells' novels,"
the charm, which has been his finest quality, is "largely
wanting"--and it is missed.

231   "Our Bookshelf." Cottage Hearth, 8 (Dec 1882), 401. Brief
review of A Modern Instance.
It is "neither a very bad book nor a very good one."
Calls for presentation of "the nobler and truer types of
husband and wife."

1882

232   "Literary Matters / Items." Boston Evening Transcript, 12
         Dec 1882, p. 6. Brief note.
              Maurice Thompson has taken a cottage in the suburbs—
         the house in which the final chapters of A Modern Instance
         were written.

233   "News and Notes." Literary World, 13 (16 Dec 1882), 462.
         Brief mention.
              Howells, in Switzerland, cannot recollect what he said
         about Dickens and Thackeray.

  *   "Howells on Dickens and Thackeray." New York Times, 17 Dec
         1882, p. 4. Rpt. from Athenaeum, No. 2874 (25 Nov 1882),
         700. See item 229.

234   "A Modern Instance." Spectator, 55 (23 Dec 1882), 1658-1659.
         Full review.
              The "strong flavour of Americanism" that pervades the
         novel causes the English reader to "fail sometimes in
         seizing the exact proportion of expressions, and conse-
         quently of thoughts too." The book is clever, but lacks
         "oneness." The fact that some parts are too elaborately
         (photographically) worked out and other parts "are wanting
         in refined detail" obstructs the "perfect realisation" of
         character.

235   "High Tea." Boston Evening Transcript, 30 Dec 1882, p. 10.
         Extended critical attack on Howells inspired by his
         Century essay.
              "The one mental window to which Mr. Howells confines
         himself evidently cramps his vision." His works feature
         "hysterical or idiotically impulsive women" and "hair-
         splitting moral quibblings."

236   NEMONA. "Our Novelists / Influence of Master Minds Upon
         Fiction." New Orleans Times-Democrat, 31 Dec 1882, p. 14.
         Note.
              While James fails to provide "the fresh, wild flavor of
         Americanism," "Howells gratifies our national vanity by
         the justice he renders us in presenting the artistic side
         of our New World life in its most agreeable guise." Like
         Hawthorne, he has given vitality to American fiction. He
         presents women more exhaustively and with more penetrating
         insight than he does men.

1883

*   "American Literature in England." <u>Studies in Literature</u>, ed.
T. M. Coan. New York: Putnam, 1883. Pp. 1-61. Rpt.
from <u>Blackwood's</u>, 133 (Jan 1883), 136-161. <u>See</u> item 238.

237   DIDIER, EUGENE L. "William D. Howells." <u>A Primer of Criti-
cism</u>. Baltimore: People's Publishing Co., 1883. Pp. 13-
18. Negative evaluation.
    Howells can write gracefully, but "we are heartily tired
of his titles, his methods and himself" (p. 14). "Mr.
Howells is never exciting; the most nervous old lady can
read him without fear" (p. 15). He will not be remembered.
[This item is a 46-page pamphlet, No. 1 in the "Primers
for the People" series.]

238   "American Literature in England." <u>Blackwood's</u>, 133 (Jan 1883),
136-161. Review of Edinburgh edition of <u>Works of W. D.
Howells</u>, with emphasis on <u>The Lady of the Aroostook</u> and
<u>A Modern Instance</u>. Rpt. <u>Studies in Literature</u>, ed. T. M.
Coan (New York: Putnam, 1883), pp. 1-61; rpt. in part,
<u>Howells / A Century of Criticism</u>, ed. Kenneth E. Eble
(Dallas: Southern Methodist University, 1962), pp. 19-33.
    Cisatlantic disagreement with Charles Dudley Warner's
evaluation of English literature turns to a condescending
review of Howells: "He is a better type of the American
novelist than Mr. James, by right of being less accomplished, and moving within a more contracted circle of
observation." He is chauvinistic. His books are stories,
not the "analytic studies" he thinks them to be. While
crediting Howells' art with some pleasantness, the review
is generally negative, motivated in part by the "sore"
copyright issue.

239   "American Novels." <u>Quarterly Review</u>, 155 (Jan 1883), 201-229.
Review essay. Rpt. in part in <u>The War of the Critics
over William Dean Howells</u>, ed. Edwin H. Cady and David L.
Frazier (Evanston: Row, Peterson, 1962), pp. 30-31.
    Highly negative comment on Howells, his evaluation of
James, and <u>A Modern Instance</u> (pp. 208-229). "Was ever
any reader kept out of bed by his desire to finish <u>Por-
trait of a Lady</u> or <u>A Modern Instance</u>?" "Dull, unspeakably
dull, Howells and James may be, but they are never improper."

240   "Contemporary Literature / Belles Lettres." <u>Westminster Re-
view</u>, 119 (Jan 1883), 138. Review of <u>A Modern Instance</u>.

1883

("Contemporary Literature / Belles Lettres")
"There reigns throughout the book an ethical standard
which is rather superfine and dilettante than truly just
and noble." The review centers on the portrayal of Bartley Hubbard.

241 [CURTIS, GEORGE WILLIAM.] "Editor's Literary Record." Harper's, 66 (Jan 1883), 314-315. Review of A Modern Instance.
After a point-by-point comparison, A Modern Instance is
pronounced inferior to Constance Fenimore Woolson's Anne
"as a work of imaginative art." The value of Howells'
social concern is recognized.

242 "Howells's A Modern Instance." Century, 25 (Jan 1883), 463-
465. Full review.
"Mr. Howells excels himself as a reporter of manners
and customs, and yet does much more." He touches on
deeper passions, his humor strikes a deeper vein, and he
has found a higher moral purpose than in his earlier works.
The work exhibits "an artistic finish of parts and con-
scientiousness of study." Howells is related to Dickens,
Thackeray, and George Eliot.

243 S. "Young Men and A Modern Instance." Century, 25 (Jan 1883),
473. Editorial.
Discussion of the defensive response of contemporary
young men to Howells' novel, especially to the disturbing-
ly accurate portrayal of Bartley Hubbard.

244 "The Macaulayflower Papers / A History of Our Own Times /
Chapter II." Life, 1 (11 Jan 1883), 16. Brief reference.
Humorous and ironic reference to "the flamboyant and
epic Howells" and to Bartley Hubbard and Ben Halleck.
Illustration of Hubbard-Howells drinking Tivoli beer.

245 "Recent Novels." Nation, 36 (11 Jan 1883), 41. Review of A
Modern Instance.
A conscientious introduction to one aspect of American
life. But it is a disagreeable novel, perhaps because
every reader finds in himself some resemblance to the
common types it contains.

246 "News and Notes." Literary World, 14 (13 Jan 1883), 13.
Mention of serialization of A Woman's Reason.
It promises to be more like the earlier than the later
novels.

247 No Entry

248   W., J. H. "The Women in Mr. Howells's Books." <u>Boston Evening Transcript</u>, 16 Jan 1883, p. 6. A column-and-a-half defense of Howells in response to "High Tea," <u>Boston Evening Transcript</u>, 30 Dec 1882, p. 10. <u>See</u> item 235.
    "Mr. Howells as a writer delineates types and not persons." "Types" are moved by influences and are "really weak, individually considered." "The very thing that distinguishes a type from a personality is that the person acts by his own force of character, the type acts through the force of some kind of influences."

249   BENTZON, TH. [M. T. BLANC]. "Les Nouveaux Romancier Américains / I. William Dean Howells." <u>Revue des Deux Mondes</u>, 53 (31 Jan 1883), 634-670. Essay.
    Focusing on <u>The Undiscovered Country</u> and <u>A Modern Instance</u>, Bentzon finds Howells typically American but capable, because of his Latin experiences, of a subtle irony. His work is marked by the psychological honesty of character portrayal and by a pervasive humor.

250   "Literary Notes." <u>Independent</u>, 35 (15 Feb 1883), 12. Brief mention of <u>A Woman's Reason</u>.
    "Mr. Howells' new novel, begun in the current <u>Century</u>, has necessitated a new edition of that number of the magazine."

251   KENDRICK. "A Literary Combination." <u>Life</u>, 1 (22 Feb 1883), 91. Full-page cartoon.
    Henry James, standing on shoulders of Howells, is still unable to attain the height of a statue of Thackeray.

252   "Parnassus Advertised." <u>Life</u>, 1 (15 Mar 1883), 128. Brief item.
    Parody of a Boston <u>Herald</u> advertisement (not seen) of <u>A Woman's Reason</u>.

253   "The Case of Mr. Howells." <u>New York Tribune</u>, 18 Mar 1883, p. 6. Brief note.
    An antagonistic press has resulted from Howells' criticism of Thackeray and Dickens.

254   "The Modest Spread-Eagle." <u>Punch</u>, 84 (24 Mar 1883), 142. Poem. Rpt. <u>Albany Evening Journal</u>, 21 Apr 1883, p. 4, and by Robert H. Woodward in "<u>Punch</u> on Howells and James," <u>American Literary Realism</u>, 3 (Winter 1970), 76-77.
    This satiric verse, a part of British response to Howells' <u>Century</u> essay on James, is headed by a quotation drawn from the essay.

1883

255   [CURTIS, GEORGE WILLIAM.] "Editor's Easy Chair." Harper's,
           61 (Apr 1883), 791-793.
           Defense of Howells for his article on James.

256   TILLEY, ARTHUR. "The New School of Fiction." National and
           English Review, 1 (Apr 1883), 257-268. Essay.
           In comparing A Modern Instance and Portrait of a Lady,
           which are alike in that both subordinate plot, elaborately
           analyze character, and study human nature "mainly in its
           wonted aspects," Tilley also points comparisons and con-
           trasts with Scott, Hawthorne, Thackeray, Balzac, Turgenev,
           Austen, and Trollope.

   *   "The Modest Spread-Eagle." Albany Evening Journal, 21 Apr
           1883, p. 4. Poem. Rpt. from Punch, 84 (24 Mar 1883),
           142. See item 254.

257   "Live and Let Live." Life, 1 (26 Apr 1883), 195. Brief
           humorous note.
           Howells gives away his ladies' hairdressing secrets.

258   "Fiction in the May Magazine." Critic, 3 (28 Apr 1883), 195.
           Brief references to the serialization of A Woman's Reason
           and to "Niagara Revisited."
           "Mr. Howells's 'touches' are so apt to be merely funny,
           that some very tender ones...are especially effective."
           "Niagara Revisited" (Atlantic) is dispiriting. Isabel's
           illusions were charming, and we don't care to hear about
           her disillusions."

259   BADGER, G. H. "Howells as an Interpreter of American Life."
           International Review, 14 (May-Jun 1883), 380-386. Essay
           review.
           Measured strictly as an interpreter of American life,
           Howells falls short. He lacks "that intensity of purpose
           which penetrates right through the externals of life and
           takes hold of its vital motives, and which pushes directly
           onward to a significant conclusion" (p. 382).

260   "New Publications." New Orleans Times-Democrat, 13 May 1883,
           p. 7. Brief notice of The Sleeping Car.
           Howells "has descended from his level to enter the
           region of the ridiculous but, withal, the eminently
           natural, while he presents a chapter from life that might
           be from the experience of most anybody, taken at random."

261   "Fiction in June Magazines." Critic, 3 (26 May 1883), 242.
           Mention of A Woman's Reason.

("Fiction in June Magazines")
　　　　Readers will continue to find pleasure in Howells'
minute touches, but his shipwreck is not better than other
people's shipwrecks, "except there are a few more sharks
in it."

262　　"A Temporary and Foolish Reaction." Literary World, 14 (16
　　　　Jun 1883), 192. Brief editorial.
　　　　Defends a critical view of Howells and James.

263　　H., M. L. "A Non-Combatant's View." Literary World, 14 (30
　　　　Jun 1883), 209. Letter to editor.
　　　　In support of Howells and James.

264　　RIDDLE, A. G. "The American Novel." Literary World, 14 (30
　　　　Jun 1883), 209. Letter to editor.
　　　　"Certainly Mr. Howells is a most intense American."

265　　MORSE, JAMES HERBERT. "The Native Element in American Fiction
　　　　/ Since the War." Century, 26 (Jul 1883), 362-375, esp.
　　　　371-375. Essay.
　　　　　　Howells and James, the two most accomplished American
writers of this period, are contrasted. Both are limited.
Both "feel the effect of the scientific critical spirit."
Howells is restricted by his journalistic tolerance: the
"shows of life" are curious to him, but not vital.

266　　"Anecdotal Photographs / Mr. W. D. Howells." Truth, 14 (16
　　　　Aug 1883), 241-243. Biographical sketch. Rpt. in part,
　　　　Boston Evening Transcript, 31 Aug 1883, p. 6.
　　　　　　Howells' "whipped-cream sort of literary composition
requires the delicate touch of a master hand, the true
spirit of the poet, the humorist, and the man of the
world to prevent it from degenerating into dulness. It
is to be feared that Mr. Howells will have a host of
imitators who will be deadly stupid."

267　　THOMPSON, MAURICE. "A 'Modern Instance' of Criticism."
　　　　Indianapolis Saturday Herald, 18 Aug 1883, p. 4. Full
　　　　review of A Modern Instance.
　　　　　　In what he describes as his own "ill-tempered nagging,"
Thompson praises Howells' skill of characterization but
mistakenly views the novel as an anti-divorce tract.
Howells is linked to James. [Scharnhorst]

　*　　"Mr. Howells in England." Boston Evening Transcript, 31 Aug
　　　　1883, p. 6. Rpt. from "Anecdotal Photographs / Mr. W. D.
　　　　Howells," Truth, 14 (16 Aug 1883), 241-243. See item 266.

1883

268   "Periodicals." <u>Boston Evening Transcript</u>, 21 Sep 1883, p. 6.
      Brief mention.
        Howells brings <u>A Woman's Reason</u> to a close, and it is
      being issued "today" in book form.

269   "Fall Book Announcements." <u>Boston Evening Transcript</u>, 25 Sep
      1883, p. 6.   Brief, non-critical mention of <u>A Little Girl</u>
      <u>Among Old Masters</u>.

270   "New Books / <u>A Woman's Reason</u>." <u>Boston Evening Transcript</u>,
      27 Sep 1883, p. 6.   Full review.
        "The structure topples a little, and suffers by compari-
      son with [Howells'] stronger works."   Again Howells "deals
      with the ethics of love and matrimony."   "The thing that
      he likes to scourge is presumption."   All of the charac-
      ters "stand in the realistic commonplaceness with which
      Howells stamps most of his coin."

271   "Literature." <u>American</u> (Philadelphia), 6 (29 Sep 1883), 393–
      394.   Review of <u>A Woman's Reason</u>.
        Howells is his own best competition, and this novel
      bears up admirably.   Portrayal of Helen Harkness is excel-
      lent, but the title should be "A Woman's Unreason."

272   "Contemporary Literature / Belles Lettres." <u>Westminster Re-</u>
      <u>view</u>, 120 (Oct 1883), 280.   Brief mention of <u>Out of the</u>
      <u>Question</u> and "At the Sign of the Savage."
        The first is clever satire, the second "a charming
      little tale brimming over with fun; French in its light-
      hearted gaiety, but with an undercurrent of sly humour
      essentially American."

273   "Contemporary Literature / Belles Lettres." <u>Westminster Re-</u>
      <u>view</u>, 120 (Oct 1883), 280.   Brief mention of <u>Italian</u>
      <u>Journeys</u>.
        "Delicate and discriminating originality" gives fresh-
      ness to trite themes.

274   RUNNION, JAMES B.   "Howells-Harte-James." <u>Dial</u>, 4 (Oct 1883),
      126-129.   Review of <u>A Woman's Reason</u> (along with Harte's
      <u>In the Carquinez Woods</u> and James's <u>Daisy Miller</u>).
        Howells' "most ambitious novel...indicates a larger and
      broader conception of the scope, the opportunities, and
      the resources of his art."

275   "Book News." <u>Philadelphia Press</u>, 5 Oct 1883, p. 7.   Brief
      review of <u>A Woman's Reason</u>.

("Book News")
"The most spontaneous and natural" of Howells' recent
novels. [Graham]

276 "New Publications / A Woman's Reason." New York Times, 7 Oct
1883, p. 6. Review.
"Is it possible...that Mr. Howells is becoming as con-
scienceless as Mr. William Black, and padding his book
with as much method, if not as much hollow gayety, as he?"
This initial response gives way to enthusiasm for Howells'
character portrayal and control.

277 "A Writer as a Talker / Chat with Howells, the Author." Baltimore American and Commercial Advertiser, 10 Oct 1883,
p. [4]. Interview.
Long introductory paragraph focuses on Howells' fine
handwriting and on his physical appearance. Howells comments on his personal experiences as a youth and in Venice,
the literary possibilities of Baltimore, and the English
tendency to produce books rather than magazines.

278 "High Tea." Boston Evening Transcript, 13 Oct 1883, p. 10.
Note.
Discussion of Howells' women. "The fact remains that
the people who know the types [Howells] holds upon his
nicely pointed pen recognize them."

279 "Literature / Recent Fiction." Chicago Daily Tribune, 13 Oct
1883, p. 9. Review of A Woman's Reason.
"The art of facile expression has in the hands of Mr.
Howells attained ideal perfection." "Like Don Juan, Mr.
Howells evidently thinks that the proper study of mankind
is woman," and he has studied them to some purpose.

280 THOMPSON, MAURICE. "A Woman's Reason." Indianapolis Saturday
Herald, 13 Oct 1883, p. 5. Full review.
Howells improves with each new novel and here seems "to
write with a clearer view of life, from a man's standpoint,
than ever before." Thompson praises the sentimentality of
Helen Harkness' "pitiful but sincerely earnest struggles"
and claims that the story is "American in every respect."
[Scharnhorst]

281 KING, ROLAND. "Hark from the Tombs! / or, A Woman's Reason /
a Novel by / W---- D---- H-w-lls." Life, 2 (18 Oct 1883),
188-191. Parody.

1883

282　"Fiction." Literary World, 14 (20 Oct 1883), 350. Review of
　　　A Woman's Reason.
　　　　　"Light and agreeable reading." Although genial and
　　　sweet tempered, Howells never avoids "the stern facts of
　　　life."

283　"American Feuilletons." New Orleans Times-Democrat, 21 Oct
　　　1883, p. 4. Editorial.
　　　　　Approves of Howells' suggestion that stories and
　　　sketches be published in newspapers. [In subsequent
　　　months the editors act on the suggestion.]

284　NEMONA. "W. D. Howells." New Orleans Times-Democrat, 21 Oct
　　　1883, p. 8. Critical evaluation.
　　　　　A lengthy analysis of the art of Howells applauds "the
　　　effect of finest realism" in his work but regrets that he
　　　fails to represent the "highest idealism." "He never
　　　reaches the grandeur of the perfect prose of Thackeray,
　　　the passion and pathos of George Eliot, or the many-sided
　　　subtle witchery of Hawthorne.... His stories, with their
　　　refinement of style and subtle power of dissection, are
　　　not as impressive as Mr. Cable's unsurpassed conceptions
　　　of pathos." The Undiscovered Country is his most charming
　　　work, Marcia Hubbard the least attractive of his female
　　　portraits, and Helen Harkness "a charming mouthpiece."
　　　"His manner of hinting and suggesting social themes is a
　　　very winning one."

285　[SCUDDER, H. E.] "The East and West in Recent Fiction."
　　　Atlantic, 52 (Nov 1883), 704-706. Review of A Woman's
　　　Reason (contrasted with Bret Harte's In the Carquinez
　　　Woods). Rpt. in part, Book News, 2 (Nov 1883), 48.
　　　　　This is the first time Howells "has allowed the story
　　　element to get the upper hand of him." There is danger
　　　that Howells' "success as an artist depends upon his real-
　　　ism, whereas the reverse should be true." One hopes the
　　　coming novelist will inherit both "the grace and distinct
　　　naturalness of Howells" and "the large, vigorous, imagina-
　　　tive vividness" of Harte.

＊　　　　. "The East and West in Recent Fiction." Book News, 2
　　　(Nov 1883), 48. Rpt. in part from Atlantic, 52 (Nov 1883),
　　　704-706. See item 285.

286　NORMAN, HENRY. "Theories and Practice of Modern Fiction."
　　　Fortnightly Review, n.s. 34 (1 Nov 1883), 870-886. Brief
　　　reference. Rpt. in part, "Modern Fiction," Critic, n.s.
　　　1 (12 Jan 1884), 15.

(NORMAN, HENRY)
   The new American school of fiction is "actuated by the
same fundamental views" as those that guide Zola, yet the
American writers "produce works of great delicacy and
purity." Howells is "a far better representative" of the
school than is James (pp. 874-875).

287   W., N. M. "Was Howells Nodding?" Literary World, 14 (3 Nov
      1883), 366. Letter to the editor.
         Challenges the digging of a well on an atoll in A Wom-
      an's Reason.

288   "Literature / Novels of the Week." Athenaeum, No. 2924 (10
      Nov 1883), 597-598. Review of A Woman's Reason.
         "An old theme pleasantly handled." The logic of the
      title is puzzling.

289   "A Woman's Reason." Saturday Review, 56 (10 Nov 1883), 604-
      605. Full review.
         Howells' more conscious attempt to form a definite plot
      is faulted: "Mr. Howells allows the scaffolding of his
      edifice to be visible from the beginning." Further, he
      "permits the reader to perceive that he is bored with
      writing." He must learn how to manage his machinery.

290   "Recent Novels." Nation, 37 (15 Nov 1883), 420. Review of
      A Woman's Reason.
         The book suffers "from appearing in the beginning to
      suggest a profundity of social motive which is really not
      to be found between its covers."

291   PURCELL, E. "New Novels." Academy, 24 (17 Nov 1883), 327.
      Review of A Woman's Reason.
         "As a student of the great enigma--woman--[Howells] is
      quite unrivalled."

292   "Book News." Philadelphia Press, 23 Nov 1883, p. 9. Brief
      mention.
         Notes Howells' introduction and commentary for A Little
      Girl Among the Old Masters. [Graham]

293   "New Publications." New York Times, 26 Nov 1883, p. 3. Re-
      view of A Little Girl Among the Old Masters, introd. by
      Howells.
         "A proud father, with just sufficient criticism not to
      snub his little girl."

1883

294　ARDEN, ALFRED. "Open Letters / Recent American Novels."
　　　Century, 27 (Dec 1883), 313-315. Review of A Woman's
　　　Reason.
　　　　　"Unquestionably Mr. Howells has never before written so
　　　finely as regards diction and style nor so acutely as re-
　　　gards observation of the ways of women in his part of the
　　　world." In detecting and defining the flaw in women's ed-
　　　ucation, he "goes as near as he dares to suggest a remedy
　　　without becoming absolutely didactic."

295　[CURTIS, GEORGE WILLIAM.] "Editor's Literary Record." Harp-
　　　er's, 68 (Dec 1883), 518-519. Review of A Woman's Reason.
　　　　　Howells has so artfully "grafted multiplied incident
　　　and vicissitude upon the stem of a slender and rather
　　　hackneyed plot" that its triteness is concealed.

296　"A Little Girl Among Old Masters." Literary World, 14 (1 Dec
　　　1883), 412-413. Review.
　　　　　Howells' comment is "the delicious element in the book,"
　　　his "grave-faced humor" coming perilously close to "making
　　　fun."

297　"The Bookshelf." Continent, 4 (5 Dec 1883), 733-734. Review
　　　of A Woman's Reason.
　　　　　"Mr. Howells exhibits both his power [stylistic] and his
　　　limitations [structural] to a greater extent than in any
　　　of his preceding volumes." The title of this one should
　　　be "A Man's Unreason."

298　NECK, L. VAN. "A Modern Instance." Life, 2 (6 Dec 1883),
　　　286-288. A satiric narrative.
　　　　　"[The author begs leave to inform Mr. W. D. Howells
　　　that there are a thousand and one 'modern instances';
　　　this one, for instance.]"

299　"New Publications." New Orleans Times-Democrat, 16 Dec 1883,
　　　p. 16. Review of A Little Girl Among the Old Masters.
　　　　　Enthusiastic reception of the drawings which suggest a
　　　talent which one day will not require an introduction by
　　　Howells.

300　"Notes." Nation, 37 (20 Dec 1883), 508. Review of A Little
　　　Girl Among the Old Masters.
　　　　　No critical comment on Howells' contribution.

301　"Literature / A Woman's Reason." Critic, 3 (22 Dec 1883),
　　　518-519. Full review.

("Literature / A Woman's Reason")
Howells' lack of sympathy for the life he described so
effectively in A Modern Instance deprived the novel of
power and reality. One finds more of that sympathy in
the portrayal of Helen Harkness. But "we still look to
Howells in vain for that undiscovered country where good
background and closer dramatic intensity shall carry our
imaginations and hold them long captive in spite of themselves."

302   WHITING, LILIAN. "Boston Days /.../ Mr. Howells' Little
      Daughter /...." New Orleans Times-Democrat, 23 Dec 1883,
      p. 7. Brief note.
      Full-paragraph appreciation of the artistic talent of
      Howells' daughter, noting that she is a niece of sculptor
      Larkin W. Mead and so has artistic background on both
      paternal and maternal sides.

303   "The Bookshelf." Continent, 4 (26 Dec 1883), 831. Brief
      mention of A Little Girl Among the Old Masters.
      "The reason for the work, even with all its originality,
      seems somewhat questionable."

304   "The Last of the Gift-Books." Academy, 24 (29 Dec 1883), 431.
      Favorable notice of A Little Girl Among the Old Masters.

                              1884

*   "Modern Fiction." Critic, n.s. 1 (12 Jan 1884), 15. Rpt. in
      part from Fortnightly Review, n.s. 34 (1 Nov 1883), 870-
      886. See item 286.

305   "New Publications." New Orleans Times-Democrat, 13 Jan 1884,
      p. 16. Review of A Woman's Reason.
      Helen Harkness is not plausible. The novel lacks the
      qualities which appeal to the sympathies of the reader.
      All of the characters, with the exception of Lord Rainford,
      are vague and unsubstantial.

306   "Books of Travel and Description." Literary World, 15 (14 Jan
      1884), 193. Brief mention of Three Villages.
      "Photographic minuteness" touched with "delicate humor."

307   "New Publications." Catholic World, 38 (Feb 1884), 718.
      Brief notice of A Little Girl Among the Old Masters.
      "Mr. Howells' running criticism on these sketches is
      interesting and amusing."

1884

308   "High Tea." Boston Evening Transcript, 16 Feb 1884, p. 6.
        Brief reference.
            Since an English writer has described Howells as "a
        benevolent Balzac," Howells "should hasten to extend his
        repertory of characters."

309   "New Books." New York Times, 10 Mar 1884, p. 3. Brief men-
        tion of The Register.
            Low-life characters would be better, since the behavior
        presented does not reflect "the received conventions among
        cultivated people."

310   "A Woman's Reason." Spectator, 57 (29 Mar 1884), 415-416.
        Full review.
            Retaining his best qualities in this work, Howells fur-
        ther "condescends to modify that lofty contempt for inci-
        dent...which he has hitherto been somewhat inclined to
        carry to excess, and which has led to some people's think-
        ing him occasionally monotonous." Gratingly unpleasant
        Americanisms are mentioned.

311   "Our 'Forty Immortals.'" Critic, n.s. 1 (12 Apr 1884), 169.
        Brief mention.
            Howells is number five in a list of forty.

312   [Untitled.] New York Times, 17 Apr 1884, p. 4. Brief note.
            Howells has published notice that he is "merely the
        adapter, not the author," of "Yorick's Love."

313   ZIMMERN, H[ELEN]. "W. D. Howells." Revue Internationale,
        2 (25 Apr 1884), 353-363. Essay.
            A routine biographical sketch prefaces a critical dis-
        cussion of five novels, Their Wedding Journey to A Modern
        Instance. Howells is one of the most effective painters
        of American life.

314   "New Publications / Three Villages." New York Daily Tribune,
        16 May 1884, p. 6. Brief review.
            "The pleasantest and in a literary sense the best of
        the three is the charming paper on 'Lexington.'" It has
        the "strong individual flavor" which sets Howells' work
        apart from the other good books of the day.

315   "Reviews / Minor Notices." Critic, n.s. 1 (7 Jun 1884), 270.
        Brief review of Three Villages.
            "The sketches all have that descriptive touch which
        could make a treatise on sawdust interesting."

316   [Untitled.]   New Orleans Times-Democrat, 8 Jun 1884, p. 4.
      A two-part story by Howells is announced for the 15 and
      22 June issues, preceded by a two-part story by James and
      followed by one by Bret Harte. James's "Pandora" was
      published on 1 and 8 June and Harte's "A Blue Grass Penel-
      ope" on 29 June and 6 July. But the Howells story never
      appeared. All three stories were to be published simul-
      taneously in the New York Sun. The Times-Democrat carried
      additional stories by James, Harte, and Lafcadio Hearn in
      subsequent Sunday issues.

317   "Well-Paid Authors." Philadelphia Press, 24 Jun 1884, p. 8.
      Brief note.
      Howells receives about $5000 for each of his serialized
      novels and a percentage when the book is published.
      [Graham]

318   "The Lounger." Critic, n.s. 1 (28 Jun 1884), 306-307. Brief
      note.
      Information on how much Howells is paid for his work.

319   "Personal and General Notes." New Orleans Daily Picayune
      (Afternoon ed.), 2 Jul 1884, p. [1]. Brief mention.
      Howells buys a home, a few doors from Dr. Holmes, in
      Boston.

320   "Our Library Table." Athenaeum, No. 2960 (19 Jul 1884), 78.
      Brief review of Three Villages.
      The paper on Lexington is superior; but when Howells
      writes history, he loses his charm.

321   "Recent Literature." Manhattan, 4 (Aug 1884), 251. Very
      brief mention of Three Villages.
      "These sketches are in Mr. Howells' best vein."

322   "New Books." New York Times, 24 Aug 1884, p. 9. Brief notice
      of Three Villages.
      The piece on Lexington is most interesting and most
      Howellsian.

323   [ROBERTSON, JOHN M.] "Mr. Howells' Novels." Westminster
      Review, 122 (Oct 1884), 347-375. Major essay. Rpt. John
      M. Robertson, Essays Toward a Critical Method (London: T.
      Fisher Unwin, 1889), pp. 149-199, and in part, The War of
      the Critics over William Dean Howells, ed. Edwin H. Cady
      and David L. Frazier (Evanston: Row, Peterson, 1962),
      p. 32.

1884

([ROBERTSON, JOHN M.])
Although Howells is a master of the language in which he
writes, his work lacks penetration. Even in his more
serious endeavors, "he has exhibited a lack of the necessary width and depth of thought--in short, deficient philosophic capacity." Robertson concludes, "One arrives at a
notion that this gifted, sympathetic, unphilosophic novelist, with his acutenesses and his blindnesses, his felici-
ties and his inefficiencies, may be a link between a past
school and a future school; an intermediate type in the
evolution of fictional art. But, remembering the fate of
intermediate types, we cannot promise him a full-bodied
immortality."

324   VERNEY, F. P. "The Americans Painted by Themselves." Contemporary Review, 46 (Oct 1884), 543-555. Essay.
Americans seem to be obsessed with gowns, position, independence ("they undertake to do everything, and to de-
cide all questions with an aplomb of ignorance utterly
startling"), and "that purely American conviction that
knowledge is heaven-born." "The almost entire absence of
an ideal of any kind, in men and women alike, of any
poetic feeling of character, is strange in so young a
literature." Many of the illustrative references are to
Howells' novels.

325   "American Books." Academy, 26 (4 Oct 1884), 214. Brief notice of Three Villages.
"Very slight and strung together by a slender thread."

326   "Fiction." Literary World, 15 (4 Oct 1884), 328. Brief notice of The Register.
"Not a very important performance."

327   "The Magazines for November." Critic, n.s. 2 (1 Nov 1884),
210. Brief mention.
"It is almost with a groan that we discover that Mr.
Howells's new serial is to be a resurrection of that
frightful Bartley Hubbard and Marcia, who may be types,
and undoubtedly are warnings, but who are inexcusably uninteresting."

328   DROCH [ROBERT BRIDGES]. "Bookishness / The Mugwump Canonized."
Life, 4 (4 Dec 1884), 311. Note.
Howells is contrasted with F. Marion Crawford, to the
latter's discredit. "Mr. Howells is a literary artist
and student of human nature." He uses dialogue as "the

1884

(DROCH [ROBERT BRIDGES])
expression of the characters he has created"--rather than
to tell a story.

329   "How We Do It.--No. 2 / By W. Dowells." Life, 4 (25 Dec 1884),
362. Epistolary satire.
"Relating to focus and method in the "Lady of the
Aroostuck."

1885

330   [BLANC, M. T.] "William D. Howells," in Les Nouveaux Ro-
manciers Américains, by "Th. Bentzon." Paris: Levy,
1885. Pp. 7-70. Critical introduction to Howells.
Focus is on The Undiscovered Country, A Modern Instance,
The Lady of the Aroostook, and to a lesser degree on Out
of the Question and A Counterfeit Presentment. Generally
favorable evaluation.

*   GOSSE, EDMUND. "To W. D. Howells." From Shakespeare to Pope.
New York: Dodd, Mead, 1885. P. iii. Dedicatory poem.
Advance publication in Critic, n.s. 4 (19 Sep 1885), 139.
See item 366.

331   DROCH [ROBERT BRIDGES]. "Bookishness / Olla-Podrida." Life,
5 (1 Jan 1885), 4. Brief reference.
"'It is the effect of contemporaneousness that is to be
given,' says Mr. Howells in excuse for his anachronisms
[see "Open Letters," Century, 29 (Jan 1885), 477]. Anachronisms are about as consistent with 'contemporaneousness'
as thefts with honesty."

332   "Notes." Critic, n.s. 3 (17 Jan 1885), 24. Brief reference.
Frederic R. Guernsey acquits Howells "of perpetrating
an anachronism" in The Rise of Silas Lapham by having a
typewriter in use in 1875.

333   "A Contemporaneous Ghost Story / Dedicated to W. D. Howells."
Life, 5 (29 Jan 1885), 60, 62. Note.
Ironic response to Howells' "Open Letter" in the January
Century.

334   "Literary Notes." Philadelphia Record, 31 Jan 1885, p. 6.
Brief reference.
Howells is fond of quoting Shakespeare. The Undiscovered
Country and The Lady of the Aroostook are Howells' personal
favorites of his works thus far. [Graham]

1885

335   "The Lounger." Critic, n.s. 3 (31 Jan 1885), 55. Brief note.
       Was Howells aware that the name Lapham is an Irish deri-
       vation, although the character is wholly New England?

336   "Mr. Howells's Operetta." Critic, n.s. 3 (31 Jan 1885), 59.
       Brief note.
       Howells went to Gilbert for suggestions.

337   "The Lounger." Critic, n.s. 3 (14 Feb 1885), 79. Brief note.
       Lapham is a New England name (geneology is traced).
       Howells apparently chose it "at haphazard."

338   "The Magazine in March." Critic, n.s. 3 (28 Feb 1885), 101.
       Brief mention.
       Reference is to The Rise of Silas Lapham and other Cen-
       tury selections: "In fiction we are having really too
       much realism."

339   WHITING, LILIAN. "Boston Days." New Orleans Times-Democrat,
       15 Mar 1885, p. 5. Brief reference.
       Howells meets "Mr. Craddock" (Mary Noailles Murfree.)

340   "By the Way." Life, 5 (23 Apr 1885), 228. Satiric note.
       On the "lightness" of The Rise of Silas Lapham being
       serialized in Century.

341   CHASE, F. E. "The Rise of Silas Slap 'Em / By W. D. Howls."
       Life, 5 (7 May 1885), 262-263. Parody of Chapter 1.
       The other thirty-nine chapters are omitted "out of con-
       sideration for our readers."

342   "Literary Notes." Philadelphia Evening Bulletin, 11 May 1885,
       p. 4. Announcement.
       Howells begins a new serial in Century, six parts
       dealing with the "perplexities of a country boy in Bos-
       ton" and the minister who advises him, illustrating "one
       of the peculiar phases of American life." [Graham]

343   "Literary Notes." Philadelphia Press, 11 May 1895, p. 11.
       Mention of Howells' introd. to Tolstoy's Master and Man.

344   DROCH [ROBERT BRIDGES]. "Bookishness / A Thoroughly American
       Success." Life, 5 (14 May 1885), 273. Brief review of
       The Rise of Silas Lapham.
       This clever novel, featuring admirable character sketch-
       ing and dialogue, is pervaded by "a gentle humor which
       sees the foibles of humanity, and yet forgives them."

345   "A Doleful Tale." <u>Life</u>, 6 (2 Jul 1885), 10.   Satiric verse.
      Inspired by <u>The Rise of Silas Lapham</u>.

346   BRYAN, CLARK W. "The Literature of the Household, a Sketch
      of America's Leading Writer of Fiction, W. D. Howells."
      <u>Good Housekeeping</u>, 1 (11 Jul 1885), 2-3. Biographical
      sketch. Rpt. <u>Good Housekeeping</u>, 12 (Jun 1891), 293-295.
      Interesting and moderately detailed, this introduction
      was endorsed by Howells as the best ever written about
      him to this point.

347   "August Magazines." <u>Boston Evening Transcript</u>, 5 Aug 1885,
      p. 6. Brief note.
      Howells brings <u>The Rise of Silas Lapham</u> "to what many
      readers may feel to be an unsatisfactory conclusion."

348   WHITING, LILIAN. "Boston Days /.../ 'The Rise of Silas Lap-
      ham' /...." New Orleans <u>Times-Democrat</u>, 9 Aug 1885, p. 8.
      Critical reaction to <u>The Rise of Silas Lapham</u> upon its
      conclusion in <u>Century</u>.
      "The story could easily have been carried forward to a
      seemingly natural, but innately vulgar denouement, and
      that it does not find this ending reveals both the artis-
      tic feeling of the author, and also still more impressive-
      ly emphasizes the delicacy and truth of his perceptions
      regarding the social types he is delineating."

349   DROCH [ROBERT BRIDGES]. "Bookishness / Why We Admire Old
      Silas Lapham." <u>Life</u>, 6 (13 Aug 1885), 90. Brief note.
      Howells "has made the central figure of his story an
      old man, unromantic, lacking refinement, a braggart, with
      many frailties, vulgarly rich--and yet the most notable
      character of recent fiction, ennobled by his transcendent
      honesty and unpretentious sincerity."

350   "Jottings." <u>Boston Evening Transcript</u>, 14 Aug 1885, p. 4.
      Brief mention.
      "The 1st words of Colonel Silas Lapham after he has lost
      all, rather than save himself by sharp practice, are true
      grit."

351   "Mr. Howells's <u>Rise of Silas Lapham</u>." <u>Boston Evening Tran-
      script</u>, 14 Aug 1885, p. 4. Major review. Rpt. Philadel-
      phia <u>Evening Bulletin</u>, 17 Aug 1885, p. 8.
      The displeasure engendered by <u>The Rise of Silas Lapham</u>
      "arises from a misunderstanding of the nature of Mr.
      Howells's work." But Howells "must go on and put down
      things as he sees them, whether we like them or no."

1885

("Mr. Howells's Rise of Silas Lapham")
Instead of creating an unreal world, Howells "does us the credit, apparently, of believing that, in this age of our civilization, we care more for conscientious studies of our actual selves." Future historians will find more of value in Howells' fiction than in our histories.

352 "New Publications / Mr. Howells's Last Story / The Rise of Silas Lapham." New York Daily Tribune, 16 Aug 1885, p. 8. Full review.
Howells does not have faith in his characters. He "tells us what he likes about his people, and what he says is consistent and natural, and for the most part they act up to the characters he has given them. But all the time he is describing them we feel that somehow he is not telling us all he thinks; that he does not think so much of them as he pretends to; and that even their best thoughts and actions would seem less noble if we only surveyed the scene from his point of view."

* "Literature." Philadelphia Evening Bulletin, 17 Aug 1885, p. 8. Review of The Rise of Silas Lapham. Rpt. from Boston Evening Transcript, 14 Aug 1885, p. 4. See item 350.

353 "Mr. Howells's Heroines." Boston Evening Transcript, 20 Aug 1885, p. 6. A letter to the editor, signed "An Every-Day American Girl."
Howells presents a variety of American men, but all of his young women lack common sense. This representative of "that much-abused class, 'Boston girls,'" calls for justice.

354 "Notes." Critic, n.s. 4 (22 Aug 1885), 84.
M. L. B. W. in Portland, Maine, submits a collection of Howells' "lapses from correct English" in Indian Summer.

355 "Some New Books / Mr. Howells's Last Novel." New York Sun, 23 Aug 1885, p. 4. Full review of The Rise of Silas Lapham. Rpt. Book News, 4 (Oct 1885), 37-38.
"Every one appreciates the almost flawless finish of Mr. Howells's literary workmanship, but it seems to us that the intrinsic capabilities of the material selected, and the amount of thought and insight involved in the author's choice of theme, are not always adequately recognized."

356 "Reviews." American (Philadelphia), 10 (29 Aug 1885), 265-266. Full review of The Rise of Silas Lapham.

54

("Reviews")
Howells' portrayal of Silas "is entirely successful, and
the whole story, designed to develop this character, and
to present it as one type of American men, has artistic
unity and completeness."

357   "The Newest Books." Book Buyer, n.s. 2 (Sep 1885), 200.
Brief notice of The Rise of Silas Lapham.
"As a study of living men and women the book is a master-
piece...."

358   PAYNE, WILLIAM MORTON. "Recent Fiction." Dial, 6 (Sep 1885),
122. Review of The Rise of Silas Lapham.
"Almost a new species of work." Howells "has never done
anything better than this picture of the self-made American."

359   "Notes." Critic, n.s. 4 (5 Sep 1885), 108.
S. H. responds to M. L. B. W. (Critic, n.s. 4 [22 Aug
1885], 84). "Our language has far more to fear from the
grammarians than from the common usage of the common
people."

360   "The Rise of Silas Lapham." Literary World, 16 (5 Sep 1885),
299. Review.
"It has the fresh, unsparing, almost pitiless realism
of A Modern Instance, but it touches throughout a higher
plane." Lapham is the protagonist in a great moral drama.
The women are less clearly wrought. Special mention of
Howells' humor.

361   "Novels of the Week." Athenaeum, No. 3020 (12 Sep 1885), 334.
Review of The Rise of Silas Lapham. Rpt. Critic, n.s. 4
(24 Oct 1885), 202.
"The book is characteristically American," and English
readers, failing to differentiate American sensibilities,
"must be content to be amused." Howells seems to have
"a want of perception as to climax, and consequently he
is rather wrong (to use a favourite expression of his) as
to the point where he should conclude."

362   "Reviews / The Rise of Silas Lapham." Critic, n.s. 4 (12 Sep
1885), 122. Full review.
"The book is one to interest and to please, even if it
does not touch the deepest springs or inspire the most
lasting and enthusiastic appreciation." Silas was "a
good 'subject,' and the author threw a sop to Cerberus by
letting him also be a good man."

1885

363 DANE, B. L. R. "Literary Bric-A-Brac." New Orleans _Times-
      Democrat_, 13 Sep 1885, p. 5. Brief reference.
          Howells in America is "frigid, cynical, impersonal and
      dry," but Howells in Italy is "glowing with color, sensu-
      ous, passionate, rhetorical and tender."

364 WHITING, LILIAN. "Boston Days /.../ Mr. Howells' New Engage-
      ment /...." New Orleans _Times-Democrat_, 13 Sep 1885, p. 5.
      Announcement of Howells' new contract with _Harper's_.
          Notes that _The Rise of Silas Lapham_ is a local novel,
      not only because Lapham is not a common type everywhere
      in America, but also because the social influences studied
      are distinctively Bostonian.

365 "Literary Notes." _Philadelphia Evening Bulletin_, 16 Sep 1885,
      p. 4. Brief reference.
          Howells' newest novel is to be of lighter tone than _The
      Rise of Silas Lapham_, involving the adventures of a pure
      country boy adrift in Boston with only a "trashy poem" for
      comfort. [Graham]

366 GOSSE, EDMUND. "Mr. Gosse to Mr. Howells." _Critic_, n.s. 4
      (19 Sep 1885), 139. Poem.
          An advance printing of the dedicatory poem to Howells
      scheduled to appear in Gosse's forthcoming _From Shakespeare
      to Pope_.

367 SMITH, G. BARNETT. "New Novels." _Academy_, 28 (19 Sep 1885),
      182. Brief review of _The Rise of Silas Lapham_.
          "A triumph of character drawing." Lapham reminds one of
      Abraham Lincoln.

368 "Howells's Last and Best Novel." _Philadelphia Record_, 26 Sep
      1885, p. 6. Review of _The Rise of Silas Lapham_.
          In this "chronical of contemporary society" Howells'
      "study of character" merits praise. But the author is un-
      necessarily sarcastic towards his hero, who is deserving
      of sympathy. [Graham]

369 "New Publications / Mr. Howells's Novel." _New York Times_, 27
      Sep 1885, p. 5. Full review of _The Rise of Silas Lapham_.
          Howells bungles the Tom-Penelope affair. Lapham's busi-
      ness crisis is overstrained. The first half of the novel
      is superior to the last.

370　"Book News." Philadelphia Press, 28 Sep 1885, p. 7.　Brief
　　　reference.
　　　　Notes the success of The Rise of Silas Lapham.　[Graham]

371　"The Bookshelf." Cottage Hearth, 11 (Oct 1885), 326.　Review
　　　of The Rise of Silas Lapham.
　　　　This is Howells' finest achievement.　He has focused on
　　　the noble and lovable traits of common people.　Howells
　　　has the kindly human feeling found in the best of Dickens
　　　and Thackeray.

*　[Howells' Last Novel.] Book News, 4 (Oct 1885), 37-38.　Rpt.
　　　from New York Sun, 23 Aug 1885, p. 4.　See item 355.

372　"Literature of the Day." Lippincott's, 36 (Oct 1885), 421-
　　　422.　Review of The Rise of Silas Lapham.
　　　　Howells advances "into the broad arena of real life,
　　　with its diversity of actors and its multiplicity of in-
　　　terests."　Social comment is implicit in the characters.
　　　The study of the businessman is strikingly similar to that
　　　of Balzac in César Biotteau.　Compared with Balzac, Howells
　　　wastes his force on non-essentials."

373　[SCUDDER, HORACE E.]　"Recent American Fiction." Atlantic,
　　　56 (Oct 1885), 554-556.　Full review of The Rise of Silas
　　　Lapham.　Rpt. in part, The War of the Critics over William
　　　Dean Howells, ed. Edwin H. Cady and David L. Frazier
　　　(Evanston:　Row, Peterson, 1962), pp. 33-34.
　　　　Howells "has convinced himself of the higher value to be
　　　found in a creation which discloses morals as well as man-
　　　ners."　But this novel, like A Modern Instance, is flawed
　　　by an "over-refinement of motive."

374　"The Rise of Silas Lapham." Saturday Review, 60 (17 Oct 1885),
　　　517-518.　Full review.　Rpt. in Critic, n.s. 4 (7 Nov
　　　1885), 224-225.
　　　　In none of Howells' novels is his Americanness more con-
　　　spicuous, and that may be the reason this one is "in many
　　　respects the best novel he has written yet."　America is
　　　in the pages of Howells' novels as no where else except in
　　　real life.

375　"The Rise of Silas Lapham." Nation, 41 (22 Oct 1885), 347-
　　　348.　Full review.
　　　　Lapham is "a literal, merciless representation," but
　　　the other characters are less than truthful.　Howells
　　　exhibits social distinctions as natural rather than arti-
　　　ficial.

1885

*   "Current Criticism." <u>Critic</u>, n.s. 4 (24 Oct 1885), 202.
      Review of <u>The Rise of Silas Lapham</u>. Rpt. from <u>Athenaeum</u>,
      No. 3020 (12 Sep 1885), 334. <u>See</u> item 361.

376   MABIE, HAMILTON WRIGHT. "A Typical Novel." <u>Andover Review</u>,
      4 (Nov 1885), 417–429. Major review of <u>The Rise of Silas
      Lapham</u>. Rpt. in part, <u>The War of the Critics over William
      Dean Howells</u>, ed. Edwin H. Cady and David L. Frazier
      (Evanston: Row, Peterson, 1962), pp. 38–41.
        After giving Howells high praise, Mabie declares war on
      his realism by asserting that <u>The Rise of Silas Lapham</u> is
      "an unsatisfactory story: defective in power, in reality,
      and in the vitalizing atmosphere of imagination...
      cold." Howells depends on the observation of science
      rather than on the insight of imagination.

377   "Novel-Writing as a Science." <u>Catholic World</u>, 42 (Nov 1885),
      274–280. Rpt. in part, <u>The War of the Critics over William
      Dean Howells</u>, ed. Edwin H. Cady and David L. Frazier
      (Evanston: Row, Peterson, 1962), pp. 35–37. Essay review
      of <u>The Rise of Silas Lapham</u>.
        Howells regards novel-writing "as science and not as
      art." The realistic trend marks "a descent, a degrada-
      tion."

378   "Recent Fiction." <u>Overland</u>, 2d Ser., 6 (Nov 1885), 553–554.
      Review of <u>The Rise of Silas Lapham</u>.
        Howells "has only to turn his scrutiny upon the most
      bare and unromantic phase of life, and the reader sees it
      in its true light." This novel has "a warmer quality"
      than Howells' previous books, but it ends unsatisfactorily.

379   "New Publications / Mr. Howells's New Italian Sketches." <u>New
      York Tribune</u>, 1 Nov 1885, p. 8. Review of <u>Tuscan Cities</u>.
      Rpt. <u>Book News</u>, 4 (Dec 1885–Jan 1886), 100–101.
        "Mr. Howells...is no longer a fresh sensation but a
      familiar favorite." In this work, "he is too often a
      cynical examiner of his impressions."

380   WHITING, LILIAN. "Boston Days /.../ Howells' Popularity /...."
      New Orleans <u>Times-Democrat</u>, 1 Nov 1885, p. 5. Brief ref-
      erence.
        Both the Boston and New York press seem to confuse popu-
      larity with art. Howells is an ideal man of business.
      His novels are regarded as having excellent commercial
      value. It is unfortunate that they exhibit so much
      "touch" and express so little.

*   "The Rise of Silas Lapham." Critic, n.s. 4 (7 Nov 1885), 224–
      225. Review. Rpt. from Saturday Review, 60 (17 Oct 1885),
      517–518. See item 374.

381   LATHROP, GEORGE PARSONS. "W. D. Howells / His Career and His
      Home." New York Daily Tribune, 8 Nov 1885, p. 3. Full-
      column (fine print) biographical sketch.
        Although Howells, in his work, draws heavily from actual
      observation, he does not permit himself the license of re-
      cording actual people as fictional characters. A brief
      anecdote in that regard. He once said, "I don't seem able
      to get very far away from to-day." That may be the reason
      for his success.

382   "Tuscan Cities." Nation, 41 (12 Nov 1885), 410. Full review.
        Although skillfully done, these papers are "an incon-
      gruous mixture of scene and incident." The collection
      lacks discrimination, a characteristic of modern realism
      in general. It lacks "any principle of selection."

383   "A Crazy Quilt." Boston Evening Transcript, 19 Nov 1885, p. 6.
      Brief note.
        "Mr. Howells's 'Mrs. Roberts' grows a shade sillier each
      year, and yet continues to be maddeningly natural." Ref-
      erence is made to an English paper that predicted Howells'
      next story "would tell how a man stepped on a girl's dress
      and nothing came of it."

384   "New Publications." New Orleans Times-Democrat, 22 Nov 1885,
      p. 8. Book publication of The Rise of Silas Lapham an-
      nounced without review.

385   DROCH [ROBERT BRIDGES]. "Bookishness." Life, 6 (26 Nov 1885),
      299. Brief comment on The Garroters.
        "There is real roaring fun in this farce, notwithstanding
      the delicate finish which one always finds in this writer's
      work."

386   "Holiday Publications." Critic, n.s. 4 (28 Nov 1885), 259.
      Brief notice of Tuscan Cities.
        Howells' "holiday mood colors even the minor incidents
      of the naïve life that Americans lead in Italy."

387   "Literature / Holiday Books." Chicago Daily Tribune, 28 Nov
      1885, p. 10. Brief notice of Tuscan Cities.
        Howells' sympathy with Italian history and scenery has
      never been "more vividly manifested."

1885

388   "Tuscan Cities." Literary World, 16 (28 Nov 1885), 435. Re-
      view.
           The book is one "to be read again and again with un-
      failing delight," although Howells perhaps gives "too
      much of the American, not to say the Ohio, point of
      view."

389   "Among the Holiday Books." Book Buyer, n.s. 2 (Dec 1885),
      312. Brief mention of Tuscan Cities.

390   "Literary Items." Boston Evening Transcript, 4 Dec 1885,
      p. 6. Brief note.
           "It is understood that Mr. Howells in his forthcoming
      first instalment of his 'Editor's Study' in Harper's
      Magazine has touched upon the subject of 'literary
      centres.'" [The subject was currently a sensitive one in
      Boston.]

391   "Tuscan Cities." Boston Evening Transcript, 5 Dec 1885, p. 7.
      Brief review.
           "It is permeated with that delicious, hazy, Italian
      atmosphere which is so restful to the reader, and which
      casts a glamour around even the commonest objects."

392   "Mr. Howells in Italy." New York Times, 6 Dec 1885, p. 5.
      Review of Tuscan Cities.
           Howells is never better than when he is "gossiping,
      with apparent aimlessness, but very real thought and
      point, about a foreign city, particularly an Italian
      city." His appreciation of the Italian people and scene
      is unusual and laudatory.

393   "Literary Notes." New York Times, 14 Dec 1885, p. 3.
           Howells has been accused of plagiarizing John Maddison
      Morton's "The Two Bonnycastles" in his Garroter's. The
      true source of Howells' farce is noted.

394   "New Publications." New Orleans Times-Democrat, 20 Dec 1885,
      p. 12. Brief review of Tuscan Cities.
           "Touches of a light and airy humor and of delicate wit
      in Mr. Howells' happiest vein...abound in his descrip-
      tions of those ancient cities of Upper Italy."

395   "Monthly Magazines / Harper's." Boston Evening Transcript,
      23 Dec 1885, p. 6. Brief notice of the new "long-promised
      department presided over by Mr. Howells."

("Monthly Magazines / Harper's")
"Its contents fully justifies the expectation of that
very large class of readers which pins its faith upon the
ability of Mr. Howells to do anything and everything
acceptably."

* [Tuscan Cities.] Book News, 4 (Dec 1885-Jan 1886), 100-101.
Review. Rpt. from New York Tribune, 1 Nov 1885, p. 8.
See item 379.

1886

396 LONGFELLOW, SAMUEL, ed. Life of Henry Wadsworth Longfellow.
New York: Ticknor, 1886. III, passim as indexed.
Scattered minor references include Longfellow's approval
of "Modern Italian Comedy" and the portrayal of Don Ippo-
lito ("In that respect this book is a stride forward"
[p. 240]). Multiple references to Howells as dinner companion. He is "a very clever and cultivated young man"
(p. 71).

397 MOORE, GEORGE. Confessions of a Young Man. London: Heine-
mann, 1886. Pp. 158-159.
"Henry James went to France and read Tourgueneff. W. D.
Howells stayed at home and read Henry James." James
"borrowed at first hand, understanding what he was borrowing. W. D. Howells borrowed at second hand, and without understanding what he was borrowing." [Helen and
Wilson Follett use this capricious judgment as a spring-
board in their essay in Atlantic, 119 (Mar 1917), 362-372.
See item 2029.]

398 "Contemporary Literature / Belles Lettres." Westminster Review, 125 (Jan 1886), 303. Review of The Rise of Silas
Lapham.
Silas Lapham is a creation of "no common kind," worthy
of comparison with characters by Dickens and Daudet. The
entire cast is an admirable gallery of illustrations of
various phases of American life and manners. What is
more important, they throw "light on many an obscure cor-
ner of human consciousness." The review misses the significance of the title.

399 SINNOTT, J. E. "The Nabob and Silas Lapham." Harvard Monthly, 1 (Jan 1886), 164-168. Review of The Rise of Silas
Lapham.

1886

(SINNOTT, J. E.)
Howells is compared with Daudet (The Nabob) and found
wanting. He seems to withdraw from deep feeling in life.

400 W., E. F. "Our Monthly Gossip." Lippincott's, 37 (Jan 1886),
106-109. Note.
An attack on Howells' portrayal of American women. He
"gives us not truth but a half-truth; and the pity is the
greater because all mankind are prone to take the half for
the whole." He develops feminine faults and weaknesses
but ignores virtues and strengths.

401 "The Lounger." Critic, n.s. 5 (9 Jan 1886), 18. Brief item.
Reports the request of a dying woman for permission to
read the advance sheets of Indian Summer.

402 CRACKETT, JOE D. "Howells, 'Craddock' and the Old School."
New Orleans Daily Picayune, 10 Jan 1886, p. 8. Literary
editorial.
In "Editor's Study" Howells condescendingly pats Miss
Murfree on the head even though she has had "the very bad
taste to turn her back on Boston and its school of vivi-
section" in her decision to learn from Dickens.

403 WHITING, LILIAN. "Boston Days /.../ Howells' Poems." New
Orleans Times-Democrat, 10 Jan 1886, p. 5. Critical
response to Poems.
The volume reveals that Howells has "the poet's suscepti-
bility to beauty." Many of the stanzas contain "a very
delicate and subtle interpretation of life," but Howells
sometimes "essays a poetic form for what is not poetic."

404 BANGS, J[OHN] K[ENDRICK]. "To W. D. Howells / On Reading His
Poems." Life, 7 (14 Jan 1886), 32. Satiric verse.

405 "Recent Publications." New Orleans Daily Picayune, 17 Jan
1886, p. 8. Very brief mention of The Garroters.
"Mr. Howells's usual annual Christmas farce."

406 DROCH [ROBERT BRIDGES]. "Bookishness / About Two Novels and
an Eminent Novelist." Life, 7 (21 Jan 1886), 49. Note.
Howells denies that a young lady in Buffalo was used as
a model for Imogene in Indian Summer.

407 "Mr. Howells's Poems." Critic, n.s. 5 (30 Jan 1886), 53-54.
Review.

("Mr. Howells's Poems")
 The moods of Heine and Arthur Hugh Clough prevail in
 Howells' "youthful and frank" ballads and verses. The
 Heine mood is preferred.

408   "Talk About Books." Chautauquan, 6 (Feb 1886), 303. Brief
 review of Tuscan Cities.
 Readers who want facts should turn to guidebooks and
 encyclopaedias; those who enjoy humorous, suggestive, and
 lifelike impressions should read Howells.

409   "Travel and Art." Atlantic, 57 (Feb 1886), 275-277. Full review of Tuscan Cities.
 "It must be conceded that, except the poets, who do
 everything best, the novelists write the most entertaining
 history, and Mr. Howells has not been denied common distinction."

410   "Literary Notes." Philadelphia Evening Bulletin, 11 Feb 1886,
 p. 4. Anecdote.
 Concerning Howells' correction of the improper rigging
 of the Aroostook upon the advice of an "old salt."
 [Graham]

411   DROCH [ROBERT BRIDGES]. "Bookishness." Life, 7 (18 Feb 1886),
 103. Brief reference.
 "Mr. Howells has been so busy recently pointing out the
 defects of Thackeray and Dickens that he has not kept the
 fly specks off his own china." Reference is to The Minister's Charge, where Howells has Nelsson born in Norway
 instead of Sweden.

412   "New Publications / Mr. Howells's New Story." New York Daily
 Tribune, 21 Feb 1886, p. 6. Full review of Indian Summer.
 Rpt. Literary News, 7 (1886), 75-76.
 Howells demonstrates his belief that "the literature of
 romantic ideals and heroic characters is a thing of the
 past." His "power of mental analysis is seen at its full-
 est in some of the passages, and he follows the various
 threads of motive with sustained discrimination."

413   [Untitled.] Boston Evening Transcript, 26 Feb 1886, p. 4.
 Editorial.
 Defends Howells against the misinterpretation apparent
 in the Boston Advertiser's (26 Feb 1886) [not seen] attack
 on him. "Only ignorance or malice would so misunderstand
 him." The "arrogant Howells" is "an invention purely of
 the paragraphers."

1886

* "Indian Summer." Literary News, 7 (Mar 1886), 75-76. Rpt.
  from New York Daily Tribune, 21 Feb 1886, p. 6. See item
  412.

414　MILLET, J. B. "The Tribute to George Fuller." Book Buyer,
  n.s. 3 (Mar 1886), 66-67. Brief mention.
  　　Appreciative mention of Howells' "charming" contribution
  to A Memorial to George Fuller.

415　"The Newest Books." Book Buyer, n.s. 3 (Mar 1886), 77. Review of Indian Summer.
  　　Howells has mastered American traits and characteristics.
  This volume contains "that delightful combination of realism, with just a flavor of idealism."

416　PAYNE, WILLIAM MORTON. "Recent Fiction." Dial, 6 (Mar 1886),
  303. Review of Indian Summer.
  　　Favorable. "It is quite as interesting as a romance of
  Dumas, although in a different way, and rather more artistic."

417　R., A. W. "Our Monthly Gossip." Lippincott's, 37 (Mar 1886),
  333-335. Note. Rpt. Book News, 4 (Apr 1886), 237-238.
  　　Indian Summer breaks in purpose and style from Howells'
  earlier work. It is internal in nature rather than external; it focuses on mind, not manner. Thus Howells has
  risen above his own standards. Here he departs from other
  novelists by giving charm to age.

418　DROCH [ROBERT BRIDGES]. "Bookishness / Love and Reason."
  Life, 7 (4 Mar 1886), 132-133. Review of Indian Summer.
  　　Considerable enthusiasm for evidence of Howells' development. "Colville is a most artistic and deft piece of literary work." The elder Corey in The Rise of Silas Lapham
  is a transition between him and Bartley Hubbard.

419　"Reviews." American (Philadelphia), 11 (6 Mar 1886), 315.
  Full review of Indian Summer.
  　　Following A Modern Instance and The Rise of Silas Lap-
  ham, Indian Summer seems "slighter than it really is."

420　"New Publications / Mr. Howells's Last Novel." New York Times,
  8 Mar 1886, p. 3. Full review of Indian Summer.
  　　The novel is "neither deep nor pathetic, but essentially
  clever and nice and neat in workmanship"--a superfine
  "wheaten cake" of the type which is beginning to appeal to
  English readers. Howells uses the Italian scene with

("New Publications / Mr. Howells's Last Novel")
artistic effectiveness, but "Silas Lapham, his red paint,
his pretty daughters, will have a larger hearing."

421   "Fiction." <u>Literary World</u>, 17 (20 Mar 1886), 103. Brief
reference.
"Mr. Howells's arena is the parlor."

422   "Reviews / Mr. Howells's <u>Indian Summer</u>." <u>Critic</u>, n.s. 5 (27
Mar 1886), 154. Full review.
The "little plot" is filled "to the brim" with human
interest, but the chief focus is on the "Indian Summer"
of life.

423   "The Bookshelf." <u>Cottage Hearth</u>, 12 (Apr 1886), 128. Brief
review of <u>Indian Summer</u>.
"The book has not the profound purpose of 'Silas Lapham,'
but its moral atmosphere is sweet and wholesome."

424   E[GAN, MAURICE F.] "A Chat About New Books." <u>Catholic World</u>,
43 (Apr 1886), 130. Notice of <u>Indian Summer</u>.
"Mr. Howells is not a great writer."

*   [<u>Indian Summer</u>.] <u>Book News</u>, 4 (Apr 1886), 237-238. Review.
Rpt. from <u>Lippincott's</u>, 37 (Mar 1886), 333-335. <u>See</u> item
417.

425   WILSON, ROBERT BURNS. "Mr. Howells and the Poets." <u>Southern
Bivouac</u>, n.s. 1 (Apr 1886), 654-655. Note. Rpt. in part,
<u>Critic</u>, n.s. 5 (10 Apr 1886), 186-187, and Philadelphia
<u>Evening Bulletin</u>, 13 Apr 1886, p. 4.
An attack on Howells' statements about poetry in the
"Editor's Study," <u>Harper's</u>, 72 (Mar 1886). "Mr. Howells
is out of temper about something, and forgets, for the
moment, the quiet and kindly dignity which ought to
characterize a magnificent success like his."

426   "Novels of the Week." <u>Athenaeum</u>, No. 3049 (3 Apr 1886), 453-
454. Review of <u>Indian Summer</u>.
Howells and James are commended for the strength of
their fiction. James has more "staying power," but
Howells "puts in his strokes more sharply, and his style
is, on the whole, brisker and more attractive." <u>Indian
Summer</u> well represents him.

427   SAINTSBURY, GEORGE. "New Novels." <u>Academy</u>, 29 (3 Apr 1886),
233-234. Review of <u>Indian Summer</u>.
It is not sensational.

1886

428   "Seven Novels." Saturday Review, 61 (3 Apr 1886), 481. Re-
          view of Indian Summer.
          Howells "in his most genial playful humour."

429   "Indian Summer." Boston Evening Transcript, 7 Apr 1886, p. 6.
          Full review.
             "Mr. Howells is, above all things, realistic. Not in the
          slightest degree imaginative or sensational or emotional,
          but thoroughly and entirely realistic."

430   "The Home of Fiction / Novelist Howells Says America Is the
          Future Field for Writers." New York Mail and Express, 10
          Apr 1886, p. 6. Interview. Rpt. in part as "Our New York
          Letter" by "Nassau," Literary World, 17 (17 Apr 1886),
          135; rpt., "Interviews with William Dean Howells," ed.
          Ulrich Halfmann, American Literary Realism, 6 (Fall 1973),
          281-284.
             Subheaded "The Romantic School Nearly Dead--The Realistic
          Ahead in Every Country Except England--Russian Novelists
          the Best in the World--How Novels Are Written."

431   "Literature of the Day / Howells' Indian Summer." Chicago
          Daily Tribune, 10 Apr 1886, p. 13. Review.
             Extensive summary. Howells has written stories "more
          vivid and interesting...but none more symmetrical or
          artistic."

432   WHITING, LILIAN. "Boston Days /.../ Mr. Howells' Criticisms /
          ...." New Orleans Times-Democrat, 11 Apr 1886, p. 5.
             An attack on the "Editor's Study" series. Howells'
          "self-sufficient arrogance and his lack of high ideals"
          are combining to destroy his reputation. He is using his
          column "to pay off old grudges." Much of his criticism
          is worthless, "not only because it is the outcome of per-
          sonal prejudice, but because it is weak and lacking in
          fibre." [These comments set the tone for Times-Democrat
          response to Howells for the next five years.]

  *   "Nassau." "Our New York Letter." Literary World, 17 (17 Apr
          1886), 135. Partial rpt. of interview in New York Mail
          and Express, 10 Apr 1886. See item 430.

433   "Book Table." Godey's Lady's Book, 112 (May 1886), 536.
          Very brief mention of The Garroters.
             "A laughable farce" that could be adapted to parlor
          theatricals.

434   COOLIDGE, JESSE. "Notes and Comments." North American Re-
            view, 142 (May 1886), 619-622. Satiric essay.
            This protest against Howells and his work, "bric-a-brac
            social studies," is filled with flamboyant images that
            move toward moral indictment. "American character is
            flabby enough now; Mr. Howells would make it flabbier
            still" (p. 621).

435   "Nassau." "Our New York Letter." Literary World, 17 (1 May
            1886), 152. Coverage of a reception given for Howells by
            the New York Author's Club.

436   DANE, B. L. R. "Literary Bric-A-Brac." New Orleans Times-
            Democrat, 2 May 1886, p. 5. Brief comment.
            After all "it isn't worth while getting into a passion
            with Mr. Howells. Nearly every month he puts a literary
            chip on his shoulder, and then is wickedly hilarious when
            the critics rush with wild wrath to knock it off."

437   "Literature." Philadelphia Evening Bulletin, 3 May 1886,
            p. 8. Brief reference.
            Howells' serial in Century is "brisk and sparkling."
            [Graham]

438   "New Publications." New Orleans Times-Democrat, 9 May 1886,
            p. 8. Review of Indian Summer.
            Howells' latest novel "might fitly serve as another
            'Modern Instance' this time of 'Much Ado About Nothing.'"
            There is less of everything in this novel than one has a
            right to expect.

439   "Recent Novels." Nation, 42 (13 May 1886), 408. Review of
            Indian Summer.
            "Mr. Howells always chooses to avoid drama and deep
            feeling; he has a right to select, but the novelist who
            persistently ignores both or mocks at both, is as false to
            life in a broad way as the novelist who is always in hys-
            terics."

440   ROGERS, W. A. "The Modern Novel." Life, 7 (20 May 1886),
            288-289. Double-page cartoon.
            Howells and James doing brain surgery.

441   [SCUDDER, HORACE E.] "James, Crawford, and Howells."
            Atlantic, 57 (Jun 1886), 855-857. Full review of Indian
            Summer.
            Howells and James "occupy themselves with similar ma-
            terial,--namely, the men and women whom their readers are

1886

([SCUDDER, HORACE E.])
  likely to meet,--and...they work from individuals to
  the general, rather than, as in Mr. Crawford's case, accept ready-made individuals out of the general lot."
  Howells continues to charm with his fidelity to life and
  his lightness of touch, but his self-imposed limitations
  are disappointing. "No large conception is required, no
  long-sustained right following a figure through devious
  ways, but merely a sympathetic penetrating vision of a
  miniature nature which discloses itself by little signs."
  "The incidents of the story are insignificant," but Effie
  Bowen is "a delightfully drawn child"--Howells' art at its
  best.

442 WEDMORE, FREDERICK. "To Millicent, from America." Temple
  Bar, 77 (Jun 1886), 241. Epistolary report of interview.
  Rpt. Critic, n.s. 6 (3 Jul 1886), 10; abstr. "Interviews
  with William Dean Howells," ed. Ulrich Halfmann, American
  Literary Realism, 6 (Fall 1973), 285.
    Howells is "a genial, downright, matter of fact, and
  withal satirical person." Among his comments on a variety
  of literary subjects is the endorsement of Murfree's The
  Prophet of the Great Smoky Mountains.

443 [HEARN, LAFCADIO.] "Sins of Genius." New Orleans Times-Democrat, 6 Jun 1886, p. 5. Editorial. Rpt. Essays on American Literature, ed. Albert Mordell and Sanki Ichikawa
  (Tokyo: Hokuseido, 1929), pp. 189-193.
    Argument against Howells' statements on the nature of
  genius. "To demand that all men of genius should live
  perfectly placid and passionless lives is about as reasonable as to demand the advent of the Millenium." Howells
  need not pose as a "Converted Idealist." "His early work,
  now resuscitated, shows that he never possessed the imaginative faculty to any remarkable degree."

444 DANE, B. L. R. "Literary Bric-A-Brac." New Orleans Times-
  Democrat, 13 Jun 1886, p. 5. Brief reference.
    "Howells can typify, but his types can never crystallize
  themselves into personages, but Thackeray can do both."

445 DROCH [ROBERT BRIDGES]. "Bookishness." Life, 7 (17 Jun 1886),
  342. Brief reference.
    Howells is to be congratulated on the "effect of con-
  temporaneousness" in Indian Summer in that it parallels
  the recent presidential romance--except that in real life
  the romance ended in marriage.

446   JAMES, HENRY. "William Dean Howells." Harper's Weekly, 30
        (19 Jun 1886), 394-395. Essay. Abridged in Book News
        Monthly, 5 (Oct 1886), 41-42; rpt. Howells / A Century of
        Criticism, ed. Kenneth E. Eble (Dallas: Southern Method-
        ist University, 1962), pp. 41-50; and rpt. in part, The
        War of the Critics over William Dean Howells, ed. Edwin H.
        Cady and David L. Frazier (Evanston: Row, Peterson, 1962),
        42-45.
          A highly favorable critical survey of Howells' work to
        date. "Other persons have considered and discoursed upon
        American life, but no one, surely, has felt it so complete-
        ly as [Howells]." "I know of no English novelist of our
        hour whose work is so exclusively a matter of painting
        what he sees, and who is so sure of what he sees."

447   "Contemporary Literature / Belles Lettres." Westminster Re-
        view, 126 (Jul 1886), 295. Review of Indian Summer.
          Like all of Howells' stories, "its interest depends far
        more on the causation of incident by the mingling and
        clashing of various skilfully portrayed types of human
        character, than on anything striking or dramatic in the
        incidents themselves."

  *   WETMORE, FREDERICK. "To Millicent, from America." Critic,
        n.s. 6 (3 Jul 1886), 241. Rpt. from Temple Bar, 77 (Jun
        1886), 241. See item 442.

448   DROCH [ROBERT BRIDGES]. "Bookishness / A Glimpse of Mr.
        Howells's Workshop." Life, 8 (8 Jul 1886), 20. Brief
        comment.
          Response to recent "Editor's Study" takes issue with
        Howells' concept of truth.

449   THOMPSON, MAURICE. "The Analysts Analyzed." Critic, n.s. 6
        (10 Jul 1886), 19-22. Address delivered to the Women's
        Club of Indianapolis. Rpt. in part, The War of the
        Critics over William Dean Howells, ed. Edwin H. Cady and
        David L. Frazier (Evanston: Row, Peterson, 1962), pp.
        46-47.
          Extensive reference to Howells as less than an "ultra
        realist." "To speak frankly of Mr. Howells, I think he
        is a genius, but a specialty all the same, a genius hold-
        ing a perfect mastery of its own field and its own method"
        --and making the mistake of thinking its specialty is the
        whole.

1886

450   "An American Novelist in His Worship / Mr. Trowells at Home--
His Aims--His Methods--Interesting Literary Gossip."
Life, 8 (22 Jul 1886), 48-49. Epistolary satire.

451   W., E. F. "Our Monthly Gossip." _Lippincott's_, 37 (Aug 1886),
225-227. Review of _The Minister's Charge_.
It is "a slough of commonplace and vulgarity." That
"the work of our chief novelist should be so distinctly
journalistic in tone" seems a pity. Howells' method is
compared briefly to that of Aristophanes.

452   WHITING, LILIAN. "Boston Life /.../ Mr. Howells Talks on His
Work in _Harper's_." New Orleans _Times-Democrat_, 8 Aug
1886, p. 5. Note.
"With true consistency to his devotion to materialism--
which he mistakes for realism," Howells never loses an
opportunity to note his own glory.

453   "Literary Notes." _Philadelphia Evening Bulletin_, 19 Aug 1886,
p. 4. Brief comment.
Howells is living alone in a large house on Beacon
Street, overlooking the Charles, and attending Music Hall
concerts where he is the center of brilliant conversation.
[Graham]

454   DROCH [ROBERT BRIDGES]. "Bookishness / More About the Weakness
of Novel Writing." _Life_, 8 (26 Aug 1886), 118. Brief reference.
Takes issue with Howells and the realists. "All that
they see they minutely chronicle, but they do not select
and generalize."

455   "Ave, Howells!" _Saturday Review_, 62 (28 Aug 1886), 279-280.
Satiric note. Rpt. in part, "Mr. Howells and the British
Aristocracy," _Critic_, n.s. 6 (11 Sep 1886), 118-119.
"Long ago he slew Thackeray and Dickens, and left us
mourning their demonstrated inferiority to William D.
Howells." Had he but fired a shot at the British aris-
tocracy, it too would have fallen.

456   "The Russian Novelists and Their Boston Critics." New
Orleans _Daily Picayune_, 29 Aug 1886, p. 6. Editorial.
In suggesting that American life lacks the material for
the darker passions found in Russian literature, Howells
is rationalizing his own failure. "He is a sort of car-
pet knight in literature, exposing in a superficial way
the smaller shams of society, and making a gentle appeal
for good manners and fair dealing." He is unable to

("The Russian Novelists and Their Boston Critics")
penetrate low life as Craddock, for instance, can. "But
Craddock is a woman of genius, and Mr. Howells is only an
accomplished man of letters."

457 WHITING, LILIAN. "Boston Days /.../ Mr. Howells Lays Down the
Law of Novel Writing /...." New Orleans Times-Democrat,
29 Aug 1886, p. 5. Note.
Howells' novels do not elevate as he says novels should.
All of his women more or less caricature "refined, cultivated, high-minded womanhood." Neither do we find in his
work a single "absolutely whole, earnest and high-minded
man." Howells' monthly comments "are becoming monotonous,
dull, and unsufferable."

458 DROCH [ROBERT BRIDGES]. "Bookishness / Social Contempt in
Fiction." Life, 8 (2 Sep 1886), 132. Brief reference.
Howellsian "realists are in doubt as to what is wholly
admirable in life, because, like so many people in this
transition period, they are giving up the old forms of
faith, and have not grasped the significance and responsi-
bilities of the new."

459 "Literature at Low Tide." Life, 8 (7 Sep 1886), 148-149.
Double-page cartoon.
Features carnival setting. Includes caricature of
Howells selling milk--"Realistic, refreshing, and intoxi-
cating."

460 "Literary Notes." Philadelphia Evening Bulletin, 11 Sep 1886,
p. 4. Brief mention.
Howells is receiving subscriptions for the purchase of
the Healy portrait of Longfellow to be placed in Harvard's
Memorial Hall. [Graham]

 * "Mr. Howells and the British Aristocracy." Critic, n.s. 6
(11 Sep 1886), 118-119. Rpt. from Saturday Review, 62
(28 Aug 1886), 279-280. See item 455.

461 "Mr. Howells, Mr. Stedman and--Genius." Critic, n.s. 6 (11
Sep 1886), 121-122. Note.
Howells as destroyer: "there surely was never image-
breaker more graceful and courteous."

462 DANE, B. L. R. "Literary Bric-A-Brac." New Orleans Times-
Democrat, 19 Sep 1886, p. 5. Brief reference.
Dane gloats at length over the way in which Edmund
Clarence Stedman, in the New Princeton Review, takes
Howells to task on the issue of "genius."

1886

463   DROCH [ROBERT BRIDGES]. "Bookishness." Life, 8 (14 Oct 1886),
        227. Note.
          Howells has, happily, reintroduced Bromfield Corey as
        the patron of Lemuel Barker. "Whatever one may think of
        Mr. Howells's theory of fiction, it must still be admitted
        that his intelligent gentlemen are most delightful com-
        panions."

464   M., E. W. "Mr. Howells's Play Acted / How A Foregone Conclu-
        sion Was Performed and Received in New York." Boston
        Evening Transcript, 19 Nov 1886, p. 6. Full review.
          "The brilliancy of the dialogue, or rather of the suc-
        cession of dialogues, is the striking thing about the
        play." Although it was well received by its critical
        audience, for the theatre-going masses the play lacks
        the necessary dramatic element.

465   "Mr. Howells's Play." New York Times, 19 Nov 1886, p. 5.
        Full review of the initial performance of A Foregone Con-
        clusion--in five acts.
          Howells, who sat in a stage box, was called forward at
        the close of the third act. Although A Foregone Conclu-
        sion contains a depth of passion not common to Howells'
        novels, it is not entirely suited to dramatic production.
        The play lacks variety and is "almost wholly made up of
        conversations between two persons." It is inferior to
        Sardou's "Daniel Rochat," which was a failure. "Priest
        and Painter," an English version of A Foregone Conclusion,
        "has for some years held a place in the repertory of Mr.
        F. W. Benson, an English actor."

466   "December Magazines / Harper's." Boston Evening Transcript,
        24 Nov 1886, p. 10. Brief notice.
          Howells' farce The Mouse Trap is fully equal to the
        earlier The Register and The Elevator.

467   BISHOP, WILLIAM HENRY. "Authors at Home. XXII. / Mr.
        Howells in Beacon Street, Boston." Critic, n.s. 6 (27
        Nov 1886), 259-261. Rpt. Authors at Home, ed. J. L. and
        J. B. Gilder (New York: Cassell, 1888), pp. 193-209.
          Description of physical setting as a tentative approach
        to an understanding of Howells as man and author.

468   "A Foregone Conclusion." Critic, n.s. 6 (27 Nov 1886), 265.
        Review of dramatic production.
          Considering the nature of its literary source, it "suc-
        ceeded better than might have been expected."

469 "News and Notes." Literary World, 17 (27 Nov 1886), 439.
Reports performance of A Foregone Conclusion at the
Madison Square Theater, New York.

470 "Amusements in New York / A. M. Palmer on Mr. Howells's Play /
...." Boston Evening Transcript, 1 Dec 1886, p. 6. Note.
Summation of the critical judgment of the theatrical
manager who produced Howells' play from edited script.
The faults of the play "may perhaps be summed up by saying
that the story is indicated rather than told"; but it is
both entertaining and interesting, and experienced editing
could make it a popular theatrical success.

471 RIDEING, WILLIAM H. "Boston Letter." Critic, n.s. 6 (4 Dec
1886), 282.
Includes a substantial preview of A Boy's Town--"a
charming bit of work, this fragment of autobiography,
quite candid and free from self-consciousness."

472 "Jottings." Boston Evening Transcript, 6 Dec 1886, p. 4.
Brief note.
"There will probably be another chance to see Mr.
Howells's A Foregone Conclusion at the Madison Square
Theatre on the afternoon of Dec. 16."

473 DROCH [ROBERT BRIDGES]. "Bookishness / The Christmas Prayer
of the Critic." Life, 8 (9 Dec 1886), 365. Verse.
References to major American writers, including Howells.

474 "New Books / The Minister's Charge." Boston Evening Transcript, 11 Dec 1886, p. 6. Review.
The novel demonstrates that Howells "can not only preach
a philosophy, but live up to it." One questions, however,
whether the "omitted chapters" in Lemuel's history are
compatible with Howells' interest in fidelity to conditions. Howells is becoming self-indulgent in his in-
creasing reliance on mouthpieces.

475 DROCH [ROBERT BRIDGES]. "Bookishness." Life, 8 (16 Dec 1886),
362. Brief reference.
Anticipates a Lemuel Barker sequel, assuming a major
role for Jessie.

476 "Literature and Art / The Minister's Charge." Chicago Daily
Tribune, 18 Dec 1886, p. 12. Full review.

1886

("Literature and Art / The Minister's Charge")
"The great soul sees that in common things lurk what is best and greatest in life." Without a reading of this novel, "no just estimate of Mr. Howells can be made."

477   DROCH [ROBERT BRIDGES]. "Bookishness / 'Process' Literature." Life, 8 (23 Dec 1886), 398. Brief reference.
"If one would live up to the principles of realism, he should immediately revise his nomenclature, and include such terms as the 'Howells' Heliotype,' the 'James' Photogravure,' and the 'Zola Electrotype.'"

478   "An American Realistic Novel." American (Philadelphia), 13 (25 Dec 1886), 153-154. Full review of The Minister's Charge.
Howells "has gone to work conscientiously, and faithfully endeavored to carry out his own precepts and exemplify his own creed." He is not entirely successful.

479   SHARP, WILLIAM. "New Novels." Academy, 30 (25 Dec 1886), 423-424. Review of The Minister's Charge.
"A book so hopelessly, so irredeemably dull, that the hearts of [Howells'] enemies must be filled with rejoiceing."

1887

480   BEERS, HENRY A. An Outline Sketch of American Literature. New York: Chautauqua Press, 1887. Pp. 269-271, 274-278. Rpt. as Initial Studies in American Letters (Cleveland: Chautauqua Press, 1895).
Howells and James are "analytic in method and realistic in spirit." Both "try to express character through manners." Howells' works are surveyed and contrasted with James's.

481   BOLTON, SARAH K. "William Dean Howells." Famous American Authors. New York: Crowell, 1887. Pp. 258-285. Rev. and enl. (New York: Crowell, 1938), pp. 258-285. Biographical introduction.
Quite superficial critical response to the novels, especially the women in them.

482   RIDEING, WILLIAM H. "William Dean Howells." The Boyhood of Living Authors. New York: Crowell, 1887. Pp. 74-85. Juvenile biography.

(RIDEING, WILLIAM H.)
This elementary sketch of Howells' boyhood emphasizes "the simplicity of the early life" and the taste for literature cultivated by Howells' father. It is framed by paraphrased passages from New Leaf Mills.

483   MONROE, HARRIET EARHART. "Statesman and Novelist / A Talk Between Senator Ingalls and Mr. Howells." Lippincott's, 39 (Jan 1887), 128-132. Dialogue. Rpt. "Interviews with William Dean Howells," ed. Ulrich Halfmann, American Literary Realism, 6 (Fall 1973), 285-287.
A recorded conversation, "stripped of the picturesque language of the speakers; but the spirit and sentiment are retained." Senator Ingalls and Howells chat about political and literary figures and about Washington as a subject for fiction.

484   "Book-Talk." Lippincott's, 39 (Feb 1887), 359-360. Review of The Minister's Charge.
"Mr. Howells takes a more humane interest in his fellows than Mr. James, for he is essentially a humorist, and humor in its higher forms is always kindly and sympathetic." Lemuel Barker is an idealization.

485   B., W. H. "Our Monthly Gossip." Lippincott's, 39 (Feb 1887), 184-186. Note.
An attack on Howellsian literary theory. Howells' "outstretched index-finger" is not "invariably safe to follow." Howells is "better in practice than in theory, and best where he is least consistent."

486   BOYESEN, HJALMAR HJORTH. "Why We Have No Great Novelists." Forum, 2 (Feb 1887), 615-622. Minor references.
Both Howells and James are silent on politics, a most vital aspect of common life (p. 617); further, most novelists, Howells being an exception, subordinate personal conviction to popular attitudes (p. 620).

487   EGAN, MAURICE F. "A Chat About New Books." Catholic World, 44 (Feb 1887), 702-705. Review of The Minister's Charge.
Howells is compared unfavorably with F. Marion Crawford, but he does have "absolute purity of tone." He is less than realistic.

488   DROCH [ROBERT BRIDGES]. "The Old and the New Style of Fiction." Life, 9 (3 Feb 1887), 62. Brief reference.
Notes factual errors in Howells' study of the short story in the current Harper's and in the first installment

1887

(DROCH [ROBERT BRIDGES])
of April Hopes. "All in all, the great apostle of Realism
is relying too much on his untrained imagination."

489   "The Minister's Charge." Critic, n.s. 7 (5 Feb 1887), 63.
       Review.
       "There is nothing anywhere in the book that is not real-
       istic, but the first half...is touched with sympathy, the
       sympathy which means insight as well as photography....
       In the last half the sympathy drops away from the author,
       and the interest correspondingly dies away in the reader."

490   "Three Novels." Saturday Review, 63 (5 Feb 1887), 198. Full
       review of The Minister's Charge.
       Condescending in tone. "Mr. Howells [ironic comparisons
       are made with Dickens and Thackeray] triumphantly avoids
       ...interesting anybody."

491   [LOGAN, ANNIE R. M.] "Recent Novels." Nation, 44 (10 Feb
       1887), 124. Review of The Minister's Charge.
       The novel is compared with James's The Princess Casa-
       massima. Howells' novel is weak because the central
       character has no significance. The narrowness of Howells'
       novels suggests "either a suppression of that part of the
       truth best worth telling," or indicates "the author's un-
       fortunately contracted vision."

492   [Untitled.] Life, 9 (17 Feb 1887), 88. Humorous paragraph.
       "Everybody seems to be down on Howells"--even his wife.

493   "Mr. Howells and Other Book-Makers." Life, 9 (3 Mar 1887),
       121. Brief reference to April Hopes.
       "When Mr. Howells tries to write the New York girl dia-
       lect his realism becomes funerealistically ridiculous."

494   UNDERHILL, ANDREW J. "Lessons in Literature." Life, 9 (3
       Mar 1887), 120. Dramatic fragment satirizing Howells'
       method. Rpt. American Literary Realism, 3 (Summer 1970),
       280-281.

495   "The Lounger." Critic, n.s. 7 (5 Mar 1887), 115. Note on
       Howells' fiftieth birthday.
       He is seventeen days older than President Cleveland.
       Both worked to make their way, each stands at the head of
       his profession in America, and they should continue for
       another twenty-five years.

496 [Untitled.] <u>Life</u>, 9 (17 Mar 1887), 144. Brief comment on
     <u>Poems</u>.
         "To a near-sighted person who can't read, they look like
     poems; but in reality they are more prosaic than anything"
     Howells has written.

497 [Untitled.] <u>Life</u>, 9 (31 Mar 1887), 172. Brief paragraph.
         Will Howells please apply his formula for detection of
     pernicious novels to the shop girls in <u>The Minister's
     Charge</u>?

498 [HEARN, LAFCADIO.] "One of Mr. Howells' Realisms." New
     Orleans <u>Times-Democrat</u>, 12 Apr 1887, p. 4. Editorial.
     Rpt. <u>Essays on American Literature</u>, ed. Albert Mordell and
     Sanki Ichikawa (Tokyo: Hokuseido, 1929), pp. 238-240.
         Howells' impressions of life are limited in range, as he
     shows when he criticizes the fancy Miss Murfree incorpo-
     rates in her studies of the Tennessee mountaineers (April
     "Editor's Study").

499 [Untitled.] <u>Life</u>, 9 (14 Apr 1887), 204. Brief reference.
         "Mr. Howells is not well satisfied with the condition
     of fiction. Perhaps the eminent realist has been reading
     W. D. H."

500 [Untitled.] <u>Life</u>, 9 (14 Apr 1887), 210. Brief reference.
         Howells is paired with John L. Sullivan in a proposed
     athletic-literary contest.

501 THOMPSON, MAURICE. "'Truth' in Fiction." <u>Independent</u>, 39
     (21 Apr 1887), 485-486. Essay.
         "Viewed in the light of literary history, how utterly
     untenable is Mr. Howells's theory of creative art in
     fiction! He seems to be unable to comprehend that there
     can be a great, safe middle ground between photography and
     thaumaturgy in the story-teller's art."

502 CLARK, SAMUEL M. "Mr. Haggard's Romances." <u>Dial</u>, 8 (May
     1887), 5-7. Brief reference.
         Anti-Howells comparison.

503 "Contemporary Literature / Belles Lettres." <u>Westminster Re-
     view</u>, 128 (May 1887), 262. Review of <u>The Minister's
     Charge</u>.
         "A wonderfully fine piece of moral and mental analysis."
     As presentations of New England life and manners, Howells'
     novels "are nothing less than what the French realists
     call 'documents humains.'"

1887

504   DANE, B. L. R. "Literary Bric-A-Brac." New Orleans Times-
           Democrat, 1 May 1887, p. 11. Note.
              Challenges Howells' assessment of the plausibility of
           the ending of Craddock's Prophet of the Great Smoky Moun-
           tains. Self-sacrifice is beyond the understanding of
           Howells and "the sleek gentlemen who are his daily asso-
           ciates."

505   "Scraps." Life, 9 (5 May 1887), 247. Brief reference.
              "An exchange says that Mark Twain and Mr. Howells walk
           around New York with their arms lovingly locked. This is
           probably done to keep them from writing in the streets."

506   "By the Way." Life, 9 (12 May 1887), 260. Brief reference.
              "Mr. Howells is a fair poet, but he must grow some be-
           fore he can wear Longfellow's old clothes."

507   [HEARN, LAFCADIO.] "Howells on Critics." New Orleans Times-
           Democrat, 29 May 1887, p. 4. Editorial. Rpt. Essays on
           American Literature, ed. Albert Mordell and Sanki Ichikawa
           (Tokyo: Hokuseido, 1929), pp. 248-250.
              "Intolerance has been a distinguishing trait of realism."
           Howells himself "violated all those principles of criticism
           he would have the rest of the world obey." Respect for
           Howells turned to antagonism when he moved from fiction to
           criticism [a trend clearly reflected in the Times-Democrat].
           He has been badly beaten in his battle.

508   [Untitled.] Life, 9 (2 Jun 1887), 302. Brief reference to
           current "Editor's Study."
              If Howells "is ever to have as much fun with the Ameri-
           can critics as they have had with him it is time he began,
           and he should keep prodding with all his might." They
           will cease attacking him when he ceases to be worthwhile.

509   "The Minister's Charge." Literary World, 18 (8 Jun 1887),
           4-5. Review.
              Contrasted with James's Princess Casamassima. In
           Howells' novel "there is an almost fatal lack of percep-
           tion of relative values." It is "in a certain way instruc-
           tive; but it is never edifying or stimulating."

510   DROCH [ROBERT BRIDGES]. "Some Truths About Criticism." Life,
           9 (9 Jun 1887), 320. Note.
              Approval of Howells on critics and criticism in the
           June "Editor's Study." Especially appreciated are his
           satiric thrusts at "women critics" and "the brutality of
           English criticism."

511 HUTTON, LAURENCE. "Literary Notes." Harper's, 75 (Jul 1887),
     2. Brief mention.
     Howells' introduction to Sebastopol is "the clearest,
     most sympathetic analysis" of Tolstoy to date.

512 REPPLIER, AGNES. "The Decay of Sentiment." Atlantic, 60
     (Jul 1887), 75. Brief reference.
     "We read The Bostonians and The Rise of Silas Lapham
     with a due appreciation of their minute perfections; but
     we go to bed quite cheerfully at our usual hour, and are
     content to wait an interval of leisure to resume them."

513 "Mr. Howells on Realism." New York Daily Tribune, 10 Jul 1887,
     p. 4. Editorial.
     "However repellant and distasteful the new school doc-
     trines of fiction may be to such as have been trained in
     the old school," Howells may be correct in his prevision
     of the emerging literature. Indeed, much in the current
     social situation supports his view. "But since it is not
     credible that materialism as a master impulse can guide
     the world to anything but disaster, and confusion, the
     prospect for the stability of the school of fiction which
     represents the prevailing cult is not brilliant."

514 "Mr. Howells on Realism / A Talk with the Novelist." New York
     Daily Tribune, 10 Jul 1887, p. 12. Rpt. in part, "Mr.
     Howells on Some Modern Novelists," Critic, n.s. 8 (16 Jul
     1887), 32; "Interviews with William Dean Howells," ed.
     Ulrich Halfmann, American Literary Realism, 6 (Fall 1973),
     287-289.
     Howells informally evaluates leading English, Russian,
     Scandinavian, and French writers.

  * "Mr. Howells on Some Modern Novelists." Critic, n.s. 8 (16
     Jul 1887), 32. Rpt. from New York Daily Tribune, 10 Jul
     1887, p. 12. See item 514.

515 "Two Opinions of Tolstoi." Literary World, 18 (23 Jul 1887),
     233. Note.
     The editor contrasts the positions of Howells and
     Maurice Thompson, with preference for that of Howells.
     Thompson is quoted from his 29 June 1887 address delivered
     before the Association of American Writers, Indianapolis.

516 "Mr. Howells Enlightens." Life, 10 (28 Jul 1887), 47. Brief
     note.
     Single-paragraph satiric response to Howells' placing
     Tolstoy above Dickens.

1887

517 BATES, ARLO. "Realism and the Art of Fiction." Scribner's,
2 (Aug 1887), 241-252. Minor reference.
This attempt to define the nature of literary realism
refers briefly to Howells on realism in the May installment of "Editor's Study" (p. 248).

518 BANGS, J. K. "Concerning Mr. Haggard." Life, 10 (11 Aug
1887), 76. Brief note.
Humorous contrast of Howells and H. Rider Haggard.

519 "Author and Critic." New Orleans Times-Democrat, 14 Aug 1887,
p. 4. Editorial.
Howells' fiction before A Woman's Reason was admirable
because it contained "something younger and more ideal,
that we miss amid the clever triflings of his later work."
One "cannot but lament the perverseness which has led
this author to devote himself to the photographing of such
types as Lemuel Barker, and the Laphams, and the silly
young lovers of April Hopes; though we are obliged to
acknowledge with a laugh, the humorous fidelity of the
reproduction." Howells' error as critic is "in wishing
to sweep from the face of the earth all literature but
the sort he prefers."

520 THOMPSON, MAURICE. "Realism and Criticism." Chicago Sunday
Times, 14 Aug 1887, Sup., p. [17]. Essay. Rpt. in part as
"Mr. Maurice Thompson on Mr. Howells," Literary World,
18 (3 Sep 1887), 281-282.
An explicitly critical attack upon Howells, who is "a
failure as a novelist" because he sees no "great good in
his own country and people." Thompson takes Howells to
task in general for his critical theory of realism--"Mr.
Howells teaches that to abjectly copy life is the whole
of worthy art"--and in particular for his praise of
Tolstoy, that "peculiar Russian." [Scharnhorst]

521 _____. "Tolstoi." Literary World, 18 (20 Aug 1887), 265-266.
Note.
Thompson's negative opinion of Tolstoy is contrasted
with Howells' favorable one.

522 "Literary Notes." Life, 10 (25 Aug 1887), 110. Brief comment.
"Mr. Howells calls himself 'we' in his contributions to
Harper's. This does not alter the fact that Mr. Howells
is a very singular individual."

523 "Book Reviews." Public Opinion, 3 (27 Aug 1887), 428. Brief
review of Dr. Breen's Practice.

("Book Reviews")
"Strong himself, why is it that Mr. Howells denies to his leading characters that mental strength and moral heroism for which he is himself so much distinguished?"

524 LANG, ANDREW. "The Manners of Critics." Forum, 4 (Sep 1887), 58-66. Essay.
Response to Howells on critics and criticism, generally receptive to his comments but unwilling to admit that English criticism is a weaker product than European criticism.

525 WALSH, WILLIAM S. "Book-Talk." Lippincott's, 40 (Sep 1887), 464-465. Note.
Howells is "the greatest American humorist. He has another of the rare marks of genius: he is sincere and genuine." Response to him is "distinctly personal." He is critically inconsistent: "his strictures on the limitations of modern criticism are strictures on the limitations of human nature."

* "Mr. Maurice Thompson on Mr. Howells." Literary World, 18 (3 Sep 1887), 281-282. Rpt. from Chicago Sunday Times, 14 Aug 1887. See item 520.

526 [Untitled.] Life, 10 (15 Sep 1887), 142. Full-page editorial.
Takes exception to Howells' enthusiasm for Tolstoy.

527 H[IGGINSON], T. W. "Women and Men / The Russian School of Writers." Harper's Bazar, 20 (17 Sep 1887), 642. Brief reference.
Challenges Howells' belief that the Russian writers are exponents of realism but sides with him, against Maurice Thompson, relative to their moral quality.

528 THOMPSON, MAURICE. "A Literary Controversy: Mr. Maurice Thompson Defends Himself Against the Abuse of a Boston Paper." Indianapolis Journal, 18 Sep 1887, p. 11. Comments responding to Literary World editorial.
Thompson attempts to soften his criticism of Howells in this interview. His position, as he states it here, is that "I am far from an enemy, personally, of Mr. Howells. The last time I saw him we parted at the threshold of my home the very best of friends, and I still am his warm friend, but I do not like his attitude and his utterances as a critic." [Scharnhorst]

1887

529   A SOUTHERNER. "Mr. Howells on the Tendency of Fiction."
      Critic, n.s. 8 (24 Sep 1887), 147-148. Note.
         Responds to Howells' comments on the narrowness of fic-
      tion ("Editor's Study") and argues that the "main essential
      tendency of the novel is to become broader and deeper in
      the study of personality, though in doing so it may become
      narrower in the variety of human types, and may of necessi-
      ty have to deal with social types less broadly representa-
      tive and powerful."

530   HUTTON, LAURENCE. "Literary Notes." Harper's, 75 (Oct 1887),
      1. Review of Modern Italian Poets. Rpt. Book News, 6
      (Nov 1887), 106-107.
         Howells' "history of poetry in Italy during the hundred
      years ending in 1870 most assuredly is neither desultory
      or slight."

531   McCABE, L. R. "Literary and Social Recollections of W. D.
      Howells." Lippincott's, 40 (Oct 1887), 547-552. Informal
      anecdotal biography.

532   DROCH [ROBERT BRIDGES]. "A Word for the Philistines." Life,
      10 (6 Oct 1887), 188. Note.
         "Mr. Howells never wrote a page which would foster weak-
      ness or despair (neither did he ever lead to heroism or
      great deeds—but that's another side of the question)."
      The last installment of April Hopes is illustrative.

533   "Literature." Philadelphia Evening Bulletin, 10 Oct 1887,
      p. 4. Brief review of Modern Italian Poets.
         "For those satiated with Howells's latest novels," this
      is a fascinating and "sufficiently instructive book."
      [Graham]

534   ALLEN, JAMES LANE. "Caterpillar Critics." Forum, 4 (Nov
      1887), 332-341. Essay.
         A rebuttal to Howells' explanation of the critical
      function in the June "Editor's Study."

535   BRADFORD, GAMALIEL, JR. "Idealism in Literature." Andover
      Review, 8 (Nov 1887), 461-468. Brief reference.
         A call for the incorporation of idealism in realism
      places Howells among realists (p. 461).

  *   "Modern Italian Poets." Book News, 6 (Nov 1887), 106-107.
      Rpt. from "Literary Notes," Harper's, 75 (Oct 1887), 1.
      See item 530.

536 THOMPSON, MAURICE. "Studies of Prominent Novelists, No. 3--
William Dean Howells." Book News, 6 (Nov 1887), 93-94.
Short literary evaluation. Rpt. in part, The War of the
Critics over William Dean Howells, ed. Edwin H. Cady and
David L. Frazier (Evanston: Row, Peterson, 1962), p. 48.
"As a novelist I should rank Mr. Howells a little below
Daudet and a little above Thomas Hardy, at the same time
I feel certain that but for his realistic hobby he could
easily go above even Daudet."

537 [Untitled.] Life, 10 (3 Nov 1887), 242. Note.
Paragraph judges Howells' use of "lady friends" to be
substandard diction.

538 "The Mistake of Cowardice." New York Daily Tribune, 8 Nov
1887, p. 4. Editorial.
Responds to public sentiment for Chicago anarchists
(e.g., Howells' letter printed in the Tribune, 6 Nov 1887,
p. 5).

539 DROCH [ROBERT BRIDGES]. "Bookishness." Life, 10 (10 Nov
1887), 260. Brief reference.
Dan, in April Hopes, deserves a better fate.

540 "Howells's Modern Italian Poets." Critic, n.s. 8 (12 Nov
1887), 241-242. Review.
"In these polished pages--as 'polished' as one of
Tennyson's poetic 'finger-tips'--we have the accomplished
portrayer of feminine logic off on a side hunt"--"excursions into the realms of poetic imagination entirely worth
following."

541 "Novels of the Week." Athenaeum, No. 3134 (19 Nov 1887), 671-
672. Review of April Hopes. Rpt. in part, "Why Mr.
Howells Interests English Readers," Boston Evening Transcript, 8 Dec 1887, p. 6.
Howells "tells no story because he has none to tell,
but occupies himself with an imaginative analysis of commonplace characters which shows his peculiar ingenuity and
originality of expression."

542 "Reviews." American (Philadelphia), 15 (19 Nov 1887), 74.
Review of Modern Italian Poets.
The excellence of the work is marred by "the poor quali-
ty of the metrical translations."

543 "The Lounger." Critic, n.s. 8 (26 Nov 1887), 274. Brief
note.

1887

("The Lounger")
On the advantage Howells gains by having plates for his books made in Edinburgh.

544 WALLACE, WILLIAM. "New Novels." _Academy_, 32 (26 Nov 1887), 350. Review of _April Hopes_.
"As dreary and cleverly written" as anything Howells has published. It is marked by his "peculiarly dry and attenuated American cynicism."

545 B., H. "The Boston Matron's English." _Boston Evening Transcript_, 29 Nov 1887, p. 6. Letter to the editor.
On Howells' diction.

546 GARLAND, HAMLIN. "Modern Italian Poets." _Boston Evening Transcript_, 30 Nov 1887, p. 6. Review.
"It is because this volume makes possible further comparative studies of literature shut out from most readers that it is chiefly notable." It also illuminates incidentally Howells' "conception of the office of poetry and fiction." The style is commended.

547 PAYNE, WILLIAM MORTON. "Recent Books on Poetry." _Dial_, 8 (Dec 1887), 183-184. Review of _Modern Italian Poets_.
The translations feature "literal faithfulness and little else."

548 "Realism." _Life_, 10 (1 Dec 1887), 301. Joke.
Suggestive of Howells' realism, taken from the autobiography of W. P. Frith: "A certain Mr. Wilkins, an artist of some repute, had painted a number of pictures of dead game, among which was a group of dead rabbits which Dr. Herring asserted were 'remarkably true to nature.'
"'Nature, sir!' replied Wilkins pompously. 'Yes, I flatter myself there is more nature in those rabbits than you usually see in rabbits.'"

549 [Untitled.] _Life_, 10 (1 Dec 1887), 300. Brief reference.
Note is taken of Howells' visit to Buffalo. The change of air should do him good. A separate comment: "A steady literary diet of _Life_, Howells and the death column ought to prolong the existence of many a worthy person."

550 "International Copyright / The Authors' Readings." _Critic_, n.s. 8 (3 Dec 1887), 281-282. Report on the Authors' Readings held in support of International Copyright.
Howells was given an enthusiastic reception and read a chapter from _April Hopes_.

*   "Why Mr. Howells Interests English Readers." <u>Boston Evening
    Transcript</u>, 8 Dec 1887, p. 6. Rpt. from <u>Athenaeum</u>, No.
    3134 (19 Nov 1887), 671-672. <u>See</u> item 541.

551   "Mr. Howells and the Plain Man." <u>Saturday Review</u>, 64 (10 Dec
    1887), 779-780. Note.
    Satiric response to Howells' literary theories includes
    a paragraph on the grasshopper metaphor.

552   "Novels." <u>Saturday Review</u>, 64 (10 Dec 1887), 794-795. Review
    of <u>April Hopes</u>.
    The reviewer gives simplified instructions as to how any-
    one can write a Howells novel. "There is nothing in this
    book to hurt the feelings of an Englishman."

553   "A Mistaken Estimate." New Orleans <u>Times-Democrat</u>, 18 Dec
    1887, p. 4. Editorial.
    Challenges Maurice Thompson's comparison of Howells to
    Daudet and Hardy. As for Daudet and Howells, "the one is
    a man of genius, and the other a man of talent who believes
    that genius means simple industry, and proves his mistake
    in every line he writes." As regards the other, "Howells
    has painted no scenes that stand out in living colors upon
    the memory; whereas Hardy throws open to us a whole pic-
    ture-gallery." [The negative view of Howells is tempered
    by a conciliatory catalogue of his occasional excellences.]

554   "New Publications / Mr. Howells's Novel." <u>New York Times</u>, 19
    Dec 1887, p. 3. Full review of <u>April Hopes</u>.
    "The analysis of an infinite number of little nothings
    to which Mr. Howells devotes his entire energies." Such
    over-refinement denies the substance of life.

555   "New Publications / Italian Literature." <u>New York Times</u>, 25
    Dec 1887, p. 11. Brief review of <u>Modern Italian Poets</u>.
    "Mr. Howells proves an able but not enthusiastic guide
    through modern Italian literature."

556   "New Publications." New Orleans <u>Times-Democrat</u>, 25 Dec 1887,
    p. 16. Brief review of <u>Modern Italian Poets</u>.
    "Perhaps W. D. Howells has never done better work."
    [A curious assessment after the limbo into which the <u>Times-
    Democrat</u> had thrown his fiction.]

557   "Book Reviews." <u>Epoch</u>, 2 (30 Dec 1887), 415-416. Review of
    <u>April Hopes</u>.

1887

("Book Reviews")
    Howells' "idealism has diminished, and the realism has increased." This is "distinctly the worst story that Mr. Howells has ever written."

1888

558   BANGS, JOHN KENDRICK. "The Rise of Hop O' My Thumb: A Parody." New Waggins of Old Tales, By Two Wags [John Kendrick Bangs and Frank Dempster Sherman]. Boston: Ticknor, 1888. Pp. 18-46. Rpt. in part, Howells / A Century of Criticism, ed. Kenneth E. Eble (Dallas: Southern Methodist University, 1962), pp. 51-53.
    A parody of The Rise of Silas Lapham.

*   BISHOP, WILLIAM HENRY. "Mr. Howells / In Beacon Street, Boston." Authors at Home / Personal and Biographical Sketches of Well-Known American Writers, ed. J[eannette] L. and J[oseph] B. Gilder. New York: Cassell, 1888. Pp. 193-209. Rpt. from Critic, n.s. 6 (27 Nov 1886), 259-261. See item 467.

559   "The Bookshelf." Cottage Hearth, 14 (Jan 1888), 24. Mention of paperback edition of A Woman's Reason.
    One of Howells' "most striking...works, introducing life under strange conditions."

560   "Contemporary Literature / Belles Lettres." Westminster Review, 129 (Jan 1888), 124. Brief review of April Hopes.
    Howells "stands unrivalled" in "the dissection of human motive." The revelation is not wholesome, but "it is undoubtedly amusing."

561   EGAN, MAURICE FRANCIS. "A Chat About New Books." Catholic World, 46 (Jan 1888), 557. Brief review of April Hopes.
    Howells' "practice...is much better than his theories."

562   PARKER, H. T. "Mr. Howells and the Realistic Movement." Harvard Monthly, 5 (Jan 1888), 145-149. Short essay.
    The analytic method of Howells' realism limits the emotional force of his fiction.

563   [WOODBERRY, G. E.] "Howells's Modern Italian Poets." Atlantic, 61 (Jan 1888), 130-135. Full review.
    Howells' great indebtedness to the Italian critics causes his essays to "exhibit an Italianated view."

([WOODBERRY, G. E.])
Howells is more a novelist than critic. He "succeeds best with the satirical poets," shows "considerable doubt and hesitation" with major poets. "His essay on Leopardi, in particular, is narrow."

564   "Mr. Howells's New Book / Realism and Love-Making / April Hopes." New York Daily Tribune, 1 Jan 1888, p. 10. Full review.
Although recognizing that Howells has instructed reviewers neither to praise nor blame, but to analyze and categorize, this reviewer finds "it is an old habit of ours to praise the first manner of Mr. Howells, and we are not sure that we wish to break it." Howells' "second manner," however, "began with the odious product of realism, Bartley Hubbard, in A Modern Instance." Now Howells has perhaps reached a third manner, in which the story may "be omitted from his variety of the realistic novel, so that the personages shall attract us as little by their actions as by their characters."

565   [HIGGINSON, THOMAS W.] "Howells's Modern Italian Poets." Nation, 46 (5 Jan 1888), 18-19. Full review.
"The book is really a chapter in the history of liberty." Howells' translations are both faithful and musical, but some of his rhymes suggest indolence.

566   "News and Notes." Literary World, 19 (7 Jan 1888), 15. Brief comment.
Attributes British spelling of certain words in Howells' novels to the fact that he has the plates prepared in Edinburgh.

567   "Recent Fiction." Critic, n.s. 9 (7 Jan 1888), 4. Brief mention of A Woman's Reason (Ticknor's Paper Series).
"An unobtrusive sermon."

568   "Jottings." Boston Evening Transcript, 13 Jan 1888, p. 4. Brief note.
"Some critics have worried about Mr. Howells's English, others about his lack of point and pith. Let anybody troubled that way read his scathing note on page three today on hangings and the substitute he proposes for the sheriff as hangman!"

569   POOL, M. L. "Women and the Realists." Boston Evening Transcript, 14 Jan 1888, p. 10. Note.

1888

(POOL, M. L.)
Entertaining satiric study of feminine critics of
Howells and James.

570 "Recent Fiction." Critic, n.s. 9 (14 Jan 1888), 17. Brief
review of April Hopes.
"Mr. Howells's work is beginning to have fewer and fewer
salient points, either for praise or blame. His stories
are a clever mosaic of bright and entertaining views of
ordinary life, with a good many pages devoted to the absolutely commonplace."

571 "Mere Fable." New Orleans Times-Democrat, 15 Jan 1888, p. 4.
Editorial.
Assumes that Howells' hope that those who are "sunk in
the foolish joys of mere fable" may see the error of their
ways is comment aimed at British rather than American
writers, and provides documentation of that position.

572 "Mr. Howells's April Hopes." Literary World, 19 (21 Jan 1888),
20. Review.
"No story at all," the novel is nevertheless charming.
Howells does not see deeply, but he reproduces what he
does see "with a poetical grace that is inimitable."

573 DROCH, ROBERT. "Types of American Fiction." Book Buyer, n.s.
5 (Feb 1888), 22 Brief comment on April Hopes.
Howells, "a court photographer to the Brahmins,...
stands in just a little awe of the high-priests. With
other Bostonian castes he takes the liberty to be satirical and patronizing...."

574 EGAN, MAURICE FRANCIS. "A Chat About New Books." Catholic
World, 46 (Feb 1888), 702. Brief reference.
Howells is compared with John Habberton.

575 WALSH, WILLIAM S. "Book-Talk." Lippincott's, 41 (Feb 1888),
283. Review of April Hopes.
It is a pity Howells turned his Harper's column "into
a pulpit for the delivery of literary sermons." Now he
feels he must conform practice to preaching. As a result,
April Hopes is his "only really tedious book."

576 [Untitled.] Life, 11 (2 Feb 1888), 58. Note.
Response to Howells' call for use of electricity in
capital punishment. The "satirical and humorous nature"
of his expression is confusing.

577 "April Hopes--Autumnal Decay." Public Opinion, 4 (4 Feb 1888), 418-419. Review of April Hopes.
    Howells' fame must rest on his earlier works. "He was fitted by talent, taste, instinct, and culture to hold a master's place in the school of romanticism."

578 "Literature." Athenaeum, No. 3145 (4 Feb 1888), 141. Review of Modern Italian Poets.
    Howells' poetry lacks the felicity of his prose, and he "is not too familiar with the classics." He does convey "in an easy, casual fashion" much solid information about the century he treats and records the alliance between politics and poetry.

579 "Literary Notes." Life, 11 (16 Feb 1888), 91. Brief reference.
    "Mr. Howells has left Buffalo, and is reported to be about to settle in New York. Mr. Howells, doubtless, found life in Buffalo too exciting."

580 [LOGAN, ANNIE R. M.] "More Novels." Nation, 46 (16 Feb 1888), 142. Review of April Hopes.
    Howells is uncharitable to both his characters and the Boston people interested in them. He digs "fathoms deep for their faults."

581 "Recent Fiction." Critic, n.s. 9 (18 Feb 1888), 80. Brief mention of A Fearful Responsibility (Ticknor's Paper Series).
    "A pleasant little story, belonging to the good old time when Mr. Howells let us like him without insisting that we should not like anybody else."

582 "A Word on Mr. Howells." Boston Post, 24 Feb 1888, p. 4. Editorial.
    Howells is criticized for his support of Zola and for his failure to understand the New England personality as evidenced by The Undiscovered Country, The Minister's Charge, and April Hopes.

583 PELLEW, GEORGE. "A Word on Mr. Howells." Boston Post, 27 Feb 1888, p. 3. Brief note.
    Responding to the note immediately above, Pellew argues that Howells is objective as a critic.

584 J. "As to Mr. Howells." Boston Post, 28 Feb 1888, p. 5. Letter to the editor.

1888

(J.)
Howells' devotion to truth prevents him from appreci-
ating fiction that presents more than a surface reality.

585   "April Hopes--A Novel." North American Review, 146 (Mar 1888),
      353-354. Review.
      "On the whole, the novel is much pleasanter reading than
      most of the author's recent works, and ends happily in
      ending so soon."

586   PAYNE, WILLIAM MORTON. "Recent Fiction." Dial, 8 (Mar 1888),
      267-268. Review of April Hopes.
      No plot. Vulgar characters.

587   "Fiction." Literary World, 19 (3 Mar 1888), 73. Brief notice
      of new edition of Their Wedding Journey.

588   "Book Notes." Boston Post, 5 Mar 1888, p. 3. Brief mention
      of new edition of Their Wedding Journey.
      It is regrettable that in his later novels Howells has
      shifted away from his "earlier and more refined art."

589   [Untitled.] Life, 11 (8 Mar 1888), 132. Note.
      "Aha, there! Mr. Comstock, Mr. Howells has been reading
      La Terre, and calls it 'a book not to be avoided by the
      student of civilization.' See him about it, if you like,
      but for goodness sake d-t s-y we t-d y-u!"

590   "By the Way." Life, 11 (15 Mar 1888), 148. Note.
      Publisher's Weekly has tabulated books in two categories:
      fiction and language. "Now, what we want to know is, under
      which head do Mr. Howells's works come?"

591   F., W. C. "Books That Have Helped." Life, 11 (15 Mar 1888),
      149. Brief mention.
      Much Ado About Nothing is listed for Howells.

592   [Untitled.] Life, 11 (15 Mar 1888), 146. Editorial.
      On Howells' enthusiasm and surprise in finding Americans
      attempting to modify their lives according to Tolstoy's
      ideas.

593   "Recent Fiction." Critic, n.s. 9 (31 Mar 1888), 152. Brief
      mention of new edition of Their Wedding Journey with sup-
      plementary chapter "Niagara Revisited."
      The realism of the supplement "must be accepted as very
      genuine."

594   "Recent Fiction." Overland, 2nd Ser., 11 (Apr 1888), 437.
        Very brief review of reissue of A Modern Instance.
        Although the book first communicates "a decided tinge
        of unpleasantness," it has "very permanent qualities of
        interest and value." [Reviews immediately following con-
        tain multiple minor references to Howells.]

595   WALSH, WILLIAM S. "Book-Talk." Lippincott's, 41 (Apr 1888),
        565-572. Short essay.
        Discussion of realism vs. romanticism centers on Howells'
        opposition to idealism.

596   DROCH [ROBERT BRIDGES]. "Nothing Is Here for Tears." Life, 11
        (5 Apr 1888), 194. Brief reference.
        Howells is referred to in a review of The Quick or the
    Dead? by Amélie Rives. He "never preached a better sermon
    than when he showed, through the clear-sighted Sewell,
    that unhappiness is not in itself praiseworthy or heroic."

597   "New Publications." New Orleans Times-Democrat, 29 Apr 1888,
        p. 16. Brief review of April Hopes.
        In its "general monotony and dullness and the inconse-
    quential behavior and often puerile talk of its tiresome
    people," it is reminiscent of Indian Summer and fails to
    measure up to "the more virile purposes and stronger meth-
    ods of A Modern Instance."

598   "The Bookshelf." Cottage Hearth, 14 (May 1888), 160. Brief
        mention of Indian Summer in paper.
        "Almost painfully truthful."

599   FAVILLE, JOHN. "Tolstoi on Immortality." Andover Review, 9
        (May 1888), 499-511. Brief reference.
        Howells' praise of "'truthfulness,' or 'realism,'" in
    Tolstoi is noted (p. 501).

600   "Notices of New Books." Godey's Lady's Book, 116 (May 1888),
        479. Brief mention of Indian Summer.
        "An exquisite story of American life in Tuscany."

601   "Recent Publications." New Orleans Daily Picayune, 27 May
        1888, p. 14. Brief review of The Minister's Charge.
        Influenced by the opinions of Henry James and George
    William Curtis, the reviewer concludes that there could
    be no finer "bit of realism."

602   "By the Way." Life, 11 (31 May 1888), 306. Brief reference.

1888

("By the Way")
   Satiric comment about author involvement with character.
"But even you, Mr. Howells, must have had some feelings
about Silas Lapham. There was a person, sir, that you almost permitted 'to live!'"

603   DROCH [ROBERT BRIDGES]. "Some Notes About New Stories."
      Life, 11 (7 Jun 1888), 322. Brief reference.
      Annie Kilburn begins well. "Is it hazardous to foresee
      a most interesting Indian summer love-affair between the
      Rev. Mr. Peck and Miss Kilburn?"

604   "Mark Twain's Library of Humour." Saturday Review, 65 (30
      Jun 1888), 803. Brief review.
      Single reference to the "attenuated humour of Mr.
      Howells."

605   "Modern Italian Poets." Princeton Review, 6 (Jul 1888), 133-
      138. Essay review.
      Were not this book presented "as the result of the care-
      ful study of many years, we should think it an essentially
      youthful work, written chiefly as a frame in which to set
      exercises in verse-translation."

606   PELLEW, GEORGE. "The New Battle of the Books." Forum, 5
      (Jul 1888), 564-573. Minor references.
      Howells, as one of the antagonists in a continuing dis-
      pute, provides background for Pellew's own understanding
      of romanticism and realism.

607   DROCH [ROBERT BRIDGES]. "Bookishness." Life, 12 (5 Jul 1888),
      6. Note.
      On Howells and Americanism versus distinction.

608   THOMPSON, MAURICE. "Mr. Howells's Poetry." Independent, 40
      (5 Jul 1888), 834. Review essay.
      Beginning with reminiscences of his own Ohio childhood,
      Thompson meditates on how far Howells has gone as revealed
      in the excellence of his poetry and regrets that his "suc-
      cess on a lower plane [i.e., his fiction]" has obscured
      his poetic work. "Whatever may be said of Mr. Howells's
      extreme notions about Tolstoi and Zola and their raw-beef
      realism, [Howells'] writings have in them a quality and a
      force of no ordinary sort, and they reflect a nature as
      strong, as pure and as true as any now speaking through
      letters."

609   [Untitled.] Life, 12 (12 Jul 1888), 16. Paragraph editorial.
      On the response to Howells' suggestion that Americans
      are snobbish.

610   D., E. A. "Mr. Howells's Ballet." New York Times, 15 Jul
      1888, p. 10. Full review of A Sea Change.
      Howells' first effort in ballet "naturally takes the
      color of his severely chaste and frigid mind." In spite
      of his continuing vogue as a novelist, Howells has been
      growing tired of the restrictions of his fiction, and so
      he has ventured into comic opera. "A Sea Change is quite
      stupid enough to be comic opera."

611   "New Books." Boston Evening Transcript, 23 Jul 1888, p. 6.
      Review of The Gambler by Franc B. Wilkie.
      It is doubtful that those who complain about Howells'
      faithful observation of the commonplace would prefer to
      substitute Wilkie's "revelations of baseness and moral
      downfall."

612   "August Magazines / Harper's." Boston Evening Transcript, 24
      Jul 1888, p. 6. Brief reference to Annie Kilburn.
      "Charming."

613   DROCH [ROBERT BRIDGES]. "The Reverberator." Life, 12 (26 Jul
      1888), 48. Review of James's novel.
      Both Flack and Bartley Hubbard represent a phase of
      journalism which "neither Mr. James nor Mr. Howells would
      claim to be the prevailing one."

614   "New Publications." New Orleans Times-Democrat, 29 Jul 1888,
      p. 8. Brief reference.
      Mention only of a cheap edition (Ticknor) of "the not
      very thrilling adventures of Lemuel Barker"--the least
      interesting of Howells' novels.

615   "Recent Publications." New Orleans Daily Picayune, 29 Jul
      1888, p. 7. Brief review of The Rise of Silas Lapham
      (Ticknor's Paper Series).
      This novel "ranks easily as the finest work Howells has
      ever done, if indeed it has ever been excelled in America....
      It is a book that business men read as much in the bank as
      women did in the boudoir when it first appeared as a serial
      in Century."

616   "New Books." Boston Evening Transcript, 30 Jul 1888, p. 6.
      Announcement of The Rise of Silas Lapham (Ticknor's Paper
      Series).
      "By many considered the best of Howells's novels."

1888

617 "The Bookshelf." Cottage Hearth, 14 (Aug 1888), 262. Brief
    mention of The Minister's Charge.
    "Rare and singular beauty, full of kindliness and of
    tenderness."

618 "New Books." Boston Evening Transcript, 9 Aug 1888, p. 6.
    Brief notice of reissue of A Sea Change.
    Readers "who imagine that the author is nothing if not
    rigidly realistic, have here an opportunity of seeing what
    he can do in the line of the idealistic fantastic."

619 DROCH [ROBERT BRIDGES]. "The Place of Home in American Fic-
    tion." Life, 12 (16 Aug 1888), 90. Brief reference.
    Howells "has given us a number of beautiful family pic-
    tures, perhaps none more genuine, and almost pathetic,
    with all its humor, than the Putneys, of Hatboro', in
    Annie Kilburn.

620 M., E. S. "Reflections." Life, 12 (30 Aug 1888), 123. Brief
    reference.
    "Mr. Howells has been censured, not because his readers
    were tired of him, but for the very reason that they
    couldn't spare him."

621 "Mr. Howells's A Sea Change." Literary World, 19 (1 Sep 1888),
    275. Review.
    "Mr. Howells's earlier farces have been in reality come-
    dies.... A Sea Change is purely and wholly farcical."

622 C., E. J. "Howells at Nahant / The American Novelist at His
    Summer Home." Boston Daily Advertiser, 20 Sep 1888, p. 5.
    Interview. Rpt. in part, Critic, n.s. 10 (6 Oct 1888),
    166-167; abstr. "Interviews with William Dean Howells,"
    ed. Ulrich Halfmann, American Literary Realism, 6 (Fall
    1973), 290.
    Howells and his home at Little Nahant are described as
    a frame for Howells' random talk about current literary
    activities.

623 "Book Table." Godey's Lady's Book, 117 (Oct 1888), 339.
    Brief mention of The Rise of Silas Lapham.
    "A noble and vivid work, with rare flashes of modern
    humor, and frequent episodes of amazing pathos."

624 "The Lounger." Critic, n.s. 10 (6 Oct 1888), 166-167. Note.
    Brief response to Howells' comments on New York as re-
    ported by an interview published in the Boston Daily Ad-
    vertiser, 20 Sep 1888, p. 5. Reprints one paragraph.

625   "Book Reviews." Epoch, 4 (12 Oct 1888), 173-174. Review of
      A Sea Change.
      "Ridiculous and merciless exposure of the hypocritical
      and conventional." Reviewer finds it singular that A Sea
      Change has not yet "been fitted with suitable music."

626   "By the Way." Life, 12 (18 Oct 1888), 214. Brief note.
      Life sides with Andrew Lang against Howells and calls
      for focus on action in fiction.

627   BOYESEN, HJALMAR HJORTH. "The Romantic and the Realistic
      Novel." Chautauquan, 9 (Nov 1888), 96-98. An "interlude"
      reference.
      Although to Howells, "more than to any other man in the
      United States, belongs the credit for having weaned the
      literary taste of the country from the crude sensational-
      ism of the earlier school of English fiction," he has not
      "fully and completely expounded his gospel of realism"
      (p. 97).

628   [Untitled.] Life, 12 (15 Nov 1888), 270. Brief reference.
      Howells' last novel is the best since The Rise of Silas
      Lapham.

629   GIBSON, CHARLES DANA. "Folly Loves the Martyrdom of Fame."
      Life, 12 (29 Nov 1888), 304-305. Double-page cartoon.
      A caricature of Howells leads the procession.

630   "December Magazines / Harper's." Boston Evening Transcript,
      5 Dec 1888, p. 10. Brief notice of A Likely Story.
      "Abounds in amusing situations and bright dialogue."

631   M., E. S. "Reflections." Life, 12 (6 Dec 1888), 323. Brief
      reference.
      Hats off to Howells for his comments (current "Editor's
      Study") on Christmas literature.

632   "Novels of the Week." Athenaeum, No. 3191 (22 Dec 1888), 847.
      Brief review of Annie Kilburn.
      "The book can only be called a description of some un-
      successful essays in philanthropy." Good subjects are not
      easy for this "most American of American novelists" to
      find.

633   "New Publications / Realism by Howells." New York Times, 24
      Dec 1888, p. 3. Full review of Annie Kilburn.
      "It is a study for a story rather than a fully-wrought
      novel, for it has little or no plot and the principal

1888

("New Publications / Realism by Howells")
character is never clearly defined." The memorable parts
of the novel are "the isolated figures which have been
studied from the life."

634 GARLAND, HAMLIN. "Annie Kilburn." Boston Evening Transcript,
27 Dec 1888, p. 6. Full review.
"That Mr. Howells has...caught and recorded unprece-
dentedly well a part of the social questioning of our day
is not a decline, but an advance in his art." Annie Kilburn is "electric with inquiry." The "artistic impartial-
ity of the book is, after all, its strong point, its
lasting value."

1889

635 HOLMES, OLIVER WENDELL. [Letter dated 10 Oct 1865.] The
Correspondence of John Lothrop Motley, ed. George William
Curtis. 2 vols. New York: Harper, 1889. II, p. 212.
Brief reference.
Holmes, writing to Motley, refers to Howells as "a young
man of no small talent. In fact, his letters from Venice
are as good travellers' letters as I remember since
'Eothn.'"

* ROBERTSON, JOHN M. "Mr. Howells' Novels." Essays Towards a
Critical Method. London: T. Fisher Unwin, 1889. Pp. 149-
199. Rpt. from Westminster Review, 122 (Oct 1884), 347-
375. See item 323.

636 DAWES, ANNA LAURENS. "The Moral Purpose in Howells' Novels."
Andover Review, 11 (Jan 1889), 23-36. Essay.
The moral element "has become the mainspring of [Howells']
conception, as well as the atmosphere of its expression,
--a distinct ethical intention" (p. 25). Special attention is given to A Modern Instance (p. 30), The Minister's
Charge (pp. 31-32), Indian Summer (p. 33), April Hopes
(pp. 33-34). Howells' novels are essentially negative:
they do not so much make us love virtue as hate vice
(p. 36).

637 ALLEN, JOHN BARROW. "New Novels." Academy, 35 (5 Jan 1889),
6. Brief review of Annie Kilburn.
A psychological study rather than a novel.

638   DAWES, ANNA L. "Some Minor Observations on the American
         Novel." Critic, n.s. 11 (5 Jan 1889), 1. Brief reference.
         Howells' "view of life is essentially and thoroughly the
         New England view."

639   "By the Way." Life, 13 (10 Jan 1889), 18. Anecdote.
         "A Hebrew scholar, last week in Boston, picked up a copy
         of one of Howells's novels.· He began at the back end,
         recognized the style, and became so interested that he
         forgot to breathe and died."

640   "Howells' Annie Kilburn / A Dull and Unprofitable Use of the
         Literary Microscope." Chicago Tribune, 12 Jan 1889, p. 12.
         Full review.
         Outstanding in Howells' latest novel are "the low level
         of its human interest and the indifference of the author
         to his own creatures." While character and situation may
         be "fully representative," their depiction is without
         moral value.

641   "William Dean Howells." Life, 13 (17 Jan 1889), 35. Brief
         satiric biography.
         Accompanied by "Life's Gallery of Beauties. No. 1"--a
         picture of Howells in the attire of a little girl.

642   "Book Reviews." Public Opinion, 6 (19 Jan 1889), 313. Re-
         view of Annie Kilburn.
         "Things do not begin in the story; they do not end
         there; a piece is merely cut off and framed for us to
         look at. We feel that any other piece would have done
         just as well." It is pessimistic rather than inspiring.

643   "The Magazines." Critic, n.s. 11 (19 Jan 1889), 34. Brief
         reference.
         Anna L. Dawes in "The Moral Purpose in Howells's Novels"
         cleverly characterizes Howells' purport.

644   "Novels." Saturday Review, 67 (26 Jan 1889), 102-103. Re-
         view of Annie Kilburn.
         Summary--from a slightly lofty point of view.

645   "Recent Fiction." Book Buyer, n.s. 6 (Feb 1889), 18. Review
         of Annie Kilburn.
         This work exhibits "a closer sympathy with the heart and
         soul of New England than the author has heretofore re-
         vealed. Howells has "uncommon skill."

1889

646   "<u>Annie Kilburn</u>." <u>Literary World</u>, 20 (2 Feb 1889), 35. Review.
Howells' philosophy is sound, his touch is clever, and
he is becoming tiresome.

647   "<u>Annie Kilburn</u>." <u>Critic</u>, n.s. 11 (9 Feb 1889), 63. Review.
"Annie Kilburn will remain as the best example of the
Puritan type of to-day." Ralph Putney and his wife "form
the plaintive note of the book."

648   "The Lounger." Critic, n.s. 11 (16 Feb 1889), 79. Brief note.
About the failure of the Boston <u>Herald</u> reviewer (item
not seen) to understand <u>Annie Kilburn</u>.

649   [LOGAN, ANNIE R. M.] "More Novels." <u>Nation</u>, 48 (21 Feb 1889),
165-166. Review of <u>Annie Kilburn</u>.
Howells "pretends to write only what he sees, and now it
appears that he doesn't see...traditional spirit and
intellect because they are no longer there to see." His
delineation of Putney leads him into excesses.

650   "Two Novels--American and French." <u>Spectator</u>, 62 (16 Mar
1889), 371-373. Review of <u>Annie Kilburn</u> (and Bourget's
<u>André Cornélis</u>).
Placing the two novels side by side establishes contrasting national climates. Howells is "singularly successful in his suggestion of moral, intellectual, and
emotional atmosphere."

651   WALSH, WILLIAM S. "Book-Talk." <u>Lippincott's</u>, 43 (Apr 1889),
605-606. Review of <u>Annie Kilburn</u>.
Clever but futile. It has "just a little redeeming
vice. There is one character who is neither good nor
stupid. This is the lawyer Alva Putney." The reviewer
investigates the function of novels.

652   BOYESEN, H. H. "The Hero in Fiction." <u>North American Review</u>,
148 (May 1889), 594-601. Scattered references to Howells.
"There is not another American novelist who has appre-
hended so deeply and portrayed so faithfully two such
types of our National life as Silas Lapham and Bartley
Hubbard" (p. 601).

653   [Untitled.] <u>Life</u>, 13 (2 May 1889), 252. Editorial paragraph.
Notes Howells' "lively criticism of Sir Walter and all
his works" in the current <u>Harper's</u>. "Mr. Howells will
not admit that, either as a novelist or moralist, Sir
Walter is a freckle on the face of Count Tolstoy."

654   "Scott's Latest Critics." <u>Saturday Review</u>, 67 (4 May 1889),
521-523. Note.
     Satirical tirade responding to Howells on Scott. "O
genius of critical terminology! O shade of Longinus!
what does Mr. Howells mean?"

655   "New Publications / New Books." <u>New York Times</u>, 6 May 1889,
p. 3. Brief review of <u>The Mouse Trap, and Other Farces</u>.
     Howells can "take a nothing and give it airy grace. A
molecule is all he wants, for the thing itself is of no
account. It is the constructive power that is everything."
There are smiles here, but nothing like a good laugh.

656   DROCH [ROBERT BRIDGES]. "Mr. Howells's Eulogy of George
Meredith." <u>Life</u>, 13 (9 May 1889), 270. Note.
     Howells' judgment of Meredith is belated, but it is,
"all in all, one of the best critical estimates of him
that we have seen anywhere."

657   BLATCH, HARRIET STANTON. "Stepniak at Home / A Chat with the
Famous Russian Nihilist About Emerson, Walt Whitman,
George Eliot and Others /...." <u>Boston Evening Transcript</u>,
18 May 1889, p. 5. Interview. Brief reference.
     Howells' books will endure because he follows "the old,
natural method."

658   DROCH [ROBERT BRIDGES]. "Bookishness." <u>Life</u>, 13 (30 May
1889), 316. Brief comment.
     Howells' farces are unified by the characters appearing
in them. "If the American woman does not object to these
portraits of herself, the American man need not worry
about them; he may, however, thank the fates which sent a
different type to his hearth and home."

659   "Fiction for Idle Summer Days." <u>Book Buyer</u>, n.s. 5 (Jun 1889),
186, 195, 196. Brief mention of <u>An Italian Summer</u> [sic],
<u>The Minister's Charge</u>, and a reissue of <u>Their Wedding
Journey</u>.
     <u>The Minister's Charge</u> represents "very fairly" Howells'
later method. <u>Their Wedding Journey</u> contrasts with the
later works in which "the social reformer and commentator
upon social tendencies supersedes the novelist."

660   LANG, ANDREW. "Unhappy Marriages in Fiction." <u>North American
Review</u>, 148 (Jun 1889), 676-686. Brief reference.
     Howells has "a most unhappy marriage in <u>A Modern In-
stance</u>, but who can be sorry for such a pair--a jealous
shrew, and a beery journalist?"

1889

661   "Book Reviews." Public Opinion, 7 (1 Jun 1889), 177. Brief
     mention of The Mouse Trap, and Other Farces.
       "Superabundance of 'small talk' mingled with the humor
     and sparkle" of which Howells is master.

662   "Boston Letter." Critic, n.s. 11 (8 Jun 1889), 286. Announce-
     ment of forthcoming Wit and Wisdom of Howells (Minnie
     Macoun's Character and Comment).

663   BROOKS, NOAH. "The Evolution of a Newspaper Paragraph."
     Critic, n.s. 11 (8 Jun 1889), 286-287. Letter to the
     editor.
       Humorous account traces the wide copying of a paragraph
     originally in the New York World, 7 Mar 1889 (not seen),
     crediting Brooks and Howells with being able to type.

664   "Mr. Howells' Farces." Literary World, 20 (8 Jun 1889), 193.
     Brief notice of two collections of the farces.

665   "Recent Fiction." Critic, n.s. 11 (8 Jun 1889), 283. Brief
     mention of The Mouse Trap.
       It "excites a gentle risibility without in the least
     taxing the reader's mental capacity."

666   "Boston Letter." Critic, n.s. 11 (15 Jun 1889), 298-299.
     Brief mention.
       Notes Howells' return to Boston and his occupancy of
     "the old Winthrop estate."

667   VAN ZILE, EDWARD S. "The Brooks-Howells Type-writer Para-
     graph." Critic, n.s. 11 (15 Jun 1889), 300. Further
     response.

668   PAYNE, WILLIAM MORTON. "Recent Fiction." Dial, 10 (Jul 1889),
     59. Brief notice of The Mouse Trap, and Other Farces and
     The Sleeping Car, and Other Farces.
       Humor in the latter group seems less forced, perhaps be-
     cause these selections were done earlier. The Californian
     in The Sleeping Car is "irresistibly comical."

669   "The Sleeping Car, and Other Farces / The Mouse Trap, and
     Other Farces." Nation, 49 (4 Jul 1889), 18. Review.
       These are "dialogued sketches" rather than farces.
     Howells has not learned "the manual of arms" for theatri-
     cal art.

670   CLARK, KATE UPSON. "Book Reviews." Epoch, 5 (19 Jul 1889),
     389. Review of The Mouse Trap.

(CLARK, KATE UPSON)
Mr. Howells' "refined--perhaps it might be called super-refined--style is exactly adapted to the slight plots and unindividualized characters of these inconsequential but charming little dramas."

671 "Native and Foreign Novelists." New Orleans Times-Democrat, 21 Jul 1889, p. 4. Editorial.
"Howells, as a novelist, is unequal to Daudet in literary art and feeling for color, and is dwarfed by comparison with Tolstoi's sombre strength. But the last word has not been spoken; for he is yet in the prime of his powers. He has proved that he is not without humor and pathos, and his endeavor to reproduce typical American scenes and characters" points in the right direction. His characters are "living personages, not ghosts." A Hazard of New Fortunes, underway, shows a firm hold on life.

672 "Recent Fiction." Critic, n.s. 12 (27 Jul 1889), 42. Brief notice of The Sleeping Car, and Other Farces.
Their "impracticable scenery" makes them unsuitable for staging.

673 LADD, GEORGE T. "The Psychology of the Modern Novel." Andover Review, 12 (Aug 1889), 134-156. Brief reference.
Generally sympathetic to realism, Ladd questions the extent to which Howells and James go. "What can be more tiresome, whether we meet it in real life or in art, than much of the conversations in the 'Bostonians' or the 'Minister's Charge'?" (p. 154)

674 THOMPSON, MAURICE. "The Alien Taint in Criticism." America (Chicago), 2 (15 Aug 1889), 631-632. Anti-Howells essay.
"The revolution now threatening our country is in its early stage. The progression will be: Realism, sensualism, materialism, socialism, communism, nihilism, absolute anarchy. Each one of these is a form of death" (p. 63]). Howells is doing his fellow-Americans a disservice by promoting foreign literature.

675 _____. "Adventures with Editors." America (Chicago), 2 (29 Aug 1889), 695. Literary reminiscence.
Thompson relates an anecdote about how, during their Crawfordsville visit, Howells accepted for the Century a poem he had a few years earlier rejected with "stiff criticism."

1889

676   THOMPSON, MAURICE. "Women in Novels." America (Chicago), 2
        (5 Sep 1889), 727-728. Essay.
        "The heroine, as Scott and Goethe and Thackeray and
        Dickens portrayed her, has given place to a sort of talk-
        ing milliner's sign, whose chief attractiveness lies in
        the absolute nonsense which she is made to utter in the
        most refined style of decorative literary art" (p. 727).
        Howells and James are instrumental in molding this new
        heroine.

677   "Literature." Independent, 41 (17 Oct 1889), 1357. Very
        brief notice of Character and Comment (selections from the
        novels of Howells by Minnie Macoun).
        A "charming" but "scrappy" compilation.

678   "Talk About New Books." Catholic World, 50 (Nov 1889), 252-
        253. Brief reference.
        Howells and The Rise of Silas Lapham are briefly con-
        trasted with Lora: The Major's Daughter by W. Heimburg.

679   "The Scope of Literature." New Orleans Times-Democrat, 3 Nov
        1889, p. 4. Editorial.
        This satiric catalogue of Howells' observations in the
        "Editor's Study" concludes that "in criticism, Mr. Howells
        seems to have become a man of one idea. His insistence is
        scarcely comprehensible."
        [In subsequent literary editorials not entered in this
        listing, brief quotations from Howells or reference to
        him frequently serve as springboards into discussions
        that do not directly pertain to him.]

680   THOMPSON, MAURICE. "The Big Bow-Wow." America (Chicago), 3
        (14 Nov 1889), 215. Anti-Howells essay.
        "I know an editor, as sweet-natured and as high and
        noble a soul as ever lived, whose humor is like mulled
        cider on a frosty morning and whose criticism, no matter
        how severe, reacts upon the sources of good temper and
        makes one chuckle and love him all the more; but, he has
        a window, a beautiful one of his own making, that looks
        upon just the particular patch of earth which he likes,
        and against this window he imagines that all the world of
        bad men are heaving immense stones...." This unnamed edi-
        tor is disproportionately influenced by Tolstoy and Jane
        Austen.

681   "Reviews." American (Philadelphia), 19 (16 Nov 1889), 93.
        Review of Character and Comment (excerpts from Howells
        selected by Minnie Macoun).

("Reviews")
"Books of this kind are enfeebling to the mental powers
of those who read them, and can certainly give no gratifi-
cation to the mutilated author."

682 WILLIAMS, FRANCIS HOWARD. "Are We Coming Back to Scott?"
American (Philadelphia), 19 (23 Nov 1889), 108-109. Short
essay.
Speculates on whether or not literature will turn back
from the realism of Howells to idealism.

683 BROOKS, NOAH. "Books of the Christmas Season." Book Buyer,
n.s. 6 (Dec 1889), 438. Brief notice of Character and
Comment (Macoun).
Selections highlight the wise and witty sayings sometimes lost in context.

684 [CURTIS, GEORGE WILLIAM.] "Editor's Easy Chair." Harper's,
80 (Dec 1889), p. 153. Brief reference to A Hazard of New
Fortunes.
"This is a story of profound interest, as vivid a tale
of distinctive life and character as we have had."
[This quotation is used as a part of the advertisement
in the subsequent issue of Harper's, Advertiser, p. 117.]

685 "Recent Publications." New Orleans Daily Picayune, 1 Dec 1889,
p. 13. Very brief mention of The Hazard of New Fortunes
(Uniform Edition).

686 "The Listener." Boston Evening Transcript, 7 Dec 1889, p. 14.
Brief reference.
Speculation as to how Howells would likely respond to
Herne's Drifting Apart, currently playing at the Grand
Opera House.

687 "Literary Items." Boston Evening Transcript, 7 Dec 1889, p. 6.
Brief note.
Howells, "who has just given to older readers a novel
full of the Christmas spirit, A Hazard of New Fortunes,"
is a contributor to the Christmas number of Harper's Young
People.

688 GARLAND, HAMLIN. "Mr. Howells's Latest Novel." Boston Evening Transcript, 14 Dec 1889, p. 10. Full-column review
of A Hazard of New Fortunes.
"No such critical study of American society has been
previously made." This "rigidly artistic" work is "the
most candid and masterly study of a city in modern
literature."

103

1889

689   "Novels." Saturday Review, 68 (14 Dec 1889), 684. Review of
       A Hazard of New Fortunes.
          Typical Saturday Review disapproval of Howells. "It
       takes a long time to read, but--a man was shot."

690   "New Publications / A Novel by Howells." New York Times,
       15 Dec 1889, p. 19. Full review of A Hazard of New For-
       tunes.
          The novel has solidarity ·and completeness its forerunners
       lacked. Howells seems "to have added to his knowledge of
       womankind," and without losing his "vivacity," he meets
       social questions more seriously. The reader is both "in-
       tellectually amused" and "morally quickened." The last
       chapter is an unnecessary addition.

691   DROCH [ROBERT BRIDGES]. "A Hazard of New Fortunes." Life,
       14 (26 Dec 1889), 358-359. Review.
          "Whatever one may think of Mr. Howells' socialism--it
       is, nevertheless, very patent that his sympathies have
       been broadened by it and an earnestness has been added to
       his character studies." As a character, Fulkerson towers
       above the rest, but "the subtilest bit of work in the book
       is Beaton."

692   "Howells' Latest Novel / Vivid Study of New York Life and
       Social Conditions." Boston Sunday Herald, 26 Dec 1889,
       p. 4. Three-column review of A Hazard of New Fortunes as
       sequel to Their Wedding Journey.
          The novel is viewed as evidence of Howells' growth. His
       sympathy for individuals "has reached out to comprehend
       the sum of personalities--humanity." Howells understands
       social forces at work. Many references to his earlier
       novels. A major review.

693   "Minor Notices." Critic, n.s. 12 (28 Dec 1889), 325. Brief
       mention of Character and Comment (Macoun).
          As satisfactory "as the perusal of a cookbook to a hun-
       gry schoolboy."

694   "Novels of the Week." Athenaeum, No. 3244 (28 Dec 1889),
       889-890. Review of A Hazard of New Fortunes.
          Howells "has adopted that fixed manner which comes to
       almost every novelist who writes much." He is "fitfully
       dramatic." He lacks focus.

1890

695   STEUART, JOHN A. "To Mr. William Dean Howells." Letters to
      Living Authors. London: Sampson Low, Marston, Searle,
      & Rivington, 1890. Pp. 191-206. Epistolary essay.
         Ironically speculates on the non-existence of the Ameri-
      can novel, asserts that Howells himself may be most repre-
      sentative, and analyzes first Howells' critical attitude
      toward England and then his merits as an artist. Portrait
      (facing p. 191).

696   [CURTIS, GEORGE WILLIAM.] "Editor's Easy Chair." Harper's,
      80 (Jan 1890), 313-314. Review of A Hazard of New For-
      tunes.
         "It is a story of real life in the truest sense, a micro-
      cosm of America, a tale which, like all works of the imagi-
      nation, reveals another world beneath itself."

697   "Mr. Howells's Hazard of New Fortunes." Critic, n.s. 13
      (11 Jan 1890), 13-14. Review.
         "The heart of modern New York is laid bare to our gaze."
      Here one finds "the core of the society we form."

698   "A Hazard of New Fortunes." Literary World, 21 (18 Jan 1890),
      20-21. Review.
         The novel has "enlarged horizon," "freer movement,"
      "stronger dramatic tone," and more attractive characters.
      Howells' more expansive art is credited to the gay atmos-
      phere of New York City.

699   SHARP, WILLIAM. "New Novels." Academy, 37 (18 Jan 1890),
      41-42. Review of A Hazard of New Fortunes.
         Whether or not Howells has earned permanence is debatable,
      but his work is "the genuine connecting link between the
      crude realists in method like Tolstoi, and the crude real-
      ists in thought like Zola." Howells' theory may be a bar-
      rier to his mastery.

700   [Untitled.] Life, 15 (23 Jan 1890), 46. Brief note.
         Satiric paragraph notes that Bronson Howard is paid
      "something like $1,000 a week" because he "has been mis-
      taken by nearsighted people" for William Dean Howells.

701   WHARTON, ANNE H. "Some Tendencies of American Fiction."
      American (Philadelphia), 19 (25 Jan 1890), 293-294. Short
      essay.
         This piece, attempting, among other things, to determine
      the role of Howellsian and Jamesian realism in American
      fiction, has a romantic coloration.

1890

702   HUTTON, LAURENCE. "Literary Notes." Harper's, 80 (Feb 1890),
         1-2. Review of A Hazard of New Fortunes.
           "Follow Mr. Howells's March about New York, oh, New-
         Yorker! no matter how much you belong here, and learn to
         know yourself."

703   "New Books." Lippincott's, 45 (Feb 1890), 291. Brief notice
         of A Hazard of New Fortunes.
           This novel contains one lurid spot: a man is shot.
         Howells brings together typical characters and "makes
         speaking effigies of them."

704   "Recent Fiction." Book Buyer, n.s. 7 (Feb 1890), 23. Review
         of A Hazard of New Fortunes.
           Howells' move from Boston to New York "appears to have
         been beneficial...in many ways"--especially in the dis-
         covery of new character types.

705   "Literature of the Day / Great Fiction--Howells' Latest Hap-
         pily Not His Last." Chicago Tribune, 8 Feb 1890, p. 13.
         Full review of A Hazard of New Fortunes.
           Subtitle reads, "Perhaps the Best of American Novels--
         A New Departure for Our Leading Novelist--Social Problems
         Set Forth--Wit and Humor, Comedy and Tragedy, Laughter
         and Tears."

706   [Untitled.] Life, 15 (13 Feb 1890), 88. Editorial paragraph.
           "Mr. Howells will need another new wig. He is accused
         of having said the other day that there is nothing left
         of Dr. Johnson but Boswell, and the contemporary press has
         since been illustrated with handfuls of his hair."

707   "Boston Letter." Critic, n.s. 13 (15 Feb 1890), 80. Brief
         reference.
           Cynical note on Howells' move to a "swell-front" apart-
         ment on Commonwealth Avenue.

708   "Book Reviews." Public Opinion, 8 (1 Mar 1890), 504. Review
         of A Hazard of New Fortunes.
           Howells is "a profound student of life in its moods and
         types, and has a richness of view which shows that he has
         grasped the nature of man in its amazing varieties of de-
         velopment."

709   P., J. "A Hazard of New Fortunes / More About Some Old
         Friends." Boston Journal, Morning Ed., 1 Mar 1890, p. [2].
         Letter. Rpt. American Literary Realism, 5 (Winter 1972),
         74-77.

(P., J.)
Fulkerson, meeting the correspondent on a New York
street, provides information on what has happened to
Howells' characters subsequent to the ending of A Hazard
of New Fortunes.

710 "Short Stories." New Orleans Daily Picayune, 2 Mar 1890,
p. 12. Editorial.
Contains brief references to Howells' claim to have discovered James.

711 "Mr. W. D. Howells's Latest Novel." Spectator, 64 (8 Mar 1890),
342-343. Full review of A Hazard of New Fortunes.
Howells has two periods. His early works are tentative
studies in the art of fiction. His more recent works have
"a body of intrinsic interest" and "an orderly narrative
movement toward a definite goal or dénouement." A Hazard
of New Fortunes combines the best of both periods.

712 THOMPSON, DAVID L. "Novelists Begin to See the Cat." Standard (New York), 7 (12 Mar 1890), 4. Note.
Howells' awareness of inequities in American life is
evident in Annie Kilburn and A Hazard of New Fortunes.

713 [Untitled.] Life, 15 (20 Mar 1890), 164. Editorial paragraph.
A "Western contemporary" accuses Howells of taking the
Dryfoos family "from a poem of Jim Riley's about a family
that were poor and happy at Griggsby Station, but lost
peace and comfort and home in getting rich." That situation, however, is not uncommon in America.

714 [SCUDDER, HORACE E.] "New York in Recent Fiction." Atlantic,
65 (Apr 1890), 563-567. Full review of A Hazard of New
Fortunes.
Here one finds greater "power of portraiture" and "deeper
truthfulness" than in the earlier novels. Howells comes
"near adjusting the ethical and aesthetic glasses with
which he views life, so that they have the same focus."
New York is presented as a mirror of modern life.

715 "Talk About New Books." Catholic World, 51 (Apr 1890), 119-
122. Review of A Hazard of New Fortunes.
Focus is on Howells' women and on Lindau.

716 CLARK, KATE UPSON. "Book Reviews." Epoch, 7 (11 Apr 1890),
158. Review of A Hazard of New Fortunes.
Howells is nearer to his characters than ever before,
but he should present more interesting people--especially
"a noble, high-minded, well-balanced woman."

1890

717   "We Shall Meet on That Beautiful Shore." Life, 15 (17 Apr
       1890), 228-229. Double-page cartoon. Rpt. American Liter-
       ary Realism, 8 (Spring 1975), 100.
           The angry spirits of Dickens, Scott, Johnson, and
       Thackeray await Howells' arrival at "Elysium Landing."
       Howells, during his passage across the Styx, is reading
       Tolstoy.

718   "Recent Fiction." Independent, 42 (24 Apr 1890), 561-562.
       Brief reference.
           Review of Charles Dudley Warner's A Little Journey in
       the World mentions Howells' "veritable romance" appearing
       in a current serial.

719   GARLAND, HAMLIN. "Mr. Howells's Latest Novels." New England
       Magazine, n.s. 2 (May 1890), 243-250. Essay. Rpt. in
       part, Review of Reviews, 1 (Jun 1890), 497; Howells / A
       Century of Criticism, ed. Kenneth E. Eble (Dallas: South-
       ern Methodist University, 1962), pp. 54-59; and The War of
       the Critics over William Dean Howells, ed. Edwin H. Cady
       and David L. Frazier (Evanston: Row, Peterson, 1962),
       pp. 48-50.
           In this major essay, Garland, both appreciative and de-
       fensive, seeks to define the nature of Howells' art by
       tracing its progression from A Woman's Reason through A
       Hazard of New Fortunes.

720   "New Publications." New Orleans Times-Democrat, 4 May 1890,
       p. 16. Review of A Hazard of New Fortunes.
           "It is a triumph of realistic art." Although it con-
       tains tedious detail, the serious purpose of the author is
       clear and takes hold of the imagination. The characters
       are fresh, original, and natural.

721   "Amusements / The Theatrical Week." New York Times, 25 May
       1890, p. 13. A lengthy response to Howells' review of
       American drama in the June Harper's.
           Howells is disappointing in his failure to offer new in-
       sights. The drama critics whom he censures have already
       commented on the things he points out now.

722   "Men of the Time." Chicago Evening Post, 26 May 1890, p. 4.
       Biographical introduction to Howells.
           "Perhaps no author of modern times has grown in breadth
       and caliber to the extent that Howells has.... His vision
       has grown keener and his knowledge of American life of to-
       day deeper."

723   BIRD, FREDERIC M. "A Hazard of New Fortunes." Lippincott's,
       45 (Jun 1890), 910-912. Full review.
           "Nobody could do better work than Mr. Howells, if he
       were not weighted down by certain dogmas of which he has
       made himself the apostle. It is not easy to be at once a
       leading novelist and a literary lawgiver and dictator."
       April Hopes illustrates that. But in A Hazard of New For-
       tunes "there are signs that Mr. Howells is becoming hap-
       pily illogical, or less heavily ridden by his perverse
       theories."

*   "In Praise of Mr. W. D. Howells." Review of Reviews, 1 (Jun
       1890), 497. Hamlin Garland's appreciation rpt. from New
       England Magazine, n.s. 2 (May 1890), 243-250. See item
       719.

724   No Entry

725   [LOGAN, ANNIE R. M.] "Mr. Howells's Latest Novel." Nation,
       50 (5 Jun 1890), 454-455. Full review of A Hazard of New
       Fortunes. Rpt. in part, The War of the Critics over
       William Dean Howells, ed. Edwin H. Cady and David L.
       Frazier (Evanston: Row, Peterson, 1962), pp. 50-51.
           "Seeing how lucidly and kindly [Howells] can translate
       the meaning of some of [New York's] innumerable vibrations,
       one regrets that he has devoted so much time to the in-
       consequent prattle and finished irony of the ladies and
       gentlemen from Boston." A Hazard of New Fortunes is great-
       er than Howells' earlier novels because it focuses on "the
       multiform life" of a great city.

726   "Recent Publications." New Orleans Daily Picayune, 8 Jun 1890,
       p. 16. Very brief mention of The Shadow of a Dream.
           "Clever, well written, and interesting."

727   DROCH [ROBERT BRIDGES]. "The Shadow of a Dream." Life, 15
       (19 Jun 1890), 354. Review.
           "There was more sentiment in The Undiscovered Country,
       more fancy, perhaps--but here are emotions and perplexi-
       ties of the deep, unreasonable sort which only wise men
       know to be nearest the reality."

728   "Novels of the Week." Athenaeum, No. 3270 (28 Jun 1890), 828.
       Brief review of The Shadow of a Dream.
           "A decidedly clever piece of work." Mr. and Mrs. March
       are becoming more precise and less involved with triviali-
       ties. Regrettably, the subject is not a "vigorous" one.

1890

729   "Contemporary Literature / Belles Lettres." Westminster Review, 134 (Jul 1890), 89-90. Review of A Hazard of New Fortunes.
       Howells' work is fine rather than powerful; there is too little action, and too much refining upon the motives of action." But Howells' name on the title page is always welcome. In this novel, Fulkerson's romance "is the prettiest and most touching bit."

730   HUTTON, LAURENCE. "Literary Notes." Harper's, 81 (Jul 1890), 1. Review of The Shadow of a Dream.
       "Notwithstanding its portrayal of much morbid conscientiousness, and of much exaggerated sensibility upon the part of all the victims of the dream," this is "a very clever sketch."

731   "Novels for Summer Days." Book Buyer, n.s. 7 (Jul 1890), 249-250. Review of The Shadow of a Dream.
       Here is further evidence that Howells' "literary art-sense [is] stronger than his fidelity to the theory of realism which he upholds as a critic."

732   "The Point of View." Scribner's, 8 (Jul 1890), 129-130. Brief reference.
       Howells makes the mistake of taking "his native contemporaries at the pitch of their aspirations rather than their deeds." Distinction must be made "between taking one's art seriously and taking one's self, the artist, so."

733   "Fiction." Literary World, 21 (5 Jul 1890), 221. Brief review of The Shadow of a Dream.
       Dreary. One garden by the sea recalls Swinburne's "Forsaken Garden."

734   "The Lounger." Critic, n.s. 14 (5 Jul 1890), 6. Brief note.
       Howells was the only author up to this point to write books on a salary. Another unnamed author is now also doing so.

735   "Novels." Saturday Review, 70 (5 Jul 1890), 18-19. Brief review of The Shadow of a Dream.
       "Mr. Howells's last novel is written in his usual jargon, or if anything rather worse than usual.... The story, as usual, is all about three very unpleasant souls."

736   "How Literary Men Work / Interesting Bits of Gossip About Their Habits." Boston Herald, 6 Jul 1890, p. 21. Brief reference.

("How Literary Men Work / Interesting Bits of Gossip About
Their Habits")
> Howells couldn't write novels amid the noise of New
> York, so he retreated to the quieter Boston environs.

737 SHARP, WILLIAM. "New Novels." Academy, 38 (12 Jul 1890),
27-28. Review of The Shadow of a Dream.
> Highly favorable response to a "remarkably subtle and
> clever" work. "Mr. Howells's humor is always delicate,
> while virile."

738 "Points of View." New Orleans Times-Democrat, 13 Jul 1890,
p. 4. Editorial.
> Since A Modern Instance, Howells' novels have "steadily
> grown in breadth and vigor." Howells' work exhibits "de-
> lightful, genial humor."

739 THOMPSON, MAURICE. "The First Novel." New Orleans Daily
Picayune, 13 Jul 1890, p. 11. Note.
> Comparison of the surprising similarities of Mme La
> Fayette's romance La Princesse de Clives and Howells' The
> Shadow of a Dream. Howells is more delicate and more
> modern. [This may be reprinted from another source, but
> it is not so indicated.]

740 CLARK, KATE UPSON. "Book Reviews." Epoch, 7 (25 Jul 1890),
397-398. Full review of The Shadow of a Dream.
> "The white, bald light of noon is still over everything."
> "Mr. Howells, as a litterateur, is a fop." This book is
> of "little value and hardly worthy" of him.

741 "Mr. Howells's Shadow of a Dream." Critic, n.s. 14 (26 Jul
1890), 44. Review.
> This "study" departs from the Howells of The Rise of
> Silas Lapham and the farces. The "dark, sad scenes" are
> lightened by "the familiar inter-connubial utterances" of
> the Marches, whom Howells again presents with Kodak-like
> exactness.

742 PAYNE, WILLIAM MORTON. "Recent Fiction." Dial, 11 (Aug 1890),
93. Review of The Shadow of a Dream.
> Howells seems again to have entered a "tentative stage."
> James is superior.

743 "Some Critics of Criticism." New Orleans Times-Democrat,
3 Aug 1890, p. 4. Editorial.
> A lengthy response to Howells' current "Editor's Study,"
> somewhat more sympathetic than usual. The "generous

1890

("Some Critics of Criticism")
tolerance" Howells extends to all conscientious creative
endeavor may one day be extended, it is hoped, to critics
who differ with his point-of-view.

744   "Literary Notes." Independent, 42 (7 Aug 1890), 1102. Short
comment.
Full paragraph applauding Howells' writing on critics
and criticism in the "Editor's Study."

745   "Notes." Nation, 51 (7 Aug 1890), 111-112. Editorial comment.
Negative reaction to Howells' attack on anonymous criticism in the August "Editor's Study." For nearly five
years Howells "has expressed his personal opinions without
let or hindrance; and the result has been a mass of judgments upon great and petty authors which is remarkable for
eccentricity, dogmatism, and the spirit of faction"
(p. 112).

746   "A Critic's Criticism of Critics." New Orleans Daily Picayune,
10 Aug 1890, p. 12. Editorial.
Defense of anonymity in newspaper criticism shifts to a
discussion of Howells. "In his intolerance of romance Mr.
Howells approaches bigotry, and in his self-assertion he
sometimes very nearly betrays the confidence of an egotist,
but he is a very able, brilliant and witty writer, and we
are ready to quarrel with the first critic who may say anything to the contrary."

747   "Books / The Shadow of a Dream." Spectator, 65 (16 Aug 1890),
213-215. Full review.
This novel "deserves special appreciation for its perfection of grouping, the novelty of its interest, and the
harmony of its colour in every detail."

748   "The Lounger." Critic, n.s. 14 (16 Aug 1890), 84. Brief note.
Howells is "a good lover and a good hater," and "some
brutal criticism, not of his own work, I am persuaded, but
of some mute inglorious author whom he has championed,"
has moved him to write the "scorcher" in the current
Harper's.

749   "The Office of Literary Critic." Boston Sunday Herald,
17 Aug 1890, p. 20. Editorial.
Takes issue with Howells' "wholesale onslaught upon the
literary critic" in the August Harper's.

750   "Saratoga / William Dean Howells Taking Notes /...." <u>New York Times</u>, 17 Aug 1890, p. 10. Gossip.
        About Howells' presence in Saratoga at the height of the season. He is writing several hours a day and has shown much interest in the Salvation Army campaign underway.

751   "Book Reviews." <u>Public Opinion</u>, 9 (23 Aug 1890), 468. Review of <u>The Shadow of a Dream</u>.
        "There is an air of Hawthorne over the whole, though the development in method and style is greatly different from Hawthorne."

752   "Current Criticism." <u>Critic</u>, n.s. 14 (23 Aug 1890), 100. Note.
        Justin McCarthy is quoted. Howells' "idealism quickens his realism and makes it gleam and glance with beauty. His realism strengthens his idealism and gives it form and substance, so that the commonest eyes can see it and recognize it and understand it."

753   "New Publications." New Orleans <u>Times-Democrat</u>, 24 Aug 1890, p. 16. Review of <u>The Shadow of a Dream</u>.
        The novel is based on another, of Howells' "intricate psychological problems" so finely drawn it could be a problem only to "the most delicately strung natures." In the denouement Howells seems to rush into catastrophe to avoid a rational commonplace termination.

754   "<u>A Boy's Town</u>." <u>Harper's</u>, 81 (Sep 1890), Advertiser, p. 222. Advertisement.
        Although <u>A Boy's Town</u> is "primarily and above all, a boy's book about boys," it will also appeal to older readers--"those whose boyhood days have long been past, but whose doings and dreamings were wonderfully like those of Mr. Howells's 'my boy' forty years ago." The book also has autobiographical interest.

755   [LOGAN, ANNIE R. M.] "More Novels." <u>Nation</u>, 51 (25 Sep 1890), 252-253. Review of <u>The Shadow of a Dream</u>.
        Howells' "admirable method of narrating ordinary events and depicting ordinary characters is applied with notable success to the narration of an unusual episode," and the characters are "not quite like everybody else." March displays more warmth than previously, but Mrs. Faulkner is "vague and unsubstantial."

756   HUTTON, LAURENCE. "Literary Notes." <u>Harper's</u>, 81 (Oct 1890), 1-2. Review of <u>A Boy's Town</u>.

1890

(HUTTON, LAURENCE)
> Each grown-up boy among Howells' readers "will find some
> one of his own peculiar characteristics, and many of his
> own particular tastes, embodied in this Boy of Mr. Howells's,
> and will wonder how Mr. Howells found him out." Youthful
> love of angling is defended against Howells' charge of
> cruelty.

757 "The Limitation of the Creative Imagination." New Orleans
> Daily Picayune, 5 Oct 1890, p. 12. Editorial.
> > Unsympathetic response to Howells' negative criticism of
> > Kipling in the current "Editor's Study." "It was hardly
> > to have been expected that a writer who so evidently loves
> > a story for its own sake would be welcomed by Mr. Howells
> > with unalloyed satisfaction."

758 "Literary Items." Boston Evening Transcript, 11 Oct 1890,
> p. 10. Brief announcement of A Boy's Town.
> > Of interest because of its autobiographical passages.

759 "Books of the Month." Atlantic, 66 (Nov 1890), 720. Brief
> review of The Shadow of a Dream.
> > Howells "has failed to make the experience real." The
> > story should have been given "a more nebulous atmosphere."

760 "A Boy's Town." Nation, 51 (13 Nov 1890), 385. Review.
> The book, which is a study of a Western town and "only
> incidentally a boy's book," is flawed by its critical,
> adult point of view.

761 RICHARDS, LAURA E. "Book Reviews." Epoch, 8 (21 Nov 1890),
> 252. Review of A Boy's Town.
> > Anyone "who wishes to study boy nature cannot do it bet-
> > ter than in these delightful pages."

762 "A Boy's Town." Literary World, 21 (22 Nov 1890), 429. Re-
> view.
> > Howells' "literary practice is so much better than his
> > theory, that it seems a pity he should ever spend his time
> > in formulating his views of the art of fiction."

763 "Briefer Notices." Public Opinion, 10 (22 Nov 1890), 166.
> Mention of A Boy's Town.
> > "Delightful and entertaining."

764 "New Publications." New Orleans Times-Democrat, 30 Nov 1890,
> p. 16. Brief notice of A Boy's Town.

("New Publications")
    "The humor is perhaps a little too dry and fine to be comprehended by the juvenile readers for whom it is intended, but older people will enjoy it."

765   "Truth and Reality." New Orleans Daily Picayune, 30 Nov 1890, p. 12. Editorial.
    Responding to Andrew Lang and to Howells in the December "Editor's Study." "Mr. Howells is well enough in his place--otherwise we should not have to say so much about him. But Mr. Howells has, perhaps, his limitations. It seems to us that a man can never understand the world quite thoroughly while he insists upon taking it literally."

766   DROCH [ROBERT BRIDGES]. "In a Boy's World." Life, 16 (4 Dec 1890), 320. Review of A Boy's Town.
    "What Mr. Howells has expressed with most felicity in this story is the aloofness of a Boy's world from the world of man, woman, or girl." For an hour or two he makes it possible for grown men to go back.

767   "Recent Fiction." Independent, 42 (4 Dec 1890), 1720. Review of A Boy's Town.
    "Mr. Howells's book is true to life in its incidents, which are strung upon a thread of reflective, retrospective analysis shimmering with refined, double-distilled humor."

768   "Novelist Howells." Buffalo Times, 17 Dec 1890, p. 1. Interview. Rpt. in part, "Interviews with William Dean Howells," ed. Ulrich Halfmann, American Literary Realism, 6 (Fall 1973), 293-294.
    Subheaded, "He Was a Guest at the Iroquois Yesterday. How He Writes Stories. The New Novels That He Is To Publish--He Tells a Times Reporter of His Work and His Views of American Literature."

769   "Christmas Autographs / American Writers Talk of Their Merriest Christmas." Boston Evening Transcript, 20 Dec 1890, p. 12. Note.
    Howells, who selects the first Christmas he can remember, is introduced as "probably one of the best known and best liked [novelists] among the more cultivated class of American readers of fiction."

770   "Notes." Critic, n.s. 14 (27 Dec 1890), 344. Brief note.
    Announces that Howells' association with Harper's will continue another year, much as in the past. Howells'

1890

("Notes")
    contracted novel with a newspaper syndicate was approved
    by Harper.

1891

771   BEERS, HENRY A. Initial Studies in American Letters. New
        York: Chautauqua Press, 1891. Pp. 63, 203-204, 210.
        Brief assessment of Howells and James.
          They have shaped recent fiction. "Their writings, though
        dissimilar in some respects, are alike in this, that they
        are analytic in method and realistic in spirit" (pp. 203-
        204).

772   "Howells, William Dean." National Cyclopedia of American Bi-
        ography. New York: White, 1891. I, pp. 281-282. Routine
        encyclopedic entry.

773   "American Fiction." Edinburg Review, 173 (Jan 1891), 31-65.
        Review essay. Rpt. in part, Literary Digest, 2 (14 Feb
        1891), 430-431.
          The work of Howells is contrasted (pp. 57-65) with that
        of George Washington Cable, Bret Harte, and Mary N. Mur-
        free. Howells best represents American realism, which is
        made up of negatives. "In his hands Americans seem to
        have lost the virility of the race.... He has no story to
        tell.... The realistic standpoint from which Howells
        writes is deadening; even the deft workmanship of the
        artist fails to galvanise it into vitality."

774   "Personalities." Independent, 43 (8 Jan 1891), 49. Brief
        note.
          On Howells' method. The plot develops as he writes, and
        incidents of daily life are woven into the story.

775   "New Publications / As Boys See It." New York Times, 11 Jan
        1891, p. 19. Review of A Boy's Town.
          Howells' book is morbid and painful. It misrepresents
        typical boyhood. It is not, in fact, a book for boys;
        but fathers and mothers may find the meaning Howells has
        placed in it.

776   "The Life of Lincoln." New Orleans Daily Picayune, 1 Feb 1891,
        p. 12. Editorial.
          Criticism of the bias that colors Howells' favorable re-
        view (current "Editor's Study") of The Life of Lincoln by
        Nicolay and Hay.

*   "American Fiction." Literary Digest, 2 (14 Feb 1891), 430-431.
      Rpt. from Edinburg Review, 173 (Jan 1891), 31-65. See
      item 773.

777   ROSS, ALBERT [LINN BOYD PORTER]. "What Is Immoral in Litera-
      ture?" Arena, 3 (Mar 1891), 438-445. Brief reference.
      "Even Howells, the delicate, soft-stepping favorite of
      the parlors," is drawn to "love that goes astray" (p. 440).

778   ROGERS, W. A. "Activity in Literary Circles / Caused by the
      Passage of the International Copyright Law." Life, 17
      (19 Mar 1891), 172-173. Double-page cartoon.
      Front center are caricatures of Howells and Twain.

779   DOLE, NATHAN HASKELL. "Boston Letter." Critic, n.s. 15
      (21 Mar 1891), 155. Brief reference.
      Although "mystery always attaches to Mr. Howells's move-
      ment," reports that he has moved to New York are accurate.

780   "Literature." Independent, 43 (2 Apr 1891), 500. Review of
      Doña Luz by Juan Valera.
      Compared erroneously with Howells' work. Attacks
      Howells' literary judgment.

781   "In a Minor Key / New York Society." New Orleans Daily
      Picayune, 5 Apr 1891, p. 10. Feature column.
      Ironic explanation of Howells' current "Editor's Study"
      comments on aristocratic and commercial society.

782   "Progress." New Orleans Daily Picayune, 5 Apr 1891, p. 12.
      Editorial.
      Realism has been written by the English greats--Thackeray,
      Eliot, Trollope--as well as by the Russian, Italian, and
      Spanish novelists Howells admires so much.

783   "Recent Publications." New Orleans Daily Picayune, 5 Apr 1891,
      p. 12. Brief review of Annie Kilburn.
      "The story is very well told" and enforces "some good
      social truth." But it is "not satisfactory. It lacks
      something, perhaps a heart."

784   "Recent Publications." New Orleans Daily Picayune, 5 Apr 1891,
      p. 12. Brief review of A Hazard of New Fortunes.
      "It is not a stupid book, but it is certainly not one
      that the reader will become so absorbed in as to forget
      to go to bed."

1891

785   "In the Library." Book Buyer, n.s. 8 (May 1891), 154-155.
      Note.
      Short discussion of the structural weakness in Howells'
      work.

786   "The Value of Criticism." New Orleans Daily Picayune, 3 May
      1891, p. 12. Editorial.
      Discussion of the function of criticism with minor illus-
      trative references to Howells.

787   "A Family Disgrace." Life, 17 (7 May 1891), 286. Joke.
      Centering on "Emerson Howeljames." "To think that you,
      the son of a Boston novelist, should be caught telling a
      story!"

788   "Literary Notes." Independent, 43 (7 May 1891), 686. Brief
      comment.
      The work of Howells is contrasted with a novel by
      Julien Gordon.

789   "The Free Parliament." Critic, n.s. 15 (30 May 1891), 282.
      Question and answer series.
      Question No. 1618 from H. H. B. M. asks if Howells pub-
      lished, about 1869, a novel entitled No Love Lost.

790   "Recent Fiction." Critic, n.s. 15 (30 May 1891), 286-287.
      Brief announcement of paperbound editions of A Hazard of
      New Fortunes and Annie Kilburn.
      Non-critical.

791   HUTTON, LAURENCE. "Literary Notes." Harper's, 83 (Jun 1891),
      4. Brief notice of Franklin Square Library editions of
      A Hazard of New Fortunes and Annie Kilburn.
      The stories reflect "the same strain of thinking" and so
      belong together. Their appearance in this form is "an en-
      couraging sign that the popular taste is by degrees being
      educated up to a proper understanding of the moral worth
      of a healthy, sensible realism in fiction."

792   "Six Volumes of Essays." Book Buyer, n.s. 8 (Jun 1891), 215-
      216. Brief notice Criticism and Fiction.
      Howells "pleads his cause with vigor and eloquence."

*   [W. D. HOWELLS.] Good Housekeeping, 12 (Jun 1891), 293-295.
      Rpt. from Good Housekeeping, 1 (11 Jul 1885), 2-3. See
      item 346.

793   "Recent Publications." New Orleans <u>Daily Picayune</u>, 7 Jun 1891,
      p. 10. Review of <u>April Hopes</u>.
        "This is a very long...and fine-spun story about two
      fools--a masculine fool and a feminine fool." Most of the
      other characters exhibit the same quality. And there are
      "yards upon yards of silly conversation."

794   "<u>Criticism and Fiction</u>." <u>Literary World</u>, 22 (20 Jun 1891),
      208-209. Full review.
        Howells' realistic stance is "almost purely amusing."
      "The good effect to be expected from [his] criticism of
      novelists and critics is largely destroyed by his bad tem-
      per and the extraordinary crudity and irrationality of his
      frequent negations."

795   "Literature." <u>Independent</u>, 43 (25 Jun 1891), 953-954. Review
      of <u>Criticism and Fiction</u>.
        "A prickly, pungent, exasperating piece of work, stuffed
      with good things and overloaded with things absurd."

796   COLE, CATHARINE. "Catharine Cole Causerie." New Orleans
      <u>Daily Picayune</u>, 5 Jul 1891, p. 9. Literary column.
        Negative response to Howells' work in general. "It is
      a very good thing, by the by, that Mr. Howells' novels are
      issued in monthly installments. His people may be Ameri-
      can [he supposedly writes for posterity], but they are not
      wildly interesting, and to have them call once a month is
      enough."

797   "Literature / Mr. Howells's <u>Criticism and Fiction</u>." <u>Critic</u>,
      n.s. 16 (11 Jul 1891), 13. Lead review.
        Howells "seems only half in a 'pucker' when he is pen-
      ning his paradoxes. His booklet abounds in truths felici-
      tously expressed."

798   "<u>Criticism and Fiction</u>." <u>Nation</u>, 53 (23 Jul 1891), 73. Re-
      view.
        "The fatal thing about this little volume is that it is
      dull." Its only value is "as an example of eccentricity."

799   HUTTON, LAURENCE. "Literary Notes." <u>Harper's</u>, 83 (Aug 1891),
      2-4. Full review of <u>Criticism and Fiction</u> and illustrative
      reference to <u>April Hopes</u> (Popular Edition).
        One need not agree with Howells in order to respect him.
      "The man who can publicly assert himself against any deep-
      ly rooted popular prejudice, as Mr. Howells has done in
      these brilliant essays of his, is, alas, so rare a charac-
      ter in this weak world of ours, that he would figure as a

1891

(HUTTON, LAURENCE)
'type,' almost as 'a creation,' if he were introduced into any realistic modern novel."

800 QUILLER-COUCH, A. T. "A Literary Causerie." Speaker, 4
(1 Aug 1891), 143-144. Review of Criticism and Fiction.
While objecting to Howells' manners, Quiller-Couch ad-
mits that in England "the love of form blinds us to reality." But Howells' "patriotism has brought him into queer
straits." He is "a worshipper of the incomplete and amor-
phous beating the tom-tom over the artistic achievements
of men and women who are, before all things, worshippers
of form." Howells focuses on the aristocratic and dyspep-
tic rather than on the toiler and on life.

801 ARCHER, WILLIAM. "The Novelist as Critic." Illustrated London News, 99 (8 Aug 1891), 175. Response to Criticism and
Fiction.
Howells' case is excellent, but he is confused in stating
his case and wrong in adopting a churlish tone towards England. The misunderstanding between "so admirable a writer" and "a large section of English criticism" is deplor-
able.

802 LUNDT, DOROTHY. "Library and Foyer." Boston Evening Transcript, 8 Aug 1891, p. 12. Brief anecdote.
About Howells' failure to find, "at a railway bookstall,
a novel which might prove a suitable travelling companion
for a young girl."

803 "The Drama in the Dog Days /.../ Mr. Howells at It Again /...."
New York Times, 9 Aug 1891, p. 13. Brief comment.
Response to Howells on drama in the current "Editor's
Study." He "moves slowly in theatrical matters." His
"false judgment of literature and art sometimes makes us
fear that his observations of contemporary life are not
so true as we have been striving to believe."

804 "A Literary Causerie." Speaker, 4 (15 Aug 1891), 202. Note.
Because Howells' language is "truculent rather than con-
ciliatory, his English critics miss all advantage they
might extract" from Criticism and Fiction.

805 "Our Library Table." Athenaeum, No. 3329 (15 Aug 1891), 223.
Review of Criticism and Fiction.
The book is not "stimulating," but it is "full of honest,
wholesome good sense," its biases notwithstanding.

806   "The Ages of Inspiration." New Orleans <u>Daily Picayune</u>, 16 Aug
       1891, p. 12. Editorial.
           Brief, negative reference to Howells. "The realism
       which Mr. Howells champions with monotonous emphasis
       amounts to an abandonment of the whole field of romance
       for the sake of a literal report of the bare facts of
       life."

807   CRANE, STEPHEN. "Howells Discussed at Avon-by-the-Sea." <u>New
       York Tribune</u>, 18 Aug 1891, p. 5. News item. Rpt. Donald
       Pizer, "Crane Reports Garland on Howells," <u>Modern Language
       Notes</u>, 70 (Jan 1955), 37-39.
           Coverage of Garland's lecture on Howells as novelist.
       Garland predicted that Howells' novels, taken together,
       "will form the most accurate, sympathetic and artistic
       study of American society yet made by an American."

808   "Some September Fiction." <u>Boston Evening Transcript</u>, 26 Aug
       1891, p. 4. Brief mention.
           Speculation about popular response to <u>An Imperative Duty</u>.

809   "Mr. Howells on Criticism." <u>Spectator</u>, 67 (29 Aug 1891), 294-
       296. Major review of <u>Criticism and Fiction</u>.
           Howells "plunges and tramples up and down in a sort of
       guagmire of theories and views which he has created partly
       out of his own head, and partly by means of quotations
       from other people." It is apparent that he has had a row
       with someone, and in the end he says nothing new.

810   WALFORD, L. B. "London Letter." <u>Critic</u>, n.s. 16 (29 Aug
       1891), 107. Brief response to <u>Criticism and Fiction</u>.
           "Mr. Howells has done good work--very good work; but
       self-applause such as he now and then gives vent to--
       never more boisterously than in <u>Criticism and Fiction</u>--
       would tarnish anything."

811   "Briefs on New Books." <u>Dial</u>, 12 (Sep 1891), 144. Review of
       <u>Criticism and Fiction</u>.
           Howells' reviews are "stimulating and suggestive"--and
       biased.

812   [SCUDDER, H. E.] "Mr. Howells's Literary Creed." <u>Atlantic</u>,
       68 (Oct 1891), 566-569. Full review of <u>Criticism and Fic-
       tion</u>. Rpt. in part, <u>The War of the Critics over William
       Dean Howells</u>, ed. Edwin H. Cady and David L. Frazier
       (Evanston: Row, Peterson, 1962), pp. 51-54.
           "The very intemperance of his zeal, the almost incoher-
       ence of his protestations, bears witness to the fact that

1891

([SCUDDER, H. E.])
his literary creed as regards criticism and fiction is
not a cool intellectual dogma, but a belief quicunque
vult." Beneath apparent contradictions and diverting
weaknesses one "discovers that his contention is for art
in its relation to human nature and human history; that
the figures whom he uses are not so much directly the subjects of his criticism as they are concrete examples of
artistic tendencies." Ultimately realism "will simply
make its contribution to art and give place to a purer
idealism."

813   "The Lounger." Critic, n.s. 16 (3 Oct 1891), 168. Brief note.
Points out striking similarities between An Imperative
Duty and Matt Crim's Was It an Exceptional Case? and quotes
from a letter in which Howells attributes the similarity
to "mere blind chance."

814   "New Publications." New Orleans Times-Democrat, 4 Oct 1891,
p. 16. Brief notice of Franklin Square Library edition
of April Hopes.
"The last novel belonging to what may be called the
author's earliest style."

815   "An Imperative Duty." New Orleans Daily Picayune, 12 Oct 1891,
p. 4. Editorial review.
"Upon the whole, An Imperative Duty does not strike us
as an important contribution to the discussion of the race
problem, and its mere literary value is not greater than
that which attaches to its author's customary portraiture
of the types with which he had already made us sufficiently
familiar."

816   DROCH [ROBERT BRIDGES]. "Several New Stories." Life, 18
(15 Oct 1891), 210. Brief review of An Imperative Duty.
Howells again preaches "a vigorous sermon against use-
less self-sacrifice which has been made a false ideal to
so many young women by writers of 'intense' fiction."

817   [Untitled.] Life, 18 (22 Oct 1891), 224. Editorial paragraph.
"It would be hard to find a finer bit of American realism than the recent advertisements of a forthcoming novel
by Mr. Howells."

818   "The Lounger." Critic, n.s. 16 (31 Oct 1891), 235. Brief
reference.
George Washington Cable has congratulated Howells "for
arresting, trying and convicting Bartley Hubbard, who has
been going around all these years as a decent fellow."

819   HUTTON, LAURENCE. "Literary Notes." Harper's, 83 (Nov 1891),
        2. Review of The Albany Depot and An Imperative Duty.
        It is likely that nearly everyone will appreciate the
        jokes in The Albany Depot because "we all appreciate
        jokes--upon somebody else!"
        "'The Color Line' which Mr. Howells draws in his latest
        story" is illustrated with a contrast of the accommodations
        offered John L. Sullivan and Frederick Douglass in the
        South and of the character of the men themselves. An Im-
        perative Duty is Howells' strongest piece of work since A
        Foregone Conclusion.

820   MATTHEWS, BRANDER. "Recent Essays in Criticism." Cosmopoli-
        tan, 12 (Nov 1891), 124-126. Full review of Criticism
        and Fiction.
        "Militant criticism." Howells' book is "a plea for
        truth in fiction. It is a request that literature shall
        be judged by life and not by the library."

821   "New Publications." New Orleans Times-Democrat, 1 Nov 1891,
        p. 16. Very brief review of Criticism and Fiction.
        This book "will chiefly serve as an awful warning to
        authors against the folly of setting up theory in opposi-
        tion to natural impulse as a guide to literary excellence."

822   "The Working Classes in Fiction." New Orleans Times-Democrat,
        1 Nov 1891, p. 4. Editorial.
        A Hazard of New Fortunes and The Quality of Mercy show
        that Howells' "deepest interest is aroused by the strenu-
        ous life of action, rather than by the cobwebby problems
        of the drawing-room."

823   DROCH [ROBERT BRIDGES]. "Bookishness." Life, 18 (5 Nov 1891),
        258. Brief mention of The Albany Depot.
        Howells "abandons himself to 'pure fun' without any
        moral intention whatever."

824   "New Publications." New Orleans Times-Democrat, 15 Nov 1891,
        p. 18. Brief notice.
        Largely situation of The Albany Depot--an amusing little
        comedy.

825   "Book Reviews." Public Opinion, 12 (21 Nov 1891), 163.
        Brief notice.
        Description of the physical appearance of the Riverside
        Press Venetian Life.

1891

826   "New Books / <u>Albany Depot</u>." <u>Boston Evening Transcript</u>, 25 Nov
      1891, p. 6. Brief review.
      If the characters possessed common sense, they would
      extricate themselves from their embarrassing positions
      "without so much of the author's evident assistance."

827   "Howells's <u>Venetian Days</u> [sic]." <u>Critic</u>, n.s. 16 (29 Nov
      1891), 298. Announcement of new two-volume edition.
      Focuses on the colored illustrations.

828   "New Publications / The Color Line." <u>New York Times</u>, 30 Nov
      1891, p. 3. Review of <u>An Imperative Duty</u>.
      "It is to us as if Mr. Howells has become super-sensi-
      tive on the art side of his topics, and was a sufferer
      from acute nervous susceptibility. The keenness of his
      observation is shown only in the by play of those charac-
      ters which have the least to do with the romance."

829   CARPENTER, G. R. "Three Critics: Mr. Howells, Mr. Moore, and
      Mr. Wilde." <u>Andover Review</u>, 16 (Dec 1891), 568-576. Essay
      review of <u>Criticism and Fiction</u> (and critical studies by
      George Moore and Oscar Wilde).
      "He who is wise will, with Mr. Moore, show a hearty zest
      for what comes to his table; like Mr. Howells, he will
      find most pleasure in fare which is simple and natural;
      and, like Mr. Wilde, he will not disdain, at the proper
      time, a dainty dish" (p. 576).

830   "Literature and Criticism." <u>Harper's</u>, 84 (Dec 1891), Adver-
      tiser, p. 16. Advertisement of <u>Criticism and Fiction</u>.
      "In these essays Mr. Howells pleads for a criticism
      which is both intelligent and honest, and a fiction which
      is true to nature and serviceable to humanity. He dis-
      cusses the scope and influence of modern criticism, the
      narrowness of modern fiction, the excellence of the Ameri-
      can short story, the rise and decline of holiday litera-
      ture, and many other topics equally interesting and impor-
      tant. Every chapter of the volume is rich in thought and
      full of pertinent suggestions to lovers of books, and
      especially to advocates of a more intelligent criticism
      and a nobler quality of fiction."

831   "Short Stories, Novels, and Farces." <u>Harper's</u>, 84 (Dec 1891),
      Advertiser, p. 22. Advertisement of <u>The Albany Depot</u>.
      "That very attractive farce...in a single dainty
      volume, by itself--the first of a series of modern clas-
      sics, to be known collectively as 'Harper's Black and
      White Series.'"

832 "Today's Literature / An Imperative Duty by W. D. Howells."
Chicago Daily Tribune, 5 Dec 1891, p. 12. Review.
"If the cleverness of the execution can ever be held to
justify the adoption of a hybrid art-form An Imperative
Duty is its own excuse for being." A "case of conscience"
is the motive for the novel.

833 "Books for Grown Folks and Little Ones." New York Herald,
6 Dec 1891, p. 26. Brief review of An Imperative Duty.
Rpt. Book News, 10 (Jan 1892), 250.
This story on the race question is "delicately written."

834 "Holiday Publications." Critic, n.s. 16 (12 Dec 1891), 332–
333. Brief notice of The Albany Depot.
Largely summary. Howells "rather reverses the alleged
order of creation, for having first tried his 'prentice
hand on making women foolish, he now applies the same
process to men."

835 "Some Christmas Books / Venetian Life by William D. Howells /
...." Boston Evening Transcript, 17 Dec 1891, p. 6.
Review of new Houghton Mifflin edition.
"It has the inescapable charm of youth," and it is not
likely Howells could do the same thing over again.

836 "New Publications / Holiday Books." New York Times, 19 Dec
1891, p. 3. Brief notice.
Details physical appearance of a gift edition of
Venetian Life.

837 COON, SPENCER H. "Mr. Howells Talks / He Predicts Much for
the Cosmopolitan." Boston Advertiser, 26 Dec 1891, p. 3.
Interview. Abstr. "Interviews with William Dean Howells,"
ed. Ulrich Halfmann, American Literary Realism, 6 (Fall
1973), 294.
Howells is reported as preferring to write novels rather
than criticism and as recognizing that his commitment to
the "Editor's Study" interrupted his fiction.

1892

838 "Novels and Tales." Book Buyer, n.s. 8 (Jan 1892), 641–642.
Review of An Imperative Duty.
That Howells "accepts frankly the obligations of the
naturalistic school is apparent...."

1892

839   [Untitled.] Bookman (London), 1 (Jan 1892), 131. Note.
        Among American writers of fiction, ranked according to
        selling power, Howells is in fourth position behind Mark
        Twain, Mrs. Burnett, and F. R. Stockton.

840   GARLAND, HAMLIN. "Mr. Howells's Plans / The Editorship of the
        Cosmopolitan a Welcome Change." Boston Evening Transcript,
        1 Jan 1892, p. 6. Interview. Rpt. in part, Critic, n.s.
        17 (9 Jan 1892), 28; "Interviews with William Dean Howells,"
        ed. Ulrich Halfmann, American Literary Realism 6 (Fall
        1973), 295-296.
        "Unquestionably Mr. Howells will be a greater power than
        ever in the radical wing of American literature, and do
        his great work at less cost to himself."

841   "Literary Notes." Boston Evening Transcript, 2 Jan 1892,
        p. 6. Brief comment.
        On the editorial restructuring of Cosmopolitan and
        Howells' new role.

842   "Writers and Books." Boston Evening Transcript, 2 Jan 1892,
        p. 6. Brief note.
        Interest in Howells' move to Cosmopolitan is expressed.
        Howells is reported as saying "it is not so important to
        me to write criticism as novels."

843   "Immortality in Literature." New Orleans Daily Picayune,
        3 Jan 1892, p. 4. Editorial.
        "Fiction, whether in prose or verse, is the attempted
        delineation of human character and human acts under the
        particular conditions which furnish the ground work or
        motive power of the theme." On that basis the realists
        --the moral branch represented by Howells and the obscene
        branch by Zola--have no greater claim to permanence than
        do the romanticists.

844   CLARK, KATE UPSON. "Book Reviews." Epoch, 10 (8 Jan 1892),
        370. Review of An Imperative Duty.
        "Mr. Howells has managed the delicate situations of his
        story with his usual skill. The characters are only those
        to which he has already accustomed us."

  *   "Mr. Howells's Plans." Critic, n.s. 17 (9 Jan 1892), 28.
        Rpt. from Boston Evening Transcript, 1 Jan 1892, p. 6.
        See item 840.

845   "An Imperative Duty." Critic, n.s. 17 (16 Jan 1892), 34-35.
        Review.

("An Imperative Duty")
    In this successful "psychologic study" Howells "has
shown himself a bold man indeed. He has rushed in, not
where angels, to be sure, but where men of broadest mind
and noblest purpose have feared to tread."

846   WINGATE, CHARLES E. L. "Boston Letter." Critic, n.s. 17
       (16 Jan 1892), 41.
           Howells' acceptance of the editorship of Cosmopolitan
       is traced to a speech entitled "The Church and Poverty"
       by John Brisben Walker.

847   BOYESEN, HJALMAR HJORTH. "Mr. Howells and His Work." Cosmo-
       politan, 12 (Feb 1892), 502-503. Essay. Rpt. The War of
       the Critics over William Dean Howells, ed. Edwin H. Cady
       and David L. Frazier (Evanston: Row, Peterson, 1962),
       pp. 55-57.
           This quick appraisal applauds Howells' strength of
       characterization, his Americanism, and his contemporane-
       ousness.

848   "Contemporary Literature / Belles Lettres." Westminster Re-
       view, 137 (Feb 1892), 224. Review of An Imperative Duty.
           "For a moment, one is half persuaded that the micro-
       scopic analysis of motive is the true function of the
       novelist."

849   MABIE, HAMILTON W. "A Year's Literary Production." Forum
       12 (Feb 1892), 797-800. Brief reference to An Imperative
       Duty.
           Demonstrates Howells' "depth and delicacy of insight"
       (p. 800).

850   BURROUGHS, JOHN. "Mr. Howells's Agreements with Whitman."
       Critic, n.s. 17 (6 Feb 1892), 85-86. Note.
           In Criticism and Fiction Howells has placed principles
       above standards and in doing so has raised criticism
       above the dogmatic method. Perhaps Whitman was the ex-
       ample which gave Howells the courage to take his stand.

851   "The Lounger." Critic, n.s. 17 (13 Feb 1892), 102. Brief
       note.
           Describes Howells' neighborhood, study, and routine in
       New York.

852   "Novels of the Week." Athenaeum, No. 3355 (13 Feb 1892), 211.
       Brief review of An Imperative Duty.

1892

("Novels of the Week")
"Remarkable for the cleverness of story" and the "neat-
ness" of plot. Some readers may resent Howells' attitude
toward women's education.

853   "A Critic's Exit." New Orleans Daily Picayune, 14 Feb 1892,
p. 12. Editorial.
On Howells' resignation from Harper's. Howells is a
better writer than critic, but in both cases his arbitrary
bias has been a limiting factor.

854   "Writers and Books." Boston Evening Transcript, 18 Feb 1892,
p. 6. Brief note.
"Mr. Howells's last story, The Quality of Mercy, has
hardly gained in the change of title, John Northwick,
Defaulter, under which it was brought out in London.

855   [LOGAN, ANNIE R. M.] "More Novels." Nation, 54 (25 Feb 1892),
154. Review of An Imperative Duty.
"The situation is described and argued with that lucidi-
ty, force, and grace which give to all Mr. Howells's
stories a rare distinction."

856   "The Lounger." Critic, n.s. 17 (27 Feb 1892), 132. Brief
note.
Reflection on "the tone of melancholy" that marks
Howells' departure from Harper's.

857   "March Magazines / Harper's." Boston Evening Transcript,
27 Feb 1892, p. 6. Brief note.
Judging from the opening chapters, The World of Chance
"promises to outrival in interest anything written by that
distinguished author."

858   "At the Circulating Library," Bookman (London), 1 (Mar 1892),
219. Mention of The Quality of Mercy.
One wishes Howells would do something new "in the matter
of womenkind. Of course he won't, for he has reached the
stage of having theories on the subject, which is fatal to
a novelist."
Reference also to Howells' "enthusiastic" preface to
Miss Craig's translation of Verga's House by the Medlar
Tree. His characteristic moralistic concern "pulls up a
frivolous reader at the Circulating Library, and gives him
pause."

859   "Writers and Books." Boston Evening Transcript, 1 Mar 1892,
p. 6. Note.

("Writers and Books")
   On Howells' Stuyvesant Square neighborhood and on his
   writing routine.

860   "Notes." Nation, 54 (10 Mar 1892), 193-194. Brief comment.
      On the occasion of Howells' departure from Harper's,
      "an expression of regard for faith, endurance, and purpose,
      though opposed."

861   "Novels." Saturday Review, 73 (12 Mar 1892), 307. Review of
      The Quality of Mercy.
         "Mr. Howells would seem to have abandoned the fatuous
      practice of leaving the story out of his romances." The
      narration is "still thoroughly niggling," but the novel
      ends because the tale is told.

862   "Novels of the Week." Athenaeum, No. 3359 (12 Mar 1892), 339.
      Review of The Quality of Mercy.
         Although the situation is strong, the novel lacks dis-
      tinction--a quality Howells has never had but which has
      never been more conspicuously absent.

863   SMITH, FRANKLIN. "An Hour with Mr. Howells." Frank Leslie's
      Weekly, 74 (17 Mar 1892), 118-119. Interview. Rpt.
      "Interviews with William Dean Howells," ed. Ulrich Half-
      mann, American Literary Realism, 6 (Fall 1973), 295-296.
         Howells compares New York with other cities as a liter-
      ary environment and speculates about possible training and
      experience which may contribute to the development of
      writers.

864   "The Listener." Boston Evening Transcript, 21 Mar 1892, p. 4.
      Note.
         On the negative response to Howells' women. "Mr.
      Howells would be acquitted by any jury of good and true
      women, the Listener fancies, of an intention to paint the
      woman of the present generation in unduly dark colors."
      Helen Harkness is "morally about as nearly perfect as
      women are found now-a-days."

865   "New Publications." New Orleans Times-Democrat, 27 Mar 1892,
      p. 20. Brief review of An Imperative Duty.
         The "cheerful conviction" about the practicality of
      racial fusion voiced by Dr. Olney, as spokesman for
      Howells, suggests "restricted opportunities for forming
      an opinion rather than...superior wisdom and liberality."

1892

866   "Contemporary Literature / Belles Lettres." <u>Westminster Re-</u>
<u>view</u>, 137 (Apr 1892), 464-465. Review of <u>The Quality of</u>
<u>Mercy</u>.
"A curious and interesting study of the working and mu-
tual re-action of widely various characters, under circumstances of painful stress and reverse." The novel is less
bound by the "quintessence of morality" which shapes much
of Howells' fiction. Pinney is an especially pleasing
creation.

867   LANG, ANDREW. "At the Sign of the Ship." <u>Longman's</u>, 19
(Apr 1892), 682-684. Satiric note. Rpt. in part, <u>Critic</u>,
n.s. 20 (16 Apr 1892), 233, and <u>The War of the Critics</u>
<u>over William Dean Howells</u>, ed. Edwin H. Cady and David L.
Frazier (Evanston: Row, Peterson, 1962), pp. 58-59.
Lang taunts Howells for his didactic tendencies and
lightly argues the cause of literature designed to enter-
tain. "To W. D. H.," a seven-stanza satiric poem, is included.

868   "<u>The Quality of Mercy</u>." <u>Harper's</u>, 84 (Apr 1892), Advertiser,
p. 4. Advertisement. Repeated May 1892, Advertiser, p. 3.
"This story will easily take rank among the best that
Mr. Howells has written. It possesses all those distinguishing qualities of invention and style which have made
his previous works so popular, and its realistic but semi-
tragic plot is most artistically wrought out from the beginning. In the delicacy of its satire on some phases of
modern life, in its skilful analysis of character and motives, no less than in the development of its leading
theme--the quality of mercy, human or divine, which is
meted out to repentant criminals--it is a story of sur-
passing interest and power."

869   [WARNER, CHARLES DUDLEY.] "Editor's Study." <u>Harper's</u>, 84
(Apr 1892), 802-803. Brief comment.
On taking over the "Editor's Study" from Howells, Warner
notes that his predecessor, by the tradition his "informing
spirit" has established, has rendered succession difficult.
Howells' criticism is characterized by an "intuitive quali-
ty," a "sincere spirit," and a "spiritual lift." "Mr.
Howells has sought the truth as it appeared to him."

870   BLATHWAYT, RAYMOND. "A Talk with 'Q'." <u>Boston Evening Tran-</u>
<u>script</u>, 2 Apr 1892, p. 16. Full-column report of inter-
view with Mr. Quiller-Couch.
He joins Howells in opposing anonymous criticism and
appreciates his serious study of women.

871 "New Publications / Howells's New Story." New York Times,
10 Apr 1892, p. 19. Review of The Quality of Mercy. Rpt.
Book News, 10 (May 1892), 403.
"Mr. Howells's morbidity is becoming more and more conspicuous. He seems to hanker after mental dissections.
He operates on abnormal growth." Two journalistic types
are of interest.

872 DROCH [ROBERT BRIDGES]. "The Quality of Mercy." Life, 19
(14 Apr 1892), 230. Review.
"You can't get at the real pleasures of life (and annoy-
ances also) as Mr. Howells does, unless you put each character in a social environment and show how it affects him,
and how he affects it.
"That is why a man who lives in a bachelor apartment,
and thinks he knows the world, is apt to be a poor judge
of motives."

* [LANG, ANDREW.] "At the Sign of the Ship." Critic, n.s. 17
(16 Apr 1892), 233. Rpt. from Longman's, 19 (Apr 1892),
682-684. See item 867.

873 "The History of David Grieve." New Orleans Daily Picayune,
17 Apr 1892, p. 18. Editorial review.
Highly favorable comments on the novel by Mrs. Humphrey
Ward. American writers, in contrast, although very admirable in their own ways, "lack feeling, or they are
either unwilling or unable to express it. It is not easy
to believe that anyone has ever dropped a tear upon Mr.
Howells' most pathetic page, and Howells is more emotional
than either James or Crawford [the three American novelists
cited]."

874 "Fiction." Literary World, 23 (23 Apr 1892), 149. Review of
The Quality of Mercy.
Perhaps Howells "judges his presentment of medium people
the best tonic for a world which needs greater moral
strength," but one wishes for characters both nobler and
more base.

875 "Today's Literature / The Quality of Mercy by William D.
Howells." Chicago Daily Tribune, 23 Apr 1892, p. 12.
Full review.
"The philosophic tendency of this work, which bears a
close and necessary relation to the literary interest,
has not been allowed to spoil the story, except for con-
firmed lotus-eaters like Miss Agnes Repplier." It will
rank with Howells' finest.

1892

876   [Untitled.] <u>Boston Evening Transcript</u>, 23 Apr 1892, p. 12.
        Editorial.
          "Mr. Howells is evidently still in the arena although
        he had retired from criticism into editorial work. [His
        poem, "Materials of a Story," copied on this page from
        <u>Harper's</u>] is a big red flag of provocation, which he
        sturdily shakes at the bull of popular fury; he is likely
        to be tossed on higher horns than any his critics have
        yet gashed his literary theories with." The editorial ob-
        jects to Howells' departure from conventional poetry in
        both idea and form.

877   COLE, CATHARINE. "Short Story Writing." New Orleans <u>Daily
        Picayune</u>, 24 Apr 1892, p. 18. Literary column.
          Includes an anecdote about Mr. and Mrs. Howells respon-
        ding to Cable's <u>The Grandissimes</u> by talking broken Creole-
        English around the house for a week. In a separate con-
        text Cole notes that Howells proved that "criticism of
        literature is only a matter of individual taste."

878   "The Contributor's Club." <u>Atlantic</u>, 69 (May 1892), 717.
        Brief note.
          A preface by Howells should be enough to guard one
        against a book because the depressing books he recommends
        weaken one's vitality.

  *   "Howells's New Story." <u>Book News</u>, 10 (May 1892), 403. Rpt.
        from <u>New York Times</u>, 10 Apr 1892, p. 19. <u>See</u> item 871.

879   "Novels and Short Stories." <u>Book Buyer</u>, n.s. 9 (May 1892),
        166-167. Review of <u>The Quality of Mercy</u>.
          Howells demonstrates "his capacity to lay bare and to
        analyze a disease that is becoming more and more common
        in the social body." Largely summary.

880   [SCUDDER, HORACE E.] "Recent English and American Fiction."
        <u>Atlantic</u>, 69 (May 1892), 702-704. Review of <u>The Quality
        of Mercy</u>.
          "Absence of sharp dramatic scenes" may focus attention
        on governing considerations, "yet we doubt if a novel has
        justified itself fully when its persons fade in the mind
        of the reader, and a few abstract principles remain as
        his chief possession."

881   "Notes." <u>Nation</u>, 54 (5 May 1892), 340-341. Brief comment.
          Howells "signalizes the beginning of his editorship of
        the <u>Cosmopolitan</u> by a number strong in variety and notable
        in the list of contributors."

882   "The Quality of Mercy." Critic, n.s. 17 (7 May 1892), 262.
      Full review.
      "The treatment of John Northwick himself, considered
      not as a character in fiction but as a study in sociology,
      is a masterly bit of psychological analysis." But the
      chief feature of the book is uninteresting conversation.

883   "Literature." Independent, 44 (12 May 1892), 664. Brief re-
      view of The Quality of Mercy.
      The novel is "on the dead level of realism." "A novel
      so perfectly written suggests a glorious possibility--the
      building of a romance on the gauge of Scott's best, with
      Howells's style to make it more than immortal! Try it
      just once, Howells."

884   "New Books / A Group of Little Books." Boston Evening Tran-
      script, 13 May 1892, p. 6. Brief note.
      The idea for Brander Matthew's In the Vestibule Limited
      may have been suggested by Howells.

885   AYRES, NELSON. "The Novelist's Materials / The Best Materials
      Yet Left for the Novel of the Future." New Orleans Daily
      Picayune, 15 May 1892, p. 18. Brief reference.
      True conjugal love is not yet treated in the novel, but
      were it presented "by some such masterly hand as Mrs.
      Ward's or Mr. Howells'," "it would command the delighted
      admiration of the myriad hearts of true men and women, who
      know its sweetness by precious experience."

886   "The Melancholy of Modern Fiction." New Orleans Daily Picayune,
      22 May 1892, p. 12. Editorial.
      "A preface by Mr. Howells, recommending a book for its
      realism, will hereafter be enough to guard one against it."

887   "Sharp Criticism of Mr. Howells / Ambrose Bierce of San Fran-
      cisco Says Harsh Things of Him." New York Times, 23 May
      1892, p. 5. News item.
      Datelined "San Francisco, May 22." Report of a Sunday
      newspaper attack by Bierce on realism, and on Howells,
      "'the master of this detestable school of literature.'"

888   "Book Reviews." Public Opinion, 13 (28 May 1892), 194. Brief
      review of The Quality of Mercy.
      When Howells studies life, "he sets himself to discern
      the motives and principles of it."

889   "About Authors." Book Buyer, n.s. 9 (Jun 1892), 211. Brief
      reference.

1892

("About Authors")
> Notes Hall Caine's failure to appreciate Howells as re-
corded in an interview with a correspondent of the St.
Louis Post-Dispatch (not seen).

890 "The Cosmopolitan Magazine,--Its Methods and Its Editors."
Review of Reviews, 5 (Jun 1892), 607-610. Note.
> Announces Howells' association with Cosmopolitan and
speculates on the contribution he will make. Full-page
sketch (p. 606).

891 CRAWFORD, T. C. "Mr. Howells / His Career, His Present Work,
and His Literary Opinions." New York Tribune, 26 Jun
1892, p. 14. Interview. Rpt. in part, Critic, n.s. 18
(16 Jul 1892), 36-37; "Interviews with William Dean
Howells," ed. Ulrich Halfmann, American Literary Realism,
6 (Fall 1973), 299-303.
> Report of two interview sessions covers a wide range of
questions dealing with such things as personal income,
source of material, advice to young writers, future expec-
tations.

892 MATTHEWS, BRANDER. "The Literary Independence of the United
States." Cosmopolitan, 13 (Jul 1892), 343-350. Brief
reference.
> The author of The Rise of Silas Lapham is among "aggres-
sively American" writers who embrace not "the slightest
suggestion of colonialism" (p. 345).

893 [WARNER, CHARLES DUDLEY.] "Editor's Study." Harper's, 85
(Jul 1892), 316-317. Full review of The Quality of Mercy.
> Howells "has never done anything else that exhibited
more subtle power" than the flight of Northwick through
Canada. "The man is fleeing from himself, and this
double action, the reality of the movement, with this
dodging of a psychological spectre, rises into the most
pitiful tragedy."

894 "Two American Societies." Author, 3 (1 Jul 1892), 54. Brief
mention.
> Howells' role in emergence of competing American liter-
ary societies is noted.

895 "New Publications." New Orleans Times-Democrat, 3 Jul 1892,
p. 20. Review of The Quality of Mercy.
> "Trollopean prolixity and iteration of the dialogue" as
means of development. "While the weakest of all Mr.
Howells' novels on the literary and artistic side, [this]

("New Publications")
is the strongest of all in its moral bearing." It is a
powerful study "of that form of commercial crime which so
especially distinguishes our modern civilization."

896   [LOGAN, ANNIE R. M.] "Recent Fiction." Nation, 55 (14 Jul
1892), 33-34. Review of The Quality of Mercy.
Howells has "done his best to lighten inseparable gloom."
His people are becoming more human than American. "The
hardness and coldness of his touch, which resulted from
limited vision, have been much modified."

*   "Mr. Howells Interviewed." Critic, n.s. 18 (16 Jul 1892),
36-37. Rpt from New York Tribune, 26 Jun 1892, p. 14.
See item 891.

897   PAYNE, WILLIAM MORTON. "Recent Books of Fiction." Dial, 13
(Aug 1892), 102. Review of The Quality of Mercy.
Mr. Howells, "who knew how to tell in artistic manner
a story of real human interest, has come back to us
again...."

898   [Untitled.] Life, 20 (4 Aug 1892), 68. Brief note.
Paragraph responding to Howells' wonder that anyone can
love New York. "If Mr. Howells really wants to love New
York he should join Tammany Hall, acquire a good-sized
pull, and then see what a lovable city this is." Portrait.

899   [Untitled.] Life, 20 (18 Aug 1892), 88. Editorial paragraph.
If Howells wonders how anyone can love New York, a visit
to Chicago during the fair will help him to understand.

900   "Briefer Mention." Dial, 13 (1 Sep 1892), 150. Brief notice
of A Letter of Introduction.
"Simply irresistible in its mirth-provoking qualities."

901   "Some Current Novels and Tales." New York Times, 4 Sep 1892,
p. 19. Brief review of A Letter of Introduction.
"Mr. Howells's fun is nice and well mannered," but his
farce is too subtle for the stage.

902   "New Books / A Letter of Introduction." Boston Evening Transcript, 15 Sep 1892, p. 6. Brief review.
The farce features "a quartette of tiresome mortals."
Although Howells' method is irritating, "there are passages so delightfully true to nature that one's outraged
fortitude often changes to admiration."

1892

903   "The Lounger." Critic, n.s. 18 (24 Sep 1892), 167. Brief
      note.
        Corrects the rumor that Howells has severed relation
      with Cosmopolitan, indicates that he will write instead
      of edit, and reminisces about the way in which "his caustic
      criticisms [in Harper's] kept the teeth of two continents
      on edge."

904   DROCH [ROBERT BRIDGES]. "The 'Hustler' in Recent Fiction."
      Life, 20 (29 Sep 1892), 174-175. Note.
        Fulkerson in A Hazard of New Fortunes, Pinkerton in The
      Wrecker (Stevenson and Osbourne), and Tarvin in The
      Naulahka (Kipling and Balestier) are amazingly alike in
      characteristics.

905   "Recent Fiction." Critic, n.s. 18 (8 Oct 1892), 190. Brief
      review of A Letter of Introduction.
        "One of those clever little farces that everyone thinks
      such capital fun when they illustrate some weak point in
      a neighbor's character, and so tiresome when they turn
      the illuminating light of humor on some act of folly of
      one's own."

906   "Howells' Development as a Novelist." New Orleans Times-
      Democrat, 16 Oct 1892, p. 4. Lengthy editorial.
        Howells' early work is slight and feminine rather than
      manly. In The Undiscovered Country he "first showed an
      inclination to break away from generalities, and lay hold
      upon the ruggedest realities of life." A Modern Instance
      revealed Howells' power, but The Minister's Charge falls
      into an "arid commonness that is repellant." Silas Lap-
      ham is an "unmistakable American product." A Woman's
      Reason, though more penetrating than either Indian Summer
      or April Hopes, is less successful as literature.
      "Howells' three great books are A Modern Instance, A
      Hazard of New Fortunes, and The Quality of Mercy; and The
      World of Chance...promises to make a fourth.: Howells
      is our strongest novelist. His "gain in vigor and robust-
      ness must strike even a casual reader."

907   "Artistic, Literary, Social, and Scientific." Book Buyer,
      n.s. 9 (Nov 1892), 443. Brief notice of A Letter of
      Introduction.
      Non-critical.

908   "Harper's Black and White Series / New Volumes / A Little
      Swiss Sojourn." Harper's, 85 (Nov 1892), Advertiser,
      p. 12. Advertisement.

("Harper's Black and White Series / New Volumes / A Little Swiss Sojourn")
"A delightful narrative of a three months' stay in Switzerland, including sketches of scenes, incidents, and impressions connected with visits to several of the most interesting localities."

909   "Pen-Pictures of Men and Places." Book Buyer, n.s. 9 (Nov 1892), 434. Brief notice of A Little Swiss Sojourn.
Howells is "never more delightful than when he is painting some foreign place and its people."

910   "Briefer Mention." Dial, 13 (1 Nov 1892), 281. Very brief notice of A Little Swiss Sojourn.
"Mr. Howells is at his best in sketches of travel."

911   "Literature / Recent Fiction." Independent, 44 (3 Nov 1892), 1564. Brief mention of A Little Swiss Sojourn.
"Next to an actual little sojourn in Switzerland we would choose to read this little book."

912   "New Books and New Editions." New York Times, 6 Nov 1892, p. 19. Brief review of A Little Swiss Sojourn.
"The little volume is pleasant and chatty."

913   "Two American Realists." New Orleans Daily Picayune, 6 Nov 1892, p. 16. Editorial.
Unfavorable reaction to Howells' The World of Chance, favorable to Wilkins' Jane Field. Miss Wilkins' portraitures "affect us with a deeper and more poignant sense of sympathy" than do Howells'. "The reason may be that Mr. Howells writes in cold blood. We suspect that he writes too much to write with contagious intensity."

914   "Literature / Recent Fiction." Independent, 44 (10 Nov 1892), 1599. Review of The Quality of Mercy.
Although the novel is a depressing one, it causes the reader to recognize that "Sir Walter never could set words together with such aptness of correlation as appears in these graceful and polished paragraphs." It is pleasing to note that Howells "has at last mustered courage to tackle landscape and weather."

915   "Traveller from Altruria." New Nation, 2 (26 Nov 1892), 701-702. Response to early installments of serialization.
Since Annie Kilburn, nationalistic ideas have become increasingly evident in Howells' work.

1892

916 "Intensity." New Orleans <u>Daily Picayune</u>, 27 Nov 1892, p. 16.
    Editorial review of <u>The World of Chance</u>.
        Howells lacks intensity, and intensity as it is incorpo-
    rated in the work of Carlyle and Scott is "one of the
    traits of genius." It also accounts for the fact that
    Scott could write more prolifically than Howells.

917 "New Books / Realistic Juvenile Fiction." <u>Boston Evening
    Transcript</u>, 20 Dec 1892, p. 6. Brief review of <u>Christmas
    Every Day and Other Stories</u>.
        Howells does not take "the dear, delightful realms of
    fantastic fiction" away from children after all.

918 "Books for the Young / Mr. Howells's <u>Christmas Every Day</u>."
    <u>Critic</u>, n.s. 18 (31 Dec 1892), 375. Brief review.
        Howells shows "an unexpected tenderness lurking in a
    corner of his capacious heart."

1893

919 THOMPSON, MAURICE. <u>The Ethics of Literary Art</u>. Hartford:
    Hartford Seminary Press, 1893. Not indexed. Brief
    references.
        Howells, along with the author of "The Ancient Mariner"
    and some others, has the ability to attract thousands of
    readers and repel none (p. 70). "What realism, so-called,
    lacks in intrinsic interest is hoped to be compensated
    for by extrinsic cleverness." This is what Howells must
    have meant by saying literary art is now finer than in the
    days of Scott (p. 72).

920 "<u>Christmas Every Day</u>." <u>Harper's</u>, 86 (Jan 1893), Advertiser,
    p. 5. Advertisement.
        "The boys and girls who become the fortunate owners of
    this volume may, indeed, have 'Christmas every Day in the
    Year,' for they will be in possession of a fund of enjoy-
    ment which will outlast the holidays and afford amusement
    through all the seasons. It is a delightful collection
    of stories written in Mr. Howells's pleasantest manner."

921 HUTTON, LAURENCE. "Literary Notes." <u>Harper's</u>, 86 (Jan 1893),
    3. Brief reviews of <u>A Letter of Introduction</u>, <u>A Little
    Swiss Sojourn</u>, and <u>Christmas Every Day, and Other Stories
    Told for Children</u>.
        "Mr. Howells, notwithstanding his theoretical bellicosity,
    is as mild a mannered man as ever scuttled a fellow-novel-
    ist's ship, or cut a companion poet's throat." <u>A Letter</u>

(HUTTON, LAURENCE)
of Introduction is "droll," Christmas Every Day is "non-sensical," and A Little Swiss Sojourn "is almost as enter-taining and quite as instructive as is [Howells'] incom-parable Venetian Life."

922   "Literature." Independent, 45 (5 Jan 1893), 22. Brief re-view of Christmas Every Day.
The stories are "just what juvenile stories should be--pure, wholesome, not loaded with sobriety nor didactics, just pure and simple fun of the kindling and irresistible kind."

923   "New York Notes." Literary World, 24 (14 Jan 1893), 11.
Brief comment.
On Howells as a literary man. "After winning a brilliant reputation as a writer Mr. Howells had the misfortune to become an editor." This accounts for his attraction to realism.

924   WINGATE, CHARLES E. L. "Boston Letter." Critic, n.s. 19
(14 Jan 1893), 22. Brief reference.
Quotations from a letter by Howells to the Secretary of the Forestry Commission in New Hampshire documents Howells' interest in preserving woodlands.

925   "New Publications." New Orleans Times-Democrat, 29 Jan 1893,
p. 24. Brief review of A Little Swiss Sojourn.
Howells is a good travel companion. "It is very doubt-ful whether the average traveler would see as much to amuse on a personal visit" abroad.

926   "New Publications." New Orleans Times-Democrat, 26 Mar 1893,
p. 20. Brief mention of Christmas Every Day.
"Mr. Howells tells stories for children which are as inimitable as those he tells for older people.

927   HARRISON, FREDERIC. "The Decadence of Romance." Forum, 15
(Apr 1893), 216-224. Brief reference.
In this celebration of traditional romance, Howells--along with George Eliot, Meredith, Stevenson, and James--is described as looking on life "from a private box" (p. 223).

928   "Two Novels." New Orleans Daily Picayune, 2 Apr 1893, p. 16.
Major editorial review of The Coast of Bohemia (and A. Conan Doyle's The Refugees).

1893

("Two Novels")
Howells is skillful in setting scenes and describing characters, but his stories lack movement. "If there could be a drama without action, Mr. Howells would be a dramatist."

929   "The World of Chance." Literary World, 24 (8 Apr 1893), 108.
Review.
"Mr. Howells appears to have turned at length from discipleship of Tolstoy, Bellamy, and other social reformers." His style "occasionally lapses into the dialect of journalism."

930   "Novels." Saturday Review, 75 (15 Apr 1893), 408. Review of The World of Chance.
"It would be interesting to see for oneself Mr. Howells's idea of a novel which--by chance--was 'boomed' by reviewers, and sold forty-three thousand copies, neither more nor less."

931   "New Novels." Athenaeum, No. 3417 (22 Apr 1893), 502. Review of The World of Chance.
"Within the limits he has imposed Mr. Howells has never done a more searching and artistic piece of work."

932   "Today's Literature / The World of Chance by William Dean Howells." Chicago Daily Tribune, 22 Apr 1893, p. 10.
Full review.
Defends Howells against the charge that his novels are uninteresting. Does a novel not have "sufficient excuse for being if it serves to stimulate thought, gratify or excite spiritual cravings, and widen sympathies?" The World of Chance has shape and freshness and richness.

933   "Contemporary Literature / Belles Lettres." Westminster Review, 139 (May 1893), 584. Brief notice of The World of Chance.
"Full of cleverness and originality" but "the ending is a little too metaphysical."

934   "Harper's Black and White Series / Latest Issues / The Unexpected Guests." Harper's, 86 (May 1893), Advertiser, p. 10. Advertisement.
"For brilliant repartee, comic situations, and unrestrained amusement, this farce will rank among the best of Mr. Howells's lighter productions."

935 HUTTON, LAURENCE. "Literary Notes." Harper's, 86 (May 1893),
     1. Review of The World of Chance.
       "That Mr. Howells is ever ready to create new journal-
     ists; that he is not forced back, for lack of material, to
     Fulkerson or Bartley Hubbard, is a never-ending marvel."
     The story told here is based upon one told in "the Third
     Reader a good many years ago."

936 "Recent Novels and Short Stories." Book Buyer, n.s. 10 (May
     1893), 154-155. Brief notice of The World of Chance.
       It is "pitched in a somewhat soberer key" than was A
     Hazard of New Fortunes.

937 "Mr. Howells as a Country Printer." Critic, n.s. 19 (6 May
     1893), 290-291. Note.
       Howells' story about his experience as a country printer
     "is interesting as illustrating the doctrine of heredity."

938 "New Publications." New Orleans Times-Democrat, 7 May 1893,
     p. 24. Review of The World of Chance.
       It might be appropriately subtitled "The Adventures of
     a Psychological Romance."

939 DROCH [ROBERT BRIDGES]. "The World of Chance." Life, 21
     (11 May 1893), 302-303. Review.
       "Mr. Howells could not have been kinder to his hero than
     to rescue him from union with a literary critic."

940 ALLEN, JOHN BARROW. "New Novels." Academy, 43 (20 May 1893),
     434-435. Brief review of The World of Chance.
       Perceptive, charming, concerned with "social, moral,
     political, and religious problems," very much in the
     Howells tradition.

941 "Novels and Tales." Christian Union, 47 (20 May 1893); 981.
     Brief review of The World of Chance.
       Less strong than A Hazard of New Fortunes, "it deals with
     very interesting phases of life, and it suggests, as its
     title implies, one of the profoundest problems of experience."

 *   [HOWELLS AND BOYESEN.] Bookman (London), 4 (Jun 1893), 79-81.
     Rpt. from McClure's, 1 (Jun 1893), 3-11. See item 942.

942 "Real Conversations.--I. A Dialogue Between William Dean
     Howells and Hjalmar Hjorth Boyesen." McClure's, 1
     (Jun 1893), 3-11. Interview. Rpt. in part, Bookman
     (London), 4 (Jun 1893), 79-81, and in Review of Reviews,
     8 (Jul 1893), 90. Rpt. Human Documents / Portraits and

1893

("Real Conversations.--I. A Dialogue Between William Dean
Howells and Hjalmar Hjorth Boyesen")
>   Biographies of Eminent Men (New York: McClure, 1895),
>   pp. 140-151; McClure's Biographies / Gladstone--Bismarck--
>   Grant--Dana--Stevenson--and Others (New York: McClure,
>   1896), pp. 140-151; "Five Interviews with William Dean
>   Howells," ed. George Arms and William M. Gibson, Americana,
>   37 (Apr 1943), 259-270 with notes 259; "Interviews with
>   William Dean Howells," ed. Ulrich Halfmann, American Liter-
>   ary Realism, 6 (Fall 1973), 24-30.
>   Boyesen's questions probe Howells' early life and liter-
>   ary career.

943 PAYNE, WILLIAM MORTON. "Recent Fiction." Dial, 14 (1 Jun
>   1893), 339-340. Review of The World of Chance.
>   One of Howells' "least admirable fictions."

* "McClure's Magazine." Critic, n.s. 19 (3 Jun 1893), 371.
>   Brief quotations from Boyesen's interview of Howells in
>   McClure's, 1 (Jun 1893), 3-11. See item 942.
>   Also portrait, "W. D. Howells at Work" (p. 368).

944 "Earliest of Summer Novels." New York Times, 5 Jun 1893, p. 3.
>   Review of The Unexpected Guests.
>   Farces are foreign to Howells. "The Unexpected Guests
>   is comedy, pure and simple, and comedy, as a general thing,
>   is very much better than farce." The people Howells
>   writes about are the people who read his books. His
>   "farces even more than his novels might be called moral
>   clinics...."

945 "Fiction for Summer Reading." Book Buyer, n.s. 10 (Jul 1893),
>   248-249. Very brief notice of The Unexpected Guests.
>   "Marked by the deftness and certainty of touch for which
>   Mr. Howells is noted."

* [HOWELLS AND BOYESEN.] Review of Reviews, 8 (Jul 1893), 90.
>   Rpt. from McClure's, 1 (Jun 1893), 3-11. See item 942.

946 HUTTON, LAURENCE. "Literary Notes." Harper's, 87 (Jul 1893),
>   3-4. Brief review of The Unexpected Guests.
>   "The brilliant, epigrammatic, satiric little comedy will
>   prove what Mr. Swiveller described as a 'boon' in fashion-
>   able summer hotels and country houses where guests are ex-
>   pected to amuse themselves, and to entertain each other."

947   "New Publications / A Traveler from Altruria." New Orleans
      Times-Democrat, 8 Jul 1893, p. 24. Review.
      A short essay supporting Howells' vision of egocentric,
materialistic man.

948   [LOGAN, ANNIE R. M.] "More Fiction." Nation, 57 (13 Jul
      1893), 31. Review of The World of Chance.
      "Mr. Howells does not write about people in order that
the reader may, first of all, like them, but that he may
understand them and recognize the truth of the delineation,
then profit thereby according to his capacity for inference."

949   "Recent Publications." New Orleans Daily Picayune, 16 Jul
      1893, p. 19. Review of The World of Chance.
      "The reader feels as though the author was short of mat-
ter, and was trying to make it hold out to fill up the
pages." The theme seems to be that everything develops
by chance. "Perhaps [the book] was written by chance, too."

950   "New Books and New Editions." Critic, n.s. 20 (5 Aug 1893),
      86. Brief review of A Little Swiss Sojourn (Harper's
      Black and White Series).
      "It is one of those prose idyls that are bound to live....
The language flows like water under the sunlit willows."

951   P., H. T. "Paul Bourget, Novelist." Boston Evening Tran-
      script, 15 Aug 1893, p. 6. News report.
      Bourget, interviewed on his arrival in New York, "pro-
fessed an intense admiration" for the work of James and
confessed he had never read Howells.

952   "Literature / Recent Fiction." Independent, 45 (24 Aug 1893),
      1154. Brief review of The World of Chance.
      Howells' "choice of subject was unfortunate to begin
with, and he treats it as if it bored him."

953   "The World of Chance." Critic, n.s. 20 (26 Aug 1893), 135-
      136. Review.
      Little of interest is found in this work except for some
details about the publishing business. Kane "combines the
analytical qualities of a Schopenhauer with the optimism
of a prose Whitman."

954   "Comment on New Books." Atlantic, 72 (Sep 1893), 420. Brief
      review of The World of Chance.
      A "shadowy" story "charged with an unfailing humor."

1893

955   HUTTON, LAURENCE. "Literary Notes." Harper's, 87 (Sep 1893),
       4. Review of My Year in a Log Cabin.
       "When the Eminent Person himself takes us into the
       chimney-corner and makes us welcome, what a warmth of
       satisfaction do we feel!"

956   "The Political Philosophy of A Traveler from Altruria." New
       Orleans Daily Picayune, 10 Sep 1893, p. 16. Major edi-
       torial review.
       The novel is a loose set of essays. "The latest tidings
       from 'Altruria' convince us that the great exponent of
       realism in American fiction is in his way an idealist,
       too." While the work may not win public acceptance be-
       cause of its socialistic views, it does furnish "food for
       reflection."

957   BAXTER, SYLVESTER. "Howells's Boston." New England Magazine,
       n.s. 9 (Oct 1893), 129–152. Essay.
       This long, illustrated study quotes Howells extensively
       and credits him with depicting "with rare fidelity the
       Boston of his day, its outer and inner character."

958   HUTTON, LAURENCE. "Literary Notes." Harper's, 87 (Oct 1893),
       3. Review of Evening Dress.
       Lowell predicted that Howells would last because he
       knew how to write. "That he knows how to write amusing
       little comedies as well as serious short stories, and
       sometimes almost tragic long stories, Mr. Lowell lived to
       see."

959   "William Dean Howells." New England Magazine, n.s. 9 (Oct
       1893), front piece.
       Portrait.

960   "Mr. Howells' Great Nationalistic Story." New Nation, 3
       (14 Oct 1893), 458. Brief review of A Traveler from
       Altruria.
       "That the leading novelist of the times should have
       turned aside from the conventional types of polite fiction
       to give his countrymen this drastic arraignment of the way
       we live now" is a good sign for the nationalistic cause.

961   "The Writer and His Hire." Dial, 15 (16 Oct 1893), 211–213.
       Note.
       Response to Howells' treatment of the subject in "The
       Man of Letters as a Man of Business," Scribner's, 14
       (Oct 1893), 429–445.

962   "New Books / A Quartette of Little Books." Boston Evening
       Transcript, 20 Oct 1893, p. 6. Brief review of My Year
       in a Log Cabin.
           Howells' descriptions of "friendly and domestic things,"
       his recollections of "familiar scene and trivial incident,"
       arouse long dormant memories.

963   M., A. N. "'The Unknown Man' and the Editors." Critic, n.s.
       20 (21 Oct 1893), 262. Letter to the editor.
           Challenges the Evening Post's distortion (not seen) of
       Howells on the inaccessibility of the magazine to new
       writers.

964   DROCH [ROBERT BRIDGES]. "Overheard in Arcady." Life, 22
       (26 Oct 1893), 261-263. Short drama. Rpt. Overheard in
       Arcady (New York: Scribner's, 1894), pp. 1-11.
           Howells' characters, in the guise of real-life people
       meeting in a parlor car between New York and Boston, take
       the liberty of discussing their creator.

965   "New Publications / New Books and New Editions." New York
       Times, 30 Oct 1893, p. 3. Brief review of My Year in a
       Log Cabin.
           "Somehow or another, when Mr. Howells writes of his boy-
       hood there is always a tinge of sadness about him."

966   "Books of the Month." Cottage Hearth, 19 (Nov 1893), Adver-
       tisements 28. Brief mention of The World of Chance.
           A perfect description of human nature.

967   BOYESEN, HJALMAR HJORTH. "Mr. Howells at Close Range."
       Ladies' Home Journal, 10 (Nov 1893), 7-8. Literary bi-
       ography.
           An introduction to Howells' opinions, literary methods,
       and personal life. Two portraits (p. 7).

968   "Mr. Howells and the Journal." Ladies' Home Journal, 10
       (Nov 1893), p. 8. Note.
           Three-paragraph announcement of Howells' "autobiographi-
       cal series" beginning in the next number.

969   "Talk About New Books." Catholic World, 58 (Nov 1893), 287-
       288. Brief mention of The Niagara Book.
           Non-critical.

1893

970   BARRY, JOHN D. "New York Notes." Literary World, 24 (4 Nov 1893), 368. Short comment.
Traces Howells' recent movements and quotes from interviews. Howells was "immensely enthusiastic" over the Chicago Exhibition and made use of his experience in A Traveler from Altruria.

971   "New Books / Howells's Latest Farce." Boston Evening Transcript, 8 Nov 1893, p. 6. Brief review of Evening Dress.
"One of the most rational, plausible bits of nonsense with which the famous exponent of realism has favored us."

972   THOMPSON, MAURICE. "A Bit of Realism." Independent, 45 (16 Nov 1893), 1534-1535. Brief reference.
Both The Rise of Silas Lapham and Fuller's Cliff-Dwellers "have worthy and valuable significance as pieces of amusing literature, while the assumption that they measure the civilizations of [Boston and Chicago] is simply preposterous."

973   "Fiction." Literary World, 24 (18 Nov 1893), 386. Brief notice of My Year in a Log Cabin.
Favorable.

974   "Our Two Novelists / Latest Stories by W. D. Howells and F. Marion Crawford." Chicago Daily Tribune, 18 Nov 1893, p. 10. Review of The Coast of Bohemia.
Although the story is tedious, the characters are well drawn.

975   "New Publications / New Novels." New York Times, 19 Nov 1893, p. 23. Full review of The Coast of Bohemia.
"Somebody ought to codify" Howells' whole system of social laws. He "has made a closer and more accurate study of the social peculiarities of American life in his time than any other writer"; but he has begun to spin too fine, and this novel seems to be "about as thin and dry a novel" as he could produce. Nevertheless, it has virtues--among them "accuracy of touch."

976   "Briefer Notices." Public Opinion, 16 (23 Nov 1893), 182. Mention of My Year in a Log Cabin.
"Most appetizing mental confectionery."

977   [ROGERS, J. R.] "More Fiction." Nation, 57 (23 Nov 1893), 394-395. Review of The Coast of Bohemia.
"Mr. Howells blunders constantly as to the facts of the life of an art student in New York."

978   "With William Dean Howells / Realist in Fiction and Altrurian
      in Philosophy." New York Times, 26 Nov 1893, p. 23.
      Interview. Rpt. with revisions in Francis Whiting Halsey,
      American Authors and Their Homes / Personal Descriptions
      and Interviews (New York: James Pott, 1901), pp. 99-109;
      rpt. "Interviews with William Dean Howells," ed. Ulrich
      Halfmann, American Literary Realism, 6 (Fall 1973), 310-
      312.
        Sub-headings include "His Ideas on Literary Criticism,
      the Drama, Novels, and Authors--His Replies to a Persis-
      tent Questioner About the Mind as a Metaphysical Entity
      and Other Subjects of General Interest."

979   DARROW, CLARENCE S. "Realism in Literature and Art." Arena,
      9 (Dec 1893), 98-113. Brief reference.
        "The great authors of the natural school, Tolstoi,
      Daudet, Howells, Ibsen, Keilland, Flaubert, Zola, Hardy,
      and the rest, have made us think and live" (p. 107).

980   "The Point of View." Scribner's, 14 (Dec 1893), 791-792.
      Note.
        Takes issue with Howells' "The Man of Letters as a Man
      of Business" in the October Scribner's.

981   "Some Other Works of Fiction." Harper's, 88 (Dec 1893),
      Advertiser, p. 9. Advertisement of The Coast of Bohemia.
        Although "radically different in many respects from The
      World of Chance ($1.50), which preceded it, [this novel]
      is worthy of as much praise as was accorded to that re-
      markably entertaining story, and will be regarded with
      equal favor by those who are so fortunate as to read them
      both."

982   WOOLLEY, CELIA PARKER. "Mr. Howells Again." New England
      Magazine, n.s. 9 (Dec 1893), 408-411. Essay. Rpt. in
      part, The War of the Critics over William Dean Howells,
      ed. Edwin H. Cady and David L. Frazier (Evanston: Row,
      Peterson, 1962), pp. 59-61.
        Woolley, in defense of Howells, attempts to establish
      the compatibility of realism and idealism and asserts the
      essential morality of Howells' work.

983   PAYNE, WILLIAM MORTON. "Recent Fiction." Dial, 15 (1 Dec
      1893), 340-341. Review of The Coast of Bohemia.
        "The manner is still that of realism, but a realism not
      too exclusive of the methods of art."

1893

984   BARRY, JOHN D. "New York Letter." Literary World, 24 (2 Dec
      1893), 426. Brief comment.
         Reference to an early Howells' play written in the man-
      ner of Ibsen before Howells had read him and to Howells'
      insistence that Yorick's Love be credited to Estimenez, a
      Spanish playwright.

985   "New Books and New Editions." Critic, n.s. 20 (2 Dec 1893),
      357. Announcement of Evening Dress (Black and White
      Series).
         Howells' art "has drawn its principles from something
      deeper than mere observation."

986   "Fiction." Literary World, 24 (30 Dec 1893), 468. Brief re-
      view of The Coast of Bohemia.
         The heroine stands in contrast "to the fantastic, irra-
      tional creature" Howells has previously presented as the
      typical American woman.

                            1894

987   ARNOLD, MATTHEW. Discourses in America. London and New York:
      Macmillan, 1894. Pp. 187-188. Brief reference.
         On Howells' depiction of New England life in his
      "charming" The Lady of the Aroostook.

  *   BRIDGES, ROBERT. "The Household of W. D. Howells." Over-
      heard in Arcady. New York: Scribner's, 1894. Pp. 1-11.
      Rpt. from Life, 22 (26 Oct 1893), 261-263. See item 964.

988   The Letters of James Russell Lowell, ed. Charles Eliot Norton.
      2 vols. New York: Harper, 1894. I, pp. 350-351. Letter.
         Lowell writing to Howells (2 Nov 1865) compliments him
      on his recent Nation articles.

989   RUTHERFORD, MILDRED. "William Dean Howells." American
      Authors / A Hand-Book of American Literature from Early
      Colonial to Living Writers. Atlanta: Franklin Printing
      and Publishing Co., 1894. Pp. 565-568. General biograph-
      ical and critical introduction.
         "Sometimes his details are very tiresome, but has not
      real life much prose in it?" Refers to Taine on Howells
      (source not traced).

990   VEDDER, HENRY C. "William Dean Howells." American Writers of
      To-day. New York and Boston: Silver, Burdett, 1894.
      Pp. 43-68 and passim as indexed. Essay. Rpt. in part,

(VEDDER, HENRY C.)
   The War of the Critics over William Dean Howells, ed.
   Edwin H. Cady and David L. Frazier (Evanston: Row, Peterson, 1962), pp. 61-63.
   A general critical introduction to Howells as artist and
   critic. More attention is given to the theory of realism
   and criticism than to specific titles although the question
   of Howells' treatment of women is raised with some emphasis.
   "Even though he occasionally aggravates us by his wrong-
   headedness, as some of us must consider it, Mr. Howells is
   easily the first living American novelist" (p. 67).

991   "Notes and News." Poet-Lore, 6 (No. 10, 1894), 527-528.
      Brief comments about "My First Visit to New England" in
      Harper's.
         Howells' "call on Emerson is one of the most quaintly
      humorous bits in the whole series of his reminiscences."

  *   "General Gossip of Authors and Writers / Literary Methods of
      William Dean Howells." Current Literature, 15 (Jan 1894),
      14. Abstr. of Boyesen in Ladies' Home Journal, 10 (Nov
      1893), 7-8. See item 967.

992   HUTTON, LAURENCE. "Literary Notes." Harper's, 88 (Jan 1894),
      3-4. Review of The Coast of Bohemia.
         This novel "is in the best of Mr. Howells's lightest
      vein, but it is as full of humorous interest and of subtle
      analysis of character as is anything that has ever come
      from the same facile pen."

993   "Fiction." Literary World, 25 (27 Jan 1894), 26. Very brief
      notice of Evening Dress.

994   CALHOUN, ALFRED R. "W. Dean Howells Talks on Literature."
      Philadelphia Press, 25 Feb 1894, p. 24. Interview. Rpt.
      in part, "Interviews with William Dean Howells," ed.
      Ulrich Halfmann, American Literary Realism, 6 (Fall 1973),
      312-314.
         The interviewer seems more eager to establish his own
      point of view than to discover Howells, who is led to com-
      ment on "Effect of Sub-Cellar Fiction Upon the Masses and
      Why It Is Liked--Stories a Source of Crime--Men Who Have
      Made Fortunes by Prostituting the Character of Their
      Readers--Change Needed in 'Family Story Papers.'"

995   "Fiction." Literary World, 25 (24 Mar 1894), 90. Brief
      reference.
         Wolcott Balestier's Benefits Forgot is favorably com-
      pared to The Rise of Silas Lapham.

1894

996   "The April Magazines." Critic, n.s. 21 (31 Mar 1894), 220.
         Brief reference.
         "Race," a poem, is cited as "unquestionably among
         [Howells'] happiest efforts in verse." The poem is copied
         here.

997   JOHNSON, CLIFTON. "The Writer and the Rest of the World."
         Outlook, 49 (31 Mar 1894), 580-582. Interview. Rpt.
         "Interviews with William Dean Howells," ed. Ulrich Half-
         mann, American Literary Realism 6 (Fall 1973), 315-319.
         Howells' comments, which explore the nature of the
         artist, his work, and their relationship to life, are
         presented as monologue.

998   MARSHALL, EDWARD. "A Great American Writer / William Dean
         Howells and His Remarkable Novels and What He Stands for
         in Literature." Philadelphia Press, 15 Apr 1894, p. 27.
         Interview. Rpt. "Interviews with William Dean Howells,"
         ed. Ulrich Halfmann, American Literary Realism, 6 (Fall
         1973), 319-323.
         Subheadings include "Not an Imposing Figure," "Politics
         and Religion," "Hopes for Immortality," "His Indian Sum-
         mer" ("The only story in which Mr. Howells might be sup-
         posed to have painted himself to even a slight extent is
         Indian Summer"), "Hard To End Stories," "Literary Methods,"
         and "Leading American Writers."

999   "Socialism and Fiction." New Orleans Daily Picayune, 13 May
         1894, p. 16. Editorial.
         Comments on Howells and Bellamy as social critics. "We
         are rather inclined to attribute [Howells'] present view
         of the great social question to his enthusiastic admira-
         tion for Tolstoi. On the other hand, it seems to us that
         the pupil is clearer and saner than his master."

1000 "James Russell Lowell / Mr. Howells Gives an Account of His
         First Meeting with Him in 1860." Boston Evening Tran-
         script, 23 May 1894, p. 5. Response to Howells' "My First
         Visit to New England" in Harper's.
         "One of the most delightful bits of autobiography printed
         for many a day."

1001 "New Publications / Mr. Howells in Various Moods." New York
         Times, 4 Jun 1894, p. 3. Review of A Traveler from
         Altruria and A Likely Story. Rpt. Book News, 12 (Jul
         1894), 431-432.
         The various characters in the novel represent the con-
         flicting elements in Howells himself as he considers "the

("New Publications / Mr. Howells in Various Moods")
subject of Socialism in its relation to the present state
of civilization in this country." The book is clever, but
it will not make converts. Howells "lacks the magnetism,
the emotional force, the fire of eloquence" required for
that. "He is always cold, satirical, given to word-hunting
and phrase-making...."
A Likely Story is "a spritely thing with a fair measure
of human nature in it."

1002 WILCOX, MARRION. "W. D. Howells's First Romance." Harper's
Bazar, 27 (16 Jun 1894), 475. Full review of A Traveler
from Altruria.
An unsparing, but helpful and suggestive, criticism of
America. A major paragraph in the review consists of
Howells' after-thoughts which he shared with Wilcox.
Howells distinguishes between a "romantic novel" and a
"romance," and scores what Tolstoy calls "impersonal
slavery."

1003 "Fiction." Literary World, 25 (30 Jun 1894), 201. Review of
A Traveler from Altruria.
"A very thin vein of thought is worked for much more than
it is worth."

1004 "A Traveler from Altruria." Critic, n.s. 21 (30 Jun 1894),
434. Review.
"The good-will of a gentle man toward his kind, the
interesting speculations of Plato, Bacon and Sir Thomas
More, the poetic dreams of William Morris and the prosaic
nonsense of Mr. Bellamy are all jumbled and shaken up together in Mr. Howells's book. The whole is served up with
a sauce à la primitive Christianity, and has to be taken
very hot; once it has cooled and settled its effect is
very disagreeable indeed."

1005 "Stories for Summer." Book Buyer, n.s. 11 (Jul 1894), 306-
307. Brief review of A Traveler from Altruria.
"A thinly disguised and somewhat acrid tract for the
times."

 *   [A Traveler from Altruria.] Book News, 12 (Jul 1894), 431-
432. Rpt. from New York Times, 4 Jun 1894, p. 3. See
item 1001.

1006 "A Traveler from Altruria." Harper's, 89 (Jul 1894), Advertiser, p. 3. Advertisement.

1894

("A Traveler from Altruria")
"This volume may be regarded as a more direct utterance
of Mr. Howells's philosophy than is to be found in any
other of his novels. The traveler comes from 'Altruria'
to visit an American friend who is stopping at a summer
hotel in the White Mountains; and, with that as a starting-
point, many phases of American life, both rural and urban,
are examined and critically discussed."

1007   "The Coast of Bohemia." Critic, n.s. 22 (7 Jul 1894), 2.
Review.
"It is a clever picture of a kind of life that really
exists in New York, but the men and women, nevertheless,
seem to be puppets playing at life." Although "pretty,"
it lacks substance.

1008   "New Novels." Athenaeum, No. 3480 (7 Jul 1894), 29. Review
of A Traveler from Altruria.
The "romance" contains much argument which is "stale,"
"dull," and unconvincing.

1009   "Book Reviews." Public Opinion, 17 (26 Jul 1894), 407. Review of A Traveler from Altruria.
Conversations only weakly characterize contemporary
society, and Howells makes few "definite propositions."

1010   "Fiction." Literary World, 25 (28 Jul 1894), 231. Very brief
notice of Five O'Clock Tea, A Likely Story, and The Mouse
Trap.
"'Trifles light as air,' but there is a place for
trifles in life, especially when they are served up so
artistically."

1011   GARLAND, HAMLIN. "Productive Conditions in American Literature." Forum, 17 (Aug 1894), 690-698. Essay. Rpt. in
part, Literary Digest, 9 (11 Aug 1894), 429.
"Veritism demands simplicity, genuineness, wholesome-
ness, perfect truth to the conditions of American life,
and unity of effect," without denying "the latitude of
personal impression of the fact" (p. 697). Howells
qualifies.

1012   "Novels." Saturday Review, 78 (4 Aug 1894), 129. Review of
A Traveler from Altruria.
"A clever economical and social novelette, a fair
specimen of Mr. Howells's finished and polished cabinet-
work."

1013   "A Traveler from Altruria." Nation, 59 (9 Aug 1894), 107.
        Full review.
            "Mr. Howells speaks the thoughts of many men of his
        time with that clearness, force, and vivacity which have
        made his fame as a novelist." He sides always with the
        workingman to the point of bias. In "some trifling social
        matters," his observation is faulty.

   *   GARLAND, HAMLIN. "Productive Conditions of American Litera-
        ture." Literary Digest, 9 (11 Aug 1894), 429. Rpt. from
        Forum, 17 (Aug 1894), 690-698. See item 1011.

1014   HUTTON, LAURENCE. "Literary Notes." Harper's, 89 (Sep 1894),
        1. Review of A Traveler from Altruria.
            "The talk is bright and sparkling, if not conclusive;
        and the book will entertain its readers, even if it will
        not move them to try to make the world the better for
        their living in it."

1015   "Howells and James as Comedy Writers." Dial, 17 (1 Sep 1894),
        124-125. Note. Brief comment motivated by Harper's Black
        and White Series.
            "Howells has made a delightful success in a little
        species peculiarly his own."

1016   SHARP, WILLIAM. "New Novels." Academy, 46 (1 Sep 1894),
        147-148. Review of A Traveler from Altruria.
            Like Mr. Homos, Howells would be "a spiritual solvent to
        precipitate sincerity." Apart from its "fundamental
        seriousness," the novel is "eminently readable."

1017   "Howells's Traveler from Altruria." Outlook, 50 (8 Sep 1894),
        396. Review.
            "The work of Mr. Howells on social reform is that of
        Count Tolstoi plus humor, minus intensity."

1018   "Literary Passions." New Orleans Daily Picayune, 9 Sep 1894,
        p. 16. Editorial review of My Literary Passions.
            In telling the story of his literary development,
        Howells has "very nearly told his wide public what sort
        of man he is, and we confess that we are not sorry that
        he has so largely anticipated the labors of future biogra-
        phers."

1019   HENDERSON, C. R. "Recent Studies in Sociology." Dial, 17
        (16 Sep 1894), 154. Brief comment on A Traveler from
        Altruria.

1894

(HENDERSON, C. R.)
Howells' traveler "leaves us angry at his rebukes, but reflecting on our deeds"--which is the function of the utopian vision.

1020   "The Lounger." Critic, n.s. 22 (29 Sep 1894), 208. Brief reference.
Notes the various places in which Howells is publishing his autobiography "on the instalment plan."

1021   "Socialism Idealized / Some Phases of Current Discontent with American Institutions / A Traveler from Altruria." New York Daily Tribune, 30 Sep 1894, p. 14. Full review.
Had Howells "written the book for the purpose of making converts to Socialism, he could scarcely have exercised his technical craftsmanship more masterfully. But had he written it as a counterblast against the follies of the whole school, from Owen to Bellamy, he could scarcely have employed the logic of the situation with more convincing force."

1022   [WARNER, CHARLES DUDLEY.] "Editor's Study." Harper's, 89 (Oct 1894), 801-802. Brief comment.
Rather nostalgic response to Howells' "My First Visit to New England" being serialized in Harper's.

1023   "'Politics but a Good Thing' / W. D. Howells's Views on the Women's Movement To Aid Dr. Parkhurst." New York Times, 13 Oct 1894, p. 9. Interview. Abstr. "Interviews with William Dean Howells," ed. Ulrich Halfmann, American Literary Realism, 6 (Fall 1973), 324.
Howells explains why "the great body of women are better than the mass of men" and suggests that novelists have been "apt to make too much distinction" between men and women.

1024   "New Books / A Traveler from Altruria." Boston Evening Transcript, 18 Oct 1894, p. 6. Brief review.
Because Howells himself is so clearly seen in all the American types he presents, one is led "to doubt the correctness of the information" brought by the Altrurian. Howells' Altruria is modelled very closely upon Plato's Republic.

1025   CRANE, STEPHEN. "Fears Realists Must Wait / An Interesting Talk with William Dean Howells." New York Times, 28 Oct 1894, p. 20. Interview. Rpt. "Five Interviews with William Dean Howells," ed. George Arms and William M.

(CRANE, STEPHEN)
    Gibson, Americana, 37 (Apr 1943), 271–274; Stephen Crane /
Selected Prose and Poetry, ed. William M. Gibson (New
York: Rinehart, 1950), pp. 227–230; 3rd ed. 1968, pp. 649–
652; Stephen Crane / Uncollected Writings, ed. Olov W.
Fryckstedt (Uppsala: Acta Universitatis Upsaliensis,
1963), pp. 79–82; American Thought and Writing / The
1890's, ed. Donald Pizer (Boston: Houghton Mifflin, 1972),
pp. 53–56; "Interviews with William Dean Howells," ed.
Ulrich Halfmann, American Literary Realism, 6 (Fall 1973),
324–326.
    The original column heading continues, "The Eminent
Novelist Still Holds a Firm Faith in Realism, but Con-
fesses a Doubt If Its Day Has Yet Come--He has Observed a
Change in the Literary Pulse of the Country Within the
Last Few Months--A Reactionary Wave."

1026   BARR, AMELIA E. "The Modern World." North American Review,
    159 (Nov 1894), 594–595. Brief reference.
        Howells' novels, along with those of Anthony Trollope,
are categorized as analytic domestic novels.

1027   [KIRK, S.] "America, Altruria, and The Coast of Bohemia."
    Atlantic, 74 (Nov 1894), 701–704. Full review of A
Traveler from Altruria and The Coast of Bohemia. Rpt. in
part, The War of the Critics over William Dean Howells,
ed. Edwin H. Cady and David L. Frazier (Evanston: Row,
Peterson, 1962), pp. 63–67.
        In the first "Mr. Howells has turned aside for a moment
from fiction, and written a confession of his faith," the
roots of which are apparent in his earlier works. The
latter is light literature in Howells' early manner but
consistent with his later thought.

1028   "Mr. Howells' Literary Autobiography." Harper's, 89 (Nov
    1894), Advertiser, p. 42. Advertisement. Rpt. American
Literary Realism, 6 (Fall 1973), facing 337.
        "My Literary Passions" appearing in Ladies' Home
Journal is Howells at his best, and no other work by him
has been more widely read. He has put into these papers
"all the charm of his personality." Portrait and photo-
graph "Mr. Howells in His New York Home."

1029   PAYNE, WILLIAM MORTON. "Recent English Novels." Dial, 17
    (1 Nov 1894), 265. Brief reference.
        Observation that Violet Hunt's The Maiden's Progress
is a novel "after the manner of Mr. Howells's farces."

1894

1030 "Publications of the Past Week." New York Times, 10 Nov 1894,
p. 3. Brief notice.
Details the physical appearance of a new gift edition
of Their Wedding Journey.

1031 "New Books and New Editions." Critic, n.s. 22 (24 Nov 1894),
349. Announcement of new white and gold edition of Their
Wedding Journey. Focuses on the illustrations by Clifford
Carleton.

1032 "Their Favorite Books / Authors Tell Which of Their Works They
Like Best." Boston Evening Transcript, 30 Nov 1895, p. 6.
Brief reference.
Howells indicates a personal preference for Indian Sum-
mer although he considers A Modern Instance his strongest
work.

1033 MARTIN, EDWARD S. "Their Wedding Journey." Book Buyer, n.s.
11 (Dec 1894), 575-577. Review of new edition.
Nostalgic comments about a young Howells who caught
fleeting sensations and crystalized them into prose "that
is as fresh and charming now as it was the day he wrote
it."

1034 THAYER, WILLIAM R. "The New Story-Tellers and the Doom of
Realism." Forum, 18 (Dec 1894), 470-480. Essay. Rpt.
in part, The War of the Critics over William Dean Howells,
ed. Edwin H. Cady and David L. Frazier (Evanston: Row,
Peterson, 1962), pp. 67-71.
The realists are "Epidermists," and "the knell of the
Epidermists has sounded." The role of Howells in the
emergence and demise of realism is discussed--quite
satirically, but with tempering appreciation--at length.

1035 "Holiday Books." Dial, 17 (1 Dec 1894), 338. Notice of new
edition of Their Wedding Journey.
Howells' "usual photographic and phonographic accuracy."

1036 "Holiday Books." Literary World, 25 (1 Dec 1894), 422. Brief
notice of new edition of Their Wedding Journey.
Illustrated by Clifford Carleton.

1037 "Fiction." Saturday Review, 78 (22 Dec 1894), 689. Review
of Their Wedding Journey.
"One incident in particular--'the first serious dispute'
--is entertaining and spirited, without being in the least
overdrawn." (Reviewer apparently does not know this
novel was among Howells' first.)

1895

1038   HOWELLS, WILLIAM COOPER. <u>Recollections of Life in Ohio / From
       1813 to 1840</u>, introd. William Dean Howells. Cincinnati:
       Robert Clarke, 1895. Rpt. with Introd. by Edwin H. Cady
       (Gainesville, Florida: Scholars' Facsimiles and Reprints,
       1963).

  *   <u>Human Documents / Portraits and Biographies of Eminent Men</u>.
       New York: McClure, 1895. Pp. 140-151. Rpt. from
       <u>McClure's</u>, 1 (Jun 1893), 3-11. <u>See</u> item 942.

1039   "Fiction." <u>Critic</u>, n.s. 23 (12 Jan 1895), 28. Brief mention
       of <u>The Garroters</u> and <u>A Likely Story</u>.
           "Little masterpieces of un-Balzacian human comedy."

1040   "Contemporary Literature / Belles Lettres." <u>Westminster Re-
       view</u>, 143 (Feb 1895), 226-229. Full review of <u>Their Wed-
       ding Journey</u>.
           "The merits of Mr. Howells' writing are very similar to
       those for which he eulogises his happy couple. He makes
       up for lack of incident by making the very best of what-
       ever will suffer itself to be made anything at all of."
       In the use of dialogue he "almost equals Wendell Holmes."

1041   "The World of New Books." <u>Philadelphia Press</u>, 16 Feb 1895,
       p. 11. Brief review of <u>A Traveler from Altruria</u>.
           Although Howells offers a shrewd criticism of modern
       society, the story is unsuccessful. [Graham]

1042   JOHNSON, CLIFTON. "Sense and Sentiment / By W. D. Howells."
       <u>Outlook</u>, 51 (23 Feb 1895), 304-305. Report on an inter-
       view. Rpt. "Interviews with William Dean Howells," ed.
       Ulrich Halfmann, <u>American Literary Realism</u>, 6 (Fall 1973),
       326-330.
           Extended comments on women, love, and marriage are pre-
       sented in monologue form.

1043   "New Publications / Reminiscences by Howells's Father." <u>New
       York Times</u>, 23 Feb 1895, p. 3. Review of <u>Recollections
       of Life in Ohio from 1813 to 1840</u> by William Cooper
       Howells, with introd. and concluding chapter by William
       Dean Howells.
           Howells' substantive contribution is summarized without
       critical comment.

1895

1044 [Untitled.] New York Times, 24 Feb 1895, p. 4. Brief editorial comment.
Expresses chagrin for the misspelling of Howells' name
in the City Directory.

1045 "The Theatrical Week /.../ Howells on Certain New Plays." New
York Times, 31 Mar 1895, p. 12. Note.
A condescending response to Howells' comment on current
English drama in the April Harper's.

1046 "Mr. Howells as a Romanticist." New York Times, 19 May 1895,
p. 4. Editorial.
Notes a recent lead article attributed to Andrew Lang
in the London Daily News (not seen) and concludes that
Howells is not a "realist by nature," that "the spirit of
romance breaks out" in his work more frequently than he
would care to admit.

1047 "Literary Notes." Philadelphia Press, 1 Jun 1895, p. 11.
Brief reference.
Mentions "Tribulations of a Cheerful Giver" in Century.
[Graham]

1048 "Literary Notes." Philadelphia Press, 8 Jun 1895, p. 11.
Briefly describes Howells' "First Impressions of Literary New York." [Graham]

1049 "New Publications / Mr. Howells as a Reader." New York Times,
26 Jun 1895, p. 3. Review of My Literary Passions.
Here one finds "probably as much of self-revelation...
as Mr. Howells' nature is capable of." There is still
doubt "whether or not Mr. Howells is not positively the
worst critic of any distinction."

1050 ROOD, HENRY EDWARD. "New York Letter." Literary World, 26
(29 Jun 1895), 201. Brief reference to My Literary Passions.
Carries "the impress of veracity." Richard Henry
Stoddard's response to the volume is quoted.

1051 "The World of New Books." Philadelphia Press, 29 Jun 1895,
p. 11. Brief note.
Announces publication of My Literary Passions, praising
Howells' chatty and entertaining style. [Graham]

1052 PECK, HARRY THURSTON. "Mr. Howells's Literary Passions."
Bookman (New York), 1 (Jul 1895), 400–402. Full review
of My Literary Passions.

(PECK, HARRY THURSTON)
    Appreciative. Considerable discussion of A Boy's Town--
a most extraordinary psychological study.

1053   DROCH [ROBERT BRIDGES]. "Mr. Howells's Literary Passions."
        Life, 26 (18 Jul 1895), 38. Review of My Literary Passions.
        In these confessions one will find "something more inter-
esting than the books referred to; he will catch the image
of the boy and the man that Mr. Howells once was, and will
make his acquaintance with delight."

1054   "Mr. Howells's Literary Passions." Independent, 47 (25 Jul
        1895), 1000-1001. Full review of My Literary Passions.
        While these "authentic confessions" are humorous and
pleasing, "the book saddens us at its close; for upon the
whole, it tells the story of a fine genius, or a fine
talent, forced out of its natural habitat by the pressure
of an influence deadly to its native characteristics."
Reference is to the disastrous effect of Tolstoy on Howells.

1055   "Mr. Howells's Literary Passions." Literary World, 26 (27 Jul
        1895), 228-229. Review of My Literary Passions.
        "Mr. Howells is refreshingly free from conventionalism
in his methods and his admirations."

1056   HUTTON, LAURENCE. "Literary Notes." Harper's, 91 (Aug 1895),
        3-4. Review of My Literary Passions.
        "No touch here of Degeneration or of anything morbid or
depressing." The atmosphere is "exhilarating, wholesome,
and inspiring." The catholicity of Howells' taste is
demonstrated.

1057   "Some Literary Autobiography from Mr. Howells." Dial, 19
        (1 Aug 1895), 78. Review of My Literary Passions.
        Appreciation of the "subjective Howells" found here.

1058   LANG, ANDREW. "The New Fiction." Illustrated London News,
        107 (3 Aug 1895), 141. Brief reference.
        Howells' "critical ears are deaf with the noise and his
eyes dim with the dust of the present." "The creation of
characters makes the novelist," and in that the new are
not clearly superior to the old.

1059   HEATON, ELIZA PUTNAM. "The Home of Miss Jewett / Ancient
        Mansion in Quaint Old Berwick Town." Boston Sunday Herald,
        18 Aug 1895, p. 29. Feature.
        Focus is on Jewett, but interesting comments on Howells
are included.

1895

1060   "The Growth of Greatness--XVI / William Dean Howells." Life,
       26 (29 Aug 1895), 138-139. Humorous note.
          "Mr. Howells has made the grievous error of differing
       from this publication on a literary question of some im-
       portance, and we still have the effrontery to regret that
       a writer so richly endowed should choose to despise his
       most artistic qualities and wander in the arid plains of
       realism." Three photo caricatures.

1061   "My Literary Passions." Nation, 61 (29 Aug 1895), 156. Re-
       view.
          Howells' "critical standards are really ethical standards
       after all." The chief interest of this work is autobio-
       graphical.

1062   "Literature." Critic, n.s. 24 (19 Oct 1895), 244. Review of
       My Literary Passions.
          "These 'Confessions of a Literary Free-Lance' are not
       more remarkable for their polish and piquancy than for
       their charming egotism and freedom from acerbity."

1063   [SCUDDER, HORACE E.] "Mr. Howells Under Tutors and Governors."
       Atlantic, 76 (Nov 1895), 701-703. Full review of My Liter-
       ary Passions.
          "The frankness of this delightful book is in its manner
       as well as in its matter." It is far more interesting as
       a narrative of Howells' life than as literary criticism,
       and its "controlling passion is far less literary than
       ethical."

1064   "Stops of Various Quills." Harper's, 91 (Nov 1895), Advertiser,
       p. 9. Advertisement.
          "All of the poems included in this volume are brief.
       Some of them illustrate the vital connection that, in pro-
       verbial philosophy, is asserted to exist between brevity
       and wit. Such are observant, discriminating. In others,
       strong feeling has driven the author's pen (for all its
       training and approved self-control) from line to line,
       until a reverential mood, or an impulsive vagrant sugges-
       tion, or a tonic and far-reaching thought has been ex-
       pressed. Of these, also, the expression is adequate,
       though it may be condensed in forty lines--or four--and
       although the strength of one at least of the poems,
       'Calvary,' might have informed four hundred pages of
       prose, and made a strong novel."

1065 "The Lounger." Critic, n.s. 24 (9 Nov 1895), 304. Brief
      note.
         Challenges Howells' finding a w in the English pronunci-
      ation of dance and bath.

1066 "'Literary Boston.'" Literary World, 26 (16 Nov 1895), 391.
      Column-and-a-half response to Howells' "Literary Boston
      Thirty Years Ago" in Harper's.

1067 "Literary Notes." Philadelphia Press, 16 Nov 1895, p. 13.
      Brief reference.
         Mentions Howells' critical introduction to May J. Ser-
      rano's translation of Galdós' latest romance, Doña
      Perfecta. [Graham]

1068 "The World of New Books." Philadelphia Press, 16 Nov 1895,
      p. 12. Brief review of Stops of Various Quills.
         Howells is too much a novelist to write poetry. He "is
      no singer." [Graham]

1069 [Untitled.] Life, 26 (21 Nov 1895), 324. Editorial paragraph.
         Reproves Howells for sharp criticism of Dickens' work.

1070 "The Lounger." Critic, n.s. 24 (23 Nov 1895), 348. Brief
      note.
         A reader attempts to correct the Lounger's misunder-
      standing of Howells' dialectic renditions.

1071 "Poetry New and Old." Literary World, 26 (30 Nov 1895), 427.
      Review of Stops of Various Quills.
         Skillful verse is sprinkled with sawdust. "The Bewil-
      dered Guest" in itself justifies the book.

1072 HUTTON, LAURENCE. "Literary Notes." Harper's, 92 (Dec 1895),
      3-4. Brief review of Stops of Various Quills.
         In Howells' prose one senses always the poet behind the
      mask of realism. In his verse-making, Howells "loses a
      certain self-consciousness and restraint."

1073 MABIE, HAMILTON W. "Books of the Holiday Season." Book
      Buyer, n.s. 12 (Dec 1895), 671. Review of Stops of Vari-
      ous Quills.
         "Mr. Howells has given us nothing so profoundly, one
      might almost say so passionately, human as these verses,
      which seem to issue from the very heart of the mystery of
      life."

1895

1074   "Some of the Important New Books." Harper's, 92 (Dec 1895),
          Advertiser, p. 10. Advertisement of My Literary Passions.
          "The names of the authors discussed...are: Goldsmith,
          Cervantes, Irving, Scott, Pope, Tolstoy, Ik Marvel,
          Charles Reader, Curtis, Heine, Dante, Zola, Hardy, Goethe,
          and Tourguenief. That will give an idea of the wide range
          of pasturage--but mostly in the high mountains, it will be
          observed. 'It carries us back,' says George Parsons
          Lathrop, 'to the pure and simple outlook of a modern man's
          unspoiled youth, and reminds us of that healthy way of
          viewing literature which helps one to live healthily and
          steer clear of degeneration and its phantasms.'"

1075   SHAW, G[EORGE] B[ERNARD]. "Told You So." Saturday Review,
          80 (7 Dec 1895), 761-762. Essay review. Rpt. Dramatic
          Opinions and Essays with an Apology, 2 vols. (New York:
          Brentano's, 1906), I, pp. 265-266; rpt. in part, Howells /
          A Century of Criticism, ed. Kenneth E. Eble (Dallas:
          Southern Methodist University, 1962), pp. 60-61, and The
          War of the Critics over William Dean Howells, ed. Edwin H.
          Cady and David L. Frazier (Evanston: Row, Peterson, 1962),
          pp. 71-72.
          Includes brief--amusing and favorable--comment on the
          performance of A Dangerous Ruffian at the Avenue Theatre.
          The piece shows, "as might have been expected, that with
          three weeks practice the American novelist could write the
          heads off the poor bunglers to whom our managers generally
          appeal when they want a small bit of work to amuse the
          people who come at eight."

1076   [HIGGINSON, THOMAS WENTWORTH.] "Recent Poetry." Nation, 61
          (12 Dec 1895), 431. Brief review of Stops of Various
          Quills.
          "Only a monotone of sadness."

1077   "Literature." Independent, 47 (12 Dec 1895), 1690-1691. Re-
          view of Stops of Various Quills.
          "Every note blown from these quills is hopelessly sorrow-
          ful or bitterly pessimistic in its mood. Mr. Howells
          avoids morbidness and seems to feel his way against atra-
          biliousness; but fluting in the chill shadow of Tolstoi
          congests, almost congeals, his Muse's breath before it
          issues from the reed."

1078   "Holiday Publications." Dial, 19 (16 Dec 1895), 388. Brief
          notice of Stops of Various Quills.
          Although not highly poetic, Howells' verses are "always
          thoughtful and virile."

1079   "The Newest Books / Poetry." <u>Boston Evening Transcript</u>, 18 Dec
      1895, p. 10. Brief, non-critical announcement of <u>Stops of</u>
      <u>Various Quills</u>.

1080   "Poetry and Verse." <u>Critic</u>, n.s. 24 (21 Dec 1895), 426.
      Brief review of <u>Stops of Various Quills</u>.
      The title apparently implies "expressions of various
      moods, not influenced by the desire to produce something
      artistic." The author has little to say.

1896

1081   ABBOTT, ELIZABETH. <u>American Literature Papers</u>. Boston:
      Lothrop, 1896. Unpaginated. Short reference.
      Howells and James are realists; they write about things
      "just exactly as they are." Neither is "of the dashing
      and lively sort," and they will not long be read since
      the things about which they write "will be forgotten in a
      few years" (last two pages of Ch. 11).

1082   CONE, STEPHEN D. <u>Biographical and Historical Sketches / A</u>
      <u>Narrative of Hamilton and Its Residents from 1792 to 1896</u>.
      Hamilton: Republican Publishing Co., 1896. P. 307.
      Brief reference.
      Howells is not included in the index, but at least one
      mention retells the story of his boyhood visit to the
      Erwin's, his homesickness, and his being taken home during
      the night.

1083   MATTHEWS, BRANDER. <u>An Introduction to the Study of American</u>
      <u>Literature</u>. New York: American Book, 1896. Passim as
      indexed.
      References to Howells are bibliographic. A small por-
      trait sketch is included (p. 231), and several of his
      books are listed in the "Brief Chronology" at the end of
      the volume.

*   <u>McClure's Biographies / Gladstone--Bismarck--Grant--Dana--</u>
      <u>Stevenson--and Others</u>. New York: McClure, 1896).
      Pp. 140-151. Rpt. from <u>McClure's</u>, 1 (Jun 1893), 3-11.
      <u>See</u> item 942.

1084   MORSE, JOHN T., JR. <u>Life and Letters of Oliver Wendell</u>
      <u>Holmes</u>. 2 vols. Cambridge: Riverside Press, 1896.
      Passim as indexed.
      Minor cordial and approving references to Howells.

1896

1085   SMYTH, ALBERT H. Bayard Taylor. Boston and New York:
        Houghton Mifflin, 1896. Passim as indexed.
           On several occasions Howells is quoted. Three Taylor
        letters to Howells are included.

1086   STEELE, ROBERT W., and MARY DAVIES STEELE. Early Dayton.
        Dayton: W. J. Shuey, 1896. Pp. 59, 60.
           Howells is briefly quoted in context of his father's
        memories of Dayton.

1087   HUTTON, LAURENCE. "Literary Notes." Harper's, 92 (Feb 1896),
        1. Review of The Day of Their Wedding.
           The Shakers are mistaken for the Quakers in this largely
        descriptive review, which focuses on the "feelin' foolish"
        sentiment characteristic of love.

1088   PECK, HARRY THURSTON. "Mr. Howells as a Poet." Bookman (New
        York), 2 (Feb 1896), 525-527. Full review of Stops of
        Various Quills.
           Sadness, just short of pessimism, pervades all the poems.
        The writing is strong, but Howells' impressions of life do
        not gain much from the metrical form.

1089   PAYNE, WILLIAM MORTON. "Recent Fiction." Dial, 20 (1 Feb
        1896), 81. Brief reference.
           Response to Howells' introduction to Mrs. Serrano's
        translation of Galdós' Doña Perfecta, challenging Howells'
        judgment of Galdós as a realist.

1090   "Literary Notes." Los Angeles Times, 2 Feb 1896, p. 31.
        Brief mention.
           A Modern Instance is third in a list of the most popular
        books in Yale College's modern novel course (following
        Lorna Doone and A Gentlemen of France). Treasure Island
        is fourth.
           Howells, Stedman, and Kipling are now using typewriters.
        The creative imagination is likely to suffer loss.
        [Nichol]

1091   "Fiction." Literary World, 27 (8 Feb 1896), 47. Review of
        Doña Perfecta by Galdós.
           Challenges Howells' opinion of the book expressed in
        his introduction to it.

1092   [Untitled.] Life, 27 (13 Feb 1896), 112. Editorial.
           Response to criticism of America by Charles Eliot Norton
        and Howells. There is more hope for us than they suggest.
        "We are not born pigs, and we don't live in a stye."

1093   FREDERIC, HAROLD. "Novels Read in London / Superiority of the
        Work Done by William Dean Howells /...." New York Times,
        16 Feb 1896, p. 17. Comment on A Boy's Town and The
        Quality of Mercy.
            A Boy's Town "has in it that universality which is a
        test of the master's work" and which makes it enjoyable
        to English readers in spite of its essential localism.
        As for The Quality of Mercy, "It seems to me that no Ameri-
        can has ever touched in fiction finer chords than vibrate
        here and there through these pages."

1094   "New Publications / A Novel by Mr. Howells." New York Times,
        19 Feb 1896, p. 10. Review of The Day of Their Wedding.
            It "may be the least bit of a laugh at bucolic manners."
        It is "the tenderest idyl, with a sad conclusion, and has
        a tinge of mysticism about it." It is also "truly
        American."

1095   "Books of the Day / Howells' Chilly Realism." Chicago Daily
        Tribune, 29 Feb 1896, p. 10. Review of The Day of Their
        Wedding.
            "It appears to be Mr. Howells' literary creed that when
        he has blown a warm bubble of romance he must finish by
        running an icicle through it. As soon as there is nothing
        left but the icicle he stops and writes 'The End.'"

1096   DROCH [ROBERT BRIDGES]. "An Idyllic Story by Mr. Howells."
        Life, 27 (12 Mar 1896), 196. Review of The Day of Their
        Wedding.
            "Mr. Howells is first and last a literary artist, im-
        mensely interested in his work and finding his greatest
        delight in new experiments." He has shown "infinite
        variety in subject and treatment." "The charm of this
        tale is its idyllic simplicity."

1097   "Bloodthirsty Civilizers." Boston Evening Transcript, 21 Mar
        1896, p. 14. Editorial.
            A scene from A Chance Acquaintance in which the Saquenay
        excursion boat delays passage for a lone Englishman is
        used as an analogue to American willingness to accept
        British military activity.

1098   "Literature." Independent, 48 (26 Mar 1896), 422. Brief re-
        view of The Day of Their Wedding.
            "Mr. Howells is writing against the grain of his true
        feelings." He should let go his "affectation of pessimism."
        The reader feels betrayed when "what he thought was a pair
        of human beings turns out to be a couple of bloodless
        effigies."

1896

1099   "Book Notices." Bachelor of Arts, 2 (Apr 1896), 719-720.
       Review of The Day of Their Wedding.
          A delightful return to Howells' "earlier, simpler man-
       ner." "Here is high art."

1100   BARRY, JOHN D. "New York Letter." Literary World, 27 (18 Apr
       1896), 120-121. Brief reference.
          Notes Howells' public praise of Crane and his early
       recognition of Crane's talent.

1101   "New Books / A Parting and a Meeting." Boston Evening Tran-
       script, 21 Apr 1896, p. 6. Brief review.
          "Its improbability does not in the least interfere with
       its interest."

1102   ALBRO, HELENA J. "The Day of Their Wedding." Bookman (New
       York), 3 (May 1896), 258-260. Full review.
          Largely summary. The novel is a delightful romance
       characteristic of Howells' early work. Lorenzo is remi-
       niscent of Lemuel Barker in The Minister's Charge.

1103   "Book Notices." Bachelor of Arts, 2 (May 1896), 860. Brief
       reference.
          In review of George Meredith's The Amazing Marriage,
       Meredith's "imaginative literature" is contrasted with
       Howells' "thoughtfully reportorial, graphic" art.

1104   "The New Books." Review of Reviews, 13 (May 1896), 630.
       Brief review of The Day of Their Wedding.
          "A pathetic little story" done with naturalness and
       realism.

1105   NORRIS, FRANK. "Theory and Reality / An Old Author and a New
       Writer Consider the Same Problem." Wave, 15 (2 May 1896),
       8. Review of A Parting and a Meeting (along with Mrs.
       J. R. Jarboe's Robert Atterbury). Rpt. The Literary
       Criticism of Frank Norris, ed. Donald Pizer (Austin: Uni-
       versity of Texas Press, 1964), 161-162.
          Critical contrast favoring Howells. While managing a
       sex problem "lightly, delicately, handling it with the
       greatest subtlety and finesse," he tells a story. Readers
       become so involved with the characters that they are un-
       aware of the author.

1106   "Their Wedding Day [sic]." Critic, n.s. 25 (2 May 1896), 307.
       Review.
          Largely summary, treated lightly. The book features
       "all the usual doorsill profundities of the realistic

("Their Wedding Day")
    novel." Howells always handles ministers much better than
    do most theological schools.

1107   "Book Reviews." American (Philadelphia), 24 (9 May 1896),
       302. Brief notice of A Parting and a Meeting.
       In itself lacks clarity.

1108   "Current Fiction." Literary World, 27 (16 May 1896), 154.
       Brief review of The Day of Their Wedding.
       Howells is "rampantly realistic."

1109   DROCH [ROBERT BRIDGES]. "Life's Tips to Summer Readers."
       Life, 27 (28 May 1896), 442. Brief mention of A Parting
       and a Meeting and The Day of Their Wedding.
       "In both Howells returns to the poetic manner which was
    the charm of his early novel, The Undiscovered Country."

1110   RICHARDS, F. T. "Life's Literary Side Show." Life, 27
       (28 May 1896), 434-435. Double-page cartoon. Rpt. in
       reduced form in Review of Reviews, 14 (Jul 1896), 109.
       Posters of literary figures mounted on side-show tent
    wall. Caricature "W. D. Howells as Weary Waggles" flanks
    entrance.

1111   PAYNE, WILLIAM MORTON. "Recent Fiction." Dial, 20 (1 Jun
       1896), 335. Brief review of The Day of Their Wedding and
       A Parting and a Meeting.
       "Mr. Howells has a weakness for queer people, and a
    disposition to find the salt of the earth where few would
    be likely to look for it."

1112   [Untitled.] Life, 27 (4 Jun 1896), 452. Note.
       Editorial paragraph disagreeing with Howells' opinion of
    tipping.

1113   "A Parting and a Meeting." Critic, n.s. 25 (6 Jun 1896),
       405-406. Review.
       This booklet is "the most perfect November pastoral in
    brown and yellow tints" Howells has produced.

1114   "Literature / Recent Fiction." Independent, 48 (11 Jun 1896),
       805. Brief review of A Parting and a Meeting.
       "If a story must have something over and above mere
    style to make it interesting," this one is scarcely medi-
    ocre. "The hero and the heroine are milksaps of the
    feeblest and shallowest sort."

1896

1115   "Current Fiction Classified / Adventists and Shakers."
       Literary World, 27 (27 Jun 1896), 204. Brief review of
       A Parting and a Meeting.
         "It is a rather tame mistake all around, even to the
       writing."

1116   NORRIS, FRANK. "Zola as a Romantic Writer." Wave, 15
       (27 Jun 1896), 3. Brief reference. Rpt. The Literary
       Criticism of Frank Norris, ed. Donald Pizer (Austin:
       University of Texas Press, 1964), pp. 71-72.
         Howells' characters "live across the street from us....
       We know all about them, about their affairs, and the story
       of their lives." Although he uses "the smaller details of
       every-day life," Howells "is not uninteresting; he is
       simply not romantic."

1117   HUTTON, LAURENCE. "Literary Notes." Harper's, 93 (Jul 1896),
       3. Review of A Parting and a Meeting.
       A "short but sweet" story.

  *   "Life's Literary Side Show." Review of Reviews, 14 (Jul 1896),
       109. Cartoon. Rpt. in reduced form from Life, 27 (28 May
       1896), 434-435. See item 1110.

1118   WILCOX, MARRION. "Works of William Dean Howells--(1860-96)."
       Harper's Weekly, 40 (4 Jul 1896), 655-656. Note.
       A survey of Howells' contributions to date, preceding
       the first serial installment of The Landlord at Lion's
       Head. Wilcox observes that Howells' early interest in
       scenery gives way to focus on human beings and concludes
       that nowhere is one to find a more able and revealing
       record of what is distinctively American life. Large
       portrait (p. 656).

1119   "New Publications / Recent Fiction." New Orleans Times-
       Democrat, 12 Jul 1896, p. 20. Very brief review of Their
       Wedding Day and A Parting and a Meeting.
         Their Wedding Day is "one of the very prettiest and
       sweetest stories Howells ever wrote." In A Parting and a
       Meeting, "the situation of Their Wedding Day is reversed."

1120   DROCH [ROBERT BRIDGES]. "Three Kinds of Gloom." Life, 28
       (30 Jul 1896), 80. Brief reference.
         In a review of Cornelia Pratt's The Daughter of a Stoic,
       The Rise of Silas Lapham is mentioned.

1121   "Book Notices." Bachelor of Arts, 3 (Aug-Sep 1896), 435-438.
       Review of Stops of Various Quills.
         Omar Khayyam and his solemnity are visible in this verse.
       "Howells prefers the optimistic theory--but is forced to
       be a pessimist" (p. 437).

1122   "Howells Discovers a Negro Poet." Los Angeles Times, 18 Oct
        1896, p. 23. Note.
            Largely quotations from Howells' introduction to collec-
        tion of Paul Dunbar's poems. [Nichol]

1123   "Book Reviews / Their Wedding Journey." Overland, 2nd ser.,
        28 (Nov 1896), 608. Very brief comment on reissue.
        A better wedding trip would be one to the Far West.

1124   "New Books / Mr. Howells' Impressions and Experiences."
        Philadelphia Press, 1 Nov 1896, p. 36. Review. Rpt.
        Book News, 15 (Dec 1896), 186.
            The opening essay, "The Country Printer," is especially
        pleasing. It clearly portrays a time and situation. "It
        is pervaded by that spirit of effervescent humor and good
        humor--two very different things--characteristic of the
        better part of Mr. Howells' writing."

1125   "Literary Notes." Los Angeles Times, 8 Nov 1896, p. 16.
            Brief mention of forthcoming A Pair of Patient Lovers and
        Ragged Lady. [Nichol]

1126   "Literary Notes." Los Angeles Times, 15 Nov 1896, p. 20.
        Brief mention.
            Announcement of Howells' forthcoming work and recogni-
        tion of Mildred Howells as an accomplished illustrator.
        [Nichol]

1127   "Mr. W. D. Howells's Impressions." Spectator, 77 (21 Nov
        1896), 730. Review of Impressions and Experiences.
            They are "sketched with microscopical detail, lighted
        up with a keen sense of humour, and also shaded with
        seriousness when occasion requires." But Howells includes
        nothing of his literary tastes!

1128   "Impressions and Experiences." Academy, 50 (28 Nov 1896),
        453. Brief review.
            Howells is not in his own element here.

1129   "Our Library Table." Athenaeum, No. 3605 (28 Nov 1896), 755.
            Very brief review of Impressions and Experiences.
            Howells' life, as he chooses to show it, "has not
        furnished matter of great interest."

1130   "Contemporary Literature / Belles Lettres." Westminster Re-
        view, 146 (Dec 1896), 706-707. Brief notice of Impres-
        sions and Experiences.
            "The fragrance of the best brand of American humour per-
        vades this brilliant collection."

1896

1131   HUTTON, LAURENCE. "Literary Notes." Harper's, 94 (Dec 1896),
        1-2. Review of Impressions and Experiences.
            "If Mr. Howells had gone to a less practical college we
        might never have had the pleasure of his Chance Acquaint-
        ance, or the benefit of the many good things we have
        gained from him since."

  *   [Impressions and Experiences.] Book News, 15 (Dec 1896), 186.
        Review. Rpt. from Philadelphia Press, 1 Nov 1896, p. 36.
        See item 1124.

1132   "Review of Books / Reminiscences by Mr. Howells." New York
        Times, 5 Dec 1896, Sat. Sup., p. 2. Full review of Im-
        pressions and Experiences.
            "It is not every man who is so safe as Mr. Howells in
        taking himself for his subject." Howells has contributed
        "a long and creditable list" of books.

1133   "Howells's Recollections of Holmes." Literary Digest, 14
        (12 Dec 1896), 171-172. Note.
            Response to the current Harper's essay. "There is a
        tenderness of touch, a fine discrimination in phrase, a
        loving analysis of character, such as few writers of our
        day are capable of exhibiting."

1134   "Mr. Howells's Impressions and Experiences." Literary World,
        27 (12 Dec 1896), 446-447. Review.
            One-half quotation. All subjects are "touched with Mr.
        Howells's distinguishing grace and felicity of phrase,
        and...[his] passionate sense of humanity."

1135   "Impressions and Experiences." Nation, 63 (24 Dec 1896),
        481-482. Full review.
            Howells "has carried his pathological studies far
        enough; let him come back to wholesome conditions, and
        once more show us some sound specimens of humanity, even
        if he has to idealize a little in doing it."

                            1897

1136   "Mr. Howells's Views." Critic, n.s. 27 (2 Jan 1897), 5. Re-
        view of "Impressions and Opinions [sic]." Rpt. in part,
        The War of the Critics over William Dean Howells, ed.
        Edwin H. Cady and David L. Frazier (Evanston: Row, Peter-
        son, 1962), pp. 72-73.
            Howells has lost heart; on the whole his impressions of
        our civilization are "too bad to be true."

1137   "Idyls in Drab." Saturday Review, 83 (16 Jan 1897), 68.
        Full review.
            Howells "was really meant to be serenely and humorously
        an idealist." In these two stories he returns from his
        militant realism to be true to himself, "and we are free
        to observe how subtle and how penetrating an observer he
        can be."

1138   "Literary Notes." Los Angeles Times, 24 Jan 1897, p. 20.
        Brief mention.
            "Maurice Thompson has no higher idea of Dickens than
        William Dean Howells has." [Nichol]

1139   PECK, HARRY THURSTON. "Living Critics / XII.--William Dean
        Howells." Bookman (New York), 4 (Feb 1897), 529-541.
        Major essay. Rpt. The Personal Equation (New York:
        Harper, 1898), pp. 3-49; and in part, The War of the
        Critics over William Dean Howells, ed. Edwin H. Cady and
        David L. Frazier (Evanston: Row, Peterson, 1962), pp. 74-
        81.
            "One cannot even touch upon [Howells'] literary criti-
        cism without feeling it is in reality only a part, and a
        comparatively unimportant part, of his wider criticism of
        life." The essay discusses Howells' abilities, his criti-
        cal concepts, his artistic accomplishments. Special con-
        sideration is given to A Boy's Town, A Modern Instance,
        The Rise of Silas Lapham, The Lady of the Aroostook, and
        Stops of Various Quills.

1140   "W. D. Howells." Bookman (New York), 4 (Feb 1897), 512.
        Portrait.

1141   "Book Notes." Citizen (Philadelphia), 3 (Mar 1897), 20.
        Brief review of Impressions and Experiences.
            Howells' "keen and practiced eye" penetrates the surface
        to reveal "human wretchedness and folly."

1142   FREDERIC, HAROLD. "How To Write a Short Story." Bookman
        (New York), 5 (Mar 1897), 44-45. Part II of a symposium
        shared with Robert Barr, Arthur Morrison, and Jane Barlow.
            Brief reference to "Howells's incomparably beautiful A
        Parting and a Meeting" accompanies the suggestion that
        Howells' work is generally too long to be classed in a
        "short" category.

1143   LEE, ALBERT. "A Bibliography of the First Editions of the
        Writings of W. D. Howells." Book Buyer, n.s. 14 (Mar
        1897), 143-147; (Apr 1897), 269-274. Descriptive listing.

1897

(LEE, ALBERT)
The April installment concludes "Part I--The Writings
of W. D. Howells" and contains entire "Part II--Books
Edited, or Contributed to, by W. D. Howells."

1144   S., E. B.   "Human Warious."   Book Buyer, n.s. 14 (Mar 1897),
188-189. Review of "Memories and Impressions [sic]"
(Compared to Isaac Zangwill's Without Prejudice).
Reminiscent essays such as these provide "so many more
cross sections of the author than are generally found in
novels."

1145   "Literary Items."   Boston Evening Transcript, 1 Mar 1897,
p. 6. Brief mention.
The first installment of The Story of a Play is "less
probable and more interesting than usual."

1146   "Notes."   Critic, n.s. 27 (13 Mar 1897), 191. Brief reference.
Major Pond has engaged Howells for fifty lyceum lectures
on "Novel-writing and Novel-reading: An Impersonal
Explanation."

1147   "Books of the Day / Mr. Howells's Impressions and Experiences."
Boston Evening Transcript, 24 Mar 1897, p. 9. Full review.
Howells "observes with a moral always, sometimes en-
forced with biting sarcasm, sometimes with wistful
resignation."

1148   "Personal."   New York Times, 28 Mar 1897, p. 16. Brief edi-
torial.
Comments on the humor and condescension in the Oswego
Times coverage (not seen) of a speech entitled "Novels and
Novel Writing" by Howells.

1149   HUTTON, LAURENCE. "Literary Notes." Harper's, 94 (Apr 1897),
1. Review of A Previous Engagement.
This comedy, "pure and simple," features "bright and
sparkling" dialogue and a plot which "turns upon what Mr.
Howells himself once termed 'hen-mindedness.'"

1150   "The Landlord at Lion's Head." Harper's, 94 (Apr 1897),
Advertiser, p. 5. Advertisement.
"The development of Jefferson Durgin, the chief figure
in this novel from a country lad to a Harvard under-
graduate, affords Mr. Howells an opportunity to contrast
two distinctive features of our social life. The city
types he presents with his familiar skill and subtle humor,
and his pictures of rustic New England are delineated with

("The Landlord at Lion's Head")
exquisite feeling both for nature and for homely character.
His study of young Durgin deserves to rank among his most
complex, searching, and finished portraits, and in Cynthia
Whitwell he has drawn one of the most interesting and
lovable women that he has as yet given us." The story im-
presses one with its "absolute reality."

1151 "Books of the Week / Mr. Howells' New Novel." Chicago Daily
Tribune, 17 Apr 1897, p. 10. Full review of The Landlord
at Lion's Head.
Howells is more effective in portraying things as they
are than as they should be. "His excursions into Altruria
are dreary, while his excursions into New England life are
always instructive, often interesting, and sometimes
pleasing." This novel combines these three desirable
qualities.

1152 "Important 'Vexed Questions.'" New York Times, 17 Apr 1897,
Sat. Sup., p. 4. Brief reference.
"Mr. Howells has finally decided that Dickens is greater
than Thackeray, and as likely as not he will presently define 'genius' and express its relation to 'talent,' if it
have any, and describe the attributes of a perfect
gentleman."

1153 "New Publications / Lyrics of Lowly Life." New Orleans Times-
Democrat, 18 Apr 1897, p. 28. Review of Paul Dunbar's
collection of verse introduced by Howells.
"If Mr. Howells were better acquainted with the negroes
and their dialect, and with existing literature for which
their peculiarities of speech and action afforded inspiration, he would see that Mr. Dunbar's dialect pieces are
far from being his best."

1154 "The Lounger." Critic, n.s. 27 (24 Apr 1897), 290. Brief
reference.
The Critic errored in citing Howells' recent work as
Impressions and Opinions and the Book-Buyer also errored
by referring to it as Memories and Impressions.

1155 "Recent Novels." Spectator, 78 (24 Apr 1897), 597. Review
of The Landlord at Lion's Head. Rpt. Book News, 15 (Jun
1897), 518-519.
An "admirable romance of north New England." The reviewer contrasts it with Gertrude Atherton's Patience Spar-
hawk and Her Times.

1897

1156 "William Dean Howells." Literary Digest, 14 (24 Apr 1897),
      761. Portrait. "Books and Authors / Novels and Tales."
      Outlook, 56 (1 May 1897), 78-79. Review of The Landlord
      at Lion's Head.
          "It required the genius of W. D. Howells to put the sum-
      mer hotel into a novel in such a way as to suggest almost
      every passion that moves men and women, and to typify in
      the hotel's evolution from a farm-house to a fashionable
      mountain resort the evolution of character of those who
      controlled its destiny."

1157 "Literary Items." Boston Evening Transcript, 8 May 1897,
      p. 20. Brief notice of The Landlord at Lion's Head.
          Howells "has produced a novel marked by rare subtlety
      in its presentation of contrasting types of character and
      by exquisite beauty in its feeling for nature."

1158 "New Books / A Previous Engagement." Boston Evening Tran-
      script, 15 May 1897, p. 20. Brief mention.
          Sketches plot and notes Howells' "felicitous style."

1159 PAYNE, WILLIAM MORTON. "Recent Fiction." Dial, 22 (16 May
      1897), 310. Brief review of The Landlord at Lion's Head.
      "Not altogether worthy of the author."

1160 "Literature / Recent Fiction." Independent, 49 (20 May 1897),
      650. Review of The Landlord at Lion's Head.
          "We recognize with pleasure the good things in this
      story"; but "since Mr. Howells dropped himself for Tolstoi
      we have no right to expect pleasing stories from his pen;
      he chooses disagreeable people and uninteresting circum-
      stances."

1161 "American Fiction." Athenaeum, No. 3630 (22 May 1897), 678.
      Brief review of The Landlord at Lion's Head.
          On other occasions Howells has had "happier inspiration,
      but he has seldom done a better piece of work."

1162 "New American Fiction." New York Times, 22 May 1897, Sat.
      Sup., p. 4. Brief review of The Landlord at Lion's Head.
          "The sense of reality one derives from the story is
      strengthened by the minuteness and clearness of Mr.
      Howells's observation." Howells can be detected behind
      his puppets.

1163 DROCH [ROBERT BRIDGES]. "The Perils of Summer Resorts in Fic-
      tion." Life, 29 (27 May 1897), 447. Includes review of
      The Landlord at Lion's Head.

(DROCH [ROBERT BRIDGES])
"What Mr. Howells is really after in a story is a Man,
and in this case the hotel business is simply incidental
to Jeff Durgin." The "action" in the story is listed.

1164   "Literary Notes." Life, 29 (27 May 1897), 438. Brief reference.
"Among the forthcoming notable works will be Mr. Howells's
thrilling tale of 'Blackbeard the Pirate; or, The Bond of
Blood.'"

1165   BARRY, JOHN D. "New York Letter." Literary World, 28 (29 May
1897), 176. Brief reference.
Howells has scheduled a trip to Carlsbad for his health.

1166   "Contemporary Literature / Belles Lettres." Westminster Review, 147 (Jun 1897), 714. Brief notice of The Landlord
at Lion's Head.
The opening is reminiscent of Nathaniel Hawthorne's
work. Howells "gives us a real live story."

1167   HUTTON, LAURENCE. "Literary Notes." Harper's, 95 (Jun 1897),
3. Review of The Landlord at Lion's Head.
Howells has given much care and thought to the portrayal
of the complex nature of Jeff Durgin.

*   "The Landlord at Lion's Head." Book News, 15 (Jun 1897), 518-
519. Rpt. from Spectator, 78 (24 Apr 1897), 597. See
item 1155.

1168   LANIER, HENRY W. "The Season's Output in Fiction." Review
of Reviews, 15 (Jun 1897), 753. Brief review of The Landlord at Lion's Head.
"One feels that as big a man as Mr. Howells, a man with
such capacity for felicitous expression and for the perception of human character--such a one ought to carry his
audience with him more surely."

1169   WELLS, BENJAMIN W. "Contemporary American Essayists." Forum,
23 (Jun 1897), 487-496. Essay.
Howells as essayist is discussed on pp. 491-494. "Mr.
Howells has the great advantage that comes from a well-
defined standard and a positive aesthetic creed"; but in
Criticism and Fiction he is "a somewhat dangerous guide,
except to those trained not only to read and understand,
but also to weigh and consider."

1897

1170   "With the New Books." Book News, 15 (Jun 1897), 506-507.
Brief review of The Landlord at Lion's Head.
Howells' readers "seek analysis, not creation, and they
will not be disappointed." Howells is "an amiable philoso-
pher who moralizes his own neighborhood."

1171   "Literature / The Landlord at Lion's Head." Critic, n.s. 27
(19 Jun 1897), 420. Full review.
"It may be taken simply as one of [Howells'] most conscientious studies of American life and conditions...."
"But probably that reader who regards the book as a piece
of special pleading, a putting of Providence on trial for
creating a world in which the Jeff Durgins are successful
and happy men, will extract from it a keener pleasure."

1172   BARRY, JOHN D. "Human Beings in New England." Book Buyer,
n.s. 14 (Jul 1897), 598-600. Full review of The Landlord
at Lion's Head.
Highly favorable. The novel reveals "the matured mind,
the sobered thought, and--it is hard to say it--the pessi-
mistic outlook." Emphasis is given to Howells' insight
into New England life and his skill in character conception and portrayal.

1173   "The Rambler." Book Buyer, n.s. 14 (Jul 1897), 558-559.
Brief note. Rpt. Literary News, 18 (Oct 1897), 313.
Howells, in giving a collected edition of his books to
a friend, recorded his opinion of each book on the fly-
leaf. Nine of his "confessions" are printed here.

1174   [LOGAN, ANNIE R. M.] "Recent Fiction." Nation, 65 (1 Jul
1897), 16-17. Review of The Landlord at Lion's Head.
Jeff Durgin ranks with Silas Lapham and Bartley Hubbard
as Howells' most vivid characterization--Durgin being perhaps the most striking and effective "for he has more of
the uncommon, the unexpected." He is not a "settled conspicuous type, but an incarnation of signs of the times."

1175   HINTON, RICHARD J. "The Howells Family." Voice (New York),
15 Jul 1897, p. 6. Biographical sketch. Rpt. Journal of
the Rutgers University Library, 14 (Dec 1950), 14-23.
A profile, containing some inaccuracies, of the William
Cooper Howells family.

1176   WELLS, CAROLYN. "ABC of Literature." Life, 30 (22 Jul 1897),
68. Limerick.

(WELLS, CAROLYN)
"H is for William Dean Howells,
    As wise as the wisest of owls;
    The subject of jokes
    Of frivolous folks,
At which he good-naturedly growls."

1177   "Book Reviews." American (Philadelphia), 27 (31 Jul 1897),
       77-79. Full review of The Landlord at Lion's Head.
       The characters "are carefully modelled in apple-dumpling
       fashion, which makes them an excellent and safe substitute
       for a richer dinner." Howells' work is exact, but lacks
       pith. (The review is highly over-written.)

1178   "Contemporary Literature / Belles Lettres." Westminster Re-
       view, 148 (Aug 1897), 231. Brief notice of The Mouse Trap.
       Howells "can unbend, when he is in the mood, to such an
       extent that he can extract the material of a comedy out of
       a harmless practical joke."

1179   "Contemporary Literature / Belles Lettres." Westminster Re-
       view, 148 (Aug 1897), 234. Brief notice of Evening Dress.
       "Charming and natural," and totally void of vulgarity.

1180   COOPER, JOHN A. "Bellamy and Howells, A Comparison and Some
       Remarks." Canadian Magazine, 9 (Aug 1897), 344-346.
       Short essay.
       Howells is relatively satisfied, Bellamy discontent.
       "Perhaps the true thinker would be a man who is slightly
       less complacent than Mr. Howells, and slightly less de-
       sirous of economic revolution than Mr. Bellamy."

1181   "A Handful of Harper's Novels." Literary World, 28 (7 Aug
       1897), 262-263. Brief review of A Landlord at Lion's
       Head.
       "The skunk-cabbage is not a soul-inspiring plant, how-
       ever carefully analyzed."

1182   "Literary Notes." Los Angeles Times, 29 Aug 1897, p. 20.
       Brief mention.
       Announcement of publication of An Open-Eyed Conspiracy
       set for 3 September by Harper & Bros. [Nichol]
       [A series of similar announcements of Howells' current
       and forthcoming publications may be found scattered through
       the subsequent "Literary Notes" and "Magazines of the
       Month" columns in the Los Angeles Times.]

1897

1183   "Literary Comment." Los Angeles Times, 5 Sep 1897, p. 14.
        Brief mention.
            Howells includes Spain's Emila Pardo Bazan among his
        three favorite novelists. [Nichol]

1184   "Mr. Howells as Editor." Los Angeles Times, 26 Sep 1897,
        p. 17. Brief note.
            Prints an acceptance letter Howells once wrote to Miss
        [Lucy] Larcom when he was editor of Atlantic, and suggests
        that authors return to the editors their letters of accep-
        tance or rejection as a great source for biographical
        material. [Nichol]

1185   "Contemporary Literature / Belles Lettres." Westminster Re-
        view, 148 (Oct 1897), 474. Very brief notice of The
        Garotters.
            In many respects the best of Howells' "'dramalettes.'"

   *   "Literary Miscellany / Mr. Howells His Own Critic." Literary
        News, 18 (Oct 1897), 313. Rpt. from Book Buyer, n.s. 14
        (Jul 1897), 558-559. See item 1173.

1186   MURRAY, D. C. "My Contemporaries in Fiction." Canadian
        Magazine, 9 (Oct 1897), 497. Brief reference.
            Howells is "more essentially a man" than is James.

1187   "With the New Books." Book News, 16 (Oct 1897), 60. Very
        brief review of An Open-Eyed Conspiracy.
            Howells at his best--"No more social problems, no more
        wearisome desire to set the world right, no prosing, a
        dear delicious American love-story at Saratoga."

1188   "Fiction from Famous Hands." New York Times, 9 Oct 1897,
        Sat. Sup., pp. 1-2. Full review of An Open-Eyed Conspiracy.
            "One of the delicately carved cherry stones which
        [Howells] flings from his hand with marvelous rapidity."
        Although it is "a trivial tale upon a hackneyed theme" and
        although the heroine is stupid and the hero a bare out-
        line, "the book is not without its piquancy and charm--
        which is only another way of saying that it is written by
        Mr. Howells."

1189   "A Mark Twainism." Los Angeles Times, 10 Oct 1897, p. 17.
        Brief note.
            Boyesen once declared that, among American writers,
        only Twain and Howells made comfortable livings from their
        books. [Nichol]

1190　"Current Fiction." Literary World, 28 (16 Oct 1897), 355.
　　　　Very brief review of An Open-Eyed Conspiracy.
　　　　It may disillusion Howells' admirers.

1191　"Fiction." Saturday Review, 84 (23 Oct 1897), 450. Brief
　　　　mention of The Garroters and Five O'Clock Tea.
　　　　　"Mere outlines, done with a turn of the wrist." "An
　　　　astonishing vivid effect is produced with half a dozen
　　　　strokes."

1192　"Contemporary Literature / Belles Lettres." Westminster Re-
　　　　view, 148 (Nov 1897), 596. Brief notice of Five O'Clock
　　　　Tea.
　　　　　"It is refreshing to turn from inflated scribblers" to
　　　　a writer who can write artistically about "the small as
　　　　well as the great things of life."

1193　"The Extraordinary Advance Sale of the Warner Library."
　　　　Harper's, 95 (Nov 1897), Advertiser, p. 18. Advertise-
　　　　ment.
　　　　　One half of this full-page advertisement of the Warner
　　　　Library is given to a portrait of Howells. The caption
　　　　reads, "William Dean Howells / America's foremost living
　　　　novelist and man of letters, has written for the Warner
　　　　Library a brilliant study of the greatest of Russian nov-
　　　　elists, Tolstoy."

1194　HUTTON, LAURENCE. "Literary Notes." Harper's, 95 (Nov 1897),
　　　　2-3. Review of An Open-Eyed Conspiracy.
　　　　　"We are always glad to renew our acquaintance with the
　　　　Marches."

1195　"A Meissonier at Saratoga." Book Buyer, n.s. 15 (Nov 1897),
　　　　364-365. Full review of An Open-Eyed Conspiracy.
　　　　　"The very tenuousness of the motive makes the fine art
　　　　of its management seem all the finer."

1196　MORRISSEY, J. J. "Disease in Modern Fiction." Catholic
　　　　World, 66 (Nov 1897), 240-248. Brief reference.
　　　　　A doctor, discussing fictional portrayal of disease,
　　　　comments on Howells' use of "the white blight" in The
　　　　Landlord at Lion's Head.

1197　[WARNER, CHARLES DUDLEY.] "Editor's Study." Harper's, 95
　　　　(Nov 1897), 961-962. Review of The Landlord at Lion's
　　　　Head.
　　　　　"It is conspicuous for its maturity.... The touch is
　　　　always that of the artist, and the touch is sure. The

1897

([WARNER, CHARLES DUDLEY])
   result is the ripened observation of certain phases of
   New England life." The personality of Howells is
   pervasive.

1198   "Mr. Howells's Trip Abroad / He Gives Some of His Impressions
   in an Entertaining Chat." New York Tribune, 10 Nov 1897,
   p. 6. Interview. Rpt. in part, Critic, 31 (13 Nov 1897),
   290; abstr. "Interviews with William Dean Howells," ed.
   Ulrich Halfmann, American Literary Realism, 6 (Fall 1973),
   330.
      Howells talks about his travels, his recent work, his
   plans for the immediate future.

1199   "Minor Mention / Some New Novels." American (Philadelphia),
   27 (13 Nov 1897), 317. Very brief review of An Open-Eyed
   Conspiracy.
      "Mr. Howells entangles his reader's curiosity from the
   start by his artless garrulity, which is one of the
   subtlest secrets of his art."

1200   "Mr. Howells at Home Again." Critic, n.s. 28 (13 Nov 1897),
   290. Interview. Rpt. from New York Tribune, 10 Nov 1897,
   p. 6. See item 1198.
      Also contains paragraph account of an interview in Paris
   in which Howells notes that American writers are becoming
   "more distinctively American." Rpt. "Interviews with
   William Dean Howells," ed. Ulrich Halfmann, American
   Literary Realism, 6 (Fall 1973), 330-331.

1201   PAYNE, WILLIAM MORTON. "Recent Fiction." Dial, 23 (16 Nov
   1897), 284. Brief review of An Open-Eyed Conspiracy.
      Howells is better in short pieces than in long ones,
   which tend to become "wearisome."

1202   DROCH [ROBERT BRIDGES]. "A Handful of Stories." Life, 30
   (18 Nov 1897), 410. Brief comment on An Open-Eyed Conspiracy.
      "Another delightful impression of Saratoga in its de-
   cline." The story ends "right," but Howells "has his
   doubts of the unalloyed happiness in store for the rash
   lovers."

1203   "Literature / Recent Fiction." Independent, 49 (25 Nov 1897),
   1546. Review of An Open-Eyed Conspiracy.
      "We would walk five miles before breakfast to take Mr.
   Howells by the hand and tell him how glad we are that he
   has at last returned from Altruria, and Bohemia, and

("Literature / Recent Fiction")
Tolstoia, and all the other fad-burdened regions, bringing under his arm this charming story of Saratoga lovers."

1204 "The New Books / I. - Some American Novels and Novelists."
Review of Reviews, 16 (Dec 1897), 753. Brief review of
An Open-Eyed Conspiracy.
"A true picture of...[a] phase of our American life and society."

1205 "Notable Recent Novels." Atlantic, 80 (Dec 1897), 859. Full
review of An Open-Eyed Conspiracy.
Howells has for so long been "almost morbidly preoccu-
pied with American types and social portents and problems
that it is a great pleasure to find him...dropping into
something like the gay and engaging manner of former
days." Mrs. March is "as defiantly impulsive and illogi-
cal, as inconsistently concerned and as incurably sympathetic with youthful romance, as ever."

1206 "A Selection of Books Suitable for Holiday Gifts." Harper's,
96 (Dec 1897), Advertiser, 39-40. Advertisement.
A full paragraph is given to three books by Howells:
An Open-Eyed Conspiracy and The Landlord at Lion's Head,
"both of which display his skill in characterization and
his finely balanced style," and A Previous Engagement, a
farce that "moves with delightful briskness." In The
Landlord at Lion's Head Howells "has produced a novel
marked by subtlety in its presentation of contrasting
types of character, and by exquisite beauty in its feeling
for nature, the opening chapters making one of the best
pictures of the New England country ever achieved in our
literature."

1207 BARRY, JOHN D. "New York Letter." Literary World, 28 (11 Dec
1897), 458-459. Note.
Brief mention of Howells' return from Europe and description of his working habits. Critics of Howells are beginning to recognize his importance as an interpreter of American life. He is a man of "extraordinary human sympathy
and nobility of character."

1208 "In Memory of Lowell." Life, 30 (16 Dec 1897), 536. Brief
reference.
Howells participates in soliciting funds for a memorial
park.

1897

1209   "The Lounger." Critic, n.s. 28 (18 Dec 1897), 384. Note.
       Briefly takes issue with John D. Barry writing to
       Literary World about the fashion to sneer at Howells'
       novels. "We are too fond of Mr. Howells and too proud of
       his accomplishment as a writer of fiction to sneer at any-
       thing he may do."

1898

1210   BATES, KATHARINE LEE. American Literature. New York: Mac-
       millan, 1898. Pp. 324-325 and passim as indexed. Nine
       scattered minor references.
           Howells is "an American product." "Something heavenly
       shines through the humdrum" (p. 325).

1211   EVANS, E. P. Beträge zur Amerikanische Litteratur- und Kul-
       turgeschichte. Stuttgart: J. G. Cotta'schen Buckhand-
       lung, 1898. Pp. 109, 125. Minor references.
           Calls for representation of Howells and other American
       authors in Tauchnitz editions.

1212   GRISWOLD, HATTIE TYNG. "William Dean Howells." Personal
       Sketches of Recent Authors. Chicago: McClurg, 1898.
       Pp. 209-228. Biographical essay.
           A rather superficial profile of a literary man, depending
       heavily on quotation from his own work. Howells lives "in
       the realm of books." Full-page portrait of Howells in fur-
       collared coat (facing p. 209).

1213   HOWE, M. A. De WOLFE. American Bookmen / Sketches, Chiefly
       Biographical, of Certain Writers of the Nineteenth Century.
       New York: Dodd, Mead, 1898. Passim as indexed. Minor
       references.
           In most cases Howells is quoted.

1214   PANCOAST, HENRY S. An Introduction to American Literature.
       New York: Holt, 1898. Pp. 311-313 and passim as indexed.
       General biographical and critical introduction.
           Howells' "books are full of characters which are the
       unmistakable outcome of our peculiar conditions." They
       "move against a background of more than photographic re-
       ality and distinctness."

  *   PECK, HARRY THURSTON. "William Dean Howells." The Personal
       Equation. New York and London: Harper, 1898. Pp. 3-49.
       Rpt. from Bookman (New York), 4 (Feb 1897), 529-541. See
       item 1139.

1215   [LOGAN, ANNIE R. M.] "Recent Fiction." Nation, 66 (6 Jan
       1898), 16. Brief review of An Open-Eyed Conspiracy.
       "Slight as the episode is, it attracts attention to a
       change amounting to transformation that American social
       life has undergone in the last ten or fifteen years."

1216   G. "Mr. Howells' Socialism." American Fabian, 4 (Feb 1898),
       1-2. Interview. Rpt. in part, Literary Digest, 16 (19 Mar
       1898), 340-341; Howells / A Century of Criticism, ed. Ken-
       neth E. Eble (Dallas: Southern Methodist University
       Press, 1962), pp. 62-64; and "Interviews with William
       Dean Howells," ed. Ulrich Halfmann, American Literary
       Realism, 6 (Fall 1973), 331-333.
       Howells is warmly hailed as a brother Socialist.
       Portrait (p. 1).

1217   "As Howells Sees Fiction / The Novelist Talks on the Tenden-
       cies of the Day." New York Sun, 6 Feb 1898, p. 3. Inter-
       view. Rpt. "An Interview with Howells," ed. James Woodress,
       American Literary Realism, 3 (Winter 1970), 71-75; "Inter-
       views with William Dean Howells," ed. Ulrich Halfmann,
       American Literary Realism, 6 (Fall 1973), 333-336.
       Subtitled "The Naturalistic School Has Come To Stay,
       Although It May Be Developed Along Physical Lines--The
       Great American Novelist To Come from the Middle West--
       Women's Place in Fiction Writing."

1218   "American Letter." Literature, 2 (26 Feb 1898), 236. Note.
       Report on and response to the New York Sun interview
       immediately above.

1219   "Authors at Home / XIX. William Dean Howells in Central Park
       South." New York Times, 26 Feb 1898, Sat. Sup., p. 136.
       Interview. Rpt. in part, Current Literature, 23 (May
       1898), 402-403; rpt. slightly rev., American Authors and
       Their Homes / Personal Descriptions & Interviews, ed.
       Francis Whiting Halsey (New York: James Pott, 1901),
       pp. 99-109; also rpt. "Interviews with William Dean
       Howells," ed. Ulrich Halfmann, American Literary Realism,
       6 (Fall 1973), 337-339.
       An impression of Howells and a description of the appro-
       priate setting of his apartment precede an exchange on
       literary matters.

1220   CARPENTER, G. R. "The Neo-Romantic Novel." Forum, 25 (Mar
       1898), 120-128. Brief reference.
       Although Carpenter concedes to Howells and Brander
       Matthews that romance may be a genus of lower order than

1898

(CARPENTER, G. R.)
literature that deals with life as it is (p. 120), the
fact remains "that any sort of theory about what art or
literature should do is of very slight importance in comparison with a knowledge of what it does do" (p. 121).

1221   "Contemporary Literature / Belles Lettres." Westminster Review, 149 (Mar 1898), 352. Brief notice of The Albany
Depot and The Unexpected Guests.
"Full of humour and originality," these farces also
feature "a delicate power of characterization."

  *   "Howells as a Socialist." Literary Digest, 16 (19 Mar 1898),
340-341. Rpt. from American Fabian, 4 (Feb 1898), 1-2.
See item 1216.

1222   "Recent Novels." Spectator, 80 (28 Mar 1898), 450. Review
of An Open-Eyed Conspiracy.
Howells' "literary patriotism has condemned him to no
taint of provincialism." When he writes as he does in
this novel, "one must forgive him even his essays in
literary criticism."

1223   DREISER, THEODORE. "How He Climbed Fame's Ladder / William
Dean Howells Tells the Story of His Long Struggle for
Success, and His Ultimate Triumph." Success, 1 (Apr 1898),
5-6. [Pseudo]-interview. Rpt. rev., "How William Dean
Howells Worked To Secure a Foothold," How They Succeeded /
Life Stories of Successful Men Told by Themselves, ed.
Orison Swett Marden (Boston: Lothrop, 1901), pp. 171-184;
as "A Printer's Boy, Self-Taught, Becomes the Dean of
American Letters," Little Visits with Great Americans, or,
Success Ideals and How To Attain Them, ed. Orison Swett
Marden (New York: Success Co., 1905), pp. 283-295; "Interviews with William Dean Howells," ed. Ulrich Halfmann,
American Literary Realism, 6 (Fall 1973), 339-344.
This success story done in the form of an interview
apparently was not based on an actual interview but is an
assemblage of unacknowledged quotations and paraphrases
from Howells' My Literary Passions. For a scholarly
exposé of Dreiser's exercise see Ulrich Halfmann, "Dreiser
and Howells: New Light on Their Relationship," Amerika-
studien (Amst), 20 (No. 1, 1975), 73-85.

1224   "Novels of American Life." Edinburgh Review, 187 (Apr 1898),
386-414. Literary essay. Rpt. in part, "American Character in American Novels," Literary Digest, 16 (25 Jun 1898),
761-762.

184

("Novels of American Life")
    The result of Howells' influence on American writers,
represented here by fifteen novelists, has been "an extraordinary concentration of intelligence upon the task of
portraying not merely individual character but the character of communities." Howells' distinctive quality is his
"pervasive, yet evasive, humor."

1225   BARRY, JOHN D.   "New York Letter."   Literary World, 29 (30 Apr
           1898), 138.   Brief reference.
           Explanation of Howells' agreement to contribute critical
       material to Literature.

1226   "Contemporary Literature / Belles Lettres."   Westminster Re-
           view, 149 (May 1898), 593.   Brief review of An Open-Eyed
           Conspiracy.
           This is "a mere fugitive effort," but "Mr. Howells has
       the incommunicable gift of style."

  *   "General Gossip of Authors and Writers / W. D. Howells at
           Home."   Current Literature, 23 (May 1898), 402-403.
           Interview.   Rpt. from New York Times, 26 Feb 1898, Sat.
           Sup., p. 136.   See item 1219.

1227   "American Fiction."   Athenaeum, No. 3680 (7 May 1898), 597.
           Very brief review of An Open-Eyed Conspiracy.
           "A capital specimen of Howells' lighter style of
       narrative."

1228   McCABE, LIDA R.   "One Never Can Tell."   Outlook, 59 (14 May
           1898), 131-132.   Brief note.
           Anecdotal piece about the scarcity of copies of Poems
       of Two Friends.

1229   DODGE, DAVID H.   "Taking a 'Turn' / or, The Literary Cake-
           Walk."   Life, 31 (26 May 1898), 437-440.   Vaudevillian
           burlesque.
           With illustrative cartoons of American authors, including
       Howells, on the convening of the Congress of American
       Authors.

1230   MARTIN, E. C.   "The Literary Outlook."   Los Angeles Times,
           29 May 1898, p. 13.   Brief note.
           Relates story of how Lowell, as editor of the Atlantic,
       once rejected one of Howells' early poems, which the maga-
       zine later printed in its entirety and commended in a re-
       view of Poems of Two Friends.   Lowell said his last judg-
       ment was the correct one.   [Nichol]

1898

1231   "The Story of a Play." Harper's, 97 (Jun 1898), Advertiser,
      p. 9. Advertisement.
        "Mr. Howells's progress in the field of American fiction
      has been so uniform, so consistent, so steadily in an up-
      ward direction, that to-day the announcement of a new work
      from his pen possesses all the elements of a literary
      event. His masterly delineation of character, his vivid
      and finely balanced style, and his keen appreciation of
      humorous situations have added day by day to his circle
      of admirers until his every work is assured a warm welcome
      and a wide reading." The best that can be said for The
      Story of a Play is that it is "a worthy successor to its
      well-known predecessors."

1232   "Mr. Howells on Mr. Bellamy." Critic, n.s. 29 (11 Jun 1898),
      391. News item.
        Reports meeting of the Social Reform Club in honor of
      Bellamy, Howells presiding.

1233   "Mr. Howells's Stories of Ohio." New York Times, 18 Jun 1898,
      Sat. Sup., pp. 396-397. Review.
      Lengthy, non-critical summary.

  *   "American Character in American Novels." Literary Digest, 16
      (25 Jun 1898), 761-762. Rpt. in part from "Novels of
      American Life," Edinburgh Review, 187 (Apr 1898), 386-414.
      See item 1224.

1234   BARRY, JOHN D. "New York Letter." Literary World, 29 (25 Jun
      1898), 200. Brief comment.
        The Story of a Play is the most important recent novel.
      The experience of the protagonist has been "curiously re-
      peated" in real life. Such real life repetition also fol-
      lowed A Hazard of New Fortunes.

1235   "Books for Summer." New York Times, 25 Jun 1898, Sat. Sup.,
      p. 414. Brief mention of The Landlord at Lion's Head.
      "The force shown in this story is remarkable."

1236   DITHMAR, EDWARD A. "The Author in Fiction / Mr. Howells's
      Launcelot Godolphin Is One of the Novelist's Most Notable
      Creations." New York Times, 25 Jun 1898, Sat. Sup., p. 424.
      Review of The Story of a Play.
        "Mr. Howells has cultivated the habits of seeing what he
      cares to see so clearly, and of setting down the results
      of his observation so accurately that the historical value
      of his novels, quite apart from their aesthetic quality,
      is an obvious fact."

1237   DROCH [ROBERT BRIDGES]. "Bookishness." Life, 31 (30 Jun
            1898), 542. Brief review of The Story of a Play. Rpt.
            Book News, 16 (Aug 1898), 723.
            Howells "has combined the light touch of his comedies
            with the more elaborate character-drawing of his serious
            novels. The result is a charming modern novel with the
            fresh grace of youth about it, and the deft craftsmanship
            of maturity."

1238   PAYNE, WILLIAM MORTON. "Recent Fiction." Dial, 25 (1 Jul
            1898), 21-22. Brief review of The Story of a Play.
            "A pleasing addition" to Howells' recent list "of
            charming trivialities." "Women are sometimes rational
            beings,...Howells's novels to the contrary notwith-
            standing."

1239   "Books and Authors / Books of the Week." Outlook, 59 (2 Jul
            1898), 588. Brief review of "The Making [sic] of a Play."
            "So vividly told that one is persuaded of its veracity
            and reality."

1240   "Recent Novels." Spectator, 81 (2 Jul 1898), 22. Review of
            The Story of a Play.
            Since Howells has emerged from his "'meticulous' mood,"
            his work has "the double merit of being at once thoroughly
            enjoyable and thoroughly American." "Whether one regards
            [this novel] as an excellent illustration of the nemesis
            that falls on any one who turns him or herself into 'copy,'
            or as a kindly yet subtle satire upon the histrionic tem-
            perament, or as a study of a thoroughly devoted yet really
            ill-assorted couple, the result is in any case an admirable
            and engrossing entertainment."

1241   JAMES, HENRY. "American Letter." Literature, 3 (9 Jul 1898),
            18. Review of The Story of a Play.
            Howells' "good nature and the tone of pleasantry" tend
            to "muffle and soften" the edges of the story, bathing it
            in a "romantic" quality.

1242   "Literature." Independent, 50, Pt. 2 (14 Jul 1898), 124.
            Brief mention of Stories of Ohio.
            "The limits of so small a book gave [Howells] little
            freedom," but it will serve well as supplementary school
            material.

1898

1243   "Magazines of the Month." Los Angeles Times, 24 Jul 1898,
       p. 11. Brief mention.
            Howells' "American Letter" in Literature names Chicago
       as having made better use of its literary possibilities
       than New York. [Nichol]

1244   "Literature." Independent, 50, Pt. 2 (28 Jul 1898), 262-263.
       Brief review of The Story of a Play.
            "Of course, the incorrigibly illogical and sweetly
       troublesome female chatters through the story, and, of
       course, there is not a hint of really strong and manly
       character in men; but there is a play of commonplace
       traits and motives that proves mildly interesting."

1245   BANGS, JOHN KENDRICK. "Literary Notes." Harper's, 97 (Aug
       1898), 1. Review of The Story of a Play.
            It is quite evident that Howells has studied his material
       at close range. "It would not be surprising should Godol-
       phin rank ultimately as one of Mr. Howells's most keenly
       analytical studies."

1246   BARRY, JOHN D. "The Story of a Play." Bookman (New York),
       7 (Aug 1898), 515-517. Full review.
            Done in the form of dialogue with the Spirit of Romance,
       who concludes her conversation by placing "her head on
       the ground in an attitude of despair."

  *   [The Story of a Play.] Book News, 16 (Aug 1898), 723. Rpt.
       from Life, 31 (30 Jun 1898), 542. See item 1237.

1247   "W. D. Howells." Book Buyer, n.s. 17 (Aug 1898), 16. Full-
       length portrait. "Yours Sincerely, W. D. Howells." Book
       Buyer, n.s. 17 (Aug 1898), front piece. Portrait.

1248   "The Story of a Play." Literary World, 29 (6 Aug 1898), 243.
       Brief review.
            "Where does Mr. Howells get the model for the extraordi-
       nary and trying women, always the same and always trying,
       which he puts into his novels?"

1249   "Reviews," Academy, 54 (13 Aug 1898), 145-146. Review of The
       Story of a Play.
            Here "Howells' method finds its most triumphant expres-
       sion." Long quotation included.

1250   "American Fiction." Athenaeum, No. 3695 (20 Aug 1898), 252.
       Review of The Story of a Play.

("American Fiction")
"One of the very best of Mr. Howells's tales without a plot. It is extremely subtle and ingenious, and yet perfectly clear throughout."

1251   "Magazines of the Month." Los Angeles Times, 21 Aug 1898, p. 18. Brief mention.
Howells' "American Letter" is the "gayest thing in Literature" (10 Aug issue). [Nichol]

1252   DROCH [ROBERT BRIDGES]. "Bookishness / Mr. Howells's Pullet Argument." Life, 32 (25 Aug 1898), 146. Response to Howells' "American Letter" in Literature.
Howells too freely ascribes a moral conscience to New England as distinct from other parts of the nation.

1253   "Chronicle and Comment." Bookman (New York), 8 (Sep 1898), 7-8. Brief comment.
Response to Howells' contributions to Literature. As a critic he is now "in such a genial mood that he will have all the young persons in the country taking to fiction if he is not careful." He "has a literary creed which he often violates in writing his own books, but which he always observes in criticizing the books of others."

1254   HYDE, GEORGE MERRIAM. "The Story of a Play." Book Buyer, n.s. 17 (Sep 1898), 146-147. Full review.
This novel is "better cushioned, has more repose, detachment, humor" than much of Howells' earlier work.

1255   "American Author-Diplomats." Critic, n.s. 30 (Oct 1898), 261. Brief reference to Venetian Days.
It is a product of Howells' consular service.

1256   "Chronicle and Comment." Bookman (New York), 8 (Oct 1898), 107. Brief note.
Howells, in declining to attend the Tolstoy dinner, notes his respect for the Russian novelist.

1257   "Mr. W. D. Howells / Consul at Venice." Critic, n.s. 30 (Oct 1898), 264. Portrait.

1258   "Recent Fiction." Nation, 67 (20 Oct 1898), 299. Notice of The Story of a Play.
"The book is almost entirely perfunctory."

1898

1259   "November Magazines." Los Angeles Times, 31 Oct 1897, p. 17.
        Brief mention.
            Notes publication of A Pair of Patient Lovers in Harper's
        and calls it a "charming story." [Nichol]

1260   "Harper's Magazine for 1899." Harper's, 98 (Dec 1898), Adver-
        tiser, p. 42. Advertisement.
            Their Silver Wedding Journey, "the tale of a sabbatical
        summer in Europe, in which the incidents of travel are
        mingled with the romantic adventures of two youthful Ameri-
        cans, whose love-story is told in Mr. Howells's best man-
        ner," will appear serially.

1261   "Current Fiction." Literary World, 29 (10 Dec 1898), 434.
        Brief reference.
            The reviewer of Bellamy's The Blindman's World challenges
        Howells' judgment of Bellamy as expressed in his introduc-
        tion to the volume.

                            1899

1262   BANGS, J[OHN] K[ENDRICK]. "The Overcoat, Being the Contribu-
        tion of Mr. Bedford Parke." The Dreamers / A Club. New
        York: Harper, 1899. Pp. 59-79.
            A parody of Howells' farces.

1263   FISHER, MARY. A General Survey of American Literature. Chi-
        cago: McClurg, 1899. Pp. 371-379, 381.
            Howells is included with James among "Later Writers."
        The introduction to him and his work is general. James
        is judged to have "a more satisfactory interpretation of
        realism" than Howells.

1264   HALE, EDWARD EVERETT. James Russell Lowell and His Friends.
        Boston and New York: Houghton Mifflin, 1899. Pp. 151,
        169, 202.
            Insignificant references to Howells relate to his associ-
        ation with the Atlantic, an invitation to contribute to
        the North American Review, and his membership in The Sat-
        urday Club. Major portions of this work were first pub-
        lished as a series in Outlook beginning 1 January 1898.

1265   McCARTHY, JUSTIN. Reminiscences. 2 vols. New York and Lon-
        don: Harper, 1899. I, pp. 194, 207-209.
            Howells has fulfilled the early promise recognized by
        Lowell. McCarthy recalls a Tavern Club conversation with
        Howells and includes a "genial" letter from him (p. 208).

1266   TRENT, WILLIAM P. "Mr. Howells and Romanticism." The Author-
        ity of Criticism and Other Essays. New York: Scribner's,
        1899. Pp. 259-267. Rpt. in part, The War of the Critics
        over William Dean Howells, ed. Edwin H. Cady and David L.
        Frazier (Evanston: Row, Peterson, 1962), p. 82.
             No matter how admirable Howells' evaluation of contem-
        porary writers may be, his antagonism toward romanticism
        is uncatholic and suggests his own inability to put him-
        self in touch with the past.

1267   WHITING, LILIAN. Kate Field / A Record. Boston: Little,
        Brown, 1899. Pp. 185, 209, 245.
             Minor references to the charm of Howells and his wife.

1268   "The Lounger." Critic, n.s. 31 (Feb 1899), 99. Brief note.
             About the St. Gaudens' medallion honoring Howells and
        his daughter. Photograph reproduction as front piece on
        facing page.

1269   BURROUGHS, JOHN. "The Vital Touch in Literature." Atlantic,
        83 (Mar 1899), 399-406. Brief reference.
             Burroughs commends Howells' style and endorses but
        qualifies Howells' evaluation of Scott (pp. 401-402).

1270   "Books of the Week / Howells' Literary Blanc Mange." Chicago
        Daily Tribune, 4 May 1899, p. 10. Review of Ragged Lady.
             "It is an actionless, passionless, love story, true to
        New England middle-class character, and ending with the
        peculiar touch of uncertainty so often affected by Mr.
        Howells." The book teems with microscopic life.

1271   "Books and Authors / Novels and Tales." Outlook, 61 (11 Mar
        1899), 602-603. Brief review of Ragged Lady.
             The novel presents average life. "There are neither
        great loves nor hates, nor temptations nor tragedies,
        save those of temperament. Perhaps Mr. Howells would
        claim that these are life's real tragedies."

1272   "Mr. Howells's Ragged Lady." New York Times, 18 Mar 1899,
        Sat. Sup., p. 164. Full review.
             There are "welcome signs of atavism" in this novel.
        "We get the full charm of the old Howells novel, enhanced
        by the deeper suggestiveness of the mature view and
        ripened experience." The reviewer does the currently un-
        fashionable thing by contrasting James and Howells in some
        detail.

1899

1273   BANGS, JOHN KENDRICK. "Literary Notes." Harper's, 98 (Apr
            1899), 1-2. Full review of Ragged Lady.
            Although the "r-less dialect" which Howells presents
            here is not convincing, the novel is both convincing and
            pleasant. "The initial complication is peculiarly Ameri-
            can in its nature." The "ensuing perplexities...are, one
            and all, easily recognizable as derived from real life,
            and there is no forcing of the note throughout."

1274   SHERMAN, ELLEN BURNS. "To the Use of Edifying." Critic, n.s.
            31 (Apr 1899), 319-320. Review of Howells' lecture on
            the novel delivered at the Social Reform Club on Universi-
            ty Place.
            "His arguments carry the conviction that sincerity alone
            can give."

1275   PALMER, HELEN M. "Mr. Howells's Ragged Lady." New York Times,
            15 Apr 1899, Sat. Sup., p. 244. Letter to the Times.
            Takes exception to one aspect of the 18 March review of
            Ragged Lady by pointing to Bartley Hubbard as "a 'deeply
            tainted soul.'"

1276   "Letters and Art / Is America 'Crippling Art?'" Literary
            Digest, 18 (22 Apr 1899), 455-456. Note.
            The views of Lilian Bell and Howells are contrasted
            through extensive quotation.

1277   "Ragged Lady." Literary World, 30 (29 Apr 1899), 131. Review.
            "It is romance, pure and simple."

1278   "Opinions of W. D. Howells / The Cycle of Poetry Has Closed
            He Thinks." New York Sun, 30 Apr 1899, p. 5. Interview.
            Rpt. in part, Literary Digest, 18 (27 May 1899), 607-608;
            "Interviews with William Dean Howells," ed. Ulrich Half-
            mann, American Literary Realism, 6 (Fall 1973), 344-346.
            Further subtitles read, "Present Tendencies in Litera-
            ture--Chances for the New Writers--Kipling's Poems--In-
            fluence of Magazines--Appreciable Changes in Literature
            in Recent Years."

1279   "Some New Novels." Book Buyer, n.s. 18 (May 1899), 322-323.
            Brief review of Ragged Lady.
            A novel for those who find entertainment "in the sane
            delights of a realism psychologically and artistically
            knowing."

1280   "W. D. Howells on War and Art." <u>New York Times</u>, 1 May 1899,
p. 6. Editorial.
    Disagrees with Howells' assertion in his <u>New York Sun</u>
(30 Apr 1899) interview that war "can inspire nothing that
is worthy in art or letters."

1281   "Novels of the Week." <u>Spectator</u>, 82 (6 May 1899), 647–648.
Review of <u>Ragged Lady</u>.
    The novel "has in full measure the sovereign qualities
of fascination and distinction." To read it after James's
<u>The Awkward Age</u> "is like emerging into a pine-wood out of
the medicated atmosphere of a sick room."

1282   HENDERSON, W. J. "War, Art and Mr. Howells." <u>New York Times</u>,
13 May 1899, Sat. Sup., p. 316. Short essay.
    Argues that Howells is wrong in his assumption that
great art cannot emerge from the war experience.

1283   "Howells, James and Co." <u>Saturday Review</u>, 87 (13 May 1899),
597–598. Review of <u>Ragged Lady</u>.
    Howells "seems to have outdone himself as an unimagina-
tive novelist."

1284   CROSBY, ERNEST H. "Homerically Danced On and Yet Not Dead."
<u>New York Times</u>, 20 May 1899, Sat. Sup., p. 336. Lengthy
letter to the <u>Times</u>.
    Comes to the defense of Howells by explaining the prob-
able idea which prompted his simplified statement on war
and art.

*   "Poetry, War, and Mr. Howells." <u>Literary Digest</u>, 18 (27 May
1899), 607–608. Rpt. in part from <u>New York Sun</u>, 30 Apr
1899, p. 5. <u>See</u> item 1278.

1285   "Summer Reading / Notes Upon New Novels." <u>Review of Reviews</u>,
19 (Jun 1899), 749. Very brief review of <u>Ragged Lady</u>.
    Howells, in avoiding social problems, returns to "his
happiest and most delicate vein."

1286   "W. D. Howells, Novelist and Critic." <u>Harper's</u>, 99 (Jun 1899),
Advertiser, p. 20. Advertisement of <u>Ragged Lady</u>.
    "There have been published in the past thirty years over
thirty volumes from the pen of the most representative man
of American letters, William Dean Howells. Mr. Howells
deserves the rank given him above for three reasons. He
has created a distinct school of fiction, he has made an
international reputation as a critic, and he has written
a volume of poems which has attracted much favorable

1899

("W. D. Howells, Novelist and Critic")
attention." Reviewers agree that the "interest and charm"
of Ragged Lady are equal to the best of Howells. Further-
more, the volume is "uniform in size and binding with our
library edition of the author's other works."

1287 "American and Canadian Fiction." Athenaeum, No. 3737 (10 Jun
1899), 719. Brief review of Ragged Lady.
Not one of Howells' best novels. Ragged Lady is "exclu-
sively American."

1288 "Fiction." Academy, 56 (10 Jun 1899), 627-628. Review of
Ragged Lady.
"Mr. Howells is a master, and the master, no matter what
his medium, always commands respect or admiration."

1289 PAYNE, WILLIAM MORTON. "Recent Fiction." Dial, 27 (1 Jul
1899), 20-21. Review of Ragged Lady.
Howells' return to Italian scenes, the source of his
"best inspiration," and his portrayal of his "gentle
heroine" contribute to the success of this novel.

1290 "Chronicle and Comment." Bookman (New York), 10 (Sep 1899),
7. Announcement of the proposed dramatization of A Hazard
of New Fortunes.
The "attachment between Conrad Dryfoos and Margaret
Vance" is to be made "pivotal."

1291 "Novel Notices." Bookman (London), 16 (Sep 1899), 168. Review of Ragged Lady.
The fact that Howells is content to tell and describe
rather than to manipulate and explain "makes his books so
marvellously lifelike and gives them their unique attraction." Portrait.

1292 "Student Lecture Course." Evanston Index, 30 Sep 1899, p. 8.
Announces Howells' lecture, "Novels and Novel Writing,"
for 21 October. [Rowlette]

1293 "Wm. Dean Howells Coming." Evanston Press, 7 Oct 1899, p. 1.
Lecture announcement.
Howells is expected to "delight" his hearers just as he
has "charmed" his readers. [Rowlette]

1294 "About Stage Folk at Home." Chicago Evening Post, 21 Oct
1899, p. 7. Announcement of Howells' public lecture.
Howells is "the most typically American of American
writers." [Rowlette]

1295   "Howells in Chicago." Chicago Evening Post, 21 Oct 1899, p. 1.
      News item.
       Announces Howells' arrival at the Palmer House, his
      lecture in Evanston and two lectures in Chicago, one pri-
      vate and one public, for 24 and 25 October respectively.
      Closes with an interview. [Rowlette]

1296   "Howells Lauds the Poets." Chicago Chronicle, 22 Oct 1899,
      p. 5. News item.
       Notes Howells' arrival the previous day, mentions his
      lecture at Evanston the previous night, closes with inter-
      view. For parallel coverage see also "Howells Tells His
      Aim," Chicago Tribune, 22 Oct 1899, p. 6. [Rowlette]

1297   "The Howells Lecture." Chicago Inter-Ocean, 22 Oct 1899, p. 34.
      Brief lecture announcement.
       See also "Lectures by Two Authors," Chicago Tribune,
      22 Oct 1899, p. 38. [Rowlette]

1298   "W. D. Howells in Chicago." Chicago Inter-Ocean, 22 Oct 1899,
      p. 6. News item.
       A notice of Howells' arrival and an interview. [Row-
      lette]

1299   "William Dean Howells / A Visitor in Chicago." Chicago Times-
      Herald, 22 Oct 1899, p. 5. News item.
       Announces Howells' public and private lectures in Chi-
      cago, describes his appearance, concludes with an inter-
      view. [Rowlette]

1300   "Howells on Writers New and Old." Chicago Times-Herald,
      23 Oct 1899, p. 6. Editorial.
       Howells' catholicity of taste for great contemporary
      authors clashes oddly with his disdain for "the great
      names of the past," such as Scott, whose The Heart of
      Midlothian is infinitely preferable to "the abominable
      mixture of finical writing and filthy suggestion called
      What Maisie Knew." [Rowlette]

1301   "Mr. Howells in the West." Chicago Record, 23 Oct 1899, p. 4.
      News item.
       Gracious welcome to Howells. Chicago is at last to hear
      "a literary man who will understand something of the
      tastes, needs, and conditions of her people." [Rowlette]

1302   [Untitled.] Chicago Journal, 23 Oct 1899, p. 4. Brief note.
       Howells strives for repose in his writing and "generally
      attains it, and so do his readers." [Rowlette]

1899

1303   "Mr. Howells' Choir Invisible." Chicago Tribune, 24 Oct 1899,
       p. 6. Brief note.
       Howells comes to Chicago accompanied by the choir invis-
       ible of his fictional characters. Will he explain why his
       admirers prefer his earlier over his later characters?
       [Rowlette]

1304   [Untitled.] Chicago Chronicle, 24 Oct 1899, p. 6. Editorial
       note.
       Howells scorns plots and seems to believe that his "mis-
       sion" is "to depict the psychological struggles of the
       Boston cab horse and the yearnings for the infinite of
       the hired man." [Rowlette]

1305   "Hear W. D. Howells Address." Chicago Record, 25 Oct 1899,
       p. 2. News item.
       Report of the private lecture presented to members of
       the Twentieth Century Club. For parallel Chicago lecture
       coverage see also "Urges the Power of Novels," Chicago
       Journal, 25 Oct 1899, p. 9; "W. D. Howells Talks of
       Novels," Chicago Chronicle, 25 Oct 1899, p. 5; "Howells,
       Teacher," Chicago Journal, 26 Oct 1899, p. 4 (a long,
       excellent appreciation by James O'Donnell Bennett); and
       "Many Listen to Howells," Chicago Chronicle, 26 Oct 1899,
       p. 4. [Rowlette]

1306   "Howells on the Novel / Justifies Realism Before the Twentieth
       Century Club." Chicago Tribune, 25 Oct 1899, p. 4. Re-
       port of lecture and interview. Abstr. "Interviews with
       William Dean Howells," ed. Ulrich Halfmann, American Liter-
       ary Realism, 6 (Fall 1973), 346-347.
       Further subtitles include "Longevity of Literary Work--
       Thoughts on Books That Live--Later He Discusses the Per-
       sonal Quality, Which, He Says, Never Varies--Problems
       Unsolved."

1307   "Amusements." Chicago Inter-Ocean, 26 Oct 1899, p. 5. News
       item.
       Ostensibly a lecture report, actually an appreciation
       of Howells' making public appearances. [Rowlette]

1308   "Howells' Lecture a Success." The Northwestern, 20 (26 Oct
       1899), 67. Brief note.
       Howells' lecture was a "rare treat." [Rowlette]

1309   "Howells on Literary Work." Chicago Times-Herald, 26 Oct
       1899, p. 6. Editorial.

("Howells on Literary Work")
   Howells' "exceptionally felicitous style" is, by his
acknowledgement, the result of "the hardest of hard work."
The novice writer is cautioned that "sustained power is
impossible without sustained work." [Rowlette]

1310   "Howells Will Write a Play." Chicago Record, 26 Oct 1899,
         p. 1. News item.
            Unable to attend a reception at Hull House, Howells
         sends his regrets and is reported as having said "that he
         intended some day to write a play specifically for presen-
         tation on the Hull House stage." [Rowlette]

1311   [Untitled.] Grinnell Herald, 27 Oct 1899, p. 3. Advertise-
         ment of lecture.
            Howells is recognized as the author of, among other
         things, Tales of Three Cities and Daisy Miller. [Rowlette]

1312   "Editorial Comment." Evanston Index, 28 Oct 1899, p. 2.
         Brief note.
            Howells, "a leader of literary thought," represented
         the Lecture Course well. [Rowlette]

1313   "Howells on Truth in Fiction." Chicago Evening Post, 28 Oct
         1899, p. 6. Editorial.
            Rejects Howells' "truth"--"exact reproduction of re-
         ality"--in favor of "truth to the ideal that lives within
         us." Argues that Howells implicitly agrees, for "he
         appreciates things that a strict application of his cri-
         teria would require him to condemn." [Rowlette]

1314   "Lecture by W. D. Howells." Evanston Index, 28 Oct 1899,
         p. 2. Lecture report.
            Howells is "one of the few great writers who are not out
         of place on the platform." See also "Famous Author Lec-
         tured," Evanston Press, 28 Oct 1899, p. 3. [Rowlette]

1315   "Books and Magazines." Des Moines Leader, 29 Oct 1899, p. 15.
         Long, competent essay.
            Advertises Howells' scheduled lecture. Reviews his
         claim to the title "Dean of the Guild of American Men of
         Letters," and urges lyceum patrons, whatever their private
         views of Howells may be, to give him an impartial hearing.
         [Rowlette]

1316   "Chat with W. D. Howells." Chicago Chronicle, 29 Oct 1899,
         p. 39. Lecture report and interview. [Rowlette]

1899

1317   "The Passing of Howells." Chicago Inter-Ocean, 29 Oct 1899,
            p. 16. Editorial.
            Howells, after having been "something of a dictator in
            fiction," is now passé; his low-key, excessively refined
            novels do not meet current demands for tales of adventure
            and valor. He does not deal with the "great emotions" and
            will not be read in the next century. [Rowlette]

1318   "Mr. Howells' Theories." Chicago Record, 30 Oct 1899, p. 4.
            Note.
            Howells' views on realism are much misunderstood. They
            are logical and "bound to prevail." [Rowlette]

1319   "College News." Grinnell Herald, 31 Oct 1899, p. 2. News
            item.
            Expresses thanks for Howells' (unscheduled and gratis)
            lecture (for the students and faculty of Iowa College).
            [Rowlette]

1320   "Howells at Drake." Des Moines Daily Iowa Capital, 31 Oct
            1899, p. 2. News item.
            Reports Howells' unscheduled appearance at Drake Univer-
            sity chapel exercises. He spoke briefly, mentioning par-
            ticularly his discomfort on the platform. [Rowlette]

1321   "William Dean Howells Here." Des Moines Iowa State Register,
            31 Oct 1899, p. 3. Lecture announcement and interview.
            [Rowlette]

1322   "William Dean Howells Here." Des Moines Leader, 31 Oct 1899,
            p. 2. News item.
            Announces the lecture, Howells' arrival, his having re-
            ceived callers. Rpt. interview excerpt from Chicago Times-
            Herald, 22 Oct 1899. [Rowlette]

1323   FAWCETT, WALDON. "Mr. Howells and His Brother." Critic, n.s.
            32 (Nov 1899), 1026-1028. Note.
            Comments on the special relationship between Howells and
            his brother Joseph, quoting extensively from Joseph's own
            reminiscences. Reference to early song by Howells.

1324   LEE, GERALD STANLEY. "Mr. Howells on the Platform." Critic,
            n.s. 32 (Nov 1899), 1029-1030. Note.
            Response to announcement of Howells' lecture tour. "We
            want to hear Howells in America to-day because he particu-
            larly belongs to us and because we particularly belong to
            him and because we are both proud of it."

1325   PRATT, CORNELIA ATWOOD. "William Dean Howells / Some Aspects
        of His Realistic Novels." Critic, n.s. 32 (Nov 1899),
        1021-1025. Essay.
            Howells "depicts chiefly a world of social relations,
        rather than a world of action...or a world of reflection."
        Although he removes love and religion from center stage,
        he has not neglected "the play of human sympathies and the
        influence of ethical considerations on conduct." Ragged
        Lady effectively demonstrates his realistic concepts.

1326   "W. D. Howells." Critic, n.s. 32 (Nov 1899). Front piece
        (facing p. 975).
            Full-page portrait of Howells reading.

1327   "Dinner for Howells." Des Moines Daily Iowa Capital, 1 Nov
        1899, p. 5. News item.
            A reception is to be given Howells by the Prairie Club
        after his lecture. Before accepting the invitation, he
        stipulated that he not be asked to speak. See also Des
        Moines Iowa State Register, 1 Nov 1899, p. 7. [Rowlette]

1328   "The Howells Lecture." Des Moines Daily Iowa Capital, 1 Nov
        1899, p. 1. Note.
            Howells is publicized as a "most entertaining speaker."
        [Rowlette]

1329   "Mr. Howells Is Entertained." Des Moines Iowa State Register,
        1 Nov 1899, p. 7. News item.
            Reports some of Howells' activities of two days, in-
        cluding his meeting a boyhood friend (W. D. Loomis) among
        his many callers, his drive around the city, his luncheon
        and reception engagements. Mentions his plans for a lec-
        ture tour on the Pacific Coast in the following spring.
        [Rowlette]

1330   "Welcome Dean Howells." Des Moines Leader, 1 Nov 1899, p. 4.
        News essay.
            Long, careful piece, partly biographical. Everyone
        knows Howells. Now that he has achieved permanency in
        literature, it is "good to see" him meeting his public
        and receiving homage from them. [Rowlette]

1331   "Dean Howells' Lecture." Des Moines Leader, 2 Nov 1899,
        pp. 2, 6. Lecture report, followed by brief mention of
        post-lecture reception.
            For parallel coverage see "Good Novels Must Be True,"
        Des Moines Iowa State Register, 2 Nov 1899, p. 4; "Howells'

1899

("Dean Howells' Lecture")
Lecture," Des Moines Daily Iowa Capital, 2 Nov 1899, p. 7;
and "Howells Talks," Des Moines Daily News, 2 Nov 1899,
p. 3. [Rowlette]

1332   "Social and Personal." Lincoln Evening News, 2 Nov 1899,
p. 5. Lecture announcement. See also Lincoln Evening
News, 3 Nov 1899, p. 3, and Lincoln Nebraska State Journal,
3 Nov 1899, p. 7. [Rowlette]

1333   "Mere Mention." Lincoln Nebraska State Journal, 3 Nov 1899,
p. 6. News item.
Announces a reception to be given by the English Club
in Howells' honor. [Rowlette]

1334   "Mr. Howells Arrives." Lincoln Nebraska State Journal, 3 Nov
1899, p. 5. News item.
Reports Howells' arrival at the Lincoln Hotel, his being
called on by Chancellor Bessey of the University of Nebraska, and others. Howells feels as if he has been lecturing
"from the beginning of time." [Rowlette]

1335   "Permanency of Howells' Work." Des Moines Daily Iowa Capital,
3 Nov 1899, p. 4. Editorial.
Disputes the Chicago Inter-Ocean editorial charge
(29 Oct 1899) that Howells will not last. [Rowlette]

1336   "Books and Men." Des Moines Daily Iowa Capital, 4 Nov 1899,
p. 3. Editorial.
A warm tribute to Howells, even a dithyramb of love.
Howells' "soul seems to be so attuned that it measurably
accords with other souls producing vibrations that please
and gratify." "Is it any wonder men love Howells?"
[Rowlette]

1337   "A Delightful Address by William Dean Howells." Lincoln
Nebraska State Journal, 4 Nov 1899, p. 3. Lecture report.
See also "William Dean Howells Gives Instruction in the
Art of Writing Books," Lincoln Evening News, 4 Nov 1899,
p. 5. [Rowlette]

1338   "Received by the English Club." Lincoln Nebraska State
Journal, 4 Nov 1899, p. 3. News item.
Reports the English Club's reception for Howells and the
satisfaction of the members. [Rowlette]

1339   "University Notes." Lincoln Nebraska State Journal, 4 Nov
          1899, p. 6. News item.
          Reports Howells' attending a musical program at the
          university chapel, the students' clamorous reception, his
          brief response. [Rowlette]

1340   "The Library Arm Chair." Ottumwa Saturday Herald, 5 Nov 1899,
          p. 2. News item.
          A movement has started to meet the necessary guarantee--
          "which of course is large"--to book a Howells lecture.
          Rpt. excerpt of Chicago Times-Herald (22 Oct 1899) inter-
          view. [Rowlette]

1341   "William Dean Howells Can Be Secured." Ottumwa Saturday
          Herald, 5 Nov 1899, p. 6. News item.
          Lyceum patrons are urged to buy "a certain number" of
          tickets to assure Howells' coming. [Rowlette]

1342   "Hot Tamales." Lincoln Evening News, 6 Nov 1899, p. 4.
          Brief mention.
          Only the "Select Few" read Howells, while the "Groaning
          Masses" read books with "some movement in them."
          [Rowlette]

1343   "William Dean Howells' Lecture." Topeka State Journal, 6 Nov
          1899, p. 5. Lecture announcement. See also Topeka State
          Journal, 7 Nov 1899, p. 5; Topeka Daily Capital, 7 Nov
          1899, p. 8; and Topeka Daily Capital, 8 Nov 1899, p. 8.
          [Rowlette]

1344   "The Coming of W. D. Howells." Topeka Daily Capital, 8 Nov
          1899, p. 4. News item.
          Announces lecture, praises Howells' personal character.
          Rpt. excerpt from Chicago Chronicle (29 Oct 1899) lecture
          report and interview. [Rowlette]

1345   "Mr. Howells Here." Topeka State Journal, 8 Nov 1899, p. 4.
          Interview. Rpt. in part, "Addenda to Halfmann: Six New
          Howells Interviews," ed. Robert Rowlette, American Liter-
          ary Realism, 8 (Spring 1975), 101-102.
          Howells talks about the habit of revision and his reac-
          tions to his first lecture tour. [Rowlette]

1346   "Many Heard Mr. Howells." Topeka State Journal, 9 Nov 1899,
          p. 5. Lecture report. Rpt. Topeka (Weekly) State Journal,
          9 Nov 1899, p. 3. [Rowlette]

1899

1347 [Untitled.] Emporia Gazette, 9 Nov 1899, p. 1. News item.
        William Allen White announces lecture, avers that the
        town will be disgraced if even standing room is left un-
        occupied. [Rowlette]

1348 [Untitled.] Emporia Gazette, 9 Nov 1899, p. 1. News item.
        White is to host a dinner for Howells prior to the
        lecture. [Rowlette]

1349 "Howells' Lecture." Emporia Daily Republican, 10 Nov 1899,
        p. 1. Lecture report. Rpt. Emporia Weekly Republican,
        16 Nov 1899, p. 2. [Rowlette]

1350 "Mr. Howells and Mr. Sheldon." Topeka Daily Capital, 10 Nov
        1899, p. 8. Letter to the Daily Capital.
        Intensely irate comment from Henry W. Roby castigating
        Howells for ignoring in his lecture the Rev. Charles M.
        Sheldon and his "ethical novel" In His Steps. [Rowlette]

1351 [Untitled.] Emporia Gazette, 10 Nov 1899, p. 1. Editorial.
        William Allen White refuses to report the lecture for
        those who did not attend, scolds those who did attend
        expecting Howells to "give a skirt dance" or "play horse,"
        commends the town for the turnout of fifteen hundred.
        [Rowlette]

1352 [Untitled.] Marion Record, 10 Nov 1899, p. 1. Very brief
        comment.
        Howells is no "great success" as a lecturer. [Rowlette]

1353 "William Dean Howells." Ottumwa Daily Courier, 11 Nov 1899,
        p. 4. News item.
        Lecture announcement, followed by a biographical sketch,
        an overview of Howells' realism, and an interview.
        [Rowlette]

1354 "William Dean Howells." Ottumwa Saturday Herald, 11 Nov 1899,
        p. 1. News item.
        Lecture announcement and unacknowledged rpt. from the
        Des Moines Leader (1 Nov 1899). [Rowlette]

1355 "William Dean Howells." Ottumwa Saturday Herald, 11 Nov 1899,
        p. 5. News item.
        Dr. F. E. Brush will introduce Howells. Howells'
        scheduled arrival is announced on same page. [Rowlette]

1356 "William Dean Howells." Ottumwa Saturday Herald, 11 Nov 1899,
     pp. 10-11. News item.
     Literary Ottumwans are taking "the greatest interest" in
     Howells' appearance. Rpts. from the Des Moines Leader
     (2 Nov 1899) and Des Moines Daily Iowa Capital (4 Nov 1899).
     [Rowlette]

1357 "Lecture on Novels." Ottumwa Daily Courier, 13 Nov 1899, p. 4.
     Lecture report. [Rowlette].

1358 [Untitled.] Ottumwa Daily Courier, 13 Nov 1899, p. 3. Brief
     mention.
     Howells says that Westerners are "not at all nervous"
     and are "very much at their ease"; Iowans say the same of
     him. [Rowlette]

1359 "William Dean Howells." Ottumwa Daily Courier, 13 Nov 1899,
     p. 3. Editorial.
     Praises Howells for his "allegiance to the American
     type," for having immortalized in fiction the "people who
     live next door to us." [Rowlette]

1360 "Howells' Lecture." Marion Headlight, 16 Nov 1899, p. 1.
     Garbled lecture report. [Rowlette]

1361 "Howells' Lecture." Emporia Times, 17 Nov 1899, p. 1. Lecture
     report.
     It was "didactic"; Howells is "a very poor reader."
     [Rowlette]

1362 "Howells' Lecture." Ottumwa Independent, 17 Nov 1899, p. 8.
     Editorial.
     Sourly berates Howells for his faulty critical judgment
     and disdains his "cold and heartless characters." Wryly
     congratulates him for having made his "system" of writing
     "a success financially." [Rowlette]

1363 "Among the Books." Indianapolis News, 18 Nov 1899, p. 10.
     Editorial.
     Expresses pleasure that the American lecture field is
     being reclaimed, after foreign domination, by Howells and
     other "literary men of the soil." [Rowlette]

1364 "The Kindness of Mr. Howells." Ottumwa Saturday Herald,
     18 Nov 1899, p. 6. News item.
     Records two instances of Howells signing autographs, one
     involving a small boy who could not get near enough to ask.
     [Rowlette]

1899

1365   "W. D. Howells Here / Talks of Indiana Writers." Indianapolis
News, 18 Nov 1899, p. 11. Interview. Abstr. "Addenda to
Halfmann: Six New Howells Interviews," ed. Robert Rowlette,
American Literary Realism, 8 (Spring 1975), 102-103.
    Authors discussed include Maurice Thompson, Lucy Furman,
John James Piatt, Lew Wallace, James Whitcomb Riley, Anna
Nicholas, and Edward Eggleston. [Rowlette]

1366   "William Dean Howells in Ottumwa." Ottumwa Saturday Herald,
18 Nov 1899, p. 6. Editorial.
    Congratulates Ottumwans who used their "blessed privi-
lege" to hear Howells and "have one good look at him before passing from this earth." [Rowlette]

1367   "A Chat with Howells." Indianapolis Journal, 19 Nov 1899,
p. 3. Interview. Abstr. "Addenda to Halfmann: Six New
Howells Interviews," ed. Robert Rowlette, American Literary Realism, 8 (Spring 1975), 103.
    Howells talks about the response to his lectures and
indicates that he most enjoyed writing The Story of a Play
because he knew he was "getting at it." [Rowlette]

1368   "For William Dean Howells." Indianapolis Journal, 19 Nov 1899,
p. 11. News item.
    Reports a dinner party for Howells. Guests included
Booth Tarkington and ex-President Benjamin Harrison. See
also "In Society," Indianapolis Sentinel, 19 Nov 1899,
p. 10. [Rowlette]

1369   "Mr. Howells and His Books." Indianapolis Journal, 19 Nov
1899, II, p. 12. Editorial.
    Laments that Howells' novels are not "popular," predicts
that they will stand as accurate "pictures of nineteenth
century life." [Rowlette]

1370   "A Splendid Audience." Indianapolis Journal, 19 Nov 1899,
p. 3. Lecture report.
    Long response to "Novels and Novel Writing" at Plymouth
Church. [Rowlette]

1371   "Talk with Mr. Howells." Indianapolis Sentinel, 19 Nov 1899,
p. 4. Interview. Abstr. "Addenda to Halfmann: Six New
Howells Interviews," ed. Robert Rowlette, American Literary Realism, 8 (Spring 1975), 103.
    Howells compares Eastern and Western writers and praises
Booth Tarkington, "an author of great promise." [Rowlette]

1372   [Untitled.] Indianapolis Sentinel, 19 Nov 1899, p. 4. Report
       of lecture.
            Additional comments following "Talk with Mr. Howells."
       [Rowlette]

1373   "William Dean Howells." Detroit Free Press, 19 Nov 1899,
       p. 11. Lecture announcement and short biographical sketch.
       [Rowlette]

1374   "Howells Pro and Con--A Clubwoman Gives Her Impression of the
       Novelist." Indianapolis Journal, 20 Nov 1899, p. 8. Note.
            An attack on Howells, especially for drawing women who
       are "not worth knowing"; charges that he "did not know any
       other kind of women"--not, at least, "before he got into
       society." [Rowlette]

1375   "Truth and Fiction." Indianapolis News, 20 Nov 1899, p. 4.
       Editorial.
            Further attack on Howells and his "worshippers." The
       world "has not been fooled" by Howells' insistence that
       the novel be true to life. [Rowlette]

1376   "W. D. Howells's Lecture." Indianapolis News, 20 Nov 1899,
       p. 8. Lecture report.
            The lecture provides the occasion for a savage attack
       on Howells, presented as the overheard, condescending re-
       marks of several lecture patrons. [Rowlette]

1377   "Truth's Place in Fiction." Detroit Free Press, 21 Nov 1899,
       p. 10. Lecture report. [Rowlette]

1378   "Will It Be Another Century of Dishonor?" Detroit Free Press,
       21 Nov 1899, p. 4. Editorial.
            Approves and expands upon Howells' remark that "a re-
       public has no business with colonial dependencies."
       [Rowlette]

1379   "William Dean Howells." Columbus Dispatch, 22 Nov 1899, p. 7.
       News item.
            Announces Howells' arrival, his being the guest of Mr.
       and Mrs. John G. Mitchell. Mrs. Mitchell (née Laura Platt)
       is his wife's cousin. [Rowlette]

1380   "William Dean Howells." Columbus Dispatch, 22 Nov 1899, p. 11.
       News item.
            Announces lecture, quotes Chicago Times-Herald praises,
       especially of Howells' pronunciation, which is free of
       all "English accent." See also Columbus Citizen, 22 Nov
       1899, p. 8. [Rowlette]

1899

1381 "Honors to Howells." Columbus Dispatch, 23 Nov 1899, p. 10.
      News item.
          Reports the Mitchells' formal reception for Howells and
      names seventy-three of the two hundred guests. [Rowlette]

1382 [Untitled.] Columbus Ohio State Journal, 23 Nov 1899, p. 3.
      Lecture announcement.
          Includes biographical sketch of Howells in Ohio and a
      list of three dozen of his titles. [Rowlette]

1383 "William Dean Howells." Columbus Ohio State Journal, 23 Nov
      1899, p. 10. Lecture announcement.
          Notes other papers' approval of Howells' "directness and
      simplicity" on the platform. [Rowlette]

1384 "Class of 1900 To Meet Howells." Hamilton Evening Democrat,
      24 Nov 1899, p. 4. News item.
          The seniors of Central High School are invited to a
      reception for Howells at the home of his uncle and aunt,
      Dr. and Mrs. Henry C. Howells. [Rowlette]

1385 "Delighted--An Incident of a Reception." Columbus Citizen,
      24 Nov 1899, p. 6. Anecdote.
          Reports incident of effusive woman who told Howells she
      had read all about him in an encyclopedia. [Rowlette]

1386 "Mr. Howells Lectures." Columbus Dispatch, 24 Nov 1899, p. 6.
      Brief report of lecture. See also Columbus Citizen,
      24 Nov 1899, p. 4. [Rowlette]

1387 "Some of Mr. Howells's Points." Columbus Dispatch, 24 Nov
      1899, p. 4. Editorial.
          Notes Ohio's pride in Howells. The points are that
      Howells, in paying tribute to other authors, "offset the
      charge of egotism that has been brought against him"; and
      that Howells "talks like an educated Ohio man" rather than
      "'so Bostonese, you know.'" [Rowlette]

1388 BOARDMAN, JOSEPH LOCKHART. "To William Dean Howells."
      Columbus Dispatch, 24 Nov 1899, p. 4. Poem.
          Ten lame couplets in tribute to Howells, bidding him
      "All hail and thrice welcome" and honoring the "Dear
      friend of my early years," the "man whom I loved as a
      boy." [Rowlette]

1389 [Untitled.] Columbus Dispatch, 24 Nov 1899, p. 4. Anecdote.
          Howells' response to the lady who read about him in the
      encyclopedia was, "Which one, madame?" [Rowlette]

1390 "William Dean Howells as His Head Makes Him--The Author from
      Phrenologist Point of View." Cincinnati Times-Star,
      24 Nov 1899, p. 8. Rpt. in part, Hamilton Evening Demo-
      crat, 25 Nov 1899, p. 6.
          Phrenologist Edgar Charles Beall finds that "Howells's
      success is distinctly indicated by the lines of his head."
      He reports the "dominant qualities" those lines reveal and
      describes Howells' head. [Rowlette]

1391 "William Dean Howells Lectures." Columbus Ohio State Journal,
      24 Nov 1899, p. 3. Lecture report.
          Loosely written. Includes brief account of the reception
      afterward at which Howells recognized some old friends.
      Only Robert Neil is named. [Rowlette]

1392 "Concerning Criticism." Columbus Citizen, 25 Nov 1899, p. 6.
      Editorial.
          Praises Howells for "refraining from destructive, fault-
      finding personal criticism." He exemplifies a "tolerably
      good rule" for critics: "Say nothing but good of the
      dead and nothing at all of the stupid." [Rowlette]

1393 "Critic and Novelist." Indianapolis News, 25 Nov 1899, p. 4.
      Editorial.
          Admonishes Howells for supporting "such barbarians as
      Tolstoy," who "seem to identify truth with ugliness, if
      not with positive filth"; the "moralist" should "make
      truth as lovely and attractive as possible." [Rowlette]

1394 "Dean Howells Has a New Serial Story." Cincinnati Enquirer,
      25 Nov 1899, p. 10. News item.
          Extremely careless item announcing a reception for
      Howells at the home of Miss (Clara) Nourse. Howells is
      "to write a new story" upon his return to New York.
      [Rowlette]

1395 "Lecture of Howells." Cincinnati Commercial Tribune, 25 Nov
      1899, p. 9. Lecture report.
          Long and discursive. Howells was introduced by John
      James Piatt. At the informal reception afterward, Howells
      was reunited with William H. Venable and John B. Peaslee.
      He declined an interview. [Rowlette]

1396 "Public Reception." Hamilton Evening Democrat, 25 Nov 1899,
      p. 6. News item.
          Announces plans for a public reception for Howells at
      the home of Mr. and Mrs. James K. Cullen. Emphasizes the
      honor Howells is doing his home town by returning and

1899

("Public Reception")
urges the public to "make Mr. Howells feel that Hamilton
has an interest in him and appreciates him as one of our
city's greatest products." See also "Howells Reception,"
Hamilton Republican-News, 25 Nov 1899, p. 5. [Rowlette]

1397 "Secret Well Kept by Howells." Cincinnati Enquirer, 25 Nov
1899, p. 2. Lecture report.
Ends with the complaint that "Mr. Howells attempted to
tell his hearers how to write a novel," then "thanked the
audience and begged them not to give away the tricks of
novel making which he had not revealed." [Rowlette]

1398 "Howells to the School Children at Central High School."
Hamilton Republican-News, 27 Nov 1899, p. 4. News item.
Describes Howells' brief appearance at the school, re-
cords his few remarks, chiefly about the old Hamilton.
See also "Howells at High School," Hamilton Evening Demo-
crat, 27 Nov 1899, p. 5. [Rowlette]

1399 "Howells Views Boyhood Scenes." Hamilton Republican-News,
27 Nov 1899, p. 5. News item.
Announces Howells' arrival, his being met by George T.
Earhart, a boyhood friend. After a reunion with his rela-
tives, Howells and Earhart toured the city, taking in the
principal landmarks and other sites important to Howells.
The same item reports an interview with Howells and his
announcement of a special lecture topic for his home town
audience, "A Boy's Town." [Rowlette]

1400 [Interview with Howells.] Hamilton Republican-News, 27 Nov
1899, p. 5. Abstr. "Addenda to Halfmann: Six New Howells
Interviews," ed. Robert Rowlette, American Literary Realism,
8 (Spring 1975), 103-104.
Howells notes the changes in Hamilton since his boyhood
years there. [Rowlette]

1401 "The Senior Class of High School Meets Howells." Hamilton
Evening Democrat, 27 Nov 1899, p. 5. News item.
Reports the Howellses' reception, emphasizing Howells'
pleasant exchanges with the students. [Rowlette]

1402 "Wm. D. Howells Interviewed." Hamilton Evening Democrat,
27 Nov 1899, p. 5. Abstr. "Addenda to Halfmann: Six New
Howells Interviews," ed. Robert Rowlette, American Literary Realism, 8 (Spring 1975), 104-105.
The interview, in which Howells reminisces about Hamilton as he knew it, follows details of his visit. [Rowlette]

1403   "Howells Tells His Life Story." Hamilton <u>Republican-News</u>,
        28 Nov 1899, p. 5. Lecture report.
            Lengthy coverage, about half of which is presented as
        direct quotations from Howells. Ends with strong tribute
        to "this wise old man," who has introduced "a new kind of
        fiction." Notes the audience's solid impression "that here
        is an honest man." [Rowlette]

1404   "Howells Tells of His Life Since Leaving Hamilton." Hamilton
        <u>Evening Democrat</u>, 28 Nov 1899, p. 5. Lecture report.
            Howells substituted a special lecture, "My Life Since I
        Left Hamilton," for only part of his regular lecture.
        [Rowlette]

1405   "Howells's Reception." Hamilton <u>Republican-News</u>, 28 Nov 1899,
        p. 5. News item.
            Reports very briefly the Cullens' reception, at which a
        "continuous line" of callers from Middletown, Oxford,
        Franklin, Trenton, College Hill, Hamilton, and elsewhere
        greeted Howells. [Rowlette]

1406   "Romance and Realism: Observations Suggested by Mr. Howells's
        Lecture." Indianapolis <u>News</u>, 28 Nov 1899, p. 11. Letter
        to the Editor [probably by Booth Tarkington].
            Laments the "endless controversy" over "the merits of
        romance and realism" occasioned by Howells' visit, defends
        Howells and realism, urges restraint in expressing views
        of authors. [Rowlette]

1407   MARTIN, EDWARD S. "Twenty-five Years After." <u>Book Buyer</u>,
        n.s. 19 (Dec 1899), 378-381. Full review of <u>Their Silver
        Wedding Journey</u>.
            This "restful" story features little excitement but "a
        great deal of entertainment and human interests enough to
        flavor every change of scene, and take the curse of instruc-
        tiveness off every description."

1408   "Mr. Howells's Books at Auction." <u>New York Times</u>, 2 Dec 1899,
        Sat. Sup., p. 811. News item.
            The sale of Howells first editions attracted little at-
        tention and low bids.

1409   "A New Novel by Mr. Howells." <u>New York Times</u>, 16 Dec 1899,
        Sat. Sup., pp. 868, 870. Review of <u>Their Silver Wedding
        Journey</u>.
            "Mr. Howells is as quietly entertaining as ever."

1899

1410 "Books of the Week." <u>Outlook</u>, 63 (30 Dec 1899), 1030. Brief
   review of <u>Their Silver Wedding Journey</u>.
    The Marches' "travel experiences comprise much that
   would be trivial if it were not for the skill with which
   Mr. Howells uses the trivial to suggest that which is il-
   luminative of human nature and character-variations."

1900

1411 BRONSON, WALTER C. <u>A Short History of American Literature</u>.
   Boston: Heath, 1900. Pp. 283-284, 346. Brief introduction. Rpt. in rev. and enl. ed. (Boston: Heath, 1919),
   pp. 304-307, 308, 456.
    "Under the influence of Tolstoi" Howells "has travelled
   far along the road of realism and social reform." His
   "more beautiful earlier sketches" and his "charming little
   farces" will likely outlive his "rather depressing realistic studies."

1412 [Untitled.] <u>Book-Lover</u>, (Autumn 1900), 5. Brief note.
    Howells considers Shakespeare, Dante, Homer, and Goethe
   "masters as regards genius, style and execution."

1413 "Recent Novels." <u>Review of Reviews</u>, 21 (Jan 1900), 119.
   Brief notice of <u>Their Silver Wedding Journey</u>.
    "A most delightful story of foreign travel in the very
   best and most charming manner."

1414 "Current Fiction." <u>Literary World</u>, 21 (6 Jan 1900), 10.
   Brief review of <u>Their Silver Wedding Journey</u>.
    "Mr. Howells beats his gold out pretty thin, but it is
   gold all the same."

1415 "Recent Publication." New Orleans <u>Daily Picayune</u>, 14 Jan
   1900, II, p. 7. Review of <u>Their Silver Wedding Journey</u>.
    "The story is by no means exciting, but flows pleasantly
   along." The Marches are pleasant traveling companions.

1416 "Literature / Mr. Howells's New Book." <u>Independent</u>, 52
   (25 Jan 1900), 257-258. Full review of <u>Their Silver Wedding Journey</u>.
    "The flavor of genius, that personal, distinguishing
   zest, comes out strong in these pages, in which Mr.
   Howells for a happy season breaks away from his paralyzing
   adoration of Tolstoi and returns to his own natural and
   very engaging self. That Tolstoi should have subordinated

("Literature / Mr. Howells's New Book")
a genius so sweet, so modern and so heartily contemporary
as Mr. Howells's is a nut for the future biographer to
crack."

1417   "The Point of View." Scribner's, 27 (Feb 1900), 251-252.
Brief reference.
Howells' admission that he has not been able to do full
justice to his literary method is used as basis for discussion of "Method and Inspiration."

1418   BARRY, JOHN D. "New York Letter." Literary World, 31 (3 Feb
1900), 43. Brief comment on A Boy's Town.
"One of the greatest records of boy life, in all its
phases, ever produced in this country."

1419   DREISER, THEODORE. "The Real Howells." Ainslee's, 5 (Mar
1900), 137-142. Interview. Rpt. "Five Interviews with
William Dean Howells," ed. George Arms and William M.
Gibson, Americana, 37 (Apr 1943), 275-282; American
Thought and Writing / The 1890's, ed. Donald Pizer (Boston:
Houghton Mifflin, 1972), pp. 62-68; "Interviews with Wil-
liam Dean Howells," ed. Ulrich Halfmann, American Literary
Realism, 6 (Fall 1973), 347-351.
A cumulative impression more than an interview. "It
does not matter whether Howells is the greatest novelist
in the world or not; he is a great character.... His
greatness is his goodness, his charm, his sincerity."

1420   "Fiction." Academy, 58 (10 Mar 1900), 205-206. Review of
Their Silver Wedding Journey.
Highly favorable response to the charm, humor, and
beauty of "'Mr. Howells's Impressionist Guide to the
Cities of Germany.'"

1421   [LOGAN, ANNIE R. M.] "Recent Novels." Nation, 70 (29 Mar
1900), 245. Brief review of Their Silver Wedding Journey.
"On the whole, Mr. Howells has conducted the Marches
over the longer part of the journey of life with great
vivacity and faithfulness to probability in character,
making a permanent contribution to literature of types of
good Americans."

1422   "New Novels." Athenaeum, No. 3780 (7 Apr 1900), 428. Review
of Their Silver Wedding Journey.
"The guide-book has been requisitioned in a way which
seems more like plunder than civilized warfare." The ingenuity of the work is that it is not tedious.

1900

1423 "Novels." Saturday Review, 89 (14 Apr 1900), 466. Review
of Their Silver Wedding Journey.
"If it were possible to banish from memory Mr. Howells
the critic, one might the more admire Mr. Howells the
novelist."

1424 "Mr. Howells's Their Silver Wedding Journey." New York Times,
12 May 1900, Sat. Sup., p. 311. Review.
"'What, after all, does it amount to? Was this thing
which has been done so well, at all worth the doing? And
we cannot heartily affirm that it was." Howells fails to
reveal "the serious meanings of life" beneath the every-
dayness on which he insists. [The questions are repeated
in subsequent reviews of Howells' work.]

1425 "The Novel of Character." New York Times, 12 May 1900, Sat.
Sup., p. 312. Editorial.
Reference to attempt of the New Orleans Times-Democrat
to start a "movement toward reaction against the pre-
vailing style of romantic fiction." Howells' novel of
character has been replaced by the novel of incident.

1426 "Recent Publications." New Orleans Daily Picayune, 13 May
1900, III, p. 3. Brief review of Their Silver Wedding
Journey.
"A love story in Mr. Howells' most characteristic manner
is woven into the history of [the Marches'] travels."

1427 "The Revolt Against Realism." New York Times, 19 May 1900,
Sat. Sup., p. 328. Editorial response to Howells' speech
before the National Sculpture Society and the Society of
Mural Painters.
Perhaps what frightens Howells about the large number
of writers of historical melodrama currently popular is
that they write well and challenge the realists
artistically.

1428 "'The Fad for Meredith.'" Chicago Evening Post Friday Literary Review, 20 May 1900, p. 4. Editorial response to
Howells' statement in a New York Sun interview [not seen]
that reading Meredith requires "critical resolution."

1429 "Fiction." Literary World, 31 (1 Jul 1900), 137. Very brief
notice of Bride Roses.

1430 FULLER, HENRY BLAKE. "Civic Federation and Literature."
Chicago Evening Post, 14 Jul 1900, p. 8. Brief reference.
"A more refined and kindly Balzac, nothing but the limi-
tations imposed by gentlemanliness itself has curtailed

(FULLER, HENRY BLAKE)
his comprehensiveness, and [Howells] will still be shining
after ninety-nine-hundredths of the rest of us--whether
federated or not--shall be extinguished and forgotten."

1431   G., W. "Crane's Friendship with Howells and Garland." New
York Times Saturday Review, 5 (21 Jul 1900), 489. Letter.
Explains how Maggie, and Crane, came to the attention
of Garland and Howells.

1432   "Books of the Week / Two Farces by Howells." Chicago Evening
Post, 4 Aug 1900, p. 5. Brief review of Room Forty-five
and Bride Roses.
The narrative lines are simple. "It is in the dialogue
and in the manner of development that the skill is dis-
played." The less successful Bride Roses might have been
written by Richard Harding Davis.

1433   "Briefer Notices." Public Opinion, 29 (9 Aug 1900), 185.
Very brief mention of Room Forty-five and Bride Roses.

1434   "Talk About Books." Chautauquan, 31 (Sep 1900), 642. Brief
mention of Three Villages.
Descriptions are "fragrant...with historical reminiscence."

1435   "Fiction." Literary World, 31 (1 Nov 1900), 223. Very brief
notice of The Smoking Car and An Indian Giver.
"Great dexterity and delicacy of expression."

1436   "Mr. Howells on Cambridge Society." New York Times, 3 Nov
1900, Sat. Sup., p. 752. Editorial response to Howells'
current articles in Harper's and Scribner's.
"Why does Mr. Howells write of the half-dozen years preceding 1872 as if they were the childhood days of a nono-
genarian in ill-health?"

1437   "Glimpses at Good Reading." Chicago Evening Post, 30 Nov
1900, p. 4. Response to first installment of Howells'
"Editor's Easy Chair" (Harper's, Dec 1900).
"The many sidedness of William Dean Howells crops out
in these introductory pages."

1438   [ALDEN, HENRY MILLS.] "Editor's Study." Harper's, 102 (Dec
1900), 159-160.
The editor, in welcoming Howells to the "Editor's Easy
Chair," recalls an anecdote about mice destroying a por-
tion of the manuscript of April Hopes. Alden praises

1900

([ALDEN, HENRY MILLS])
  Howells' ability to bring "us strange gossip of ourselves,
  probing our modern mood and consciousness," and assures
  the reader that in Howells' forthcoming "interpretations
  of life we shall know his heart as well as his thought."
  Released from the restrictions of the fictional form,
  Howells will have opportunity to "more fully unbosom
  himself."

1439   "Books of the Week / Howells at His Best." Chicago Daily
       Tribune, 1 Dec 1900, p. 10. Full review of Literary
       Friends and Acquaintance.
         "Best of all, it preserves the glow of the writer's
       youthful enthusiasm, shot through with just enough flashes
       of maturer criticism to give it piquancy."

1440   "Holiday Books / Howells the Well Beloved." Chicago Evening
       Post, 1 Dec 1900, p. 9. Full review of Literary Friends
       and Acquaintance.
         Howells' modesty and the youthfulness of his impressions,
       among other attributes, give the book its charm. It is
       more "than a series of literary biographies incrusting a
       literary autobiography; it is replete with discerning
       criticism, kindly always, but always just." Here is a
       whole literary education. Students should read the things
       Howells mentions, and write about them with the same felic-
       ity if possible.

1441   "Mr. Howells's Literary Friends." Literary World, 31 (1 Dec
       1900), 256-257. Review of Literary Friends and Acquaint-
       ance.
         "Mr. Howells is at his best in writing like that which
       this book contains."

1442   [CHADWICK, J. W.] "Mr. Howells and His Friends." Nation, 71
       (13 Dec 1900), 474-475. Full review of Literary Friends
       and Acquaintance.
         "The spirit of these recollections is, if possible, more
       admirable than their form."

1443   J., E. G. "Mr. Howells's Memories." Dial, 29 (16 Dec 1900),
       490-492. Review of Literary Friends and Acquaintance.
         A book to "be prized not only as a rich repository of
       literary anecdote and portraiture, but for its autobio-
       graphical value, and...for its vein of criticism."

1900

1444   "Recent Publications." New Orleans Daily Picayune, 16 Dec
           1900, III, p. 5. Review of Literary Friends and Acquaint-
           ance.
              Howells' impressions of people worth knowing recorded
           "in a breezy, intimate way, make this book a very valuable
           record of American celebrities."

1445   "Mr. Howells / His Personal Recollections." New York Times,
           22 Dec 1900, Sat. Sup., p. 947. Full review of Literary
           Friends and Acquaintance.
              "Nothing else Mr. Howells has given us is so worthy of
           immortality."

1446   "Up-to-Date Book Reviewing." Independent, 52 (27 Dec 1900),
           3096-3099. Brief reference.
              Howe's The Story of a Country Town "bid fair to drop
           still-born from the press when Mr. Howells breathed into
           it the breath of popular approval by going out of his way
           to declare it a personal discovery of unique promises"
           (p. 3097).

1447   WALSH, WILLIAM S. "William Dean Howells Believes in the
           Future." New York Herald, 30 Dec 1900, V, p. 13. Inter-
           view. Abstr. "Interviews with William Dean Howells," ed.
           Ulrich Halfmann, American Literary Realism, 6 (Fall 1973),
           351.
              Discussing the current state of literature, Howells con-
           cludes that fiction is the best form of contemporary
           expression.

1901

 *   [DREISER, THEODORE.] "How William Dean Howells Worked To Se-
           cure a Foothold." How They Succeeded / Life Stories of
           Successful Men Told by Themselves, [ed.] Orison Swett
           Marden. Boston: Lothrop, 1901. Pp. 171-184. Rpt.
           slightly revised from Success, 1 (Apr 1898), 5-6. See
           item 1223.

1448   HALSEY, FRANCIS WHITING, ed. "William Dean Howells in Central
           Park South, New York." American Authors and Their Homes /
           Personal Descriptions & Interviews. New York: James Pott,
           1901. Pp. 99-109. Rpt. slightly revised from New York
           Times, 26 Feb 1898, Sat. Sup., p. 136. See item 1219.
              Portrait "Mr. Howells at His Office Desk" (facing
           p. 100).

1901

1449   HARKINS, E[DWARD] F[RANCIS]. "William Dean Howells." Little
        Pilgrimages / Among the Men Who Have Written Famous Books.
        Boston: Page, 1901. Pp. 11-25. Introductory literary
        biography. Also published in Famous Authors (Men) (Boston:
        Page, 1901), pp. 11-25.
            Routine, non-critical. Intended for the "reading public."
        Portrait (in both volumes as front piece).

1450   NEWCOMER, ALPHONSO GERALD. American Literature. Chicago:
        Scott, Foresman, 1901. Pp. 298-300 and passim as indexed.
        Routine introduction.
            "All readers must grant [Howells] a deep insight into
        character, a power of exceptionally accurate and vivid
        portraiture, both of people and of scenes, and a never
        failing humor and charm of style."

1451   STILLMAN, WILLIAM JAMES. The Autobiography of a Journalist.
        2 vols. Boston and New York: Houghton Mifflin, 1901.
        I, pp. 98, 336, 370. Minor references to Howells' consular
        appointment.

1452   [STREAMER, VOLNEY.] Book Titles from Shakspere. Privately
        printed, 1901; expanded edition, 1911.
            The first edition lists thirteen Howells titles and
        sources; the 1911 edition lists sixteen novel titles and
        one play title. In both cases Howells is shown as drawing
        far more heavily from Shakespeare than has any other author
        included.

1453   "Mr. Howells' Books at Auction." Book-Lover, 2 (Spring 1901),
        232. Brief note.
            Report on New York sale of first editions of Howells'
        books.

1454   "Notes on the Season's Books." Review of Reviews, 23 (Jan
        1901), 115-116. Brief mention of Literary Friends and
        Acquaintance.
            Who is better qualified than Howells to surround liter-
        ary figures "with the 'atmosphere' of the literary Boston
        and literary New York of a generation ago?"

1455   STEDMAN, EDMUND C. "Mr. Howells and His Friends." Book Buyer,
        n.s. 21 (Jan 1901), 549-556. Full review of Literary
        Friends and Acquaintance.
            "We have no other man who can draw upon a more striking
        and inclusive master-roll." The first impressions Howells
        records reveal "the personality of the observer." Largely
        summary. Twelve illustrations including nine portraits of
        Howells' acquaintances.

1456   "Mr. Howells's First Visit to New England." Literary Digest,
       22 (26 Jan 1901), 114–115. Review of Literary Friends
       and Acquaintance.
          "With the perspective of years behind him [Howells]
       looks back with a fine sense of reverence, but a more
       critical eye." Largely quotation.

1457   GILDER, JEANNETTE L. "Mr. Howells and Some of His Friends."
       Critic, 38 (Feb 1901), 165–168. Review of Literary
       Friends and Acquaintance.
          Largely appreciative summary with extensive quotation.
       Howells is "so frank, so modest, so genial."

1458   "Talk About Books." Chautauquan, 32 (Feb 1901), 562. Brief
       review of The Smoking Car and The Indian Giver.
          Mostly summary. Appreciation for "cheerful moments"
       provided by Howells.

1459   HELLMAN, GEORGE S. "The Reminiscences of Mr. Howells."
       Bookman (New York), 13 (Mar 1901), 67–71. Review of
       Literary Friends and Acquaintance.
          "The veneration done to Human Worth—herein lies the
       greatest charm of Mr. Howells's reminiscences." From his
       record of his own "idyllic and yet strenuous days,"
       Howells emerges as an idealist, "if idealism in life means
       ...belief in the value and permanence of the noble quali-
       ties in human nature, and faith, based on this permanence,
       in a universal purpose making for good."

1460   "The Point of View." Scribner's, 29 (Apr 1901), 505. Brief
       reference.
          Howells' position on American poetry provides basis for
       discussion of the American temperament.

1461   "Talk About Books." Chautauquan, 33 (Apr 1901), 104–105.
       Brief review of Literary Friends and Acquaintance.
          "Charm that is born of judicious reminiscence." Repro-
       duction of painting of Howells and Bayard Taylor in 1860
       (p. 105).

1462   FULLER, HENRY BLAKE. "Howells Flays Professor Wendell."
       Chicago Post, 6 Apr 1901, p. 13. Note.
          Fuller flays Howells and his negative reaction to
       Barrett Wendell's Literary History of America. "Behold
       him now at last throwing the kindly mask of the advocate
       and showing the stern face of the judge—of the hanging
       judge in the black cap."

1901

1463 FIELD, ROSWELL M. "Boom Books Arraigned / Need of a John the
         Baptist To Decry Evil Ways / Make Straight Literary Paths /
         Roswell Field Joins Henry B. Fuller in Declaiming Against
         Substitution of Splutterature for Literature." Chicago
         Post, 20 Apr 1901, p. 4. Column-and-a-half news essay.
            While endorsing Howells' "recent arraignment of the
         American public for devotion to the trashy novel," Field
         notes that Howells may in large measure be "responsible
         for the catastrophe, since in the generous plentitude of
         his nature he has encouraged men to write who might be
         more profitably employed in honest agricultural pursuits,
         and in marking out a literary path for other men, for
         which they were totally unfitted and with which they were
         wholly at variance."

1464 "The Literary Man as Hero-Worshipper." Academy, 60 (20 Apr
         1901), 339-340. Review of Literary Friends and Acquaint-
         ance.
            Howells recalls his own "intercourse with the greater
         gods of the craft...in a humble and grateful spirit."
         Extensive quotation.

1465 "Music and the Drama." Chicago Post, 1 May 1901, p. 4. Short
         essay.
            Full-column support of Howells' opposition to "book
         plays," as revealed in a New York Sunday Herald interview
         by Pendennis (not seen).

1466 "Literature." Independent, 53 (2 May 1901), 1025. Review of
         Literary Friends and Acquaintance.
            Cheerful anecdotes lacking elevation or real criticism.

1467 "Books of the Week." Outlook, 68 (11 May 1901), 133. Brief
         notice of THE NIAGARA BOOK.
            "The only guide to Niagara of any literary or scientific
         importance."

1468 "'Romanticistic' vs. 'Poetic.'" New York Times, 11 May 1901,
         Sat. Sup., p. 336. Brief note.
            Howells' criticism of two poetic dramas by Stephen
         Phillis ("The New Poetic Drama," North American Review,
         172 [May 1901], 794-800) is challenged.

1469 NORRIS, FRANK. "Frank Norris' Weekly Letter." Chicago
         American, 25 May 1901, p. 8. Brief reference.
            Dreiser's Sister Carrie is the best realistic novel since
         A Modern Instance.

1470   "Literary Recollections." <u>Bookman</u> (London), 20 (Jun 1901),
            121. Review of <u>My</u> [sic] <u>Literary Friends and Acquaintance</u>.
            Howells' modesty and frankness impress one. The range
            of his appreciations is limited to the proper, the cul-
            tured, and the "recognisably great."

1471   "<u>Literary Friends and Acquaintance</u>." <u>Athenaeum</u>, No. 3840
            (1 Jun 1901), 686-687. Full review.
            Howells "seems to go out of his way to write unpleasant-
            ly" about the English. A "note of melancholy" is perva-
            sive. None of Howells' other books has greater general
            interest.

1472   "<u>Literary Friends and Acquaintance</u>." <u>Spectator</u>, 86 (1 Jun
            1901), 807-808. Review.
            Largely descriptive. The first part of the book is best
            because it reveals Howells. It is a pity he succeeded so
            well in keeping himself out of the narrative.

1473   "Mr. Howells's <u>A Pair of Patient Lovers</u>." <u>New York Times</u>,
            8 Jun 1901, Sat. Sup., p. 405. Full review.
            One can only be grateful for Howells' work--"for its
            sincerity, for its charm, for its pathos and joyousness,
            and for the serene simplicity that hides so much art."

1474   "Novels of the Week." <u>Spectator</u>, 86 (29 Jun 1901), 979-980.
            Review of <u>A Pair of Patient Lovers</u>.
            Howells' "chief title to distinction...is that he is at
            once extremely subtle and perfectly wholesome." His
            achievements are not lessened by "his consistent refusal
            to denationalise his genius."

1475   "Collections of Short Stories." <u>Literary World</u>, 32 (1 Jul
            1901). Short review of <u>A Pair of Patient Lovers</u>.
            "The literary cat playing with the social mouse." Al-
            though slight in theme and limited in action, the stories
            show Howells' understanding of women. His ability with
            conversation and his "always good-natured and amusing
            thrusts at the weaknesses and waywardness of the human
            heart."

1476   "Fiction." <u>Academy</u>, 61 (6 Jul 1901), 13. Brief review of
            <u>A Pair of Patient Lovers</u>.
            Howells is at his best.

1901

1477   "The Book-Buyer's Guide." Critic, 39 (Aug 1901), 182. Re-
        view of A Pair of Patient Lovers.
            Coming to Howells after reading stories of adventure
        "is like making harbor after a storm." This work seems
        unusually full of his "quick and charming thought-play."

1478   "Summer Novels." Book Buyer, n.s. 23 (Aug 1901), 50. Brief
        review of A Pair of Patient Lovers.
            "If one must now and then regret that this fine artist
        expends the hard-earned skill and delicacy of the master
        on the carving of cherry-stones, it remains a pleasure to
        recognize the master's skill."

1479   "Novels." Saturday Review, 92 (17 Aug 1901), 212. Review
        of A Pair of Patient Lovers.
            "The most attractive part of this collection of short
        stories is their cover, which would be quite fine in a
        cheap way if the medallion of the author might be
        eliminated."

1480   "Short Stories." Athenaeum, No. 3853 (31 Aug 1901), 282.
            Review of A Pair of Patient Lovers. Highly favorable.
            Howells' "analytic insight" is rich, as is Meredith's.
        Howells and James are "living refutations" of negative
        attitudes toward American fiction. In "dignity and sim-
        plicity of diction," Howells stands superior.

1481   SWIFT, LINDSAY. "Boston as Portrayed in Fiction." Book
        Buyer, n.s. 23 (Oct 1901), 197-204. Short reference.
            One paragraph on Howells credits him with the discovery
        of modern Boston in literature.

1482   CARRUTH, FRANCES WESTON. "Boston in Fiction / Part I--The
        Old North End." Bookman (New York), 14 (Nov 1901); 236-
        254; "Part II--About the Common" (Dec 1901), 364-385;
        "Part III--The Back Bay District" (Jan 1902), 507-521;
        "Part IV--Suburban Boston" (Feb 1902), 590-604. A four-
        part illustrated description of Boston as recorded in lit-
        erary sources.
            Reference to Howells and his work in the form of comment,
        quotation, and pictures is frequent, especially in the
        second and third installments.

1483   "William Dean Howells." Outlook, 69 (16 Nov 1901), 713. An
        appreciation.
            Howells "represents a democratic type of Americanism."
        Lowell, Hawthorne, and Holmes "loved and honored man, but
        shrank a little from men. Mr. Howells is filled with a

("William Dean Howells")
deep and passionate sympathy for men; the sadness of the
world penetrates his spirit; the sorrows of the race
mingle with his life." Full-page portrait, drawn from
life by Alfred Houghton Clark (p. [712]).

1484   "The Book-Buyer's Guide." Critic, 39 (Dec 1901), 581–582.
Brief review of Heroines of Fiction.
"However unkind Mr. Howells may be to the heroines of
his own creating, toward the heroines of other people he
is invariably generous, bringing to their treatment def-
erence and insight and charm."

1485   "New Holiday Books and New Editions." Book Buyer, n.s. 23
(Dec 1901), 416. Brief review of Heroines of Fiction.
Howells' skill in building "voluble and highly suggestive
ladies from a single rib--or other bone--of human characteristic, has been of great service to him in his analysis
and appreciation of various 'Heroines of Fiction.'"

1486   SULLIVAN, T. R. "Italian Journeys." Book Buyer, n.s. 23
(Dec 1901), 361–364. Full review.
The value of a book of travel depends upon the knowledge
of the traveler, and this adventurer is well equipped.
Howells records his keen observations with delicacy of expression. Four illustrations of Joseph Pennell reprinted
from this new edition.

1487   "Heroines of Fiction." Literary World, 32 (1 Dec 1901), 215.
Review.
Howells, who is so well acquainted with modern fiction,
discusses it "with the realism of colored portraiture and
the effects of actual life."

1488   "Mr. Howells's Italian Journeys." Literary World, 32 (1 Dec
1901), 222. Announcement of new edition.
"Mr. Howells is never better than in writing like this."

1489   "Heroines / Those Famous in Fiction Estimated by Mr. Howells."
New York Times, 7 Dec 1901, Sat. Sup., p. 944. Full review of Heroines of Fiction.
Howells' analyses of literary heroines is generally
valid.

1490   "The Holiday Books." Outlook, 69 (7 Dec 1901), 902. Brief
notice of Heroines of Fiction.
These studies in criticism will often arouse dissent,
but they offer "abundant suggestion, very delicate characterization, and...charm of manner."

1901

1491   BURTON, RICHARD. "Mr. Howells Talks of Fiction." Dial, 31
        (16 Dec 1901), 506-507. Review of Heroines of Fiction.
        "Mr. Howells is that rare thing, a genuine essayist."

1492   "Holiday Publications." Dial, 31 (16 Dec 1901), 516. Notice
        of the revised Italian Journeys.
        "A thorough revision...done with painstaking care."

1493   NORRIS, FRANK. "A Plea for Romantic Fiction." Boston Evening
        Transcript, 18 Dec 1901, p. 14. Brief reference. Rpt.
        The Literary Criticism of Frank Norris, ed. Donald Pizer
        (Austin: University of Texas Press, 1964), pp. 75-78.
        Realism can be "respectable as a church and proper as a
        deacon--as, for instance, the novels of Mr. Howells."

1494   [LOGAN, ANNIE R. M.] "Heroines of Fiction." Nation, 73
        (19 Dec 1901), 479-480. Full review.
        This work is broader than the title indicates. It is
        Howells' "most extensive and important contribution to
        critical literature." "What comes out most sharply is
        the American view of the right use of fiction, of its im-
        portance in literature, and of the methods by which its
        best and most enduring effects may be attained."

1495   "Literature / Heroines and Mr. Howells." Independent, 53
        (26 Dec 1901), 3087-3088. Review of Heroines of Fiction.
        One finds here "no lack of the sort of judgments which
        will call forth dissent or stir up antagonism." But
        Howells has the merit of supporting and making clear "his
        theoretical dicta."

                            1902

1496   ABERNETHY, JULIAN W. American Literature. New York: Merrill,
        1902. Pp. 438-445 and passim as indexed. General bio-
        graphical and literary introduction.
        "That Howells is superior to [his] restricted literary
        creed is pretty thoroughly attested by his wide popularity"
        (p. 441).

1497   HALSEY, FRANCIS WHITING. Our Literary Deluge / and Some of
        Its Deeper Waters. New York: Doubleday, Page, 1902.
        P. 39. Glancing reference only.
        The fact that writers like Howells are considered suc-
        cessful does not mean they have been "most widely read."

1498   PERRY, BLISS. Study of Prose Fiction. Boston and New York:
        Houghton Mifflin, 1902; rev. 1920. Passim as indexed.
        Minor references.
            Howells is compared with Matthew Arnold (p. 46), George
        Eliot (p. 110), and Nathaniel Hawthorne (p. 272). Brief
        mention of his contemporary American quality (p. 40) and
        his deliberate choice of the commonplace (p. 225).

1499   ROBERTSON, JOHN M. "Mr. Howells' Recent Novels (1890)."
        Criticisms. 2 vols. London: A. and H. Bradlaugh Bonner,
        1902. I, pp. 111–121.
            In Howells' early work "were manifest the delicate facul-
        ty of style, the felicity of phrase and epigram, the humor,
        the variable power of portraiture, that mark his latest
        books, along with the same phrases of wandering philosophy
        and erratic sentimentalism" (p. 112). Howells lacks a
        masculine mental fibre.

1500   FRANKLIN, VIOLA PRICE. "Lowell's Appreciation of Howells."
        Methodist Review, 84 (Jan 1902), 112–115. Essay.
            Tracing the relationship between the two men, Franklin
        quotes extensively from the letters Lowell wrote to
        Howells. Lowell was early impressed by Howells' ability,
        and his suggestions and criticism undoubtedly became a
        factor in Howells' success.

1501   MATTHEWS, BRANDER. "Mr. Howells as a Critic." Forum, 32
        (Jan 1902), 629–638. Essay. Rpt. Howells / A Century of
        Criticism, ed. Kenneth E. Eble (Dallas: Southern Methodist
        University, 1962), pp. 65–77, and in part, The War of
        Critics over William Dean Howells, ed. Edwin H. Cady and
        David L. Frazier (Evanston: Row, Peterson, 1962), pp. 83–
        90.
            A major attempt to evaluate Howells as critic concluding
        that although Howells may have been "over-strenuous" and
        "somewhat careless of proportion" on occasions, his doc-
        trines were not new, but "rooted in truth, and the truth
        shall surely prevail."

1502   "The Point of View / Doctors of Letters." Scribner's, 31
        (Jan 1902), 123–124. News coverage.
            The awarding of honorary degrees by Yale University on
        the occasion of its 200th anniversary. Howells was one of
        eight authors so honored.

1902

1503   NORRIS, FRANK. "An American School of Fiction? A Denial."
       Boston Evening Transcript, 22 Jan 1902, p. 17. Brief
       reference. Rpt. The Literary Criticism of Frank Norris,
       ed. Donald Pizer (Austin: University of Texas Press,
       1964), pp. 108-111.
           Of all the writers of American fiction, Howells has had
       "the broadest vision." Yet he has had no successors.

1504   "Lowell and Howells." Harper's Weekly, 46 (25 Jan 1902), 101.
       Note.
           Largely a summary of Viola Price Franklin's "Lowell's
       Appreciation of Howells" in the Methodist Review, 84
       (Jan 1902), 112-115.

1505   "Mr. Howells's Study of Heroines." Literary Digest, 24 (8 Feb
       1902), 195. Review of Heroines of Fiction.
           "One quarter of keen, critical observation, really en-
       lightening, and three quarters genial superfluity."
       Portrait.

1506   "Literature / Heroines of Fiction." Times Literary Supple-
       ment, 14 Feb 1902, pp. 33-34. Full review.
           The book "abounds in unkind remarks" about the British.
       In his concern with the "Nice Girl," Howells "has missed
       the real meaning of his own classification. He never
       once, so far as we can make out, makes the remark that the
       most life-like heroines are drawn by women." Another gen-
       eralization that seems not to occur to him "is that hero-
       ines as a class are too young... Let Mr. Howells keep
       his Nice Girls; give us their aunts and their (well-pre-
       served) mammas."

1507   "Heroines of Fiction." Athenaeum, No. 3880 (8 Mar 1902),
       301-302. Full review.
           "Mr. Howells's opinions are held with so little zest,
       point, or vivacity, so little are we interested in what
       he has to say, that we hardly care to dispute them." The
       reviewer's tone suggests both hurt and dignity.

1508   "River Trip for W. D. Howells / Novelist, After Visiting
       Brother in the West, To Go Down the Ohio by Steamboat."
       New York Times, 10 Mar 1902, p. 1. News item datelined
       "Ashtabula, Ohio, March 9."

1509   "Literary Notes." Independent, 54 (3 Apr 1902), 821. Brief
       note.
           Supports Howells' judgment of Longfellow's sonnets.

1510   "About Books and Bookmen." Chicago Evening Post, 12 Apr 1902,
        p. 10. Brief announcement of forthcoming The Kentons.
        It is written with "the delicacy and precision of treat-
        ment" that have made Howells famous.

1511   FULLER, HENRY BLAKE. "W. D. Howells's Return to Fiction in
        His New Novel The Kentons / The Place Held by the Finished
        Novelist Between the Advocates of Aristocratic and Demo-
        cratic Ideals in Literature." Chicago Evening Post,
        26 Apr 1902, p. 9. Full two-column review.
        Howells' work stands between the extremes called for by
        Brander Matthews and Mrs. Elia Peattie. Howells ranks
        among "the Things Established." He has mastered both de-
        tail and characterization. "Jane Austin is always before
        his eyes, and the preparation of social documents for the
        instruction of posterity seems to be his constant aim."

1512   "Library of Current Literature." Booklover's Bulletin, No. 21
        (1 May 1902), 141. Brief review of The Kentons.
        "Mr. Howells possesses the keenest appreciation of the
        meaning and influence of the most trivial nuances of talk
        and gesture upon the feeling and action of his characters."

1513   ["W. D. Howells."] Booklover's Bulletin, No. 21 (1 May 1902),
        134. Note.
        On Howells' industry: "'inspiration is perspiration.'"

1514   "Recent Fiction / Mr. Howells's The Kentons." New York Times,
        3 May 1902, Sat. Sup., p. 298. Full review.
        "It is an engaging--and an enraging--book." The charac-
        ters are perfectly portrayed but they are "deadly
        commonplace."

1515   "Book Reviews." Public Opinion, 32 (8 May 1902), 601. Review
        of The Kentons.
        "For down-to-the-ground truth in every possible detail
        of commonplace and uninteresting facts," Howells has never
        gone farther.

1516   "Books of the Week." Outlook, 71 (10 May 1902), 135. Brief
        review of The Kentons.
        "In some of Mr. Howells's stories he is entertaining;
        in some he is subtle; in some he combines the two things--
        and to this class belongs The Kentons."

1902

1517   "Mr. Howells's New Book." New York Times, 10 May 1902, Sat.
        Sup., p. 312. Review of The Kentons.
            A postscript to the review a week earlier points out
        the "young clergyman" as a new type, recognizes that
        Howells, almost alone among novelists, ignores the con-
        ventions of novel writing, and concludes that Howells
        "sees and hears, but fails to divine."

1518   "Notes on Novels." Academy, 62 (10 May 1902), 481-482. Brief
        notice of The Kentons.
            "A characteristic Howells."

1519   "Fiction / Mr. W. D. Howells." Times Literary Supplement,
        16 May 1902, p. 139. Review of The Kentons.
            "How can the showman give any one who has not read this
        book any idea of the dainty, delicate wit that plays in
        and out and round about every page...? There has been
        nothing better since Cherbuliez, and it is not spoilt, as
        Cherbuliez too often spoilt even his more exquisite come-
        dies, with a dash of melodrama thrown in at the end."

1520   "Books and Authors." Living Age, 233 (24 May 1902), 511.
        Brief review of The Kentons.
            "The most ardent American might be content to rest his
        case for the soundness and sweetness of our domestic ideal
        on such a presentation as The Kentons."

1521   "Fiction." Academy, 62 (24 May 1902), 530. Brief review of
        The Kentons.
            "Delicate and humorous character-drawing."

1522   KAUFFMAN, REGINALD WRIGHT. "From Readers / Mr. Howells's The
        Kentons." New York Times, 24 May 1902, Sat. Sup., p. 353.
        Letter to the Times challenges the Times reviewer.
            Little great fiction focuses on ladies and gentlemen.
        "The 'just-as-good-as-you-are' people have never before
        been adequately treated by any other novelist. They may
        not be pleasant people, and they may not be in the majori-
        ty, but they are distinctly American and distinctly re-
        publican. They are the price we must pay for our form of
        government."

1523   "William Dean Howells / The Latest Likeness of the Distin-
        guished Novelist and Man of Letters." Chicago Evening
        Post, 24 May 1902, II, p. 1. Portrait photograph.

1524   HALSEY, FRANCIS W. "Some Books To Read This Summer." Review of Reviews, 25 (Jun 1902), 707. Brief mention of The Kentons.
    "Many are the amusing situations which the author's fertile fancy evolves." Portrait (p. 700).

1525   "The Kentons." Book News, 20 (Jun 1902), 760. Full review.
    "The secret of unattractiveness is its spirit of realism."

1526   "The Kentons." Literary World, 33 (1 Jun 1902), 84. Short review.
    "There is not an incident in this book, not a character, worth the microscopical observation bestowed upon either."

1527   PAYNE, WILLIAM MORTON. "Recent Fiction." Dial, 32 (1 Jun 1902), 387-388. Brief review of The Kentons.
    Mostly summary. This story "of commonplace people in commonplace relations" is well suited to Howells' powers.

1528   [LOGAN, ANNIE R. M.] "Novels, Mostly of American Life." Nation, 74 (12 Jun 1902), 470. Review of The Kentons.
    The novel records "the failure of culture to improve character, and the failure of that American policy... which prevents a direct and serious exercise of parental authority." Howells seems "to have fallen back on observations made twenty years ago."

1529   "A Book of Real Americans." Literary Digest, 24 (14 Jun 1902), 815. Review of The Kentons.
    No matter how many protests one may lodge against the work of Howells, "it is he alone who can give a true picture of life in this country." He "alone has the distance necessary for a true perspective."

1530   "New Novels." Athenaeum, No. 3894 (14 Jun 1902), 748. Brief review of The Kentons.
    Bright but empty.

1531   PEATTIE, ELIA W. "Mrs. Peattie Writes of Howells, Mary MacLane, and Owen Wister." Chicago Daily Tribune, 21 Jun 1902, p. 19. Literary feature.
    Howells has "introduced us to the folk we had been carefully avoiding all our lives." He puts no "trappings" on them, but presents them as they are. Howells is "a force for good which is underestimated."

1902

1532   "Novel Notes." Bookman (London), 22 (Jul 1902), 144. Brief
       review of The Kentons.
           In addition to Howells' usual literary effectiveness,
       "The Kentons is an interesting presentment of parental
       patience."

1533   "Mr. Howells and The Kentons." Harper's Weekly, 19 Jul 1902,
       p. 947. Review.
           "Mr. Howells has never succeeded better in drawing
       familiar types with a skill and charm of divination that
       impart fresh human interest to their commonplace signifi-
       cance, and by a wonderful sympathy and understanding
       brings out the hidden romance of their apparently ordinary
       lives." Most of the three-column, full-page review takes
       the form of a tribute to Howells, "the most highly sensi-
       tized reflector of the modern mind in American conscious-
       ness," noting the increasing respect given him in critical
       and literary circles.

1534   "Library Table." Current Literature, 33 (Aug 1902), 242.
       Brief review of The Kentons.
           "It is with the ordinary that Mr. Howells does his most
       extraordinary work; and when one finishes reading the story
       of this very ordinary family, one knows the extraordinary
       beauty and subtlety of every-day life."

1535   "Novels." Saturday Review, 94 (9 Aug 1902), 175. Review of
       The Kentons.
           The Kentons alive would not be interesting, but one
       wonders at Howells' skill in portraiture.

1536   BROWN, EDITH BAKER. "Moral Hesitations of the Novelist."
       Atlantic, 90 (Oct 1902), 545-548. Brief reference.
           Howells and Stevenson, far apart in "artistic convic-
       tion," are parallel in "moral feeling." But in the area
       of moral judgment, Howells is inconclusive (pp. 545-546).

1537   MATHER, FRANK JEWETT, JR. "Literature." Forum, 34 (Oct-Dec
       1902), 221-230. Essay review with full discussion of The
       Kentons (pp. 221-223).
           The Kentons "not only exemplifies Mr. Howells' familiar
       qualities at their best, but is as well a most keen and
       kindly satire of American society. Herein lies the dif-
       ference from other novels of his to which it bears a super-
       ficial likeness."

1538   "Some New Essays / Mr. Howells's Latest Volume of Collected
            Papers." New York Times, 18 Oct 1902, Sat. Sup., p. 708.
            Review of Literature and Life.
                Perhaps because Howells does not permit himself, like
            Thackeray, to chat with his readers in his novels, he is
            especially chatty and confidential in this miscellaneous
            volume. "It is evident that life exists for Mr. Howells
            only as literature in the rough," and it is a "pity he
            cannot enjoy some things without the novelist's
            sophistication."

1539   "Pony Baker." New York Times, 25 Oct 1902, Sat. Sup., p. 737.
            Review.
                The story is told "as only Mr. Howells can tell a story.
            The boy nature is true to a hair."

1540   SMALLEY, GEORGE W. "Men of Letters / Personal Recollections
            and Appreciations." McClure's, 20 (Nov 1902), 55-65.
            Brief reference.
                On Howells' intolerance of the "unlettered" world,
            especially as comprised of people of fashion (p. 55).
            Portrait (p. 59).

1541   [The Flight of Pony Baker.] Booklover's Bulletin, No. 28
            (1 Nov 1902), 396. Brief mention.
                Ranks Howells' story with Aldrich's The Story of a Bad
            Boy and Twain's The Adventures of Tom Sawyer.

1542   "The Personal Essay." Literary Digest, 25 (1 Nov 1902), 565.
            Review of Literature and Life.
                An established writer "may write about that which inter-
            ests himself, and he may be sure it will interest others."
            Howells is one of the few writers who can do such personal
            writing well. Portrait.

1543   "The Books of the Week." Public Opinion, 33 (6 Nov 1902),
            597. Brief review of Literature and Life.
                Minute details, "that sometimes clog the wheels" of
            Howells novels, "are really delightful when taken by
            themselves."

1544   "Books of the Week." Outlook, 72 (8 Nov 1902), 611. Brief
            review of The Flight of Pony Baker.
                The boys "are just the wholesome sort of amiable young
            savages that healthy boys are sure to be when they are
            not perverted by artificial conditions."

1902

1545   "Literature." Independent, 54 (13 Nov 1902), 2717-2718.
       Brief review of Literature and Life.
       Howells at his best.

1546   HALE, EDWARD E., JR. "The Dean of American Letters." Dial,
       33 (16 Nov 1902), 323-325. Full review of Literature and
       Life.
       Previously Hale had selected Irving and Lowell "as the
       representative men of letters of their times." Here he
       confers a similar honor on Howells.

1547   "Life, and A Man of Letters." Academy, 63 (22 Nov 1902),
       553-554. Full review of Literature and Life.
       In Howells' mind "literature, the expression, overshadows
       life, the fact." Howells has "a passion for words, with
       which he so plays about the unessential as almost to per-
       suade us that the unessential matters."

1548   "The Book-Buyer's Guide." Critic, 41 (Dec 1902), 582. Very
       brief review of The Flight of Pony Baker.
       "As good women have no pasts, so good books deserve no
       criticism." This one is recommended.

1549   "Holiday Books, New and Old." Book Buyer, n.s. 25 (Dec 1902),
       459. Brief notice of Literature and Life.
       Favorable.

1550   KNAUFFT, ERNEST. "The Season's Books for the Young." Review
       of Reviews, 26 (Dec 1902), 753. Brief review of The
       Flight of Pony Baker.
       Howells' "touches of uncompromising realism" make his
       book "sui generis in contrast to the machine-made boys'
       book."

1551   "Literature and Life." Book News, 21 (Dec 1902), 250-251.
       Brief review.
       "The articles are scraps, as it were, but they are some
       of the best scraps." Howells "has the touch that awakens
       response."

1552   "Books for the Young." Dial, 33 (1 Dec 1902), 407. Brief
       mention of The Flight of Pony Baker.

1553   "Children's Books." Literary World, 33 (1 Dec 1902), 206-207.
       Brief mention of The Flight of Pony Baker.
       The excellence of the book lies in "the verisimilitude
       of its style to the sensations, emotions, and expressions
       of the average boy."

1554   "Literature and Life." Literary World, 33 (1 Dec 1902), 201–
          202. Review.
             Howells' essays are "extremely clever."

1555   "Three Good Stories About Children." Literary Digest, 25
          (6 Dec 1902), 755. Brief review of The Flight of Pony
          Baker.
             It is the child's point of view which sets this story
          apart.

                              1903

1556   BURTON, RICHARD. Literary Leaders of America. New York:
          Chautauquan Press, 1903. Pp. 314–315. Brief comment.
             "Mr. Howells has steadily produced a series of fictional
          studies which the future social historian is likely to
          recognize as the most comprehensive and truthful survey
          of certain sections of Eastern life--especially that in
          cities--ever made by an American novelist."

1557   FISKE, HORACE SPENCER. Provincial Types in American Fiction.
          New York: Chautauquan Press, 1903. Pp. 11–42. Rpt.
          Port Washington, New York: Kennikat Press, 1968.
             Chapter 2 is an extensive and non-critical summary of
          The Rise of Silas Lapham, "a convincing portrayal of a
          self-made Yankee type."

1558   HIGGINSON, THOMAS WENTWORTH, and HENRY WALCOTT BOYNTON. A
          Reader's History of American Literature. Boston: Hough-
          ton Mifflin, 1903. Pp. 3, 236, 248–252. General
          assessment.
             The first Western writer to become an Eastern literary
          leader, "Mr. Howells is without an equal among his English-
          speaking contemporaries as to some of the most attractive
          literary graces. Unless it be in Mr. James, he has no
          rival for half-tints, for modulations, for subtle phrases
          that touch the edge of an assertion yet stop short of it"
          (p. 249). Rather than being an expansive Westerner,
          Howells is a "miniature artist" (p. 251).

1559   NORRIS, FRANK. "An American School of Fiction." The Responsi-
          bilities of the Novelist. New York: Doubleday Page, 1903.
          P. 196 (not indexed).
             In A Modern Instance and The Rise of Silas Lapham,
          Howells, "American to the core," provided the foundation
          for a "fine, hardy literature, that promised to be our
          very, very own"; but he has had no serious followers.

1903

1560   TRENT, WILLIAM P. A History of American Literature. Short
       Histories of the Literatures of the World: XII, ed.
       Edmund Gosse. London: Heinemann, 1903. Pp. 444, 568,
       591.
           Brief references in connection with James Russell Lowell
       and George William Curtis.

1561   TROWBRIDGE, JOHN TOWNSEND. My Own Story / With Recollections
       of Noted Persons. Boston and New York: Houghton Mifflin,
       1903. Pp. 319, 369.
           Minor references to Howells as editor of Atlantic and to
       his comments on Whitman.

1562   [WHITELOCK, WILLIAM WALLACE.] "The Otherwise Men." The Liter-
       ary Guillotine. New York and London: John Lane, 1903.
       Pp. 238-262.
           A farcical and satiric report of a meeting of the Liter-
       ary Emergency Court investigating, among other things, the
       relationship between literature and business. A fictive
       Howells says they cannot possibly be separated. He de-
       fines "the highest order of fiction, as my own, somewhat
       in this manner: an insistence upon the unessential until
       the meeting of extremes" (p. 257).

1563   MOWBRAY, J. P. "Mr. Howells's Réchauffé." Critic, 42 (Jan
       1903), 21-26. Review of Literature and Life.
           Howells' "singularly mobile intellectuality...ex-
       presses a capricious acumen--an uncertain and restless
       cognition, which to the psychologist might indicate a cer-
       tain absence of intellectual mooring, but which to us is
       only the play of a volatile fancy that cannot rest long on
       any coign of vantage; a gayety of heart that preserves for
       us all the varying moods of youth."

1564   "The Points of View / Every-day People in Fiction." Scribner's,
       33 (Jan 1903), 123-124. Note.
           Response to Howells' observation that English readers are
       more receptive to "every-day American" types in fiction
       than are American readers. Howells is not simply interested
       in "every-day" people but in the beauties which illuminate
       them.

1565   PRESTON, HARRIET WATERS. "The Latest Novels of Howells and
       James." Atlantic, 91 (Jan 1903), 77-82. Full review of
       The Kentons (and The Wings of the Dove). Rpt. in part,
       The War of the Critics over William Dean Howells, ed.
       Edwin H. Cady and David L. Frazier (Evanston: Row, Peter-
       son, 1962), pp. 91-92.

(PRESTON, HARRIET WATERS)
Howells, to an unusual degree, has always been a personal writer. He "was ever more interesting than his
theme or his thesis, and infinitely more amusing." Never
has this fact been more conspicuous than "in the truly
vapid story of the Kentons." Howells was at his best in
A Foregone Conclusion. The influence of Tolstoy on his
work has been exaggerated.

1566   SMITH, MINNA. "The Flight of Pony Baker." Reader, 1 (Jan
       1903), 284-285. Review.
       "It is intensely native."

1567   "Literature and Life." Spectator, 90 (10 Jan 1903), 55. Re-
       view.
       Largely descriptive. Contains some qualifications of
       Howells' advice to young contributors.

1568   BARRY, WILLIAM. "Mr. Howells' Essays." Bookman (London),
       23 (Feb 1903), 214. Review of Literature and Life.
       Howells "is never without a point of interest, and if
       you look to his meaning you will perceive that his devo-
       tion to literature is nothing else than faith and hope in
       a more perfect human life."

1569   BOYNTON, H. W. "Books New and Old / Literature and Life."
       Atlantic, 91 (Feb 1903), 261-262. Full review.
       Boynton investigates the condition of life as it relates
       to the intimacy Howells seeks to establish between litera-
       ture and life.

1570   C., H. D. "Literature and Life." Reader, 1 (Feb 1903), 395.
       Howells, unlike many later novelists, is a man of
       letters.

1571   MUZZEY, DAVID SAVILLE. "Views of Readers on Recent Books /
       [The Kentons]." World's Work, 5 (Feb 1903), 3138. Con-
       tribution to a symposium.
       "Mr. Howells writes about real men and women in real
       circumstances. His incomparable gifts of insight into
       the springs of action, of mastery of colloquial English,
       and of humor refined to the utmost delicacy of suggestion,
       redeem everything that he writes from the least taint of
       triviality or commonplaceness."

1903

1572 [LOGAN, ANNIE R. M.] "Literature and Life." Nation, 76
         (12 Feb 1903), 138. Review.
            Here one finds "a clear impression of the kind of man
         Mr. Howells is, and of the things that most attract his
         imagination and engage his sympathies. These things are
         recognizable by all Americans as fragments of common exper-
         ience...."

1573 GARLAND, HAMLIN. "Sanity in Fiction." North American Review,
         176 (Mar 1903), 336-348. Rpt. in part, The War of the
         Critics over William Dean Howells, ed. Edwin H. Cady and
         David L. Frazier (Evanston: Row, Peterson, 1962), pp. 92-
         99.
            Major essay centers on Howells. He, "more than any other
         of our writers, has demonstrated that a public exists for
         a sane and wholesome novel. In his development can be
         traced the broadening scope of our literature, and, above
         all, its deepening humanity--its altruism."

1574 "Literature and Life." Athenaeum, No. 3935 (28 Mar 1903),
         393-394. Full review.
            "Mr. Howells is prone to take a somewhat easy line...
         and practises an economy of thinking which is not quite
         hospitable to the faithful reader." He is qualified to be
         more incisive.

1575 "The Point of View / A Displacement." Scribner's, 33 (May
         1903), 635-636. Note.
            Howells is mentioned, along with Zola, Kipling, Meredith,
         and James, as dealing "with the actual, or with the logic
         of the actual." "Imagination is no longer the ruler, but
         the handmaid. Its former place is occupied by Observation."

1576 "William Dean Howells." Bookman (New York), 17 (Jun 1903),
         343. Portrait. Rpt. reduced, 24 (Dec 1906), 317.

1577 PEATTIE, ELIA W. "Howells' Questionable Shapes / A Pleasing
         Return to the Old Manner." Chicago Daily Tribune, 6 Jun
         1903, p. 14. Full review.
            These stories are "alive with ideas." Howells "has
         remembered, by happy chance, that life is not all frivoli-
         ties and trifles."

1578 "20th Century Ghosts." Public Opinion, 34 (18 Jun 1903), 795.
         Review of Questionable Shapes.
            "Visions, created as only Mr. Howells can create, worth
         seeing."

1579   "Fiction / Questionable Shapes." Times Literary Supplement,
        19 Jun 1903, p. 193. Review.
        "Here is the modern 'scientific' or 'psychological'
        ghost-story, in which the interest attaches not to what
        was seen, but to how it came to be seen." The first story
        in the collection is best.

1580   "Notes on Novels." Academy, 64 (20 Jun 1903), 610. Brief
        notice of Questionable Shapes.
        "In Howells' subtle and subjective manner."

1581   "Fiction." Academy, 64 (27 Jun 1903), 633. Review of
        Questionable Shapes.
        "Mr. Howells' method is that of Edgar Allen Poe raised
        to its ultimate power."

1582   "Novels." Spectator, 90 (27 Jun 1903), 1037-1038. Review of
        Questionable Shapes.
        Again Howells demonstrates "that subtlety of analysis
        need not involve the slightest sacrifice of wholesomeness."
        His American bias charms English readers. "Though One Rose
        from the Dead," the most striking story in this volume, is
        a "variation on themes suggested by Professor William
        James's Will To Believe."

1583   HENNEMAN, JOHN BELL. "The National Element in Southern Litera-
        ture." Sewanee Review, 11 (Jul 1903), 345-366. Minor
        references.
        Howells' poetic beginnings are reflected in his descrip-
        tive Venetian Days and Italian Journeys (p. 350). Although
        he was not of New England birth, he is closely identified
        with Boston (p. 351). A Modern Instance and The Rise of
        Silas Lapham exhibit his strong American emphasis (p. 360).

1584   MacDONALD, QUENTIN. "Lorgnettes." Book News, 21 (Jul 1903),
        868-870. Review of Questionable Shapes.
        These stories place "Mr. Howells in a more up-to-date
        position." They are "at once wholesome in thought and
        irreproachable in expression."

1585   "Questionable Shapes." Literary World, 34 (Jul 1903), 168.
        Review.
        "In encroaching on the field of the romanticists. Mr.
        Howells has strictly maintained his identity." The inci-
        dents are used to develop character "in some of its most
        subtle expressions."

1903

1586 VORSE, M. H. "Certain Overlooked Phases of American Life."
      Critic, 43 (Jul 1903), 83-84. Note.
         Howells has avoided the provincialism of most American
      writers by searching for truth instead of picturesqueness,
      thus coming to focus on our national virtues. The Kentons
      is an illuminating study of American family life.

1587 "Short Stories." Athenaeum, No. 3950 (11 Jul 1903), 59. Re-
      view of Questionable Shapes.
         "The question that occurs to an unprejudiced reader of
      Mr. Howells's stories is whether the trouble of perusal is
      repaid."

1588 "Writers and Readers." Reader, 2 (Aug 1903), 220-221. Brief
      profile and list of major works.
         Full-page seated protrait (p. 221).

1589 "Literature / Questionable Shapes." Independent, 55 (13 Aug
      1903), 1932-1933. Full review.
         Howells' "disposition for developing the nerves and
      emotions of his characters into psychic details often
      renders his novels morbid and tedious," but the method
      works to better advantage in his short stories.

1590 "American Literature." Saturday Review, 96 (15 Aug 1903), 212.
      Brief mention of Questionable Shapes.
         "The tales...are really intensely human and the workman-
      ship is of the best."

1591 [ROUTH, JAMES E., JR.] "Books Reviewed--Fact and Fiction."
      Critic, 43 (Oct 1903), 374-375. Review of Questionable
      Shapes.
         "Mr. Howells has, as usual, subtilized romance until one
      wonders if there be anything else in life but pure thought,
      with perhaps a little gray matter as an unavoidable sub-
      stratum."

1592 "Epistolary Fiction." Public Opinion, 35 (8 Oct 1903), 473.
      Review of Letters Home.
         Howells' "finer touches" appear in the letters of the
      old gentleman.

1593 "Notes on New Novels." Dial, 35 (16 Oct 1903), 263-264.
      Brief notice of Letters Home.
         Howells' "understanding of the feminine mind...relates
      him to Anthony Trollope."

1594 "A Story by Howells." New York Times, 17 Oct 1903, Sat. Sup.,
      p. 731. Review of Letters Home.
      The story deals with old themes which Howells treats
      "with even more than his usual sensitiveness of perception
      and charm of expression." His people are very real, and
      the New York life in which they move is shown "in all its
      keen, crude, many-sided actuality."

1595 "Recent Fiction." Literary World, 34 (Nov 1903), 307. Review
      of Letters Home.
      An old device cleverly handled. The descriptions of
      New York life are "the more valuable part of the book."

1596 STILLÉ, KATE BLACKISTON. "Letters Home." Book News, 22 (Nov
      1903), 290. Review.
      The drama of New York is on every page, and truth is ex-
      posed. "Gems are scattered everywhere, too smoothly
      polished, and too much alike to arouse enthusiasm."

1597 "Fiction Reviews." Academy, 65 (7 Nov 1903), 499. Brief re-
      view of Letters Home.
      The greatest "proof of a novelist's mastery of his art"
      is perhaps his "ability to tell a story convincingly in
      letters." Howells does.

1598 "New Novels." Athenaeum, No. 3968 (14 Nov 1903), 646. Review
      of Letters Home.
      Howells "is now writing better essays than novels. But
      this as a novel is not negligible by any means."

1599 "Books of the Year." Independent, 55 (19 Nov 1903), 2740.
      Brief notice of Letters Home.
      "Diverting."

1600 "Some Late Works of Fiction." Chicago Daily Tribune, 28 Nov
      1903, p. 15. Review of Letters Home.
      Old themes are presented with freshness and originality.
      "Mr. Howells has never done anything better than this
      microscopic view of nicely differentiated individualities."

1601 ARTHUR, RICHARD. "The Poetry of W. D. Howells." Booklovers,
      2 (Dec 1903), 569-571. Review of Stops of Various Quills.
      The collection "contains in parvo much of the nineteenth-
      century spirit-anguish which Tennyson voiced in magno, the
      painful perplexity and confusion produced in the sensitive,
      sincere, idealistic mind and soul by the impact of scien-
      tific fact and philosophical deduction on inherited and
      cherished religious faith and traditions, and the trouble

1903

(ARTHUR, RICHARD)
of personal problems of life which modern conditions seem
to have rendered more acute" (p. 571). Full-page line
portrait (p. 570).

1602 "The Book-Buyer's Guide." Critic, 43 (Dec 1903), 578. Review
of Letters Home.
Howells' humor "is part of the very fabric of his work."

1603 D., J. S. "Letters Home." Reader, 3 (Dec 1903), 104-105.
Brief review.
Because of its humor and story--"above all by its match-
less setting-forth of our great city of New York"--it is
exceptional.

1604 "The Fiction of the Season." Outlook, 75 (5 Dec 1903), 849.
Brief review of Letters Home.
Never has Howells "disclosed the delicacy and refinement
of his art more clearly" than here. The story belongs with
his "light studies of character and manners."

1605 [LOGAN, ANNIE R. M.] "Recent Fiction." Nation, 77 (24 Dec
1903), 507-508. Review of Letters Home.
Howells "has never had any ill-feeling for romance, but
has long pursued romantic nonsense with a sacred rage."
This distinction has never been so clearly made as in
Letters Home.

1904

1606 CONWAY, MONCURE DANIEL. Autobiography / Memories and Experiences of Moncure Daniel Conway. 2 vols. New York:
Houghton Mifflin, 1904. I, pp. 307-310, 426-432 (erro-
neous index). Short references.
Quotes from the Ohio State Journal Howells' early praise
of the Dial (Cincinnati, ed. Conway) and records Conway's
enthusiasm for Howells and his early work (pp. 307-310).
Warm memories of a visit with the Howellses in Venice
(pp. 426-432).

1607 FIELD, MRS. JAMES T. Charles Dudley Warner. Contemporary
Men of Letters Series. New York: McClure, Phillips,
1904. Pp. 47ff (unindexed).
Between Warner and Howells was "the friendship of a life
time" (p. 47). Letters from Warner to Howells, occasionally responding to Howells' work, are extensively quoted.
On re-reading Italian Journeys: "What felicity, what

(FIELD, MRS. JAMES T.)
delicacy. Your handling of the English language charms me
to the core, and you catch characters and shades--nu-an-ces
--of it" (p. 67). Warner challenges Howells to write a
novel into which one can dive without feeling "that we are
to strike bottom in the first plunge" (p. 68).

1608 PAYNE, WILLIAM MORTON. "Introduction." American Literary
      Criticism, sel. and ed. William Morton Payne. New York:
      Longmans, Green, 1904. P. 33. Brief reference.
      Howells has written "in so genial a fashion as to dis-
      arm the opposition even of those who are farthest from
      sharing his opinions." Two pieces by Howells, "The Art of
      the Novelist" and "Tolstoy," are included.

1609 WENDELL, BARRETT, and CHESTER NOYES GREENOUGH. A History of
      Literature in America. New York: Scribner's, 1904.
      Pp. 395-397, 398. Brief introduction.
      Howells "has written so much, so faithfully, and in a
      spirit at once so earnestly American and so kindly, that
      it is hard to say why he has not achieved more certainly
      powerful results. His chief limitation seems to be a kind
      of lifelong diffidence, which has forbidden a feeling of
      intimate familiarity even with the people and scenes of
      his own creation" (p. 396).

1610 HORWILL, HERBERT W. "Literature." Forum, 35 (Jan-Mar 1904),
      395-401. Review essay with brief comment on Letters Home
      (pp. 400-401).
      "Except for the multitude of misprints, there is nothing
      whatever to irritate" in Letters Home. "More entertaining
      than the narrative is the self-delineation of the
      characters."

1611 "Novels." Spectator, 91 (23 Jan 1904), 136. Review of
      Letters Home.
      "What Hazlitt would have called 'the perfection of Mr.
      Howells's inestimable art' has seldom been more deftly
      displayed than in this novel." The way in which Howells
      contrives to see New York through the eyes of a stranger
      is commended."

1612 "The Great American Novel." Reader, 3 (Feb 1904), [328].
      Brief reference.
      Howells announces his intention to go to Southern France
      and make one more attempt to write it.

1904

1613   "The Lounger." Critic, 44 (Feb 1904), 99. Brief passage.
At the beginning of their careers, the names of Howells
and James were usually coupled. Since then James has com-
pletely changed his style, but Howells has altered his
very little. The Son of Royal Langbrith opens more enter-
tainingly in the North American Review than did The
Ambassadors.

1614   VAN WESTRUM, A. SCHADE. "Mr. Howells on Love and Literature."
Lamp [Book Buyer], n.s. 28 (Feb 1904), 27-31. Report of
an interview. Rpt. "Interviews with William Dean Howells,"
ed. Ulrich Halfmann, American Literary Realism, 6 (Fall
1973), 352-356.
"Mr. Howells follows the development of our literature,
and that of several other literatures, far more closely
than do most successful writers, who are generally too
busy with their own work to pay more than passing attention to that of others." Portrait by Zaida Ben-Yusuf
(p. 26).

1615   "Mr. W. D. Howells Reading His Morning Mail in the Kittery
Point Post-Office." Critic, 44 (Mar 1904), 201. Snap-
shot.

1616   ATHERTON, GERTRUDE. "Why Is American Literature Bourgeois?"
North American Review, 178 (May 1904), 771-781. Rpt. in
part, The War of the Critics over William Dean Howells,
ed. Edwin H. Cady and David L. Frazier (Evanston: Row,
Peterson, 1962), pp. 100-104.
An attack on restrictive aspects of realism. "Nevertheless, the main current of Realism--or would it not be
better to call it Littleism?--flowed placidly on." Direct
reference to Howells (pp. 774-775).

1617   CONWAY, MONCURE D. "My Hawthorne Experience." Critic, 45
(Jul 1904), 21-25. Brief reference.
Notes meeting of Howells and Hawthorne and Hawthorne's
sending Emerson a note saying, "I find him worthy" (p. 23).

1618   BROOKS, SYDNEY. "William Dean Howells, D. Litt. (Oxon)."
Harper's Weekly, 48 (23 Jul 1904), 1136, 1140. News
feature.
Report on commemoration week at Oxford includes brief
reference to Howells' receiving the degree of D. Litt.
Howells was greeted by "a hearty, long-continued cheer of
the utmost kindliness." The tribute, in Latin, of the
regius professor, is included in the report (p. 1140).

1619 "American Literature." Saturday Review, 98 (27 Aug 1904),
276. Brief mention of Letters Home.
"A highly sophisticated novel, which does not stir the
depths of experience." It is "pervaded by [Howells']
charming humour."

1620 HUTTON, LAURENCE. "The Literary Life." Critic, 45 (Sep 1904),
227-238; (Oct 1904), 321-331; (Nov 1904), 426-437; (Dec
1904), 557-567; 46 (Jan 1905), 43-57; (Feb 1905), 146-157;
(Mar 1905), 241-246. Minor references to Howells in Vol.
46, pp. 50, 51, 150.
The entire piece, expanded for separate publication
(Laurence Hutton, Talks in a Library with Laurence Hutton
[New York: Putnam's, 1905]), includes several additional
references to Howells. See item 1637.

1621 "A Tale of Self-Deception." Public Opinion, 37 (27 Oct 1904),
537. Review of The Son of Royal Langbrith.
"A mellow product."

1622 WILLIAMS, TALCOTT. "With the New Books." Book News, 23
(Nov 1904), 172. Brief review of The Son of Royal Lang-
brith.
"Is there for the novelist, too, a dead-line of fifty?
As he knows more of life, is he less facile in letters?"

1623 "The New Novels / Qualities of Real Greatness in the Latest
Work of Mr. Howells." New York Times, 5 Nov 1904, Sat.
Sup., p. 748. Review of The Son of Royal Langbrith.
The novel "deals with the commonplace people--if people
are ever commonplace." Although it is "essentially a
story of the middle-aged," Howells has also "caught and
fixed upon his canvas in masterly fashion the elusive
spirit of self-centered, auto-happy youth; its position
toward its own and other generations; its distinctive
temperamental qualities." Unfortunately, Howells too
frequently misses "the soul of the human...in his
minuteness of surface work."

1624 PAYNE, WILLIAM MORTON. "Recent Fiction." Dial, 37 (16 Nov
1904), 310-311. Review of The Son of Royal Langbrith.
This is one of the finest books Howells has written,
"one of the best American novels of our time."

1625 [LOGAN, ANNIE R. M.] "More Novels." Nation, 79 (24 Nov
1904), 419. Full review of The Son of Royal Langbrith.
"The interest of the tale is not meant to lie in action
and incidents, but in characterization and discussion of

1904

([LOGAN, ANNIE R. M.])
the question at issue ['a delicate moral question involved
in the suppression of an important truth']; and as the
principle characters fail in energy of any sort, while the
situation suffused by the question is exceptional, almost
improbable, interest never rises to the point of agitation."

1626 "A Strong Novel by Mr. Howells." Literary Digest, 29 (26 Nov
1904), 729-730. Review of The Son of Royal Langbrith.
"There is a flavor of Hawthorne to this study, with its
smothering pressure of the basic forces of conscience,
pride, and love"--something also "of the oppressive incubus
of a Nemesis which the Greek tragedians wrought into their
dramatic poems lives in these pages through the fermenting
presence of the reputation of Royal Langbrith."

1627 MILLER, ALICE DUER. "A Few Novels." Lamp [Book Buyer], 29
(Dec 1904), 448. Review of The Son of Royal Langbrith.
Here Howells has subordinated detail to main idea. Perhaps because he treats his women more objectively than
men, they are "always more vivid and more attaching."

1628 MOSS, MARY. "Mr. Howells's The Son of Royal Langbrith."
Bookman (New York), 20 (Dec 1904), 372-374. Full review.
Because Howells "observes afresh from his own shifting
point of view, this late book shows all the vigour and
spontaneity of feeling which we were wont to associate
with impressionable youth."

1629 "Recent Fiction." Literary World, 35 (Dec 1904), 378. Review of The Son of Royal Langbrith.
"A bigger, and successful, attempt to show the more
emotional and more vital side of life."

1630 "The Son of Royal Langbrith." Reader, 5 (Dec 1904), 130-131.
Review.
The characters are usual in conception. The humor is a
fundamental part of the fabric. "The book has the authori-
ty of a sermon without any of the dreadful manner."

1631 "Literature / Howells's Latest Novel." Independent, 57
(1 Dec 1904), 1270-1271. Review of The Son of Royal
Langbrith.
This novel is "startlingly like Ibsen," until Howells'
"old, drolling, half-indolent Americanisms" and gossip
about the characters eases the sense of tragedy. Although
the novel is generally strong, the dialogue of the young
people is overly bold.

1632   "Fiction / The Son of Royal Langbrith." Times Literary Sup-
          plement, 2 Dec 1904, p. 379. Review.
          This "very shrewd and delicate story," like other books
       by Howells, "has the background of sensitive, affectionate
       humour, almost romantic in its perennial freshness, that
       has nothing to do with a merely literary skill." Seeing
       Howells' story through Howells' eyes "means that the story
       is illuminated with the writer's personality."

1633   "New Novels." Athenaeum, No. 4023 (3 Dec 1904), 761. Review
          of The Son of Royal Langbrith.
          "Howells far afield under the influence of a theory."

1634   "A Review of the Season's Books." Outlook, 78 (3 Dec 1904),
          869. Brief review of The Son of Royal Langbrith.
          "It presents a series of complications which may fairly
       be said to constitute a plot, and its central motive is
       a very interesting moral problem which is treated with
       great breadth and intelligence."

1635   "Fiction." Academy, 67 (17 Dec 1904), 615. Review of The
          Son of Royal Langbrith.
          "This novel is an excellent illustration of Mr. Howells'
       most characteristic merits and defects; possessing in full
       degree his quiet controlled style, his precision and deli-
       cacy in psychological analysis, it yet conveys an impres-
       sion of coldness that a non-American reader might almost
       call tedious."

                                 1905

  *   DREISER, THEODORE. "A Printer's Boy, Self-Taught, Becomes
          the Dean of American Letters." Little Visits with Great
          Americans, or, Success Ideals and How To Attain Them, ed.
          Orison Swett Marden. New York: Success Co., 1905.
          Pp. 283-295. Rpt. from Success, 1 (Apr 1898), 5-6. See
          item 1223.

1636   HIGGINSON, THOMAS WENTWORTH. Part of a Man's Life. Boston
          and New York: Houghton Mifflin, 1905. Pp. 57, 296.
          Minor references.
          Howells is "always penetrating, and commonly accurate."

1637   HUTTON, LAURENCE. Talks in a Library with Laurence Hutton,
          recorded by Isabel Moore. New York: Putnam's, 1905.
          Pp. 257, 262, 263, 296, 298, 374, 390, 416-417, 425.

1905

(HUTTON, LAURENCE)
    The references to Howells are anecdotal and minor and
are not included in the volume index. Several of them did
not appear in Hutton's earlier version, "The Literary Life,"
Critic, Sep 1904 - Mar 1905. See item 1620.

1638   "Howells, William Dean. Son of Royal Langbrith." Book Review
       Digest, 1 (1905), 177. Brief summary.

1639   CHAMBERLAYNE, E. S. "Mr. Howells' Philosophy and The Son of
       Royal Langbrith." Poet Lore, 16 (Autumn 1905), 144-151.
       Full review.
       "Mr. Howells has become one of the chief elements in
our American literary weather." Like the weather, he is
both abused and indispensable. In the story of Dr. Anther
in The Son of Royal Langbrith, Howells has written "one
of the oldest forms of popular tragedy"; but "the lasting
value of the work will be found in its self-revelation of
the author."

1640   CARY, ELISABETH LUTHER. "William Dean Howells: A Point of
       View." Lamp [Book Buyer], n.s. 29 (Jan 1905), 597-604.
       Critical survey of major works.
       Howells' widening vision is based on his appreciative
perception of the commonplace. "No other novelist has
recorded the spectacle of our constantly changing civilization with such a quick and joyous sensibility to its
shifting impressions."

1641   "The Lounger." Critic, 46 (Jan 1905), 18-20. Brief note.
       Negative reaction to Howells' position on international
copyright.

1642   "The Season's Notable Fiction." Review of Reviews, 31 (Jan
       1905), 116. Brief mention of The Son of Royal Langbrith.
       "The subject is one of essential tragedy."

1643   "An Apology for Piracie." Dial, 38 (1 Jan 1905), 3-5. Note.
       Refutation of Howells' "whimsical plaint" about the
copyright situation (December "Editor's Easy Chair").

1644   "Novels." Spectator, 94 (7 Jan 1905), 22. Review of The Son
       of Royal Langbrith.
       "The setting and treatment are entirely characteristic
of Mr. Howells;...they illustrate once more the workings
of that subtle yet wholesome mind which has always found
its happiest inspiration in the delineation of the finest
traits of distinctively American types."

1645   "About New Books." Canadian Magazine, 24 (Feb 1905), 385-386.
       Review of The Son of Royal Langbrith.
       "As a literary production it sorely lacks the fire of
       genius." Howells should hire an editor.

1646   HARWOOD, C[HARLOTTE]. "A Writer Who Knows His Subject."
       Critic, 46 (Feb 1905), 184. Review of The Son of Royal
       Langbrith.
       "A dainty dish" marred only by excessive realistic
       detail.

1647   "The Point of View / How Much Per Annum?" Scribner's, 37
       (Apr 1905), 508. Brief reference.
       Howells, "with a masculine authority, possesses us
       easily of all needed information in regard to the finan-
       cial standing of his people."

1648   PENDENNIS [W. de WAGSTAFFE]. "Mr. Howells Talks About Fiction
       and Fiction Writers." New York Times, 30 Apr 1905, Mag.
       Sec., p. 2. Interview. Rpt. "Interviews with William
       Dean Howells," ed. Ulrich Halfmann, American Literary
       Realism, 6 (Fall 1973), 356-360.
       Subheaded "Evolution of the American Novel Since the
       Civil War--The 'Scarlet Letter's' Position in American
       Literature--As to the Short Story--Supply and Demand in
       the Book World." Amply illustrated with pencil sketches.

1649   "Degrees from Columbia for 1,137 Recipients /.../ Several
       Honorary Degrees Conferred /...." New York Times,
       15 Jun 1905, p. 5. News story.
       Doctor of Letters was conferred on Howells, introduced
       by Harry Thurston Peck, who applauded Howells' work as
       fiction that is "true as truth itself." The two-paragraph
       introduction is quoted.

1650   HARTMAN, LEE F. "Mr. Howells and the Logic of Love." Harper's
       Weekly, 49 (17 Jun 1905), 871. Review of Miss Bellard's
       Inspiration.
       An hors d'oeuvre by a master. "Variations on the theme
       of love are always welcome; Mr. Howells has improvised
       ingeniously and well." Largely summary. Portrait.

1651   "Miss Bellard's Inspiration." New York Times, 17 Jun 1905,
       Sat. Sup., p. 389. Brief review.
       "Mr. Howells has not lost any of his cunning in por-
       traying the delightfully illogical phrases of the feminine
       mental processes."

1905

1652   "This Week / Some New Honorary Degrees." Outlook, 80 (24 Jun
       1905), 457. News item.
        The honorary Doctor of Letters conferred on Howells by
       Columbia University reflects credit on both the recipient
       and the university.

1653   "Fiction / Miss Bellard's Inspiration." Times Literary Sup-
       plement, 30 Jun 1905, p. 209. Review.
        "Mr. Howells walks delicately, like a cat over a break-
       fast-table, along the little twists and turns of women's
       moods and fancies." Because he is so intent on those
       twists and turns, he fails to see the woman.

1654   "Columbia Honors Mr. Howells." Harper's Weekly, 49 (1 Jul
       1905), 956. News item.
        Harry Thurston Peck's presentation comments. Howells'
       fiction, the basis of his fame, is "as true as truth
       itself."

1655   "Books of the Week." Outlook, 80 (8 Jul 1905), 643. Brief
       review of Miss Bellard's Inspiration.
        "Mr. Howells has never written a more thoroughly charac-
       teristic or delightful story than this latest study of the
       inconsequential woman." The serious thesis does not impede
       the happy style.

1656   "New Novels." Athenaeum, No. 4054 (8 Jul 1905), 41. Review
       of Miss Bellard's Inspiration.
        "Mr. Howells pleasantly disappoints one with this
       story." It is saved by its cynicism.

1657   "Novels / Miss Bellard's Inspiration." Spectator, 95 (22 Jul
       1905), 124-125. Review.
        Howells seems to be returning to "the American comedy
       of manners. In this sphere no one else has shown pre-
       cisely the same talent." This is "a very clever and
       shrewd study of one type of American girl."

1658   "Chronicle and Comment." Bookman (New York), 21 (Aug 1905),
       566. Brief reference.
        Speculation as to how Howells responds to critics and
       reviewers.

1659   COOPER, FREDERIC TABER. "Mr. Howells's Miss Bellard's Inspira-
       tion." Bookman (New York), 21 (Aug 1905), 610-612. Full
       review.
        "Mr. Howells is like an artist who, in picturing a
       cyclone or a thunderstorm, has chosen to work in pastels

(COOPER, FREDERIC TABER)
  instead of oils." This novel is more important in the
  context of Howells' work than it is standing alone.

1660 [LOGAN, ANNIE R. M.] "Recent Fiction." Nation, 81 (3 Aug
        1905), 101. Brief review of Miss Bellard's Inspiration.
        "It may be a horror of sentimentality that makes Mr.
        Howells so shy of sentiment. Yet the power of expressing
        sentiment is a valuable grace of life, and, without it,
        fiction, even brilliant fiction, has a certain aridity."

1661 "An Incubated Inspiration." Literary Digest, 31 (5 Aug 1905),
        187. Review of Miss Bellard's Inspiration.
        Howells did not intend to do something important. The
        novel is "dainty and amusing," and the irony is "suavely
        expended."

1662 "Book Reviews / Mr. Howells' Latest." Public Opinion, 39
        (26 Aug 1905), 283. Review of Miss Bellard's Inspiration.
        Largely summary of a novel that is amusing and "spread
        out very thin."

1663 WILLIAMS, TALCOTT. "With the New Books." Book News, 24 (Sep
        1905), 31. Brief review of Miss Bellard's Inspiration.
        Howells' "classic tradition" will not save him. "Young
        men and women with literary aspirations will vote it dull."

1664 PAYNE, WILLIAM MORTON. "Recent Fiction." Dial, 39 (1 Sep
        1905), 115. Brief review of Miss Bellard's Inspiration.
        "A charm altogether out of proportion to its pretensions."

1665 "Fiction by Various Hands." Critic, 47 (Nov 1905), 452. Re-
        view of Miss Bellard's Inspiration.
        Commonplace characters behave in a most commonplace
        manner. Style is the only inducement offered by the book.

1666 HARRIS, MRS. L. H. "Our Novelists." Independent, 59 (16 Nov
        1905), 1171-1175. Brief reference.
        Comparative comments on Howells and his contemporaries.

1667 "A Review of the Important Books of the Year." Independent,
        59 (16 Nov 1905), 1152. Brief mention of Miss Bellard's
        Inspiration.
        "This young woman shows the kind of inspirations that
        still cling like entangling fairy-webs to a woman's mind
        who has evoluted into the poetically philosophical
        attitude."

1905

1668   "Mr. Howells in England." Spectator, 95 (18 Nov 1905), 810-
           811. Full review of London Films.
           "Mr. Howells has given to the Americans, perhaps con-
           sciously, a favourable likeness of a friendly people, and
           unconsciously has given to the English a true picture of
           an American friend."

1669   "Literature / London Films." Independent, 59 (23 Nov 1905),
           1227-1228. Full review.
           "It would be a mistake to suppose that Mr. Howells could
           think a thorn [about the British] and not wrap it in roses
           and say it. The roses will be voluminous, and the thorn
           hardly perceptible, but it will be there."

1670   "London Films." Athenaeum, No. 4074 (25 Nov 1905), 717-718.
           Full review.
           Not since Emerson's English Traits has an American
           writer observed England "with such acuteness and written
           with such insight." Howells is less comprehensive than
           Emerson, and more personal. Here he demonstrates why he
           is "one of our foremost writers of English to-day."

1671   "A Review of the Season's Fiction." Review of Reviews, 32
           (Dec 1905), 757. Brief review of Miss Bellard's Inspira-
           tion.
           This slight love story "embodies a maturity of concep-
           tion, a surety of view, a subtle phraseology, an exquisite
           use of irony, and, withal, a sedate, appeasing dignity."

1672   WHITTEN, WILFRED. "London and 'A Year Hence.'" Bookman (Lon-
           don), 29 (Dec 1905), 140. Review of London Films.
           Howells "strives to bring home to his readers the in-
           calculability of London."

1673   WILLIAMS, TALCOTT. "With the New Books." Book News, 24 (Dec
           1905), 234. Brief mention of London Films.
           "The ease, the grace, and the care of long practice are
           in these pages."

1674   "Holiday Publications." Dial, 39 (1 Dec 1905), 381-382.
           Brief notice of London Films (contrasted with James's
           English Hours).
           The "films" are in Howells' "happiest analytic vein."

1675   [MARKS, ALFRED.] "London Films." Nation, 81 (14 Dec 1905),
           490. Review.
           "Instead of the indiscriminate and brutal fidelity of
           the material film, Mr. Howells's mental kodak encloses

1905

([MARKS, ALFRED])
films capable of receiving the choice impressions of a
mind poetical and artistic."

1676   "American Notes." Academy, 69 (30 Dec 1905), 1353. Review
of London Films.
The book is pleasing, but "the continual references to
America...make it provincial and mar its unity."

1906

1677   HEARN, LAFCADIO. The Life and Letters of Lafcadio Hearn, ed.
Elizabeth Bisland [Wetmore]. 2 vols. Boston and New York:
Houghton Mifflin, 1906. I, p. 332. Letter to H. E.
Krehbiel (Jun 1884).
"In making the acquaintance of Howells, you have met
the subtlest and noblest literary mind in this country,--
scarcely excepting that prince of critics, Stedman; and
you have found a friend who will aid you in climbing
Parnassus, not for selfish motives, but for pure art's
sake."

1678   PENNELL, ELIZABETH R. Charles Godfrey Leland / A Biography.
New York: Houghton Mifflin, 1906. Passim as indexed.
Inconsequential references.

  *   SHAW, [GEORGE] BERNARD. "Told You So." Dramatic Opinions and
Essays with an Apology. 2 vols. New York: Brentano's,
1906. I, pp. 265-266. Rpt. from Saturday Review, 80
(7 Dec 1895), 761-762. See item 1075.

1679   TRAUBEL, HORACE. With Walt Whitman in Camden. 5 vols. Vol.
I--Boston: Small, Maynard, 1906; Vol. II--New York:
Appleton, 1908; Vol. III--New York: Kennerley, 1914;
Vol. IV--Philadelphia: University of Pennsylvania Press,
1953; Vol. V--Carbondale: Southern Illinois University
Press, 1964. Passim as indexed in each volume.
A large number of minor references to Howells. Whitman's
opinion of him wavered erratically between warmth and pique.

1680   "Howells, William Dean. Certain Delightful English Towns."
Book Review Digest, 2 (1906), 166. Brief comment.
It is delightful to see England through Howells' eyes.

1681   "London Films." Reader. 7 (Jan 1906), 226. Brief review.
Howells "takes a delightfully whimsical, gently satirical, yet admirably sane view" of the English.

1906

1682   "The New Books." Review of Reviews, 33 (Jan 1906), 128.
        Brief review of London Films.
        Howells contrasts, "in his own illuminating and humorous
        style, English and American conditions, particularly in
        New York and London."

1683   "Notes on New Novels." Atlantic, 97 (Jan 1906), 51. Brief
        notice of Miss Bellard's Inspiration.
        "Almost more than flesh and blood can bear."

1684   "The Book-Buyer's Guide / Belles Lettres." Critic, 48 (Feb
        1906), 189. Brief review of London Films.
        Howells' style "is lucidity itself."

1685   DWIGHT, H. G. "American Political Workers Abroad." Bookman
        (New York), 23 (May 1906), 263-280. Brief reference
        (p. 265).
        Notes "the happiest conjunction of Arcadian periods"--
        impressionable youth and idyllic Grand Canal rents--in
        Howells' Venetian years.

1686   "The Grand Canal in Venice, showing the two consulates of Mr.
        W. D. Howells...." Bookman (New York), 23 (May 1906), 262.
        Photograph.

1687   PECK, HARRY THURSTON. "Twenty Years of the Republic (1885-
        1905) / Part XVII--The Transformed Republic." Bookman
        (New York), 23 (Jun 1906), 388-411. Short passage.
        One column (p. 409) records Howells' importance "as a
        pourtrayer of the American life of his generation."
        Portrait (p. 393).

1688   "Comment on Current Books." Outlook, 83 (23 Jun 1906), 483.
        Brief mention of Under the Sunset.
        Identifies four of the ten stories included.

1689   "The Book-Buyer's Guide / Fiction." Critic, 49 (Jul 1906),
        93. Brief notice of Under the Sunset.
        Descriptive.

1690   HENDERSON, ARCHIBALD. "Aspects of Contemporary Fiction."
        Arena, 36 (Jul 1906), 1-10. Brief reference.
        "While Mr. James may be called the historian of fine
        consciences, and Mrs. Wharton the historian of morbid
        consciences, Mr. Howells may be called the historian of
        uninteresting personages and banal events." Howells has
        told us many things, but he has failed to tell us of our-
        selves (pp. 6-7).

1691 TWAIN, MARK. "William Dean Howells." Harper's, 113 (Jul 1906),
      221-225. Essay. Rpt. What Is Man? and Other Essays (New
      York: Harper, [1917]), pp. 228-239; Howells / A Century
      of Criticism, ed. Kenneth E. Eble (Dallas: Southern Meth-
      odist University, 1962), pp. 78-87; The Complete Essays of
      Mark Twain, ed. Charles Neider (Garden City, N. Y.: Double-
      day, 1963), pp. 400-407; in part, The War of the Critics
      over William Dean Howells, ed. Edwin H. Cady and David L.
      Frazier (Evanston: Row, Peterson, 1962), pp. 104-106.
          Twain examines Howells' style, which to him has been "a
      continual delight and astonishment," and finds it has not
      been impaired by the passage of time. "In the sustained
      exhibition of certain great qualities--clearness, compres-
      sion, verbal exactness, and unforced and seemingly uncon-
      scious felicity of phrasing--he is, in my belief, without
      his peer in the English-writing world" (p. 221).

1692 "Notes." Dial, 41 (1 Jul 1906), 21. Mere mention of Under
      the Sunset.

1693 "Western Short Stories." New York Times, 11 Aug 1906, Sat.
      Sup., p. 446. Brief review of Under the Sunset.

1694 [WRIGHT, WILMER C. F.] "Certain Delightful English Towns."
      Nation, 83 (29 Nov 1906), 462. Brief review.
          "What will endear its pages to every reader is its un-
      failing humor, its nice balancing of emotions and aesthetic
      impressions by one on whom no charm whether of setting or
      human association was thrown away."

1695 CAWEIN, MADISON. "With Howells Abroad / The Place of Mr.
      Howells in English Literature--The Charm of His New Book
      of Travel in England." New York Times, 30 Nov 1906, Lit.
      Sup., pp. 789-790. Lead review of Certain Delightful
      English Towns.
          Howells' "kinship to Henry James, to Walter Pater is un-
      mistakable, in the rich unfolding of his art, the absolute
      repose of style, which is the highest art and which bears
      so subtle a relation to the deeply psychological mind."
      But Howells' quality as homorist and wit sets him apart.

1696 HAYES, JOHN RUSSELL. "In Picturesque Lands with Holiday Books."
      Book News, 25 (Dec 1906), 235-236. Brief review of Certain
      Delightful English Towns.
          Howells sees with American eyes, but "'the spirit of
      place' is always vividly realized."

1906

1697   "The Season's New Books / Notes on Recent American Publica-
        tions." Review of Reviews, 34 (Dec 1906), 753. Brief
        mention of Certain Delightful English Towns.
           Howells has "his own inimitable way of catching the
        dominant spirit of every locality."

1698   "Holiday Books of Travel." Dial, 41 (1 Dec 1906), 391. Brief
        notice of Certain Delightful English Towns.
           Appreciative.

1699   "Fifty of the Year's Best Books for Holiday Gifts." Literary
        Digest, 33 (8 Dec 1906), 856. Review of Certain Delight-
        ful English Towns.
           "Suave, humorous observation of ordinary things which
        gives one the sense of the highest reality." Portrait
        (p. 855).

1700   BOWDOIN, W. G. "A Selection from the Year's Holiday Books."
        Independent, 61 (22 Dec 1906), 1397. Brief notice of
        Certain Delightful English Towns.
           Howells "travels with open eyes" and writes "with a keen
        regard for the value of an incident and with full apprecia-
        tion of the humorous."

1907

1701   GODKIN, EDWIN LAWRENCE. Life and Letters of Edwin Lawrence
        Godkin, ed. Rollo Ogden. 2 vols. New York: Macmillan,
        1907. I, pp. 166, 307; II, pp. 52, 73. Minor references.
           A letter to Howells (I, p. 307) and one to Lowell (II,
        p. 73) reflect Godkin's warm appreciation of Howells'
        performance.

1702   LAWTON, WILLIAM CRANSTON. A Study of American Literature.
        New York: Globe School Book Co., 1907. Pp. 83, 327-328.
        Introductory comments.
           In Modern Italian Poets Howells, so typical of Western
        man, misses the "large element"--"the unbroken relation
        to the whole historic past, above all to classical antiq-
        uity" (p. 327). His work has little room for anything
        other than "the daily doings and sayings of average men."

1703   "Howells, William Dean. Between the Dark and the Daylight."
        Book Review Digest, 3 (1907), 209. Brief notice.
           Description and listing of story titles.

1704   "Howells, William Dean. Through the Eye of the Needle."
        Book Review Digest, 3 (1907), 209. Brief summary.

1705   S., M. "The American Novelist Fulfills His Three Score Years
        and Ten." New York Times, 24 Feb 1907, Mag. Sec., p. 2.
        Half-page feature item.
            Subtitled, "A Sketch of the Career and Work of William
        Dean Howells, Who Has Interpreted the Nation's Life to It-
        self--About To Celebrate His Seventieth Birthday, He May
        Look Back with Pride upon a Worthy Performance Worthily
        Recognized." Howells' work comprises more than a personal
        achievement: "it is a National asset."

1706   "The Seventieth Birthday of America's Leading Novelist." New
        York Times, 24 Feb 1907, Pictorial Sec., p. 1. Full-page
        spread.
            Brief recognition with photographs of Howells and two of
        his homes.

1707   VAN WESTRUM, A. SCHADE. "Mr. Howells and American Aristocra-
        cies." Bookman (New York), 25 (Mar 1907), 67-73. Essay.
            Howells' interest in the American's fundamental "aristo-
        cratic instinct" is traced through three stages in major
        works from A Chance Acquaintance to Letters Home.

1708   "A Day We Like To Honor." New York Sun, 1 Mar 1907, p. 8.
        News item.
            Brief recognition of Howells' seventieth birthday.

1709   [Untitled.] Nation, 84 (7 Mar 1907), 212-213. Editorial.
            An appreciation on the occasion of Howells' seventieth
        birthday.

1710   [Untitled.] Bellman, 2 (9 Mar 1907), 274. Editorial.
            On the occasion of Howells' seventieth birthday. With
        Howells "the novel has become social, not to say
        socialistic."

1711   "Authors Who Are a Present Delight. / XXI. / William Dean
        Howells." Journal of Education, 65 (21 Mar 1907), 311-312.
        General introduction.
            "Some critics have thought that they could trace the in-
        fluence of Longfellow on Howells' diction as well as on
        the range of his work, both in prose and poetry."

1907

1712 "Mr. Howells and Relics of Feudalism." Spectator, 98 (23 Mar
1907), 450-451. Full review of Certain Delightful English
Towns.
"Mr. Howells is one of those just and genial observers
who can make comparisons without offense. A writer whose
sympathies are sufficiently keen never needs to point his
criticisms with disparagement."

1713 "England and Yesterday." Times Literary Supplement, 29 Mar
1907, p. 100. Full review of Certain Delightful English
Towns.
"Words, on these charming pages, have forgotten that
they are only words. They are colours, half-colours,
gentle shadows and tones and moods of feeling, scents
even. They weave a chain as fast as it is fragile between
the heart of one American at least and the hearts of all
the English who care to read what he says." [A prefatory
note discourages subscribers from ordering the book through
The Times Book Club since the publisher chose not to supply
it "on ordinary trade terms."]

1714 "The Bookman's Table." Bookman (London), 32 (Apr 1907), 32.
Review of Certain Delightful English Towns.
"Much that is obviously intended to amuse evokes merely
a sense of tedium, and in going over ground rich beyond
measure in historical and romantic reminiscence, the
author, only too often, fails signally to move or thrill
us."

1715 "Certain Delightful English Towns." Athenaeum, No. 4146
(13 Apr 1907), 435. Full review.
Howells' "magisterial appreciation comes as a surprise."
His American humor becomes "tender whimsicality."

1716 "A Howells Novel." New York Times, 20 Apr 1907, Sat. Sup.,
p. 255. Announcement of Through the Eye of the Needle.
In the introduction Howells "comments upon American ways
in a strain of kindly irony."

1717 "Fiction." A. L. A. Booklist, 3 (May 1907), 135. Very brief
review of Through the Eye of the Needle.
The contrast between "Altrurian ways and world ways forms
the chief interest of the book."

1718 WILSON, CALVIN DILL, and DAVID BRUCE FITZGERALD. "A Day in
Howells's 'Boy's Town.'" New England Magazine, n.s. 36
(May 1907), 289-297. Anecdotal essay.

254

(WILSON, CALVIN DILL,...)
> Escorted by George T. Earhart, a boyhood friend and companion of Howells, the authors tour Hamilton, Ohio, and pick up anecdotal reminiscences of the Howells family.

1719 "Current Fiction." Nation, 84 (9 May 1907), 434-435. Review of Through the Eye of the Needle.
> Howells' Altruria differs only slightly from other famous utopias. It is interesting that with his "deep love of humanity as he finds it, the apostle of realism in American fiction should care to spend (almost waste) his precious gifts upon such a toy of the imagination as the island of Altruria."

1720 RICE, M. GORDON PRYOR. "Homos of Altruria." New York Times, 11 May 1907, Sat. Sup., p. 297. First-page review of Through the Eye of the Needle.
> "Mr. Howells treats of exciting conditions with clearness of vision and with his unerring firmness and lightness of touch." In his enthusiasm for humanity, he, like nearly all Socialist writers, may ignore too much what "our uncompromising forefathers called 'original sin.'"

1721 "Among the New Books." Chicago Daily Tribune, 18 May 1907, p. 9. Review of Through the Eye of the Needle.
> Howells "makes Altruria seem the pleasantest and simplest sort of place to inhabit, and America amazingly difficult." Idleness appears to be the greatest offense against society.

1722 "Literature / To Altruria Thru Anarchism." Independent, 62 (23 May 1907), 1207-1208. Review of Through the Eye of the Needle.
> Howells' indictment "of the stupidity, the unreasonableness and the injustice of life in our cities" is convincing, but he does not show how we can reach Altruria. He seems, at least momentarily, to have lost his "lambent humor."

1723 "Fiction / Through the Eye of the Needle." Times Literary Supplement, 24 May 1907, p. 165. Review.
> Although "it will inspire no crusades," the book offers "very graceful fancy." Howells should be thanked "not least for a deft and witty introduction which is an almost faultless little piece of irony."

1907

1724   "Novels." Spectator, 98 (25 May 1907), 836. Review of
        Through the Eye of the Needle.
            "The scheme of his romance brings [Howells] into closer
        touch with the crude actualities of modern civilisation."
        The novel is "an impeachment of the American people" and
        calls for "a return to the simple life."

1725   COOPER, FREDERIC TABER. "Heroines in Fiction and Some Recent
        Novels." Bookman (New York), 25 (Jun 1907), 389-390, 394.
        Review of Heroines of Fiction (pp. 389-390) and briefer
        notice of Through the Eye of the Needle (p. 394).
            In the "genial and suggestive essays" that make up
        Heroines in Fiction, Howells was not simply revealing per-
        sonal taste; "he was instinctively applying the surest
        and most delicate criterion by which to judge the strength
        and quality of a novel." Through the Eye of the Needle
        is a "kindly satire," which exhibits Howells' faith in the
        American woman. Howells takes neither himself nor his
        utopian subject too seriously.

1726   "For the Reader of New Fiction / Through the Eye of the
        Needle." Book News, 25 (Jun 1907), 689. Review.
            "America is at no point spared in the minute analysis
        of her various phases and aspects."

1727   "A Review of the Season's Fiction." Review of Reviews, 35
        (Jun 1907), 761. Brief review of Through the Eye of the
        Needle.
            "A cogent criticism of every important phase of Ameri-
        can life."

1728   VAN WESTRUM, A. SCHADE. "Altruria Once More." Bookman (New
        York), 25 (Jun 1907), 434-435. Full review of Through
        the Eye of the Needle.
            "Mr. Homos the social philosopher is more interesting,
        helpful and suggestive to see than is Mrs. Homos the Al-
        trurian enthusiast. Hers is the headlong lust of prosely-
        tism of the convert." "The downtrodden American domestic
        servant...continues to be the object of [Howells']
        commiseration."

1729   "A Guide to the New Books." Literary Digest, 34 (1 Jun 1907),
        885-886. Review of Through the Eye of the Needle.
            Howells' style has "arrived at its perihelion....
        Delicate, and wholly unassuming, it springs from the
        purest sources of English and still maintains the full
        flavor of its modernity." Portrait (p. 885).

1730   "Hughes His Choice, Says W. D. Howells." Boston Herald,
       10 Jun 1907, p. 2. Interview. Abstr. "Interviews with
       William Dean Howells," ed. Ulrich Halfmann, American Liter-
       ary Realism, 6 (Fall 1973), 360-361.
           Subtitled, "Calls New York Governor Good Man for Presi-
       dent and Then Warms Up--Tells What He Didn't Come to Bos-
       ton For--Found Theatre Bad, Vaudeville Declining, James
       and Mark Twain Good."

1731   "Best Books for Summer Reading." New York Times, 15 Jun 1907,
       Sat. Sup., pp. 381-382. Brief review of Through the Eye
       of the Needle.
           Scant summary and observation that English Royal Society
       has recently experimented with a one-rail electric train
       such as Howells describes.

1732   "Comment on Current Books." Outlook, 86 (15 Jun 1907), 339.
       Review of Through the Eye of the Needle.
           "The effectiveness of this arraignment of American
       social life is much enhanced by Mr. Howells's inimitable
       way of putting things."

1733   "New Novels." Athenaeum, No. 4157 (29 Jun 1907), 786. Brief
       review of Through the Eye of the Needle.
           "Unhappily, these sociological criticisms are not con-
       veyed in an interesting form of fiction."

1734   "Our Own Times." Reader, 10 (Jul 1907), 215-216. Note.
           Howells, "who has so long and so delightfully demon-
       strated for us the wonderful simplicity of complex things,"
       is recognized on his seventieth birthday. The inevitable
       Howells-James contrast.

1735   ATWOOD, VERNON. "The Hammock Novel, and Others." Putnam's,
       2 (Aug 1907), 619. Review of Through the Eye of the
       Needle.
           "The book expresses the author's resentment against a
       civilization like our own, in which religion so ineffec-
       tually tempers the law of struggle under which we live."

1736   "Our Library Table." Athenaeum, No. 4166 (31 Aug 1907), 237.
       Brief review of Minor Dramas.
           "Merely short stories in dialogue form." They deal
       principally with one group of people.

1737   CORTISSOZ, ROYAL. "New Books Reviewed / Howells's Through
       the Eye of the Needle." North American Review, 186
       (Sep 1907), 127-130. Review.

1907

(CORTISSOZ, ROYAL)
    As he was at the beginning of his career, so Howells
remains--"a seeker after truth." But now "the light is
softer, mellower, and the emotions roused in the artist
are somehow more tenderly sympathetic."

1738   "William Dean Howells." Chautauquan, 48 (Oct 1907), 267-269.
       Brief tribute.
       On the occasion of Howells' seventieth year. "No one
has interpreted the average American, man and woman, as
has Mr. Howells in a long series of sane, accurate, realistic novels." The Rise of Silas Lapham "perhaps deserves
the title of 'the greatest American novel.'" Howells'
later social novels reveal him as an idealist. Full-page
portrait (p. 269).

1739   "New Books of the Autumn Season." New York Times, 19 Oct
1907, Sat. Sup., p. 664. Brief announcement of Between
the Dark and the Daylight.
       "The stories are graceful social pictures, written with
charm and humor."

1740   [FRANCIS, SUSAN M.] "The Atlantic's Pleasant Days in Tremont
Street." Atlantic, 100 (Nov 1907), 716-720. Reminiscent
note.
       Howells, as assistant editor, "did his work, the
greater part of the actual editorial labor, at his home
in Cambridge or at the University Press" (p. 717). He
frequently shared in the luncheons brought in daily from
the Parker House (p. 718). Brief reference to Howells'
editorial reform and to his "small, dark room" on Park
Street (p. 720).

1741   GILMAN, ARTHUR. "Atlantic Dinner and Diners." Atlantic, 100
(Nov 1907), 646-657. Reminiscent essay.
       Multiple minor references to Howells, his presence and
his role at various Atlantic dinners.

1742   VAN WESTRUM, A. SCHADE. "Mr. Howells's Between the Dark and
the Daylight." Bookman (New York), 26 (Nov 1907), 275-
276. Full review.
       Descriptive rather than critical. Each of the seven
stories is presented separately.

1743   "Novels." Spectator, 99 (9 Nov 1907), 717. Brief review of
Between the Dark and the Daylight.
       "Howells uses his delicate analytical methods in the
description of abnormal states of brain and consciousness."

1744   "Four of the Notable Ex-Editors of the <u>Atlantic Monthly</u>."
       <u>Literary Digest</u>, 35 (16 Nov 1907), 757.
       Includes routine portrait of Howells.

1745   "The Season's Books / Novels and Tales." <u>Outlook</u>, 87 (23 Nov
       1907), 624. Brief review of <u>Between the Dark and the Day-
       light</u>.
         "When we can read Mr. Howells, why should we waste our
       time in other forms of mental refreshment?"

1746   "Short Stories." <u>Athenaeum</u>, No. 4179 (30 Nov 1907), 686.
       Brief review of <u>Between the Dark and the Daylight</u>.
         "'The Chick of the Easter Egg' is true humor according
       to the best definition, being a mixture of love and fun."

1747   "The New Books of the Month." <u>Book News</u>, 26 (Dec 1907), 306–
       307. Brief review of <u>Between the Dark and the Daylight</u>.
         "Though these seven stories deal with rather morbid men-
       tal states, Mr. Howells has invested them with such human
       feeling and such subtle artistry that they are wholly
       charming."

1748   "Holiday Publications." <u>Dial</u>, 43 (1 Dec 1907), 377. Notice
       of new edition of <u>Venetian Life</u>.
       Appreciative.

1749   "Literature." <u>Independent</u>, 63 (5 Dec 1907), 1377. Brief
       review of <u>Between the Dark and the Daylight</u>.
         The stories are "queer and creepy without being exactly
       supernatural." Editha is "the same old, inconsequent and
       exasperating" heroine Howells has drawn so often he can
       do so with little effort.

1750   "Travel and Description." <u>Literary Digest</u>, 35 (14 Dec 1907),
       918. Notice of rev. and enl. ed. of <u>Venetian Life</u>.

1751   "Current Fiction." <u>Nation</u>, 85 (26 Dec 1907), 590. Review of
       <u>Between the Dark and the Daylight</u>.
         Only the first of the stories, "A Sleep and a Forgetting,"
       has "real dignity, expressing as it does something of Mr.
       Howells's full power."

1752   "Gertrude Atherton Assails 'The Powers' / A Narrow Standard
       of Taste Imposed by the Howells School, She Declares,
       Effectually Checks Originality in American Literature /
       Severe Criticism of Some of Our 'Best Sellers' Develops
       the Fact That Europe Offers Wider Fields for the Best

1907

("Gertrude Atherton Assails 'The Powers'...")
Literary Effort." New York Times, 29 Dec 1907, V, p. 2.
Rpt. Current Literature, 44 (Feb 1908), 158-160.
Nearly full-page interview establishes Atherton's atti-
tude toward what she calls "the Magazine School" of
Howellsian realists.

1753 "Say Good-by to Howells." New York Sun, 29 Dec 1907, p. 7.
News item.
Coverage of luncheon given by Col. Harvey in honor of
Mr. Howells and Mildred on the eve of their departure for
Italy. The literary guests traveled to Lakewood by special
car.

1754 [GILL, W. A.] "'The Literary Supremacy of Mr. Howells.'"
New York Sun, 31 Dec 1907, p. 4. Editorial.
Response to Gertrude Atherton's attack on the Howells
canon. "By unwearying loyalty to this canon Mr. Howells
has created a gallery to which, 'middle class' though it
be, posterity will resort for the truest pictures of American life in his time. Long life to him, man and artist!"

1908

1755 ALDEN, HENRY MILLS. Magazine Writing and the New Literature.
New York and London: Harper, 1908. Pp. 52, 54, 180.
Brief references.
Insignificant comments on Howells' association with the
Atlantic, the first appearance of Venetian Sketches, and
his position as leader in the new movement in literature.

1756 GREENSLET, FERRIS. The Life of Thomas Bailey Aldrich. Boston
and New York: Houghton Mifflin, 1908. Passim as indexed.
Rpt. Port Washington, N. Y.: Kennikat Press, 1965.
Numerous scattered references.
Some items are anecdotal in nature, some based on quotations from Howells--reminiscences, impressions, letters on
matters literary and otherwise. Portrait of Howells in
1866 (facing p. 82).

1757 WINTER, WILLIAM. Other Days / Being Chronicles and Memories
of the Stage. New York: Moffat, Yard, 1908. P. 354.
Brief reference.
Lawrence Barrett's first London lyceum engagement was
in "Yorick's Love," adapted for him from the Spanish original by Howells.

1758   "Howells, William Dean. Christmas Every Day." Book Review
           Digest, 4 (1908), 180. Brief description.
           "A charmingly told tale."

1759   "Howells, William Dean. Fennel and Rue." Book Review Digest,
           4 (1908), 180. Brief description.
           "A satirical and delicate touch."

1760   "Howells, William Dean. Roman Holidays and Others." Book
           Review Digest, 4 (1908), 180. Brief description.
           "Quiet, capacious observation, poetic vision, and ripe
           reflection characterize these impressions."

1761   "Howells, William Dean, and others. Whole Family." Book Re-
           view Digest, 4 (1908), 181. Brief mention.
           Identifies contributors.

1762   COOPER, FREDERIC TABER. "The Many Italies." Bookman (New
           York), 26 (Jan 1908), 509-512. Brief comment.
           The last paragraph focuses on the revised Venetian Life.
           "No more delightfully sympathetic and vividly personal im-
           pression of the City of Canals has appeared in English."

1763   "Literary News and Criticism." New York Daily Tribune, 4 Jan
           1908, p. 5. Brief review of Between the Dark and the Day-
           light.
           Pathological elements are "tinged with a psychic signifi-
           cance." The seven stories are "somewhat ambiguous in
           effect."

1764   "The Charm of Venice." Nation, 86 (9 Jan 1908), 38. Brief
           notice of revised and enlarged edition of Venetian Life.
           Howells' "fugitive essays on Venetian life...are still
           the best in their field."

1765   "Letters and Art / Our Literary Tyrant." Literary Digest,
           36 (11 Jan 1908), 57-58. Literary news.
           Coverage of Gertrude Atherton's attack on Howells in
           the New York Times interview. "A New Picture of William
           D. Howells" (p. 57).

1766   "Why Have We Not More Great Novelists?" Current Literature,
           44 (Feb 1908), 158-160. Note.
           Gertrude Atherton's assessment of the debilitating in-
           fluence of Howells on American literature (29 Dec 1907
           New York Times interview) is contrasted with David Graham
           Phillips' more optimistic view and his belief that Ameri-
           can writers are hindered by too close study of the liter-
           ary style of Europe.

1908

1767   "Mr. W. D. Howells's Latest Romance / Fennel and Rue, a New
       Illustration of the Novelist's Ironic Powers--A Pleasant
       Story." New York Times, 21 Mar 1908, Sat. Sup., p. 151.
       Review.

1768   "Current Fiction." Nation, 86 (2 Apr 1908), 309. Review of
       Fennel and Rue.
           "Mr. Howells's new story has at least two refreshing
       elements--it presents a novel situation, and instead of
       dealing with unpleasant immoralities, it concerns itself
       with excessive morality."

1769   "Comment on Current Books." Outlook, 88 (11 Apr 1908), 838.
       Very brief review of Fennel and Rue.
           The "pervasive spirit of mild and humorous social satire
       reminds one of certain of Mr. Howells's earlier books."

1770   "Fiction / Fennel and Rue." Times Literary Supplement, 16 Apr
       1908, p. 126. Review.
           Howells' new novel "may be looked upon as the type of
       fiction, and, indeed, as a sort of epitome of the American
       mind, as regards both its qualities and its shortcomings."

1771   "Literature." Independent, 64 (23 Apr 1908), 925. Brief re-
       view of Fennel and Rue.
           "We can forgive Mr. Howells much for old love's sake,
       but what we cannot forgive is his assumption that Miss
       Shirley is an adorable young woman."

1772   "Fiction." A. L. A. Booklist, 4 (May 1908), 156. Very brief
       review.
           Quotes review from Nation. Adds, "Expensive [at $1.50]
       for length of story."

1773   VAN WESTRUM, A. SCHADE. "Mr. Howells's Fennel and Rue."
       Bookman (New York), 27 (May 1908), 281-282. Review.
           This is "a chip from Mr. Howells's literary workshop,
       delicately carved and polished, yet, highly finished
       though it be, a by-product none the less."

1774   "New Novels." Athenaeum, No. 4201 (2 May 1908), 537-538.
       Brief review of Fennel and Rue.
           Howells' "wit and sense of character nowadays seems
       attenuated."

1775   "Novels." Spectator, 100 (2 May 1908), 710. Review of
       Fennel and Rue.

("Novels")
> Like "intellectual novelists on both sides of the Atlan-
> tic," Howells "deals in motives which are subtle, recon-
> dite, at times even sophisticated." His novels "do not
> leave off on a note of interrogation or a cry of despair,"
> however, but "tend to promote a sane if tempered optimism."
> Here Howells keeps "a story which trembles on the verge of
> morbidity pure and sweet throughout."

1776   ALDEN, HENRY MILLS. "William Dean Howells / Recollections of
a Fellow-Worker." Book News, 26 (Jun 1908), 729-731.
Note.
> An impression of Howells as a man of feeling. Full-page
> portrait (p. 730).

1777   MABIE, HAMILTON WRIGHT. "The Story of Mr. Howells' Career."
Book News, 26 (Jun 1908), 733-734. Note.
> "In season and out of season he has told the truth as
> he saw it, with a quiet and winning persuasiveness which
> has humanized our noisy activities." Two portraits at
> ages 21 and 38.

1778   "For the Reader of New Fiction." Book News, 26 (Jun 1908),
784-785. Review of Fennel and Rue.
> "It certainly requires the art of a Howells to elaborate
> and embellish so slight a theme"--and in doing so to cause
> the reader to enjoy lingering with him.

1779   MAXWELL, PERRITON. "Howells the Editor." Book News, 26 (Jun
1908), 735-738. Note.
> A survey of Howells' editorial experience and praise of
> his editorial ability. "He is to-day chiefest of his
> class, because he was born with that rarest of literary
> gifts, the instinct for selection, the feel and know-how
> of right and wrong purveyance of the multitude." Two
> portraits.

1780   PENDENNIS [W. de WAGSTAFFE]. "The Personality of Mr. Howells /
A Study at Close Range." Book News, 26 (Jun 1908), 739-
741. Interview. Rpt. in part, "Interviews with William
Dean Howells," ed. Ulrich Halfmann, American Literary
Realism, 6 (Fall 1973), 361-362.
> Although Howells was born in Ohio, "New England adopted
> his literary destiny, and in New England he found the
> germ of his ambition."

1908

1781   "A Review of the Season's Fiction." Review of Reviews, 37
(Jun 1908), 760-761. Review of Fennel and Rue.
The impulsive question "It's clever, but is it art?"
gives way to another: "It's art, but is it clever?" In
subsequent paragraphs Howells is contrasted favorably with
Jack London, Upton Sinclair, Gouverneur Morris, and Ellen
Glasgow.

1782   "William Dean Howells." Book News, 26 (Jun 1908), front
piece. Portrait.
Portrait No. 261 in Book News Monthly's portrait series.

1783   PAYNE, WILLIAM MORTON. "Recent Fiction." Dial, 44 (1 Jun
1908), 350-351. Brief notice of Fennel and Rue.
Howells has "surpassed his own previous efforts in spin-
ning a considerable story out of a trifling incident."

1784   THOMAS, EDITH M. "Mr. Howells's Way of Saying Things." Putnam's, 4 (Jul 1908), 443-447. Short essay.
"'Style--it is the man.'" The excellence and versatili-
ty of Howells' style is a reflection of Howells the man.

1785   "William Dean Howells a Literary Optimist / Although Master-
pieces Are Not Being Published, He Says, There Is an Annual
Average of Excellent Literature Being Issued To-day."
New York Times, 26 Jul 1908, V, p. 5. Interview. Rpt.
"Interviews with William Dean Howells," ed. Ulrich Half-
mann, American Literary Realism, 6 (Fall 1973), 363-368.
Subheadings include "Not Many Masterpieces," "Literary
Sentimentalism," "Sketchy Literature," "Ways of Young
Writers," "The American Free Library," "The Profits of
Writing."

1786   CARY, ELISABETH LUTHER. "A Half-Dozen Problem Novels." Putnam's, 4 (Aug 1908), 618. Brief review of Fennel and Rue.
With "a wonderfully artful artlessness," Howells com-
municates a moral motive.

1787   COLBY, F. M. "The Casual Reader, Curiosities of Literary
Controversy." Bookman (New York), 28 (Oct 1908), 124-126.
Note.
In defending Howells against William Winter's attack
(cf. the visit to see Whitman at Pfaff's as reported by
Winter in "Memories of Authors" running serially in the
Saturday Evening Post), Colby himself attacks "Howells's
spinster-like intemperance in matters of propriety"
(p. 125).

1788 "Personal and Particular." Book Monthly, 6 (Oct 1908), 10-11.
Note.
How Howells plans a novel: "Evolution is a law in all
things."

1789 KELLY, FLORENCE FINCH. "The Whole Family and Its Troubles /
Co-operative Novel by Twelve Leading Literary Lights
Achieves an Impression of the Comedy of Confusion." New
York Times, 23 Oct 1908, Lit. Sec., p. 590. Review.
"Mr. Howells and Mr. James, are, of course, the star
performers in this company of twelve," and the rest have
all tried "to play up to them and to carry on a harmonious
method of treatment."

1790 "The Season's Important Books / Travel in Many Lands." Independent, 65 (19 Nov 1908), 1180. Review of Roman Holidays.
Although Italy is "the country of Mr. Howells's love,
...England is most potently the country of his racial
allegiance."

1791 "Notes on Books for Children." Nation, 87 (26 Nov 1908), 522.
Brief review of Christmas Every Day.
"A certain zest."

1792 "Books for Very Little People." New York Times, 28 Nov 1908,
Sat. Sup., p. 702. Review of Christmas Every Day.
Non-critical.

1793 GAINES, CLARENCE H. "New Books Reviewed / The Whole Family."
North American Review, 188 (Dec 1908), 928-930. Review.
Although a collaborative effort, "the whole narrative
is one in atmosphere, one in temperament of style, and
one in spirit." The Whole Family "seems very typical of
the 'new literature' in this country."

1794 "Juveniles." Book News, 27 (Dec 1908), 278. Brief notice of
Christmas Every Day.
A "well-known writer relaxes just long enough to write
a wonderful fairy-tale."

1795 "The Season's Books for Children." Review of Reviews, 38
(Dec 1908), 764. Very brief notice of Christmas Every
Day.
"It is written with grace, lightness of touch, brillian-
cy, and literary charm."

1908

1796   "Some Books of the Holiday Season." Review of Reviews, 38
        (Dec 1908), 760. Brief notice of Roman Holidays and Others.
        Non-critical description.

1797   "Holiday Publications." Dial, 45 (1 Dec 1908), 409. Brief
        notice of Roman Holidays and Others.
          "That humorous circumstantiality in treating the common-
        place."

1798   "Current Fiction / The Whole Family." Nation, 87 (3 Dec 1908),
        552. Review.
          "Mr. Howells leads off with a chapter so good that one
        fancies a superior Kentons might have developed if it had
        been for him to write the rest."

1799   "One Hundred Holiday Books." New York Times, 5 Dec 1908, Sat.
        Sup., p. 756. Very brief review of Roman Holidays and
        Others.
          "There is no sadness in these pages, nothing but a joy
        and a mellow philosophy" typical of the author.

1800   "Brief Reviews of Late Books / Mr. Howells's Holidays." New
        York Times, 12 Dec 1908, Sat. Sup., p. 774. Review of
        Roman Holidays and Others.
          "The habit Mr. Howells formed many years ago of writing
        charmingly about his holiday doings still clings to him,
        and manifests itself strikingly in his latest book."
        Largely summary.

1801   "Comment on Current Books." Outlook, 90 (12 Dec 1908), 844.
        Brief notice of Christmas Every Day.
          "Charm, delicacy, and tenderness."

1802   "Fifty of the Year's Best Books." Literary Digest, 37 (12 Dec
        1908), 901. Brief mention of Roman Holidays and Others.
        Howells' altered impressions of Italy are interesting.

1803   "Current Fiction / Roman Holidays and Others." Nation, 87
        (24 Dec 1908), 633. Full review.
          Those who associate Howells with literary partisanship
        "will marvel at the urbanity that pervades his latest
        book." "One would need to command as rich and delicate
        an assortment of epithets as Mr. Howells himself in order
        to do justice to this book." Howells is viewed favorably
        in contrast to other travel writers such as Henry James
        and Edith Wharton.

1909

1804   BIGELOW, JOHN. Retrospections of an Active Life. 5 vols.
New York: Baker and Taylor (vols. I-III); Doubleday,
Page (vols. IV and V), 1909-1913. I, p. 299. Brief
reference to an early (1860) evaluation of Howells.

1805   "Introduction." A Modern Instance by William Dean Howells.
The Riverside Literature Series. Boston: Houghton Mifflin,
1909. Pp. iii-x.
This commercially tailored summary statement of Howells'
literary career appears also in other Riverside editions
of Howells' novels.

1806   A Manuel of American Literature, ed. Theodore Stanton / In
Collaboration with Members of the Faculty of Cornell University. New York and London: Putnam's, 1909. Pp. 198-
201, 342-343, and passim as indexed. General biographical
and critical introduction.
Howells, "the apostle of latter-day realism," is used
as source for judgments of other American writers and is
noted as an influence on Edward Eggleston and Wolcott
Balestier.

1807   VENABLE, EMERSON, ed. "William Dean Howells." Poets of Ohio.
Cincinnati: Robert Clarke, 1909. Pp. 349-350.
Brief biographical sketch precedes six poems by Howells.
Bibliography.

1808   WILKINSON, WILLIAM CLEAVER. "William Dean Howells as Man of
Letters." Some New Literary Valuations. New York and
London: Funk and Wagnalls, 1909. Pp. [9]-73. Full chapter estimate.
"The fact is that Mr. Howells's literary industry and
fruitfulness have been extraordinary" (p. 12). "As far
as mere form of expression goes, Mr. Howells is one of the
great masters" (p. 15) who moves "far beyond the reach of
mere cleverness" (p. 18). His work is characterized by
humor and wit (pp. 18-20), psychological insight (p. 20),
pathos "penetrated with thought" (pp. 21-24), dramatic
quality (pp. 24-25). His verse is not equal in quality
to his prose (pp. 27-34). He falls short of being the
ideal critic because of his "complaisance...the well-bred
inclination to conform" (pp. 34-39). His diction is flawed
by pedantry (pp. 39-47). Humor "everywhere aerates and
illumines what Mr. Howells writes" (pp. 47-61). His novels
lack the largeness associated with Tolstoy and Scott
(pp. 65-70). A Modern Instance may have more lasting value
than any of his other single contributions (pp. 70-73).

1909

1809   WINTER, WILLIAM. "Vagrant Comrades." Old Friends / Being
       Literary Recollections of Other Days. New York: Moffatt,
       Yard, 1909. Pp. 89-92. Brief comment.
          Winter asserts that Howells' account of meeting Whitman
       was in large measure fiction.

1810   "Howells, William Dean. Mother and the Father." Book Review
       Digest, 5 (1909), 215. Brief notice.
          Description of "the three phases."

1811   "Howells, William Dean. Seven English Cities." Book Review
       Digest, 5 (1909), 215. Brief notice.
          Descriptive.

1812   MABIE, HAMILTON WRIGHT. "Essays in Travel." Book News, 27
       (Feb 1909), 453. Review of Roman Holidays and Others.
          "Mr. Howells travels with so little weight of luggage
       in the form of systematic knowledge that we hardly realize
       how illuminating he is, and what an instinct he has for
       getting away from the commonplace, and how casually he
       lifts a clear light of intelligence in obscure places."

1813   "Literature." Independent, 66 (4 May 1909), 489. Brief review
       of Roman Holidays and Others.
          "We can only be humbly grateful that we are the fortunate
       sharers of [Howells'] double wealth of former and later
       reminiscences."

1814   BROOKS, VAN WYCK. "Mr. Howells at Work at Seventy-Two."
       World's Work, 18 (May 1909), 11547-11549. Report of an
       interview. Rpt. "Five Interviews with William Dean
       Howells," ed. George Arms and William M. Gibson, Ameri-
       cana, 37 (Apr 1943), 283-287; "Interviews with William
       Dean Howells," ed. Ulrich Halfmann, American Literary
       Realism, 6 (Fall 1973), 368-371.
          Brooks observes, "It is only rare minds who are impressed
       by common things." Full-page portrait at beginning of pic-
       torial section.

1815   "Roman Holidays and Others." Spectator, 102 (1 May 1909),
       703-704. Review.
          Largely summary. Howells is youthful, delightful.

1816   "Brief Reviews of Lately Published Books / The Mother and the
       Father." New York Times, 29 May 1909, Sat. Sup., p. 342.
       Review.
          This psychological study is "strangely searching and
       poignant." As a transcript of life, it is somewhat

("Brief Reviews of Lately Published Books / The Mother and the Father")
>decadent; but it was probably intended to be read symbolically rather than literally.

1817   "General Literature." A. L. A. Booklist, 5 (Jun 1909), 169.
Very brief review of The Mother and the Father.
"The psychology of these crucial experiences has been translated into speech that is remarkable for its simplicity and directness and for its beauty of thought and depth of feeling."

1818   "The New Books." Review of Reviews, 40 (Jul 1909), 123.
Brief review of The Mother and the Father.
This "exquisite poem...., while neither rhyme nor strictly blank verse, is of the real Victorian flavor."

1819   "The Lounger." Putnam's, 6 (Sep 1909), 755-756. Note.
Reference, largely as quotation, to William Winter's negative response to Howells at Pfaff's.

1820   "Autumn Book List / Travel and Description." New York Times, 22 Oct 1909, Lit. Sec., p. 634. Brief notice of Seven English Cities.
Non-critical.

1821   "Boy Heroes in Many Books." New York Times, 13 Nov 1909, Sat. Sup., p. 709. Review of Boy's Life (selections from Howells arranged for school use by Percival Chubb).
Non-critical.

1822   "Notable Books of the Season / Travel and Exploration." Independent, 67 (18 Nov 1909), 1144-1145. Brief review of Seven English Cities.
This slight volume is a delight "because it reveals so gracefully the beauty of the purely technical side of [Howells'] talent, the playful ease with which it can turn the least promising of material into something worth the doing, and so superlatively well worth the reading."

1823   "Editions." A. L. A. Booklist, 6 (Dec 1909), 145. Brief notice of Boy's Life.
"Libraries should have the original works."

1909

1824 "General Literature." <u>A. L. A. Booklist</u>, 6 (Dec 1909), 118.
   Brief review of <u>Seven English Cities</u>.
   "One or two" of these sketches are below Howells' stan-
   dard (but which ones are not specified).

1825 "New Books Reviewed." <u>North American Review</u>, 190 (Dec 1909),
   839. Very brief review of <u>Seven English Cities</u>.
   "Is the book Mr. Howells's little revenge, his Quip
   Modest, for <u>The American Scene</u>?"

1826 "The Season's Books for Children." <u>Review of Reviews</u>, 40
   (Dec 1909), 766. Very brief notice of <u>Boy's Life</u>.
   "Pictures in the 'retrospect.'"

1827 "Some Books of the Holiday Season." <u>Review of Reviews</u>, 40
   (Dec 1909), 760. Brief notice of <u>Seven English Cities</u>.
   "Leisurely literary meanderings."

1828 "Holiday Publications." <u>Dial</u>, 47 (1 Dec 1909), 459. Appreciative notice of <u>Seven English Cities</u>.
   "As gossippy and entertaining as ever."

1829 "The New Books." <u>Outlook</u>, 93 (4 Dec 1909), 788. Brief notice
   of <u>Seven English Cities</u>.
   "As a literary travel companion [Howells] is even more
   enjoyable than as a critic and story-writer."

1830 "Some of the Best Books for Children." <u>Literary Digest</u>, 39
   (4 Dec 1909), 1018. Brief notice of <u>Boy's Life</u>.
   Non-critical.

1831 "Literature." <u>Independent</u>, 67 (9 Dec 1909), 1318. Review of
   <u>The Mother and the Father</u>.
   Largely summary. "Mr. Howells should have given the
   woman four or five children and then written a drama of
   life, but--in prose."

1832 "<u>Seven English Cities</u>." <u>Athenaeum</u>, No. 4285 (11 Dec 1909),
   724-725. Full review.
   That this "shrewdly written and entertaining book" was
   obviously written for American readers "makes it all the
   more amusing and instructive for perusal in England."

1910

1833   EGGLESTON, GEORGE CARY.   Recollections of a Varied Life.   New
       York: Holt, 1910. Pp. 148-150, 204-205, 258. Brief
       references.
          Eggleston was "stunned" by Howells' invitation to write
       reminiscences of Southern army life for the Atlantic. He
       notes Howells' plan for the series and his personal response
       to the first two installments (pp. 148-149). Quotes Howells'
       speculation on the ethics of anonymous criticism (pp. 204-
       205).

1834   HEARN, LAFCADIO. The Japanese Letters of Lafcadio Hearn, ed.
       with introd. by Elizabeth Bisland [Wetmore]. Boston and
       New York: Houghton Mifflin, 1910. Pp. 126, 215. Brief
       references.
          In a letter to Basil Hall Chamberlain (25 Jun 1893), "I
       don't like Howell's [sic] books because I detest the kind
       of people he writes about" (p. 126). Again (14 Dec 1893),
       "Howells portrays the ugliest and harshest commonplaces of
       a transient democracy" (p. 215).

1835   MAUDE, AYLMER. The Life of Tolstoy / Later Years. London:
       Constable, 1910. P. 560. Very brief reference.
          Tolstoy was "particularly sympathetic towards Howells."

1836   PHELPS, WILLIAM LYON. "William Dean Howells." Essays on
       Modern Novelists. New York: Macmillan, 1910. Pp. 56-81.
       General evaluation.
          This early introduction to Howells, the "Reticent Real-
       ist," is protective, defending him against the 1907 attack
       of Gertrude Atherton, insisting that his artistic concepts
       may be open to criticism but that his ethics are not.
       Howells is a creative rather than critical writer. His
       work is divided into two periods: before and after Tol-
       stoy. Phelps gives major attention to A Modern Instance,
       Howells' most powerful novel, and to The Kentons. In-
       cludes chronological listing of book publications (pp. 272-
       278).

1837   STEDMAN, LAURA, and GEORGE M. GOULD. Life and Letters of
       Edmund Clarence Stedman. 2 vols. New York: Moffat, Yard,
       1910. Passim as indexed. Frequent brief references.
          Widely varied and generally fragmented, mostly reminis-
       cent and anecdotal in nature. Numerous letters to and
       from Howells.

1910

1838   "Howells, William Dean. Imaginary Interviews." Book Review
        Digest, 6 (1910), 195. Brief description.
            Howells' philosophizing is enjoyable, no matter what the
        subject.

1839   "Howells, William Dean. My Mark Twain." Book Review Digest,
        6 (1910), 196. Brief description.
            Here is "an intimacy and an understanding which will de-
        light all lovers of the genial humorist."

1840   "Chronicle and Comment / Mr. Howells as Critic." Bookman
        (New York), 30 (Jan 1910), 451-452. Note.
            Response to Howells' evaluation of Meredith. Someone
        ought to throw a bomb at Howells' "tidy little theory of
        art," which admits Zola and Eden Phillpotts but rejects
        Meredith and Thackeray. Howells' comments have nothing
        to do with criticism, "but only with the prohibition of
        variety."

1841   "Books / Impressions of England." Spectator, 104 (29 Jan
        1910), 151-152. Review of Seven English Cities.
            Largely summary detail with asides, both appreciative
        and defensive.

1842   "Chronicle and Comment / A Letter from Mr. Phillpotts." Book-
        man (New York), 31 (Mar 1910), 17-18. Letter and comment.
            The introduction to the letter centers on the editorial
        assertion that according to Howells "the first step in
        art is the disembowelment of the artist." Eden Phillpotts
        in the letter attempts to explain Howells' position on
        artistic intrusion by showing that it relates to form, not
        content.

1843   "The New Books." Review of Reviews, 42 (Oct 1910), 510.
        Brief notice of My Mark Twain.
            "Sympathetic and tender." Photograph of "Mark Twain
        and William Dean Howells at Lakewood in 1908."

1844   "Ricus." "A Suppressed Novel of Mr. Howells." Bookman (New
        York), 32 (Oct 1910), 201-203. Note.
            Reference is to Private Theatricals. The author specu-
        lates about source and the reason the work was not given
        book publication.

1845   "Briefs on New Books." Dial, 49 (1 Oct 1910), 238. Brief
        notice of My Mark Twain.
            Appreciative.

1846   "A Guide to the New Books." Literary Digest, 41 (1 Oct 1910),
        553. Review of My Mark Twain.
        Descriptive and non-critical.

1847   BOYNTON, H. W. "Mr. Howells's Mark Twain / A Book That Throws
        Interesting Side-Lights on a Many-Yeared and Memorable
        Friendship." New York Times, 8 Oct 1910, Lit. Sup.,
        p. 557. Full review.
            "Mr. Howells is as incapable as Mark Twain himself of
        whitewashing the subject of his study." The collection
        of Howells' reviews of Twain's work trace a gradual change
        in attitude "from one of good-humored recognition of an
        entertaining humorist to one of strong admiration for a
        force in modern letters."

1848   "Notes." Nation, 91 (27 Oct 1910), 395. Brief response to
        My Mark Twain.
            "The record has, of course, a charming anecdotal
        interest."

1849   "General Literature." A. L. A. Booklist, 7 (Nov 1910), 105.
        Very brief review.
            "A delightful record of a friendship...with a kindly
        and just appreciation of Mark Twain's personality and work,
        of both of which Mr. Howells has many intimate and new
        things to say."

1850   "Notable Books of the Year / Essays and Literary Studies."
        Independent, 69 (17 Nov 1910), 1096. Brief mention of
        Imaginary Interviews.
            "Inimitable style, even tho[ugh] the substance is some-
        what attenuated."

1851   "Mr. W. D. Howells on Mark Twain." Spectator, 105 (19 Nov
        1910), 864. Review of My Mark Twain.
            Suggests that Twain picked up the episode of three liter-
        ary men in a Western mining camp from The Golden Butterfly
        (1876).

1852   "Literary Notes." Independent, 69 (24 Nov 1910), 1161.
        Announcement of In After Days (a collection of essays on
        "the future life" to which Howells contributed.)

1853   "Mr. Howells in the Easy Chair." Times Literary Supplement,
        24 Nov 1910, p. 465. Review of Imaginary Interviews.
            The essays are less "charming in the lump" than separate-
        ly. The book is too big, "too pompous for its contents,"

1910

("Mr. Howells in the Easy Chair")
and "it seems probable that Mr. Howells has never been quite at ease in his easy chair." He is not really an essayist.

1854   "The Honour of Meeting." Spectator, 105 (26 Nov 1910), 898-899. Review of Imaginary Interviews.
The reviewer spends more time discussing the honor we attach to meeting prominent figures than he does evaluating Howells' "pleasant" book.

1855   "Notes." Nation, 91 (1 Dec 1910), 526. Brief response to Imaginary Interviews.
"The book scarcely prompts one to a review of Mr. Howells's ideas, which contain nothing that is in any way revolutionary."

1856   "Literature / And Yet the Essay." Independent, 69 (22 Dec 1910), 1399. Brief notice of My Mark Twain.
A "genial little volume." Portrait of Howells and James.

1857   "Our Modest American Academy." Literary Digest, 41 (24 Dec 1910), 1201. Note.
A brief descriptive sketch of the Academy indicating Howells' involvement. Portrait of twenty-three members.

1911

1858   HALLECK, REUBEN POST. History of American Literature. New York: American Book, 1911. Pp. 373-376 and passim as indexed.
General assessment of "the foremost leader of realism in modern American fiction, the man who has influenced more young writers than any other novelist of the last quarter of the nineteenth century." His best work belongs to his middle period. "Before this, his mastery of character portrayal had not culminated, and later, his power of artistic selection and expression was not so strictly exercised." Portrait (p. 373).

1859   HARRISON, MRS. BURTON [CONSTANCE CARY]. Recollections Grave and Gay. New York: Scribner's, 1911. P. 338. Passing reference.
In the context of an "Authors' Readings" session.

1860   JEWETT, SARAH ORNE. Letters of Sarah Orne Jewett, ed. Annie
       Fields. Boston and New York: Houghton Mifflin, 1911.
       Pp. 226-227. Short comment.
          A prefatory note expresses regret that letters offered
       by Howells arrived too late for inclusion. Jewett recalls
       Howells' rejection of "Lady Ferry," one of her stories.

1861   PORTER, GEORGE H. Ohio Politics During the Civil War Period.
       New York: Columbia University Library, 1911. Not indexed.
          The political position of W. C. Howells is referred to
       on pages 62 and 89n, but quick paging disclosed no refer-
       ence to W. D. Howells.

1862   "Howells, William Dean. Parting Friends." Book Review Digest,
       7 (1911), 242. Brief summary.

1863   "New Books." Literary Digest, 42 (7 Jan 1911), 31. Brief
       notice of Imaginary Interviews.
          Howells "has never been in happier vein than in these
       thirty sparkling lucubrations."

1864   "The Point of View." Scribner's, 47 (May 1911), 635. Brief
       reference.
          Minor mention of Howells in a discussion of "ageology."

1865   "Volumes from the Writers of Fiction and Fact / Mr. Howells's
       Farce." New York Times, 27 Aug 1911, Sat. Sup., p. 520.
       Review of Parting Friends.
          "It is all very slight, very humorous, and very Howells-
       esque."

1866   "Literary Notes." Independent, 71 (14 Sep 1911), 597. Brief
       notice of Parting Friends.
          "Mr. Howells's touch is as delicate as ever, and his
       little dialog has the sparkle of life."

1912

1867   HARPER, J[OSEPH] HENRY. The House of Harper / A Century of
       Publishing in Franklin Square. New York and London: Harp-
       er, 1912. Pp. 318-330 and passim as indexed. Scattered
       references.
          The comments, which trace Howells' association with the
       Harpers, are generally laudatory. Howells own "modest"
       statement summarizing that relationship is included
       (pp. 319-327). Portrait (facing p. 328).

1912

1868   PERRY, BLISS. The American Mind. Boston and New York:
        Houghton Mifflin, 1912. Not indexed.
            Incidental reference to the "unmatched artistry" of the
        "novels of international observation" by James and Howells
        (p. 51).

1869   "William Dean Howells at 75 / Tributes from Eminent Americans
        to Our Foremost Man of Letters." Boston Evening Tran-
        script, 24 Feb 1912. III, p. 2. A full-page spread col-
        lated with introductory statement by William Stanley
        Braithwaite.
            Items included, in order, are these:
            John D. Long, "The Art of an American Trollope."
            Brander Matthews, "As a Spokesman for the Country / Mr.
        Howells Our Most Faithful Interpreter...."
            Mary E. Wilkins Freeman, "The Permanency of Mr. Howells /
        Often Obscured, but Never Replaced, by Flashy Writers."
            Henry Mills Alden, "Strongest in His Human Naturalness /
        A Genius Who Gained by the Petty Tricks He Avoided."
            Florence Earle Coates, "William Dean Howells." [Poem.]
            George W. Cable, [Telegram].
            Henry Van Dyke, "Henry Van Dyke on Howells's Realism /
        A True Realist Because He Understands the Romance of Life."
            Robert Underwood Johnson, "A Stylist of the Very First
        Order / Precision, Clearness, Grace His Chief Distinctions."
            Robert Herrick, "A Warm Champion of the Truth / Whose
        Strength Is in the Quality of His Audience."
            George Edward Woodberry, "An American, but Yet Cosmo-
        politan / A Writer as Ambassador of Letters Abroad."
            Alice Brown, "As 'The Man Behind the Book' / The Author
        as He Discloses Himself in His Works."
            Bliss Perry, "A Skillful Painter of Our Types / The
        Genuine American Portraits from Mr. Howells' Brush."
            J. Berg Esenwein, "All Races Fused in Howells' Ameri-
        canism / The Many Tendencies Blended in His Balanced
        Product."
            W. E. Burghardt Dubois, "As a Friend of the Colored
        Man / Quick To Discover the Negro's True Standing and
        Qualities."

1870   ROOD, HENRY. "W. D. Howells, at 75, Talks of Old Literary
        New York." New York Times, 25 Feb 1912, V, p. 4. Inter-
        view. Rpt. "Interviews with William Dean Howells," ed.
        Ulrich Halfmann, American Literary Realism, 6 (Fall 1973),
        376-382.
            Subtitled "Dean of American Authors, in Reminiscent
        Mood, Recalls Other Days and Other Faces--Distinguished
        Folk Will Observe His Birthday Anniversary Next Friday."

1871   "William Dean Howells." New York Times, 1 Mar 1912, p. 10.
            Brief note.
            Recognition of his seventy-fifth birthday.

1872   "Mr. Howells Beaming on 75th Birthday." New York Sun, 2 Mar
            1912, p. 10. Interview. Brief abstr. "Interviews with
            William Dean Howells," ed. Ulrich Halfmann, American
            Literary Realism, 6 (Fall 1973), 382.
            Howells talks of ease in writing, better pay, and his
            scheduled birthday dinner.

1873   "Mr. Taft Leads in Praise of Howells." New York Sun, 3 Mar
            1912, p. 11. News item.
            Coverage of seventy-fifth birthday celebration hosted
            by George Harvey. Includes brief biographical detail,
            tributes, and a summary of Howells' speech.

1874   "Taft Joins in Praise of William Dean Howells." New York
            Times, 3 Mar 1912, pp. 1 and 8. News item.
            Account of seventy-fifth birthday celebration, includes
            summary of Howells' comments and guest list.

1875   "William Dean Howells." Independent, 72 (7 Mar 1912), 533-534.
            Editorial.
            An appreciative general summary of Howells' contribution.
            Portrait (p. 533).

1876   CLARKSON, HELEN WARRELL. "Our Debt to Mr. Howells." Harper's
            Weekly, 56 (9 Mar 1912), 6. Letter to the editor.
            "Surely never was there so sensitive a scale as his with
            which to weigh the literary balance, nor so just a sense
            of what is best and living in literature." Howells' fic-
            tion, taken together, comprises "The Great American Novel."

1877   "A Tribute to William Dean Howells / Souvenir of a Dinner
            Given to the Eminent Author in Celebration of His Seventy-
            Fifth Birthday." Harper's Weekly, 56 (9 Mar 1912), II,
            27-34. Special supplement. Rpt. in part, North American
            Review, 212 (Jul 1920), 1-16.
            Includes a full narrative account ("In Honor of Mr.
            Howells / Some of the Memorable Happenings at Last Week's
            Birthday Dinner to the Dean of American Letters"), com-
            plete with speeches, testimonials, and the dramatic
            reading presented by Silas Lapham (played by James Barnes);
            also a full-page portrait, a double-fold photograph of the
            assembled diners at Sherry's, and a list of the guests.

1912

1878   "A Woman's Tribute to Mr. Howells." Literary Digest, 44
        (9 Mar 1912), 485. Note.
            Because women are not always pleased with Howells' work,
        Literary Digest cites Mary E. Wilkins Freeman's tribute
        to Howells in the Boston Evening Transcript, 24 Feb 1912,
        III, p. 2. Portrait, "Mr. Howells' Serene Evening of
        Life."

1879   "Mr. Howells's Seventy-Fifth Birthday: The President's Speech /
        Mr. Howells's Reply." Outlook, 100 (16 Mar 1912), 568-569.
        News coverage of the New York dinner.

1880   "America's Foremost Living Man of Letters." Current Litera-
        ture, 52 (Apr 1912), 461-463. Note.
            A survey of critical response to Howells on the occasion
        of his birthday. Portrait (p. 463).

1881   JAMES, HENRY. "Literary Recollections / By Mr. James / A
        Letter to Mr. Howells." North American Review, 195 (Apr
        1912), 558-562. Rpt. Howells / A Century of Criticism,
        ed. Kenneth E. Eble (Dallas: Southern Methodist Univer-
        sity, 1962), pp. 88-93, and The War of the Critics over
        William Dean Howells, ed. Edwin H. Cady and David L.
        Frazier (Evanston: Row, Peterson, 1962), pp. 106-109.
            An enthusiastic tribute on the occasion of Howells'
        seventy-fifth birthday.

1882   SANBORN, F. B. "Literary Recollections / By Mr. Sanborn / A
        Letter to the Chairman." North American Review, 195
        (Apr 1912), 562-566.
            A reminiscence and tribute on the occasion of Howells'
        seventy-fifth birthday.

1883   "Chronicle and Comment / Mr. Howells on Rag-Babies." Bookman
        (New York), 35 (Jul 1912), 451-452. Brief comment.
            Howells' fight against the rag-baby of romance was a
        losing one. He was not a very good fighter. As for
        realism, he "had a great talent for doing the thing and
        none whatever for telling how to do it--and surely in his
        case the one was enough."

1884   [Untitled.] Bookman (New York), 35 (Jul 1912), 510. Note
        prefatory to "The Coming," a poem by Howells.
            Sketches the background of the poem, which Howells pre-
        pared for an editorial convention when he was associated
        with The Ohio State Journal.

278

1885 W[ILLIAM] D[EAN] H[OWELLS] and T[HOMAS] S[ERGEANT] P[ERRY].
"Recent Russian Fiction / A Conversation." North American
Review, 196 (Jul 1912), 85-103. Interview. Rpt. "Inter-
views with William Dean Howells," ed. Ulrich Halfmann,
American Literary Realism, 6 (Fall 1973), 382-391.
The conversation does indeed focus on Russian fiction
and not on an evaluation of Howells or his opinion of it.

1886 WYATT, EDITH FRANKLIN. "A National Contribution." North
American Review, 196 (Sep 1912), 339-352. A personal
appreciation. Rpt. Great Companions (New York: Appleton,
1917), pp. 113-142.
"In his life-long service for the realization of truth,
both as a constructive critic and as a creative artist,
Mr. Howells has, I think, made for his nation an immortal
contribution to the cause of social sympathy and genuine
common understanding which is the great end of all letters."

1887 LESSING, O. E. "William Dean Howells." Das Literarische
Echo, 15 (1 Nov 1912), 155-161. Introductory essay. Rpt.
Brücken über den Atlantik (Berlin und Leipzig, 1927),
pp. 139-149.
Emphasizes Howells' realistic affinity with the litera-
ture of Europe and his Americanism. Portrait (p. 158).

1888 DIPLOMATICUS. "A Portrayer of the Commonplace." Westminster
Review, 178 (Dec 1912), 597-608. A critical estimate.
"To all intents and purposes Howells is a descriptive
writer; he is seldom narrative because he seldom conde-
scends to write anything worth narrating. His 'novels'
are a tissue of trivial incidents in family life, told
with an inimitable charm and an aptness and truth that in-
vest them with a freshness and interest they by no means
intrinsically possess" (p. 598). Howells distorts the
reality of American life by disproportionate representation of materialism.

1913

1889 LODGE, HENRY CABOT. Early Memories. New York: Scribner's,
1913. Pp. 68, 344-346. Brief references.
An appreciation of A Boy's Town (p. 68). Favorable profile of Howells as man and artist, briefly measuring his
accomplishment (pp. 344-346).

1913

1890 LONG, WILLIAM J. American Literature. Boston: Ginn, 1913.
Pp. 457, 460-462. Brief introduction.
Howells is a "representative realist." Although his
works lack the heroic, his characters sometimes become
tiresome, and his feminine characters are shallow, he has
given us "some of the best pictures of American society
'in the making' that have ever appeared in literature."

1891 MACY, JOHN A. "Howells." The Spirit of American Literature.
Garden City, N. Y.: Doubleday, Page, 1913. Pp. 278-295
and passim as indexed. Rpt. in part, The War of the
Critics over William Dean Howells, ed. Edwin H. Cady and
David L. Frazier (Evanston: Row, Peterson, 1962),
pp. 110-113.
Howells' "American birth and training preserved him.
But he has never been the man he might have been if he had
not come under the enervating spell of obsolete pieties
[the Old Boston influence]" (p. 280). Howells, with
James, "accepted the self-imposed limitations of realism,
but they could not accept its profound privilege of tell-
ing the truth" (p. 282). Extended comment on A Modern
Instance, Annie Kilburn, and The Lady of the Aroostook.
Bibliographic note (pp. 294-295).

1892 NORTON, CHARLES ELIOT. Letters of Charles Eliot Norton / with
Biographical Comment, ed. Sara Norton and M. A. DeWolfe
Howe. 2 vols. Boston and New York: Houghton Mifflin,
1913. Passim as indexed. Brief comments.
Wide assortment of references to Howells both as man
and as artist, e.g., in an 1874 letter to James Russell
Lowell, "Howells came in to dine with [Longfellow];
plump and with ease shining out from his eyes. He has
passed his poetic stage, and bids fair to be a popular
American author" (II, p. 33).

1893 "Howells, William Dean. Familiar Spanish Travels." Book
Review Digest, 9 (1913), 266. Brief description.

1894 "Howells, William Dean. New Leaf Mills." Book Review Digest,
9 (1913), 266. Brief summary.

1895 TRITES, W. B. "William Dean Howells." Forum, 49 (Feb 1913),
217-240. A critical estimate.
On the occasion of the publication of the first six
volumes of the Library Edition of Howells' work. Trites's
comments are interesting, rather personal, and somewhat
superficial. "The mind rarely gifted, the ideal conditions, the unconquerable literary passion--granted these

(TRITES, W. B.)
> things, the only other need was a life's devotion. This
> he has given gladly, and his works remain. They are
> America's most splendid contribution to literature"
> (p. 240).

1896   STIMSON, SAM S. "Howells Discovers a New Literary Light,
W. B. Trites." New York Times, 16 Feb 1913, Mag. Sec.,
p. 8. Feature on Trites.
> Howells' early approval of Trites, who seemed to him
> "to possess the distinctive mark of genius," is used as
> the introduction to this feature on the younger writer.

1897   "Fiction." A. L. A. Booklist, 9 (Mar 1913), 299. Brief
review of New Leaf Mills.
> "The country life of the Middle West in the period fol-
> lowing the Mexican War is depicted so graphically as to
> give the story the effect of a transcript from actual ex-
> perience, which it no doubt in part is."

1898   HERFORD, OLIVER. "Celebrities I Have Not Met: William Dean
Howells." American Magazine, 75 (Mar 1913), 95. Satiric
poem and drawing.
> On Howells' kindness to "Literary Fledglings."

1899   "Latest Books as the Critic Sees Them /.../ William Dean
Howells Paints Portraits in Words." New York Sun, 1 Mar
1913, p. 10. Review of New Leaf Mills.
> The portraits of the parents are singled out for com-
> ment. Impending tragedies heighten interest; but, "in
> accordance with the laws of Howells's realism," they never
> take place.

1900   "New Leaf Mills / Mr. Howells's Latest Novel a Forceful Bit
of Art." New York Times Review of Books, 2 Mar 1913,
p. 111. Full review.
> Howells' book has three values: it is a vivid and
> interesting story, a penetrating psychological study, and
> an important historical document.

1901   E[DGETT], E[DWIN] F[RANCIS]. "Books of the Day—A Novel by
Mr. Howells / His Chronicle of Life in the Middle West."
Boston Evening Transcript, 5 Mar 1913, p. 22. Review of
New Leaf Mills.
> "Idealism in contrast with the practical exigencies of
> life." Extensive quotation.

1913

1902   "A Novel by W. D. Howells / Characteristic Study of Earlier
       American Life in the Middle West." Springfield Sunday
       Republican, 23 Mar 1913, p. 35. Review of New Leaf Mills.
          Howells "essays the role of the social historian rather
       than in any large sense of the romanticist." Howells'
       "quietism" is compared with that of Alphonse de Chateau-
       briand in The Keynote.

1903   "The New Books." Outlook, 103 (29 Mar 1913), 734. Brief re-
       view of New Leaf Mills.
          "A piece of unconscious art" marked by "sincerity, sim-
       plicity, and naturalness."

1904   "Literature and Art / The Story of a Swedenborgian Paper Mill."
       Current Opinion, 54 (Apr 1913), 317. Review of New Leaf
       Mills.
          Largely copied from New York Times Review of Books,
       2 Mar 1913, p. 111.

1905   "Literature and Art / William Dean Howells' Latest." Current
       Opinion, 54 (Apr 1913), 317. Review of New Leaf Mills.
          Little direct comment on the novel. The reviewer com-
       ments on a disagreement over Howells between Theodore
       Roosevelt and The Westminster Review and takes issue with
       both. "Howells neither deserves to be called this age's
       greatest novelist, nor does he lack a keen insight into
       the workings of moral law."

1906   "Fiction." Spectator, 110 (5 Apr 1913), 584-585. Review of
       New Leaf Mills.
          The work "is marked by an absence of mannerism and an
       unstudied ease more often associated with youth than age."
       Situational humor approaches tragi-comedy.

1907   "Reviews of New Books / Other Novels of the Season." Literary
       Digest, 46 (5 Apr 1913), 780, 782. Review of New Leaf
       Mills.
          The skill of the narrator lends interest to a "placid"
       theme.

1908   [BOYNTON, H. W.] "Current Fiction / New Leaf Mills." Nation,
       96 (24 Apr 1913), 415-416. Full review.
          "This is the Howells of A Boy's Town."

1909   "Howells as a Victim of the 'Dead Hand' in American Fiction."
       Current Opinion, 54 (May 1913), 411. Note.
          A three-column summary of John Albert Macy's "revolu-
       tionary and highly provocative" criticism of Howells in
       The Spirit of American Literature.

1910   "Some Novels of Morals and Manners." Review of Reviews, 47
        (May 1913), 630. Brief review of New Leaf Mills.
            Western pioneers are more entertaining than their de-
        scendants, "the occupants of Chicago sky-scrapers" (refer-
        ence is to Robert Herrick's One Woman's Life).

1911   "Literature and Art / Mr. Howells' Latest 'Discovery.'"
        Current Opinion, 54 (Jun 1913), 490. Brief note.
            Howells says W. B. Trites's work has the mark of genius.

1912   "The New Books of the Month." Book News, 31 (Jun 1913), 790.
        Very brief comment on New Leaf Mills.
            "Mr. Howells grows more and more dull. His fiction
        exhibits all those finicky touches which adhere to a man
        who devotes more attention to the form than to the matter."

1913   PAYNE, WILLIAM MORTON. "Recent Fiction." Dial, 54 (1 Jun
        1913), 463. Brief review of New Leaf Mills.
            "It is a book which helps us to understand our fore-
        bears of a generation or two ago, and is an undeniably
        veracious transcript of their life."

1914   "The New Books / New Leaf Mills." Independent, 74 (5 Jun
        1913), 1302-1303. Full review.
            "Nothing in the later school of novelists is cleaner,
        more just to the conditions of the times, and fuller of
        interest to those who seek a lesson in the tendency of
        our home life today."

1915   MATTHEWS, BRANDER. "American Character in American Fiction."
        Munsey's, 49 (Aug 1913), 796-797. Review of New Leaf
        Mills.
            The art of fiction is finer in each succeeding genera-
        tion, and Howells ought not to have been condemned for
        saying so. In this latest novel, "the quiet and restful
        portrayal of a group of very American characters in very
        American conditions" is marked by "mellow charm," "simple
        grace," and "absolute sincerity." The novel, on a high
        artistic plane, strikes "the austere note of inevitability."

1916   GILL, WILLIAM ARTHUR. "Some Novelists and the Business Man /
        II. In America." Atlantic, 112 (Oct 1913), 506-515.
        Brief reference to The Rise of Silas Lapham (pp. 508,
        512).
            "The book embodies in a very human instance the question
        which has since become so prominent in American novels"
        (p. 512).

1913

1917   "Critical Reviews of the Season's Latest Books /.../ Views
         of Many Lands." New York Sun, 25 Oct 1913, p. 10. Brief
         mention of Familiar Spanish Travels.
            "No pleasanter travelling companion than William Dean
         Howells can be wished for."

1918   "Recent Reflections of a Novel-Reader." Atlantic, 112 (Nov
         1913), 701. Review of New Leaf Mills.
            "Put forth without accent or emphasis, this little book,
         to which one somehow is fain to apply the intimate adjec-
         tives gentle and loving, is not only a tribute to a type
         of character whose beauty becomes clearer with our in-
         creasing perception of man's limitations, but it is also
         the sunset-comment of one long-lived, and kind, and wise,
         upon the social ferment of these latter days."

1919   "The New Books." Outlook, 105 (15 Nov 1913), 598. Brief re-
         view of Familiar Spanish Travels.
            Howells "has a way of dealing with the most familiar
         localities with an intimacy, a humor, and a continuous
         friendliness which give beaten paths a certain novelty."

1920   "The Hundred Best Books of the Year / Familiar Spanish
         Travels." New York Times Review of Books, 30 Nov 1913,
         p. 679. Brief review.
            Howells is not provincial, but "he shows a rather sur-
         prising disability to understand Spanish Christianity."

1921   "The Hundred Best Books of the Year / New Leaf Mills." New
         York Times Review of Books, 30 Nov 1913, p. 665. Review.
            "It is, in fact, a novel of thoughts, rather than of
         deeds." Howells' "vivid descriptions of the Middle West
         of pioneer days" make the novel "a real contribution to
         history, as well as a fascinating psychological study."
         Portrait.

1922   "General Literature." A. L. A. Booklist, 10 (Dec 1913), 141.
         Very brief review of Familiar Spanish Travels.
            "Delightful and entertaining, keenly observant but not
         too critical," Howells' "passion for Spain in some situa-
         tions was evidently more reminiscent than present."

1923   TASSIN, ALGERNON. "The Christmas Pen and Brush." Bookman
         (New York), 38 (Dec 1913), 387-389. Review of Familiar
         Spanish Travels.
            "On every page...is revealed the charm of Mr. Howells's
         personality, the mellowness and gentility of which makes
         every book of his one more privilege."

1913

1924　"Holiday Publications." _Dial_, 55 (1 Dec 1913), 480.　Brief
　　　　notice of _Familiar Spanish Travels_.
　　　　Appreciative.

1925　[NORTHRUP, G. T.]　"_Familiar Spanish Travels_."　_Nation_, 97
　　　　(11 Dec 1913), 567.　Review.
　　　　"Mr. Howells's powers of close observation have not
　　　　diminished with years."

1914

1926　METCALF, JOHN CALVIN.　_American Literature_.　Richmond:　B. F.
　　　　Johnson, 1914.　Pp. 369, 370, 371.　General biographical
　　　　and critical introduction.
　　　　"It seems a little strange that so consummate an idealist
　　　　as Emerson should furnish a text for so ardent a realist
　　　　as Howells, and it is doubtful whether the Concord sage
　　　　would have agreed with the novelist's application of it."

1927　UNDERWOOD, JOHN CURTIS.　"William Dean Howells and Altruria."
　　　　Literature and Insurgency / Ten Studies in Racial Evolu-
　　　　tion.　New York:　Mitchell Kennerley, 1914.　Pp. 87-129.
　　　　Rpt. in part, _Howells / A Century of Criticism_, ed. Ken-
　　　　neth E. Eble (Dallas:　Southern Methodist University, 1962),
　　　　pp. 78-87, and _The War of the Critics over William Dean_
　　　　Howells, ed. Edwin H. Cady and David L. Frazier (Evanston:
　　　　Row, Peterson, 1962), pp. 113-117.
　　　　A negative assessment of the essential softness and
　　　　weakness of Howells' work.　Howells is an incurable senti-
　　　　mentalist, who has so far "misread, and tried so long to
　　　　misinterpret, the meaning and purpose of history, of evo-
　　　　lution, of civilization, of democracy, of science."　But
　　　　insofar as he has shown "that simplicity, naturalness and
　　　　beauty are bed-rock characteristics in American literature
　　　　and life," "has made war on injustice, on pretentiousness
　　　　and deceit," and "has charmed us and opened our minds and
　　　　our hearts, we owe him a debt that we shall not lightly
　　　　pay."

1928　"Howells, William Dean.　_Seen and Unseen at Stratford-on-Avon_."
　　　　Book Review Digest, 10 (1914), 268.　Brief description.

1929　"New Books Reviewed / _Familiar Spanish Travels_."　_North_
　　　　American Review, 199 (Mar 1914), 30-31.　Review.
　　　　Howells has the "fine power of blending subjective im-
　　　　pression with clearly visualized fact, yet of distin-
　　　　quishing the two in such a way that neither is the outward
　　　　truth vitiated nor the personal impression dimmed."

1914

1930   "W. D. Howells Is 77 / Author Celebrates Birthday at Boston--
        Many Congratulations." New York Times, 2 Mar 1914, p. 1.
        News item.
            Howells "predicts all that is good and golden for the
        future."

1931   "Topics of the Week." New York Times Review of Books, 8 Mar
        1914, p. 110. Editorial on the occasion of Howells'
        seventy-seventh birthday.
            Howells "has never had much respect for mere traditions,"
        has always been "a man of the present hour." His novels
        "constitute the best and most veracious study that exists
        of our social life in the last half of the nineteenth
        century."

1932   "Travel Books." Literary Digest, 48 (21 Mar 1914), 630. Brief
        review of Familiar Spanish Travels.
            Howells is "the best writer of pure English" in America,
        "the sweet philosopher, the complete optimist."

1933   KILMER, JOYCE. "Shakespeare and Bacon / Pleasant Discourse
        from Two Amiable Ghosts Frequenting Stratford-on-Avon /
        Reported by William Dean Howells." New York Times Review
        of Books, 10 May 1914, p. 225. Lead review of The Seen
        and Unseen at Stratford-on-Avon.
            "Mr. Howells is a most satisfactory medium": his ghosts
        are "explicit, loquacious"--"in the likeness of mankind."
        This is "a delightful fantasy, and Mark Twain himself
        could not have given it a droller realism."

1934   "Topics of the Week." New York Times Review of Books, 10 May
        1914, p. 228. Editorial comment on The Seen and Unseen at
        Stratford-on-Avon.
            "The humorous treatment of an essentially humorous theory
        commends itself for its appropriateness."

1935   BRAITHWAITE, WILLIAM STANLEY. "Books of the Day--Mr. Howells
        at Stratford / Shakspeare [sic] and Howells / A Meeting
        with Disembodied Spirits at Stratford-on-Avon." Boston
        Evening Transcript, 16 May 1914, III, p. 10. Review of
        The Seen and Unseen at Stratford-on-Avon.
            "If all the 'romantic fiction' of our generation, and
        the generation before it, was as superstructurally roman-
        tic and as fundamentally realistic, as this fantasy of Mr.
        Howells's converse with the disembodied spirits of Shak-
        speare and Bacon at Stratford, not even the critical
        powers of a hundred Howells could bring this particular
        kind of fictional method into contempt."

1936   "The Newest Books." <u>Independent</u>, 78 (25 May 1914), 324.
        Very brief notice of <u>The Seen and Unseen at Stratford-on-</u>
        <u>Avon</u>.
           "Amusing, human and sympathetic."

1937   PEARSON, EDMUND LESTER. "Books and Men / Mr. Howells's Shake-
        spearean Fantasy." <u>Nation</u>, 98 (28 May 1914), 630. Re-
        view of <u>The Seen and Unseen at Stratford-on-Avon</u>.
           Largely summary. "The book would have been an agreeable
        book even if no ghosts had come from the grave--but I am
        glad they did come."

1938   "Literature and Art / Mr. Howells' Latest Discovery." <u>Current</u>
        <u>Opinion</u>, 54 (Jun 1914), 490. Brief mention.
           Howells finds "the distinctive mark of genius" on the
        work of W. B. Trites.

1939   "With Shakespeare and Bacon at Stratford-on-Avon." <u>Dial</u>, 56
        (1 Jun 1914), 470. Review of <u>The Seen and Unseen at</u>
        <u>Stratford-on-Avon</u>.
           A "genial and witty fantasy" sparked by "lightness of
        touch and fertility of invention."

1940   "Arts Academy Chartered / Membership Never To Exceed 50 /
        William Dean Howells President." <u>New York Times</u>, 11 Jun
        1914, p. 10. News item datelined "Albany, June 10."

1941   "Some Books of the Week." <u>Spectator</u>, 112 (20 Jun 1914), 1041.
        Very brief notice of <u>The Seen and Unseen at Stratford-on-</u>
        <u>Avon</u>.
           Non-critical.

1942   MOORE, E. C. "<u>The Seen and Unseen at Stratford-on-Avon</u>."
        <u>Book News</u>, 32 (Jul 1914), 546. Review.
           It is "perfect in the fantastic gayety of its treatment
        of a light and charming story."

1943   "William Dean Howells as a Medium." <u>Current Opinion</u>, 57 (Jul
        1914), 51. Response to <u>The Seen and Unseen at Stratford-</u>
        <u>on-Avon</u>.
           Howells' "brilliant attack" on the "'Bacon-is-Shake-
        speare' heresy."

1944   "Topics of the Week." <u>New York Times Review of Books</u>, 30 Aug
        1914, p. 364. Brief note.
           Editorial summary of Howells' first autobiographical
        paper in the September <u>Harper's</u>, expressing the hope that
        many installments will follow.

1914

1945   "Other Books Worth While." Literary Digest, 49 (19 Sep 1914),
       519. Brief review of The Seen and Unseen at Stratford-on-
       Avon.
       "This delightful tale is told in a spirit of mischief
       and delicious humor." Its "only fault is its brevity."

1946   "The New Books / Mr. Howells in Stratford." Outlook, 108
       (30 Sep 1914), 281-282. Full review of The Seen and Un-
       seen at Stratford-on-Avon.
       "Mr. Howells took a great risk when he brought the
       ghosts of Shakespeare and Bacon to the banks of the Avon,
       but he did not overtax his skill; the shadowy figures
       bring no ghostly chill with them, and their talk is hap-
       pily compounded of wit and knowledge."

1947   "General Literature." A. L. A. Booklist, 11 (Oct 1914), 69.
       Very brief review of The Seen and Unseen at Stratford-on-
       Avon.
       "Pleasant but slight."

1948   "Academicians Hear Brieux on Theatre." New York Times, 20 Nov
       1914, p. 8. News item.
       Full-column coverage of the joint meeting of the Ameri-
       can Academy of Arts and Letters and the National Institute
       of Arts and Letters. Howells introduced the main speaker.

1949   [KILMER, JOYCE.] "'War Stops Literature,' Says W. D. Howells /
       Dean of American Authors Does Not Believe That Such Con-
       flicts as the Present Furnish the Novelist, Poet, or
       Dramatist with the Material for Masterpieces." New York
       Times, 29 Nov 1914, Mag. Sec., p. 8. Interview. Rpt.,
       Joyce Kilmer, Literature in the Making (New York: Harper,
       1917), pp. 3-15, and (Port Washington, N. Y.: Kennikat
       Press, 1968), pp. 3-15; "Five Interviews with William Dean
       Howells," ed. George Arms and William M. Gibson, Americana,
       37 (Apr 1943), 288-295; "Interviews with William Dean
       Howells," ed. Ulrich Halfmann, American Literary Realism,
       6 (Fall 1973), 392-396.
       In addition to a discussion of the failure of war to
       motivate great literature, Howells is led to comment on
       Russian fiction, contemporary poetry, current social
       problems, Ibsen. Large three-column portrait.

1950   GARNETT, EDWARD. "Some Remarks on American and English Fic-
       tion." Atlantic, 114 (Dec 1914), 747-756. Scattered
       respectful references to Howells.
       No younger writer has been equally able to "paint with
       such subtle flexibility of insight and such breadth of
       vision the portrait of his generation" (p. 748).

WILLIAM DEAN HOWELLS: A RESEARCH BIBLIOGRAPHY

1915

1951   KELLNER, LEON. <u>American Literature</u>, trans. Julia Franklin.
Garden City, N. Y.: Doubleday, Page, 1915. Pp. 178-184.
First ed., <u>Geschichte der Nordamerikanischen Literatur</u>
(Leipzig, 1914).

       This relatively early German appreciation of the full
scope of American literature groups James and Howells together as psychological writers. They deal with enigmas
of character. Their distinguishing characteristic is
"finesse." In this "self-conscious art," the artist too
often, "in his effort not to be dominated by matter, com-
mits the mistake of renouncing matter altogether" (p. 184).

1952   PATTEE, FRED LEWIS. <u>A History of American Literature Since</u>
<u>1870</u>. New York: Century, 1915. Pp. 197-217 and passim
as indexed.

       Howells' early taste favored "literary artists and
finishers" rather than "stormy creators" (pp. 199-200).
Not a genius, "he was a man of talent of the Pope-Macaulay
order," depending more on "exquisite skill" than on inspiration (p. 201). His realism is an eighteenth- rather
than nineteenth-century type that might be labeled "classi-
cism." It is Richardsonian—"realism of the <u>Pamela</u> order"
(pp. 212-213). Bibliography (pp. 218-219).

1953   SPRAGUE, De WITT CLINTON. "William Dean Howells." <u>Famous</u>
<u>Living Americans</u>, ed. Mary Griffin Webb and Edna Lenore
Webb. Greencastle, Ind.: Charles Webb, 1915. Pp. 260-
274. Biographical essay.

       "Mr. Howells's literary creed and active performance
have been to conform his truth to the outer reality, and
not to deform the picture of reality to match a questionable truth" (p. 260). This is the essential difference
between realism and romanticism (p. 271). When "this
broad-hearted, clear-seeing American portrayed in his
novels such of his countrymen as worked with their hands
and rendered possible the <u>cultua</u> of the elegant social
epicureans, the latter lamented Mr. Howells's departure
from his earlier high artistic standards" (p. 270). Full-
page portrait (p. 261).

1954   THAYER, WILLIAM ROSCOE. <u>John Hay</u>. 2 vols (Vols. 36-37 in the
American Statesmen Series). Boston and New York: Houghton
Mifflin, 1915. Passim as indexed.

       Multiple references trace the relationship of the two men.
Includes eleven letters Hay wrote to Howells. Heading
above Ch. 1 is <u>The Life and Letters of John Hay</u>.

1915

1955   "New Books." <u>Catholic World</u>, 100 (Jan 1915), 550-552. Review
        of <u>The Seen and Unseen at Stratford-on-Avon</u>.
            The "misty theology [reference is to 'Shakespeare's
        fancied account of the Great Beyond'] seems a trifle at
        variance with Shakespeare's very human and substantial
        view of life." A "smoothing down of--shall we call them--
        'certain originalities of diction,' might not be amiss."

1956   "Current History." <u>New York Times Review of Books</u>, 9 May 1915,
        p. 180. Editorial.
            Response to Howells on war in an article entitled "Why?"
        in current <u>North American Review</u>. Howells' idealism does
        not neutralize his sympathies.

1957   JAMES, HENRY. "Mr. and Mrs. James T. Fields." <u>Atlantic</u>, 116
        (Jul 1915), 21-31. Brief references.
            Howells ("my super-excellent friend and confrère") edi-
        torially cultivated in the <u>Atlantic</u> soil the seeds of the
        new American novel (p. 26) and apparently intervened in
        James's behalf (p. 28).

1958   NICHOLSON, MEREDITH. "The Open Season for American Novelists."
        <u>Atlantic</u>, 116 (Oct 1915), 456-466. Brief references.
            Continuing the debate set off by Edward Garnett's
        December 1914 article in the <u>Atlantic</u>, Nicholson commends
        Howells' "high-minded devotion" (p. 457) and <u>The Rise of
        Silas Lapham</u>, "our best novel of business" (p. 460).

1959   "National Institute Honors Howells / His Letter, Thanking It
        for Gold Metal, Says Fashion in Novels Has Changed /...."
        <u>New York Times</u>, 20 Nov 1915, p. 6. News item.
            Full-column coverage of the annual meeting of the insti-
        tute in Boston prints Howells' letter.

1960   "Mr. Howells and Dr. Eliot." <u>New York Times</u>, 21 Nov 1915,
        Sec. 2, p. 18. Editorial.
            In honoring Howells and Charles W. Eliot, the American
        Academy and its associate Institute have honored themselves.

1961   MABIE, HAMILTON W. "William Dean Howells / The Presentation
        Address by Hamilton W. Mabie at the Boston Meeting of the
        Academy and Institute of Arts and Letters." <u>Outlook</u>, 111
        (1 Dec 1915), 786-787. Rpt. <u>American Academy Proceedings</u>,
        2 (Nov 1916), 51-52.
            The Gold Metal is awarded to Howells. "Mr. Howells,
        divesting the novel of the dramatic aids of station, pas-
        sion, and adventure, has brought into view those elements

1915

(MABIE, HAMILTON W.)
of character and of circumstance which, in the newest as
in the oldest world, give life permanent interest." Full-
page portrait (p. 798).

1962 "Bars Ford Party from War Zone." New York Times, 2 Dec 1915,
pp. 1-2. News item.
Coverage of Henry Ford's peace crusade. Howells, in declining Ford's invitation to accompany him on a peace
voyage to Europe, wrote, "Very sorry I cannot go with you.
I wish you luck if the first conditions of peace are the
abolition of militarism, the restoration of the conquered
countries to their people, with full immunity from the
conquerors, and the establishment of liberty and democracy"
(p. 2, col. 3).

1963 "The Dean of American Letters." Independent, 84 (6 Dec 1915),
p. [383]. Full-page portrait.
The sub-caption reads, "In recognition of his work as a
novelist the National Institute of Arts and Letters has
awarded to William Dean Howells the gold medal, which is
its highest tribute to attainment in any of the arts."

1964 "Current Poetry." Literary Digest, 51 (11 Dec 1915), 1381.
Brief note.
"The Lonely Land," a poem by Madison Cawein, "illustrates
the accuracy of Mr. Howells's criticism," which is briefly
quoted.

1916

1965 PAINTER, F[RANKLIN] V. N. Introduction to American Literature / Including Illustrative Selections with Notes.
Boston: Sibley, 1916. Pp. 315, 351-354. Introductory
sketch.
Routine. Howells "attempts to describe life as it is";
to his credit "he avoids portraying the criminal and the
obscene" (p. 354).

1966 SHACKLETON, ROBERT. The Story of Harper's Magazine, 1850-1917.
New York and London: Harper, 1916. Brief comment.
Roll-call of types of literature and writers published
in Harper's. The concluding chapter (pp. 54-60) outlines
Howells' association with the magazine.

1967 "Howells, William Dean. Years of My Youth." Book Review
Digest, 12 (1916), 279. Brief description.

1916

1968   "Vers Libre and Fiction by Mr. Howells / A Series of Clever
        Stories and Essays in Poetry in His Forthcoming Volume
        The Daughter of the Storage." New York Times Review of
        Books, 2 Apr 1916, p. 117. Full-page lead review.
            "The eagerness and freshness of [Howells'] mind, accen-
        tuated rather than dimmed with the passing of years," has
        led him to use forms so new they are difficult to evaluate.
        His characters are always "thoroughly realized, individual
        and convincing." He resists the didactic, displaying his
        subjects dramatically from all sides, admitting no con-
        clusion, "simply posing the facts with a delicate sort of
        justice, leaving the reader to decide for himself, to
        think for himself." Portrait.

1969   "Casual Comment." Dial, 60 (13 Apr 1916), 369. Brief mention.
            Initial response to serialization of The Leatherwood
        God--"unsparing realism."

1970   MOORE, REBECCA D. "Fiction for the Hard-to-Please." Pub-
        lisher's Weekly, 89 (15 Apr 1916), 1315. Review of The
        Daughter of the Storage.
            "The atmosphere of nearness and friendliness."

1971   "Mark Twain, Mr. Howells." New York Times Review of Books,
        30 Apr 1916, p. 184. Lead editorial responding to the
        first installments of The Mysterious Stranger and The
        Leatherwood God.
            Twain and Howells are "revered masters of the story
        art" sometimes mistakenly assigned to an "older school of
        fiction." The two stories now being serialized are marked
        by their "essential contemporaneousness" in that they
        focus on "humanity's religious strivings," which is a
        subject currently attractive.

1972   "New Tributes to the Irrepressible Youth and Vitality of
        William Dean Howells." Current Opinion, 60 (May 1916),
        352. Note.
            Cites William Cooper Howells as source for The Leather-
        wood God. Portrait.

1973   "Reviews of New Books / Novels by...Howells...and Others."
        Literary Digest, 52 (20 May 1916), 1467. Brief review
        of The Daughter of the Storage.
            "Mr. Howells always portrays real life, even ordinary
        life, and he is convincing because of his adherence to
        truth."

1974   [Untitled.] New York Times Review of Books, 28 May 1916,
        p. 224. Editorial.
            Howells' deviation from his pattern in The Leatherwood
        God--"this does not imply, of course, that psychology, or
        even mysticism, is not involved in the realistic study of
        our modern life"--has excited much curiosity. Howells
        has just published an explanation, quoted here, of the
        basis for his study.

1975   [BOYNTON, H. W.] "Current Fiction / The Daughter of the
        Storage." Nation, 102 (8 Jun 1916), 622. Brief review.
            "Nothing could better illustrate a change in fashion
        which has taken place during the past quarter-century than
        comparison of this collection with any group of tales by
        any popular story-teller of this generation."

1976   "New Novels / The Daughter of the Storage." Times Literary
        Supplement, 15 Jun 1916, p. 286. Review.
            Although both the stories and the verse have commendable
        qualities, in general "Mr. Howells conceived them in far
        too tolerant a mood."

1977   "Fiction." A. L. A. Booklist, 12 (Jul 1916), 482. Very brief
        review of The Daughter of the Storage.
            "All readable and human, told with the characteristic
        quiet, assured, sympathetic manner of the author."

1978   "Fiction." Wisconsin Library Bulletin, 12 (Jul 1916), 322.
        Very brief mention of The Daughter of the Storage.
        The stories show no lessening of power.

1979   B[RAITHWAITE], W[ILLIAM] S[TANLEY]. "A Howells Miscellany /
        The Daughter of the Storage and Other Things." Boston
        Evening Transcript, 1 Jul 1916, III, p. 6. Review.
            The varied pieces have Howells' "unmistakable touch of
        expression and his rich observation of life. The essence
        of humor which ever played gently but firmly through all
        Mr. Howells' writings glows in the serious fabric of his
        characterization and purpose."

1980   "Fiction." Spectator, 117 (1 Jul 1916), 20-21. Review of
        The Daughter of the Storage.
            "While Mr. Howells is in the main concerned with the
        portraiture of highly educated and fastidious people, he
        generally manages to show the core of simplicity and sound
        humanity which remains under somewhat sophisticated ex-
        teriors." His style has "the peculiar flavor of good
        talk."

1916

1981   "All Sorts of Stories." <u>Independent</u>, 87 (3 Jul 1916), 32.
     Very brief notice of <u>The Daughter of the Storage</u>.
     The initial story has been enjoyed for fifty years.

1982   "Changing Humor." <u>New York Times Review of Books</u>, 20 Aug 1916,
     p. 324. Editorial.
       Support of Howells' analysis of changes in American
     humor (September installment of "Editor's Easy Chair").

1983   "A Howells Miscellany." <u>Springfield Sunday Republican</u>, 17 Sep
     1916, p. 15. Review of <u>The Daughter of the Storage</u>.
       Here "Mr. Howells is the portrayer, as often before, of
     psychological indecision." The verse included in the
     volume is not "overwhelmingly brilliant."

1984   "Five Hundred Leading Autumn Books." <u>New York Times Review
     of Books</u>, p. 412. Brief notice of <u>The Leatherwood God</u>.
       Nancy and Squire Braile are memorable characters.
     Portrait sketch (p. 397).

1985   COOPER, FREDERIC TABER. "The Story of a False Prophet."
     <u>Publisher's Weekly</u>, 90 (21 Oct 1916), 1403. Review of
     <u>The Leatherwood God</u>.
       One finds again "that infinite patience in detail which
     has always been a marked characteristic of Mr. Howells's
     delicate artistry."

1986   "A Posthumous Novel by Mark Twain /.../ <u>The Leatherwood God</u>,
     by William Dean Howells /...." <u>New York Times Review of
     Books</u>, 29 Oct 1916, pp. [453], 460. Front-page review.
       Notes the challenge of Howells' subject because of its
     "inherent difficulties"--"the dangers of offense."
     Portrait.

1987   E[DGETT], E[DWIN] F[RANCIS]. "Mr. Howells's Vigorous Romanti-
     cism / The Great Apostle of Realism Writes a Romantic
     Story of Events in His Native Ohio." <u>Boston Evening Tran-
     script</u>, 1 Nov 1916, II, p. 8. Full review of <u>The Leather-
     wood God</u>.
       This romance by Howells "sets all his pet theories to
     naught, and it proves how impossible it is for any man,
     no matter how strong he may be in the faith, to practice
     always what he preaches." Portrait.

1988 "New Novels / The Leatherwood God." Times Literary Supplement,
        16 Nov 1916, p. 548. Full review.
           "It is only when one puts it down that one realizes,
        with that glow of pleasure proper to such an experience,
        the perfect wholeness, the rightness, the art of the tale."

1989 PEATTIE, ELIA W. "Mr. Howells' Story of a Religious Imposter."
        Chicago Daily Tribune, 18 Nov 1916, p. 7. Review of The
        Leatherwood God.
           "Regard for sacred traditions and the convictions of
        others" kept Howells from pointing "the disillusioning
        moral of all religious supermen from Christ to Dowie."

1990 "Reviews of New Books / A Novel by W. D. Howells." Spring-
        field Daily Republican, 20 Nov 1916, p. 6. Review of The
        Leatherwood God.
           "An unusual volume, purely American in spirit and im-
        pulse." Howells' "deeper purpose" is "to show that a
        sophisticated environment does not destroy human credulity."

1991 BOYNTON, H. W. "Some Outstanding Novels of the Year." Nation,
        103 (30 Nov 1916), 507-508. Very brief comment on The
        Leatherwood God.
           "The episode itself is of universal interest; there are
        Dylkses in all places and ages; but the setting, the atmos-
        phere, and in a sense the meaning of the picture are Ameri-
        can, are of ourselves."

1992 "Fiction." Wisconsin Library Bulletin, 12 (Dec 1916), 453.
        Very brief mention of The Leatherwood God.
           A "curious, absorbing story."

1993 "Literature and Art / A New Novel from the Dean of American
        Letters." Current Opinion, 61 (Dec 1916), 411. Mention
        of The Leatherwood God.
           "A skilful study of the psychology of those self-styled
        prophets" who impose themselves upon others.

1994 "Literature / Fiction." Athenaeum, No. 4612 (Dec 1916), 596.
        Brief notice of The Leatherwood God.
           "Thin, but no doubt Mr. Howells expects his readers to
        appreciate the breadth of real reverence for the God ideal
        which lies behind the old magistrate's rather cynical
        philosophy."

1916

1995   "New Books." Catholic World, 104 (Dec 1916), 397. Brief
       mention of The Leatherwood God.
           The theme is unworthy of Howells' pen, "although it
       illustrates well the power men like [John] Alexander
       Dowie, or women like Mrs. Baker Eddy, possessed to delude
       the ignorant multitudes."

1996   "The New Books / Novels and Short Stories." Review of Reviews,
       54 (Dec 1916), 678. Brief review of The Leatherwood God.
           A real situation and real people are clothed by Howells
       "with the vivid texture of his fine literary art and sym-
       pathetic understanding."

1997   "New Books Reviewed." North American Review, 204 (Dec 1916),
       938-939. Full review of The Leatherwood God.
           "The irony of the story is masterly; it somehow exalts
       rather than belittles human nature, while it shows how
       near the heart the greatest folly really lies."

1998   "American Ideals in Two Men of Letters / Autobiographical
       Volumes by the Late Richard Watson Gilder and W. D.
       Howells Rich in Experiences Illustrating the Country's
       Growth in Life and Thought." New York Times Review of
       Books, 3 Dec 1916, pp. 529, 539. Lead review of Years of
       My Youth.
           Parallels between the two men, as the embodiment of
       American self-development, are traced. Portrait, "Mr.
       Howells Thirty Years Ago."

1999   "Review of New Books / The Evolution of a Writer." Spring-
       field Daily Republican, 4 Dec 1916, p. 6. Review of
       Years of My Youth.
           Basically a summary of biographical facts contained in
       the volume. Howells reveals himself "psychologically as
       he would analyze his characters in a novel." Reviewer
       notes Howells' tendency to end sentences with prepositions
       but concludes that he "would rather have Mr. Howells use
       two prepositions at the end of a sentence than not to end
       it at all!"

2000   E[DGETT], E[DWIN] F[RANCIS]. "The Years of Mr. Howells's
       Youth / The Famous Novelist Tells the Story of His Early
       Days Amid the Romantic Scenes of the Middle West." Boston
       Evening Transcript, 6 Dec 1916, III, p. 5. Review of
       Years of My Youth.
           "A fascinating mingling of coherence and discursiveness."
       "There is nothing ephemeral in it.... Whether we agree or
       not with his literary theories, we cannot fail to commend
       his practice of them."

2001   "The Boyhood of Mr. Howells." Times Literary Supplement,
        7 Dec 1916, p. 585. Review of Years of My Youth.
        Howells "belongs to a world of Middle America from which
        everything but language more and more deeply divides us."

2002   "Reviews of New Books." Literary Digest, 53 (9 Dec 1916),
        1550. Brief review of Years of My Youth.
        Howells for the first time has taken center stage.

2003   QUINN, ARTHUR H. "The Thirst for Salvation." Dial, 61 (14 Dec
        1916), 534-535. Full review of The Leatherwood God.
        "The story deals with primitive emotions in a primitive
        state of society." It is not in the style of Howells'
        "great period." It lacks a "deeply significant character."
        But unity of plot, coherence of motive, and pictorial
        character drawing "make a real contribution to our novels
        of American life."

2004   "The New Books / The Quack Prophet." Independent, 88 (25 Dec
        1916), 550. Brief review of The Leatherwood God.
        A master study "of human credulity in general."

2005   "Mr. Howells's Reminiscences." Spectator, 117 (30 Dec 1916),
        834-835. Review of Years of My Youth.
        "A revelation of self that is never tedious or complacent."

1917

2006   CLARK, JOHN SPENCER. The Life and Letters of John Fiske.
        2 vols. Boston and New York: Houghton Mifflin, 1917.
        I, pp. 378, 406; II, pp. 208-209. Brief references.
        Fiske dedicated his first book to Howells (I, p. 406).
        He recommended The Undiscovered Country to his wife as
        "magnificent"--"by far the best thing Howells has yet
        done."

2007   DALY, JOSEPH FRANCIS. The Life of Augustin Daly. New York:
        Macmillan, 1917. Pp. 147-148, 231-233, 367, 566.
        In a letter (29 Oct 1874) Mark Twain urges Daly to ask
        Howells for a play since "I think he is writing" one. On
        14 November Howells responds to Daly and discusses the
        nature of what he has in mind (pp. 147-148). On 24 April
        1876 Howells sent Daly "The Parlor Car" accompanied by a
        modest letter, and on 9 May 1876 he reacts, with sustained
        modesty, to Daly's favorable response (pp. 231-233).
        Howells was reluctant to "naturalize" a German comedy,

1917

(DALY, JOSEPH FRANCIS)
suggesting Italian or Spanish ones--or Björnson's "Bank-
ruptcy"--instead (p. 367). On 11 January 1893 Howells
proposed "The Mouse Trap" to Daly (p. 566).

2008   DAVIS, RICHARD HARDING. Adventure and Letters of Richard
Harding Davis, ed. Charles Belmont Davis. New York:
Scribner's, 1917. Pp. 60-61, 63, 132, 199. Brief
references.
Minor reminiscences of meetings with Howells, stressing
his pleasantness.

*   GARLAND, HAMLIN. A Son of the Middle Border. New York: Macmillan, 1917. Pp. 383-390. Rpt. with revisions from
Bookman (New York), 45 (Mar 1917), 1-7. See item 2030.

2009   HARVEY, ALEXANDER. "William Dean Howells." A Hazard of New
Fortunes, by William Dean Howells. Modern Library ed.
New York: Boni and Liveright, [1917]. Pp. ix-xiv.
Introduction.
Three facts about the work of Howells challenge attention: "In the first place he is a literary artist--per-
haps one of the very greatest of literary artists. In
the next place he is the champion of realism against romanticism. Finally he had no college education. He is a
self-taught man." His "quiet" humor "is steeped in fla-
vors that are Gallic"; it has "a quality almost Celtic in
its gusto."

2010   _____. William Dean Howells / A Study of the Achievement of
a Literary Artist. New York: B. W. Huebsch, 1917.
This enthusiastic, but basically unscholarly, appreciation of Howells' genius is not without censure. "His
realism is without reality" because he hever really penetrates the surface to view the ultimate. His art is
"great art, but it is art and nothing more. It is not
truth in the large, but an accumulation of little truths
exquisitely arranged." In the extensive and highly un-
conventional index, pithy summary comments, more entertaining than instructive, accompany the subject entry.

2011   JAMES, HENRY. The Middle Years. New York: Scribner's, and
London: W. Collins, 1917. Not indexed.
A single reference to breakfast with Howells, "insidious
disturber and fertiliser of that state [innocence] in me"
(p. 34).

2012 JOHNSON, CLIFTON. "Preface by the Illustrator." Years of
My Youth by William Dean Howells. New York: Harper, 1917.
The illustrator, who traced the movement of Howells
through Ohio seeking the molding influence of the environment, did not find it. He found great change and only
curious awareness of the genius nurtured there. Sixteen
Ohio scenes photographed by Johnson illustrate this
edition.

* KILMER, JOYCE. "War Stops Literature." Literature in the
Making / By Some of Its Makers. New York and London:
Harper, 1917. Pp. 3-15. Interview. Rpt. from New York
Times, 29 Nov 1914, V, p. 8. See item 1949.

2013 PAINE, ALBERT BIGELOW, ed. Mark Twain's Letters / Arranged
with Comment. 2 vols. New York: Harper, 1917. Passim
as indexed.
The many letters exchanged by Howells and James are
illuminated by Paine's comments.

2014 SULLIVAN, THOMAS RUSSELL. Passages from the Journal of Thomas
Russell Sullivan 1891-1903. Boston and New York: Houghton
Mifflin, 1917. Pp. 12, 21, 99, 111.
Brief references to Howells' support of a realistic play
"Margaret Fleming" (p. 12), to Howells as pallbearer at
Lowell's funeral (p. 21), as breakfast companion (p. 99),
and a source for The Minister's Charge (p. 111).

* TWAIN, MARK. "William Dean Howells." What Is Man? / And
Other Essays. New York: Harper, 1917. Pp. 228-239.
Rpt. from Harper's, 113 (Jul 1906), 221-225. See item
1691.

* WYATT, EDITH FRANKLIN. "A National Contribution." Great
Companions. New York: Appleton, 1917. Pp. 113-142.
Rpt. from North American Review, 196 (Sep 1912), 339-352.
See item 1886.

2015 "Howells, William Dean. Buying a Horse." Book Review Digest,
12 (1917), 218. Brief description of reprint of an early
sketch.

2016 "Howells, William Dean. Daughter of the Storage, and Other
Things in Prose and Verse." Book Review Digest, 12 (1917),
278. Very brief notice.

1917

2017   "Howells, William Dean. Leatherwood God." Book Review
            Digest, 12 (1917), 279. Very brief notice.

2018   BOYNTON, H. W. "Some Stories of the Month." Bookman (New
            York), 44 (Jan 1917), 504. Review of The Leatherwood God.
            "Mr. Howells has always stood aggressively for realism,
        but has practised romance more than he has preached it."

2019   "Fiction." A. L. A. Booklist, 13 (Jan 1917), 176. Review of
            The Leatherwood God.
            "Notable for its literary style as well as for its de-
        lineation of the life of the pioneer settlers."

2020   "General Literature." A. L. A. Booklist, 13 (Jan 1917), 173.
            Very brief review of Years of My Youth.
            Howells' intimate reminiscences of early life are "inter-
        esting in themselves and as being typical pictures of the
        time in Ohio."

2021   MENCKEN, H. L. "Suffering Among Books." Smart Set, 51 (Jan
            1917), 266-272. Full review of The Leatherwood God
            (pp. 266-268). Incorporated in part, "The Dean," Preju-
            dices / First Series (New York: Knopf, 1919), pp. 52-58;
            rpt. in part, A Mencken Crestomathy (New York: Knopf,
            1949), p. 490.
            For twenty years the work of Howells ("on the whole, a
        superficial novelist") has been "hymned and fawned over."
        "Intrinsically," The Leatherwood God "is little more than
        a stale anecdote, and the dressing that Dr. Howells gives
        it does not lift it very far above this anecdotal quality."

2022   "The New Books / American Biography and Autobiography."
            Review of Reviews, 55 (Jan 1917), 99. Review of Years of
            My Youth.
            To his contemporaries the title seems appropriate to
        every period in Howells' career, even the present.
        Portrait.

2023   "Reviews of New Books." Literary Digest, 54 (13 Jan 1917),
            82. Review of The Leatherwood God.
            "The story is episodic and religiously psychological,"
        but its special value lies in the characters.

2024   "The New Books / Two Men of Letters." Independent, 89 (22 Jan
            1917), 153. Review of Years of My Youth (and Richard Wat-
            son Gilder's Letters).
            Howells' "unpretentious record" is "a valuable addition
        to our social history."

2025   "Reviews of New Books / Mr. Howells' Recollections of His
       Youth." <u>Literary Digest</u>, 54 (27 Jan 1917), 199, 202.
       Review of <u>Years of My Youth</u>.
       "Never was literary man more thoroughly to the manner
      born."

2026   "Notes." <u>Nation</u>, 104 (22 Feb 1917), 217-218. Brief response
       to <u>Years of My Youth</u>.
       "The narrative is throughout charming, adroit, gently
      whimsical, abounding in fine feeling and human wisdom."

2027   MULLET, MARY B. "His Friends Greet William Dean Howells at
       Eighty / Still Young in Everything but Years, Say Writers
       Who Delight To Tell of His Achievements in Literature and
       His Ready Helpfulness to Beginners." <u>New York Sun</u>, 25 Feb
       1917, p. 10. Full-page illustrated presentation.
       Basic credit is given to Mary Mullet, but contributions
      by Booth Tarkington, Douglas Z. Doty (editor of <u>Century</u>),
      Hamlin Garland, Charles Hanson Towne, and Thomas Sargent
      Perry are included. All are tributes in a reminiscent
      vein.

2028   "Chronicle and Comment / Mr. Howells's Anniversary." <u>Bookman</u>
       (New York), 45 (Mar 1917), 17-19. Note.
       Brief recognition of Howells' eightieth birthday judges
      him to be "the most faithful interpreter of American life
      of the last generation." Photograph of Howells in his
      garden at Kittery Point, Maine (p. 19).

2029   FOLLETT, HELEN THOMAS, and WILSON FOLLETT. "Contemporary
       Novelists: William Dean Howells." <u>Atlantic</u>, 119 (Mar
       1917), 362-372. Essay. Rpt. with revisions, Helen and
       Wilson Follett, <u>Some Modern Novelists</u> (New York: Holt,
       1918), pp. 99-123; rpt. in part, <u>The War of the Critics</u>
       <u>over William Dean Howells</u>, ed. Edwin H. Cady and David L.
       Frazier (Evanston: Row, Peterson, 1962), pp. 118-127.
       This attempt to place Howells in perspective on the
      occasion of his eightieth birthday begins, "William Dean
      Howells is quite the most American thing we have produced."
      James and Howells, both listed as "Novelists of Yesterday,"
      are contrasted as "Cosmopolitan and Provincial." The
      authors discuss the penalties Howells elected to pay in
      order to achieve his permanent importance.

2030   GARLAND, HAMLIN. "Meetings with Howells." <u>Bookman</u> (New York),
       45 (Mar 1917), 1-7. Reminiscent essay. Rpt. with re-
       visions, <u>A Son of the Middle Border</u> (New York: Macmillan,
       1917), pp. 383-390; <u>Roadside Meetings</u> (New York:

1917

(GARLAND, HAMLIN)
Macmillan, 1930), pp. 55-65; and <u>Bookman</u> (New York), 70 (Nov 1929), 246-257.
From "antagonism to conversion," Garland traces his response to Howells and narrates their eventual meeting which Garland labels "the most important literary event of my life."

2031 _____. "William Dean Howells, Master Craftsman." <u>Art World</u> 1 (Mar 1917), 411-412. Tribute to Howells on his eightieth birthday.
He remains, as he has been for half a century, "the most beneficent force in American literature." Excellent portrait (facing p. 411).

2032 "Mr. Howells at Eighty." <u>New York Times</u>, 1 Mar 1917, p. 12. Editorial.
Emphasis is on the variety and extent of Howells' work and on his continuing "youthful spirit." "His novels are a portrait gallery of American character."

2033 BUTCHER, FANNY. "Tabloid Book Review." <u>Chicago Sunday Tribune</u>, 4 Mar 1917, II, p. 5. Brief comment.
Lead paragraph devoted to reminiscence about an interview with Howells. His gentleness and sophistication are emphasized.

2034 [Untitled.] <u>New York Times Review of Books</u>, 4 Mar 1917, p. 76. Editorial.
An expression of gratitude to Howells for his contribution to "our intellectual progress." Special mention is made of his introduction of Russian literature to American readers.

2035 "Howells, Octogenarian." <u>Outlook</u>, 115 (14 Mar 1917), 454. Note.
Felicitations to Howells on his eightieth birthday. "In all his books he touched real life closely and truly, but his much-discussed realism was never of the crass and heavy type to which humor and grace are strangers."

2036 "Honor W. D. Howells / Wilson and Roosevelt Send Letters of Birthday Praise." <u>New York Times</u>, 22 Mar 1917, p. 9. News item.
On the occasion of Howells' eightieth birthday.

2037   "Birthday Tributes to Wm. D. Howells / 125 Eminent Americans
Send Letters of Appreciation of His Character and Writing /
Some Were in Verse / Cass Gilbert Says the Writer Had Done
More To Cultivate Good Taste in Architecture Than Archi-
tects." New York Times, 25 Mar 1917, I, p. 9. News cover-
age.
    In addition to Gilbert, other quoted tributes are from
Woodrow Wilson, Brander Matthews, Walter Prichard Eaton,
Percy Mackaye, James Lane Allen, Theodore Roosevelt,
Charles W. Eliot, William Gillette, and Henry Cabot Lodge.

2038   "Celebrating the Eightieth Birthday of William Dean Howells."
Current Opinion, 62 (Apr 1917), 278. Note.
    The many tributes to Howells show "greater familiarity
with his towering reputation than with his novels themselves."

2039   HACKETT, FRANCIS. "William Dean Howells." New Republic, 10
(21 Apr 1917), Spring Literary Review Sup., 3-5. Negative
review of Alexander Harvey's William Dean Howells / A Study
of the Achievement of a Literary Artist. Rpt. Horizons /
A Book of Criticism (New York: B. W. Huebsch, 1918),
pp. 21-30.
    Howells "is the one American figure on whom literary
criticism has failed to focus as it should, and from
whose large intentions and richly freighted performances
too few national writers have renewed themselves."

2040   ALDEN, HENRY MILLS. "Editor's Study." Harper's, 134 (May
1917), 903-904. Appreciation.
    Howells is the very Howells of his work. "All his
readers feel inclined to indite a love letter to him instead of sending him perfunctory congratulations." [So
too does Mr. Alden.]

2041   "Howells, at Eighty, Receives Notable Tributes as the Dean
of American Letters." Current Opinion, 62 (May 1917),
357. Note.
    Some of the fifteen hundred tributes from distinguished
men and women are singled out and quoted. Portrait.

2042   "Some Mark Twain Letters / to William Dean Howells and Others /
Arranged, with Comment, by Albert Bigelow Paine." Harper's,
134 (May 1917), 781-794.
    Paine finds in the letters "a kind of tender playfulness
that answered something in Howells's makeup, his kindly
humor, his wide knowledge of a humanity which he pictured
so faithfully and amusingly to the world" (p. 781).
Portrait (p. 787).

1917

2043   LAWRENCE, C. E. "William Dean Howells." <u>Bookman</u> (London),
        52 (Jun 1917), 88-91. Appreciation. Rpt. <u>Living Age</u>,
        294 (21 Jul 1917), 173-177.
           "Considering all things, the measure and standard of
        Mr. Howells' literary achievements are of sterling quali-
        ty and high ideal." The major novels are surveyed to
        demonstrate characteristics. Three portraits and an illus-
        tration from <u>The Day of Their Wedding</u>.

*   ____. "William Dean Howells." <u>Living Age</u>, 294 (21 Jul 1917),
        173-177. Rpt. from <u>Bookman</u> (London), 52 (Jun 1917), 88-91.
        <u>See</u> item 2043.

2044   "August Fiction." <u>New York Times Review of Books</u>, 22 Jul 1917,
        p. 272. Editorial.
           Response to Howells on fiction in the August <u>Harper's</u>,
        taking only slight exception to his views.

2045   "Topics of the Times / A Realist Judges a Realist." <u>New York
        Times</u>, 24 Aug 1917, p. 6. Editorial.
           Draws attention to Howells' forthcoming review of Gar-
        land's <u>A Son of the Middle West</u> [sic] in the 26 August
        <u>New York Times Review of Books</u>. "A critic more competent
        to review this particular book could not possibly have
        been found."

2046   "A Lesson Needed by Critics." <u>New York Times</u>, 29 Aug 1917,
        p. 8. Editorial.
           Commends a principle of criticism exhibited by Howells
        in his review of Garland: to praise has as much critical
        validity as to condemn.

2047   "Collapse of the Howells Realism in the Light of Freudian Ro-
        manticism." <u>Current Opinion</u>, 63 (Oct 1917), 270-271.
        Review of Alexander Harvey's <u>William Dean Howells / A
        Study of the Achievement of a Literary Artist</u>.
           Non-critical. Extensive quotation.

2048   FOLLETT, HELEN THOMAS. "Mr. Howells and the Anglophobe."
        <u>Dial</u>, 63 (11 Oct 1917), 331-333. Review of Alexander
        Harvey's <u>William Dean Howells / A Study of the Achieve-
        ment of a Literary Artist</u>.
           Not a book--rather a tirade, a miscellany, a preface to
        an index.

2049   "War as Seen by Famous Authors." New York Times, 2 Dec 1917,
        II, p. 8. Feature article.
            A collection of "autographed opinions on the war by
        famous American and English authors" includes a single
        statement by Howells: "'May the war for liberty win
        equality and fraternity, too.'"

2050   "Notable Books in Brief Review / William Dean Howells." New
        York Times Review of Books, 16 Dec 1917, pp. 561-562. Re-
        view of Years of My Youth and Alexander Harvey's William
        Dean Howells.
            The majority of the space is devoted to highly negative
        comment on Harvey's treatment of Howells. A single para-
        graph is given to the new, illustrated edition of Years
        of My Youth, "one of the most delightful autobiographies
        ever written."

1918

2051   BROOKS, VAN WYCK. Letters and Leadership. New York: B. W.
        Huebsch, 1918. Pp. 39-43. Brief comment.
            The Civil War has not really enlarged Americans ideo-
        logically. Howells has given us "the comédie humaine of
        our post-bellum society" and in emphasizing the "smiling
        aspects" has declared artistic bankruptcy (pp. 38-40).
        His work is restricted by a narrow perspective. He is
        less than a great novelist because his experience is no
        wider or deeper than that of the characters he creates
        (p. 43).

*   FOLLETT, HELEN THOMAS, and WILSON FOLLETT. Some Modern
        Novelists / Appreciations and Estimates. New York: Holt,
        1918. Pp. 99-123. Rpt. with revisions from Atlantic,
        119 (Mar 1917), 362-372. See item 2029.

*   HACKETT, FRANCIS. "William Dean Howells." Horizons / A Book
        of Criticism. New York: B. W. Huebsch, 1918). Pp. 21-30.
        Rpt. from New Republic, 10 (21 Apr 1917), Sup., 3-5. See
        item 2039.

2051A   SCHWARTZ, HENRY B. "The Americanism of William Dean Howells."
        Methodist Review, 101 (Mar 1918), 226-232. Essay.
            Howells is a "truly American novelist," who is under-
        estimated by critics who fail to see the complexities
        which lie beneath the commonplace surface of his novels.

1918

2052   "Howells Sticks To Buying / Tells Liberty Loan Boosters He Is
        Too Old for Press Agent Job." New York Times, 19 Apr 1918,
        p. 11. News item.
            Release of Howells' letter in which he declines to write
        Liberty Loan publicity for the Treasury Department.

2053   "Briefer Mention." Dial, 64 (9 May 1918), 460. Brief refer-
        ence.
            Recall of Howells' "faithful picture" of the Ohio River
        country in Years of My Youth, now in an illustrated edition.

                              1919

2054   BOYNTON, PERCY H. A History of American Literature. Boston:
        Ginn, 1919. Pp. 412–422 and passim as indexed.
            Biographical notes and general assessment. "The pre-
        ëminent figure in the field of American fiction during
        the last half century has been William Dean Howells"
        (p. 412).

2055   BRONSON, WALTER C. A Short History of American Literature.
        Rev. and enl. Boston: Heath, 1919. Pp. 304–307, 308,
        456. First ed., 1900. See item 1411.
            This edition adds a comparison of Howells and James.
        "While pursuing truth Mr. Howells has not wholly escaped
        the danger of the commonplace in subject and point of
        view; he nowhere has the distinction of Henry James; and
        it may be doubted whether much of his fiction will long
        survive the test of changing interests and tastes."

2056   CAIRNS, WILLIAM B. "Introduction." Annie Kilburn by William
        Dean Howells. Harper's Modern Classics. New York:
        Harper, 1919. Pp. iii–xvi.
            Howells' novels "are portrayals of life as it appears
        to a keen, kindly, and idealistic observer, widely read
        and widely experienced, interested in the myriad problems
        that life raises, but having no propaganda to advance and
        no pet theories to maintain." Annie Kilburn is "a story
        with commonplace characters, commonplace incidents, slight
        plot, and no set moral purpose"; but by "selection and
        portrayal" Howells shows how meaningful seemingly trivial
        things are.

2057   DICKEY, MARCUS. The Youth of James Whitcomb Riley / Fortune's
        Way with the Poet from Infancy to Manhood. Indianapolis:
        Bobbs-Merrill, 1919. Pp. 3, 375.
            Incidental mention only.

2058   ELLSWORTH, WILLIAM W. A Golden Age of Authors / A Publisher's
       Recollection. London: Grant Richards, 1919. Passim as
       indexed.
       A half dozen minor references.

2059   HOWE, M[ARK] A[NTHONY] DeWOLFE. The Atlantic Monthly and Its
       Makers. Boston: Atlantic Monthly Press, 1919. Passim
       as indexed.
       Extensive reference to Howells and his association with
       the Atlantic. No other editor gave as many years to the
       Atlantic. Ink-sketch portrait (p. [60]).

2060   MENCKEN, H. L. "The Dean." Prejudices / First Series. New
       York: Knopf, 1919. Pp. 52-58. Rpt. Howells / A Century
       of Criticism, ed. Kenneth E. Eble (Dallas: Southern
       Methodist University, 1962), pp. 94-98, and The War of
       the Critics over William Dean Howells, ed. Edwin H. Cady
       and David L. Frazier (Evanston: Row, Peterson, 1962),
       pp. 127-130.
       Incorporates essence of Mencken's review of The Leather-
       wood God, Smart Set, 51 (Jan 1917), 266-268. See item
       2021. Elaborates a negative view of Howells.

2061   TUCKER, WILLIAM JEWETT. My Generation / An Autobiographical
       Interpretation. Boston and New York: Houghton Mifflin,
       1919. P. 396. Incident reference.
       Howells as guest at York Harbor.

2062   "An Author's Author." New York Times Review of Books, 13 Apr
       1919, p. 192. Editorial.
       Response to Howells' introduction to the new Modern
       Library Edition of Daisy Miller. Although one may lack
       Howells' "enthusiastic appreciation" of James's work, his
       critical estimate has "the rare virtue of reasonableness
       to recommend it."

2063   ALDEN, HENRY MILLS. "William Dean Howells." Bookman (New
       York), 49 (Jul 1919), 549-554. Critical biography. Rpt.
       in part, "William Dean Howells," Review of Reviews, 61
       (Jun 1920), 644.
       "The intimacy between life and literature seems to reach
       its fullest possibilities in the writings of William Dean
       Howells" (p. 549).

1919

2064   REID, FORREST. "William Dean Howells / I." Irish Statesman,
        1 (27 Sep 1919), 333-334; "William Dean Howells / II"
        (4 Oct 1919), 359-360. Critical survey in two parts of
        Howells' novels.
            Howells' realism lacks imagination and is "largely a
        matter of photographic accuracy." The Rise of Silas Lap-
        ham is his most representative work.

2065   "Howells in Forty Lessons." New York Times Review of Books,
        7 Dec 1919, p. 712. Editorial.
            Satiric comment on the teaching of writing, especially
        by such correspondence schools as the one which offered
        its services to Howells.

                            1920

2066   ALDRICH, MRS. THOMAS BAILEY [LILIAN (WOODMAN)]. Crowding
        Memories. Boston and New York: Houghton Mifflin, 1920.
        Passim as indexed.
            Largely anecdotal reminiscences--Howells' difficulty in
        arranging for his marriage, Bret Harte's visit to Boston
        with Howells as host, association with Mark Twain (relying
        heavily on quotations from Literary Friends and Acquaint-
        ance). Portrait (facing p. 88).

2067   BROOKS, VAN WYCK. The Ordeal of Mark Twain. New York:
        Dutton, 1920. Not indexed. Pp. 16, 17, 19, 27, 31, 33,
        68, 71, 101, 102, 107, 116, 117, 121, 123, 124, 125, 130,
        134, 144, 155, 160, 162, 165, 166, 170, 172, 174, 182-183,
        185, 209-211, 221, 222, 248, 250, 258, 261. Rpt. in part,
        The War of the Critics over William Dean Howells, ed.
        Edwin H. Cady and David L. Frazier (Evanston: Row, Peter-
        son, 1962), pp. 131-134.
            All minor references. A few are anecdotal. Most quote
        things Twain and Howells said to or wrote each other.

2068   JAMES, HENRY. The Letters of Henry James, sel. and ed. Percy
        Lubbock. 2 vols. New York: Scribner's, 1920. Passim
        as indexed.
            In addition to two score letters addressed to Howells,
        a half dozen minor references are made to him, James's
        "constant companion and literary confidant" (I, p. 10).
        In a letter to his brother William, James expresses
        pleasure with the success of a Howells play, adding, "but
        I should have been afraid of the slimness and un-scenic
        quality of the plot" (I, p. 60).

                            308

* LOWELL, JAMES RUSSELL. The Function of the Poet / and Other
Essays, ed. Albert Mordell. Boston and New York: Houghton
Mifflin, 1920. Pp. 146-152. Rpt. from North American
Review, 103 (Oct 1866), 610-613. See item 11.

2069 "Howells, William Dean. Hither and Thither in Germany."
Book Review Digest, 16 (1920), 269. Brief description.

2070 "Howells, William D. Vacation of the Kelwyns." Book Review
Digest, 16 (1920), 269. Non-critical summary.

2071 "Then and Now." New York Times Review of Books, 18 Jan 1920,
p. 24. Editorial.
  Response to Howells' current "Editor's Easy Chair," on
the influence of war on national life and literature.
Takes slight issue with Howells' emphasis on pre-Civil
War New England literature and scores his failure to consider the role of Whitman.

2072 "William D. Howells Is 83 / Author, Ill with Influenza, Passes
His Birthday in Bed." New York Times, 2 Mar 1920, p. 11.
Brief news item.
  Datelined "Savannah, Ga., March 1."

2073 MATTHEWS, BRANDER. "Choosing America's Great Short Stories /
William Dean Howells Compiles an Anthology, as Interesting
for Its Omissions as Its Inclusions, of Famous Modern
Stories." New York Times Review of Books, 18 Apr 1920,
pp. 179, 182. Lead review of The Great Modern American
Stories.
  After questioning some selections and other omissions,
Matthews concludes, no other collection of American short
stories "has gathered into a single volume so many of the
masterpieces of this fascinating form."

2074 "Briefer Mention." Dial, 68 (May 1920), 666. Brief mention
of Hither and Thither in Germany.
  Howells, by ignoring the war and maintaining a tranquil
and orderly style, imparts "an almost antiquarian flavour"
to his book.

2075 "Howells, 'Dean of Novelists,' Dies of Influenza at 84 /
Leading Figure in American Letters for 55 Years--Had
Varied Career." Brooklyn Daily Eagle, 4 o'clock ed.,
11 May 1920, pp. 1-2. News story.
  "He was a constant stimulus to our literature." His
early novels are "the best source for a study of the social
life of New England, and for a notable type the life of

1920

("Howells, 'Dean of Novelists,' Dies of Influenza at 84...")
New York City, from the Civil War to 1890." "Certain
limitations of temperament and a rather narrow and obsti-
nately held theory of what the art of the novelist should
be, did much to restrict the scope of his work and in
later years to turn him from his greatest field of fiction
to that of literary journalism, in which he never had an
equal in this country." [A more definite attempt to
assess Howells' contribution than usually found in the
news stories of his death.]

2076 "Novelist Who Died To-Day." Chicago Daily News, 11 May 1920,
p. 5. Portrait (from the New York Herald service).

2077 "W. D. Howells, Noted Author, Dies Aged 83 / Novelist Succumbs
to Attack of Influenza at Home in New York City / Was a
Prolific Writer." Chicago Daily News, 11 May 1920, p. 1.

2078 "William Dean Howells." Boston Evening Transcript, 11 May
1920, p. 13. Full-column editorial tribute.
"He belongs to the whole of America; and if there was a
local touch upon him, a tang in him of some strong and
native soil, it came from Ohio." "He was not only the re-
corder but the illuminator of our common American life.
Though he scorned the 'romance,' and accepted the name of
'realist,' he never for a moment was merely the realist.
His people moved in the strong light of an almost more
than living characterization. They remain more real than
reality."

2079 "William Dean Howells." Brooklyn Daily Eagle, 4 o'clock ed.,
11 May 1920, p. 6. Editorial.
"Leaving behind him a very large volume of work, of
fiction, of criticism, and of description, there is not a
word of it which he might have wished to blot and there
is constant and enduring evidence of large powers of observation, of a style whose charm is seldom to be matched,
of lambent humor which softens life even while it searches
it, and of high ideals."

2080 "William Dean Howells Dead." Boston Globe, 11 May 1920,
pp. 1, 9. News story.
Coverage of Howells' death, datelined "New York, May 11,"
is followed by full-column review of Howells' life. Portrait (p. 1).

2081   "William D. Howells Dead / End Came This Morning to Famous
        Novelist / In His 83 Years the Dean of American Writers
        Had Published More Than Seventy-One Volumes," Kansas City
        Star, 11 May 1920, p. 19.

2082   "Wm. Dean Howells Dead / Greatest of the Modern American
        Novelists / A Literary Leader for Half a Century / Death
        Follows a Recent Influenza Attack / Burial To Be in Cam-
        bridge, His Former Home / Editor of the Atlantic Monthly
        Many Years / Also Dramatist, Essayist, Critic and Poet /
        Master of Narrative and Literary Style." Boston Evening
        Transcript, Last ed., 11 May 1920, p. 1.

2083   "William Dean Howells, Interpreter of America / His Own
        Country Ever the Background for His Writings--Novelist of
        International Distinction, Poet, Essayist and Dramatist."
        Boston Evening Transcript, 11 May 1920, p. 13. Major five-
        column illustrated coverage.
            For fifty years Howells "was a recognized contributor to
        that class of American writing which measures up to the
        standards of classicism and which has found its way to the
        shelves devoted to 'the best literature.'...In his re-
        lation to the history of the development of the American
        novel, Howells was the Fielding of American literature."
        Howells was the portrayer of American life, the constant
        lookout for new talent, the leader of a new school.
        Anecdote about Howells being mistaken for a minister.

2084   "Dean Howells, Novelist, Dies." San Francisco Examiner,
        12 May 1920, p. 2. Ten-line announcement of death.

2085   "Hold Rites Today for W. D. Howells / Noted Men To Attend
        Services for Novelist Who Died in New York." Washington
        Post, 12 May 1920, p. 7.

2086   "Howells Gone Into Elysium / Famous Author Passes on at a
        Venerable Age / Was Contemporary of Twain, Protege of
        Lowell / Son of the Publisher of a Weekly Newspaper."
        Los Angeles Daily Times, 12 May 1920, p. 2.
            "Exclusive dispatch" datelined New York. Routine survey
        of life and work. Portrait.

2087   "Howells, Noted Author, Dead in N. Y. at 83 / Belonged to
        Literary Coterie in Cambridge Famous in the Seventies /
        Champion of Realism / Devoting Himself at 33 to Novel
        Writing, He Produced Two Every Year." San Francisco
        Chronicle, 12 May 1920, p. 13.
            Survey of life and work. Portrait.

1920

2088   "Last Tribute to Howells / Funeral Services in New York Today--
Ashes To Be Brought to Cambridge." <u>Boston Post</u>, 12 May
1920, pp. 1, 10. Full news story.
Review of Howells' literary career, portrait (p. 1),
and list of "Prominent Works" (p. 10).

2089   No Entry.

2090   "'Life Was Always Full of Literature' / Howells's Single Sen-
tence Characterizes His Career in the World of Letters."
<u>New York Tribune</u>, 12 May 1920, p. 8.
Contains brief quoted reactions to Howells' death by
Hamlin Garland, Owen Wister, Dr. Lyman Abbott, Henry Cabot
Lodge, and E. V. Lucas, the English writer.

2091   "The Passing of Mr. Howells." <u>Chicago Daily News</u>, 12 May 1920,
p. 8. Editorial.
Writer claims to now be the sole survivor of "the smallest
economic society on earth," a society for "the total abolition of money" founded on the concept proposed by Howells
in <u>A Traveler from Altruria</u>.

2092   "Prominent Men Pay Tribute to Memory of Famed Novelist /
William Dean Howells, Noted Man of Letters, Dies at His
Home Near New York." <u>Rocky Mountain News</u>, 12 May 1920,
p. 4.
Associated Press release datelined "New York, May 11."
[Much of the provincial coverage of Howells' death and
funeral was obviously drawn from the same or a similar
source.]

2093   "Simplicity Marks Funeral of Howells." <u>Brooklyn Daily Eagle</u>,
4 o'clock ed., 12 May 1920, p. 2.

2094   "Simplicity Marks Howells's Funeral / Elaborate Service Omitted
at Author's Request / Dr. Percy Stickney Grant Conducts
Ceremony in Church of the Ascension." <u>New York Evening
Post</u>, 12 May 1920, p. 9.

2095   "W. D. Howells Dies Suddenly at 83 / Dominant Figure in
American Letters Succumbs to Attack of Influenza / Funeral
Set for Today / His Fellow Authors Pay Tributes to Great
Realist's Life and Work." <u>New York Times</u>, 12 May 1920,
p. 11.
Two-and-a-half column news story. Portrait by Orlando
Rowland.

2096 "W. D. Howells, Novelist, Dies / Dean of American Fiction
   Writers Passes Away in Sleep at 83 Years / His Ashes Will
   Come to Cambridge." <u>Boston Herald</u>, 12 May 1920, p. 13.

2097 "William Dean Howells." <u>Boston Herald</u>, 12 May 1920, p. 18.
   Editorial. Eulogistic.

2098 "William Dean Howells." <u>New York Sun and New York Herald</u>,
   12 May 1920, p. 10. Editorial.
    Howells was unique; "he had neither predecessors nor
   successors in his field." No other man has recorded his
   era "more broadly or accurately."

2099 "William Dean Howells." <u>New York Times</u>, 12 May 1920, p. 10.
   Editorial.
    "It is his novels that most praise him." "He has ex-
   pressed the comedy and the tragedy of ordinary American
   lives."

2100 "William Dean Howells." <u>New York Tribune</u>, 12 May 1920, p. 12.
   Editorial.
    He was "a victim of a Frankenstein Monster that he
   helped to call into existence"--caught between traditional
   romance and continental realism. "Mr. Howells was bigger
   than his works."

2101 "William Dean Howells." <u>New York World</u>, 12 May 1920, p. 12.
   Editorial.
    Howells may longest be remembered for his work rooted
   in Ohio.

2102 "William Dean Howells." <u>Springfield Daily Republican</u>, 12 May
   1920, p. 10. Editorial.
    Howells' success is attributed to his "integrity of ar-
   tistic purpose."

2103 "William Dean Howells Called into Unknown." Atlanta <u>Constitu-
   tion</u>, 12 May 1920, p. 4.

2104 "Wm. Dean Howells Dies in 84th Year / Demise of Noted American
   Author and Editor Comes Suddenly in Hotel / Funeral This
   Morning / Contracted Influenza Last Winter / Son and
   Daughter at Bedside." <u>New York Sun and New York Herald</u>,
   12 May 1920, p. 11.
    Survey of life and work, quoting from Howells himself.

1920

2105 "William Dean Howells, Novelist, Is Dead at 83 / Dean of
Alumni of the Tribune Staff Succumbs at Apartment Here
After an Attack of Influenza / Began as Reporter at 14 /
Appointed by Lincoln as Consul to Venice in 1861; Books
Were Widely Read." New York Tribune, 12 May 1920, p. 8.
Review of life and work spread over five columns.
Portrait.

2106 "Wm. Dean Howells, Novelist, Is· Dead / Lowell's Successor as
Atlantic Monthly Editor Passes." New Orleans Times-
Picayune, 12 May 1920, p. 5.

2107 "W. Dean Howells, Writer, Dies Here / Patriarch of American
Men of Letters Sleeps to His End, Unknowing / Leaves
Product of Many Years of Virile Thought / Authorship a
Gift / First Work Published in 1860--Was Mark Twain's
Mentor." New York World, 12 May 1920, p. 13.
Survey of life and work plays up the Mark Twain
connection.

2108 "William Dean Howells Wrote of After Life in 'Editor's Easy
Chair' /.../ Touch Upon New and Old Beliefs." New York
Evening Post, 12 May 1920, p. 9.
Reprints August 1919 installment of "Editor's Easy
Chair" with brief, non-critical introduction.

2109 "William Dean Howells's Death Ends Long Literary Career / He
Was America's Most Distinguished Man of Letters and One
of the Last of a Notable Group--His Work as Novelist and
Critic--Realist Who Interpreted Contemporary American
Life." Springfield Daily Republican, 12 May 1920, p. 9.
Substantial evaluation. Portrait.

2110 "Admirers Throng Funeral of William Dean Howells." Rocky
Mountain News, 13 May 1920, p. 24. Brief news story.

2111 "Funeral Services for W. D. Howells Held." San Francisco
Chronicle, 13 May 1920, p. 15. Brief coverage.

2112 "Many Pay Tribute to W. D. Howells / Noted Writers, Editors,
and Publishers Among Those Who Attend Funeral." New York
Sun and New York Herald, 13 May 1920, p. 9.
Lists names of many attending.

2113 "Plain Funeral Service for W. Dean Howells / Noted Persons
Attend, but Dr. Grant Does Not Deliver a Eulogy." New
York World, 13 May 1920, p. 13.

2114   "Simple Rites Mark Howells' Funeral / Exercises at Church of
        the Ascension Symbolic of Novelist's Life and Wishes /
        Plan Memorial Services / Author's Body Will Be Cremated
        and the Ashes Taken to Cambridge, Mass." New York Times,
        13 May 1920, p. 11.

2115   "Simplicity Marks Funeral Services for Wm. D. Howells / Church
        of Ascension Filled with Representatives of Literary, Edu-
        cational, and Artistic Circles; No Eulogy." New York
        Tribune, 13 May 1920, p. 8.
            Lists names of many attending.

2116   "U. C. Tributes to Wm. Dean Howells." San Francisco Examiner,
        13 May 1920, p. 8. Brief news story.
            Memorial services for Howells were held at the Univer-
        sity of California Faculty Club. William Morris Hart is
        quoted.

2117   BRISBANE, ARTHUR. "Today." San Francisco Examiner, 14 May
        1920, p. 22. Brief editorial mention.
            "To the day of his death he was a democrat, sympathizing
        with those that had need of sympathy."

2118   "The Late W. D. Howells." Athenaeum, No. 4698 (14 May 1920),
        634. Tribute.
            "Howells was, from the beginning of his career, a con-
        vinced believer in an American national literature; and
        his writings, facile, polished, and of an equable excel-
        lence, amounting to little less than a hundred volumes,
        are the expression of his conviction." As a critic he
        was suave rather than penetrating.

2119   "William Dean Howells." Washington Post, 14 May 1920, p. 6.
        Editorial.
            "The mild realism which he taught and practiced was very
        different from the continental variety. He did not fall
        under the sway of the French naturalistic school." Al-
        though he is currently out of fashion, readers will return
        to him.

2120   "Books in Brief." Nation, 110 (15 May 1920), 661. Brief re-
        view of Hither and Thither in Germany.
            "The deftest hand that ever drove an American pen has
        here cut away the meandering narrative" of Their Silver
        Wedding Journey and retained descriptive passages that
        are "as easy as an eagle, as flexible as a serpent, as
        natural and clear as a brook going about its business!"

1920

2121   "The Listener." Boston Evening Transcript, 15 May 1920,
         Part 2, p. 6. Tribute.
            In seeing through people, Howells "saw through whatever
         of evil there was in them, and beheld the good on the
         other side of it. That he could see through both the
         good and the evil to the other side of both of them, as
         Nietzsche assumed to do, he never for a moment pretended."
         The reference to Howells and James in Gilbert's song in
         "Patience" is not to the authors but to the London depart-
         ment store of Messrs. Howells & James. Two of Howells'
         poems, "Song the Oriole Sings" and "Thanksgiving," are
         reprinted.

2122   VAN DOREN, CARL. "William Dean Howells / The Last of America's
         Three Greatest Literary Figures in the Past Generation."
         New York Evening Post, 15 May 1920, III, pp. 1, 13. Fea-
         ture article.
            "In the sustained exhibition of certain great qualities--
         clearness, compression, verbal exactness, and unforced and
         seemingly unconscious felicity of phrasing--he is, in my
         belief, without his peer in the English writing world."
         Van Doren deals specifically with various facets of
         Howells' contribution. Portrait (p. 1).

2123   GILMAN, LAWRENCE. "Dean of American Letters / A Tribute from
         One Who Worked with Him." New York Times Review of Books,
         16 May 1920, pp. 254-255. Eulogistic piece.
            "William Dean Howells is dead, and there passes America's
         most eminent man of letters and one of the wisest, gentlest,
         most lovable of men." Large three-column portrait sketch
         from photograph.

2124   "Howells and James." New York World, 16 May 1920, Ed. Sec.,
         p. 2. Editorial.
            Howells will endure because he was "an artist who re-
         spected his material," but "Henry James was the more
         original, the profounder artist, of the two."

2125   "The Survival of Howells." New York Tribune, 16 May 1920,
         II, p. 1. Editorial.
            Because Howells was the best literary workman of his
         time and because he, more than any other, "is the fic-
         tional social historian of the second half of the nine-
         teenth century," his work will endure.

2126 "William Dean Howells." Atlanta Constitution, 16 May 1920,
p. 10. Editorial.
Focuses on his eagerness to help young writers develop.

2127 "William Dean Howells." Kansas City Star, 16 May 1920, Sec.
C, p. 30. Editorial.
"As a novelist, Howells did one supreme thing. He
placed realism in America upon a sure footing. He reported American life faithfully." As further distinctions,
"he made good women interesting," and he told stories without drawing attention to his "manner of expression."

2128 "Howells Estate $165,000 / Will Gives $1,000 and Watch Bought
in 1863 to Grandson." New York Times, 19 May 1920, p. 23.
News item.

2129 "William Dean Howells." Outlook, 125 (19 May 1920), 109–110.
Tribute. Rpt. in part, "William Dean Howells," Review of
Reviews, 61 (Jun 1920), 644.
"He interpreted life as he saw it, but he well knew
that fancy, idealism, and romance itself may be a part of
reality. Aridity was not a part of realism as he prac-
ticed it."

2130 [GARLAND, HAMLIN?] "From Venice as Far as Belmont." Boston
Evening Transcript, 22 May 1920, III, p. 5. Tribute.
An appreciative and reminiscent review of an acquaintance. "Of his essential democracy there is no more question than of his scholarship. He earned all his rewards
and merited all his honors." Two photographs of his study
and a pen-and-ink sketch of "Red Top," the house Howells
built on Somerset Street, Belmont.

2131 GARLAND, HAMLIN. "William Dean Howells' Boston / A Posthumous
Pilgrimage." Boston Evening Transcript, 22 May 1920, III,
p. 4. Feature.
A substantial article that focuses more directly on Garland's reminiscent appreciation of Howells than it does
on the five Boston houses (pictured) in which Howells
lived. A perceptive section is subheaded "Howells' Struggles with His Boston."

2132 RATCLIFFE, S. K. "William Dean Howells." New Statesman, 15
(22 May 1920), 195–196. Bio-critical survey and tribute.
The fact that Howells has never had a regular publisher
in England "is a staggering comment on the intellectual
relations of England and America."

1920

2133   "William Dean Howells." Nation, 110 (22 May 1920), 673.
        Tribute.
            "As an author Mr. Howells was so prolific during the
        sixty years between his earliest book and his latest that
        he amounts almost to a library in himself. As an editor
        and critic he was so influential that he amounts almost
        to an academy."

2134   "Mr. Howells." Literary Digest, 65 (29 May 1920), 34-35.
        Note.
            Surveys newspaper response to the death of Howells,
        noting that "his work will now come into a period of
        severer testing, since it is recognized that he painted
        an age that has passed." Two portraits.

2135   ERSKINE, JOHN. "William Dean Howells." Bookman (New York),
        51 (Jun 1920), 385-389. Critical assessment. Rpt. in
        part, The War of the Critics over William Dean Howells,
        ed. Edwin H. Cady and David L. Frazier (Evanston: Row,
        Peterson, 1962), pp. 135-137.
            Postponing judgment of Howells' place in literature,
        Erskine notes the basic complexity of his work, especially
        as it relates to the American fusion of realism and ro-
        mance. In his total work, Howells became, "as he wished
        to be in each of his novels, a faithful mirror of his time
        and place."

2136   "The Gossip Shop." Bookman (New York), 51 (Jun 1920), p. 512.
        Death notice.

2137   "William Dean Howells." Review of Reviews, 61 (Jun 1920),
            562. Front piece portrait with biographical caption.
            "He was a critic of marked power and acumen, and as a
        writer of essays and travel sketches a worthy successor
        of Irving."

   *   "William Dean Howells." Review of Reviews, 61 (Jun 1920),
            644. Rpt. from Outlook, 125 (19 May 1920), 109-110, and
        from Bookman (New York), 49 (Jul 1919), 549-554. See
        items 2129 and 2063.

2138   "W. D. Howells, Printer, Journalist, Poet, Novelist." Liter-
        ary Digest, 65 (12 Jun 1920), 53-54, 57. Short note.
            Anecdotal, biographical detail drawn from Howells' own
        work and from newspaper accounts. Photograph of Howells
        seated on ground, leaning against a tree (p. 53).

2139   "Mr. Howells in England." Literary Digest, 65 (19 Jun 1920),
        37. Note.
        "Unlike Henry James, Mr. Howells can not be called an
        'internationalist.'" This judgment is elicited from En-
        glish sources.

2140   DRAKE, FRANK C. "William Dean Howells Helped This Young Man
        Write a Play." Literary Digest, 65 (19 Jun 1920), 56, 58.
        Note.
        Summary introduction and extensive quotation from an
        article which appeared in the New York World (not seen)
        relating to Howells' guidance in the dramatization of A
        Hazard of New Fortunes.

2141   "Dean of American Literature / The Safe and Sane Genius of
        William Dean Howells." Current Opinion, 69 (Jul 1920),
        93-96. Note.
        Impressions on the occasion of Howells' death. "Howells
        is an age past and gone forever. He was, as it were, the
        last and most perfect flower of American 'realism.'"
        Portrait (p. 95).

2142   FRÉCHETTE, ANNIE HOWELLS. "William Dean Howells." Canadian
        Bookman, 2 (Jul 1920), 9-12. Note.
        A personal and essentially non-literary reminiscence by
        Howells' sister.

2143   "The Gossip Shop." Bookman (New York), 51 (Jul 1920), 601-602.
        Announcement of The Great Modern American Stories (an
        anthology prepared by Howells).
        Non-critical. It was delayed "due to the printing
        plates being side-tracked between Albany and New York."

2144   LAPPIN, HENRY A. "The Passing of W. D. Howells." Catholic
        World, 111 (Jul 1920), 445-453. Bio-critical comment.
        Essentially an apology for Howells in the context of
        the new bold temper in literature. "The Rise of Silas
        Lapham...is surely Howells' finest novel" (p. 450).

2145   MARTIN, EDWARD S. "W. D. Howells." Harper's, 141 (Jul 1920),
        265-266. Tribute.
        We have not lost Mr. Howells. "He has merely stopped
        work. We have what he did in wonderful measure." Full-
        page portrait (facing p. 265).

1920

2146   PHELPS, WILLIAM LYON. "An Appreciation." North American Re-
        view, 212 (Jul 1920), 17-20. Incorporated in Howells,
        James, Bryant and Other Essays (New York: Macmillan,
        1924), pp. 156-180.
            "The four pillars on which [Howells'] fame securely rests
        are A Modern Instance, The Rise of Silas Lapham, Indian
        Summer, and The Kentons."

2147   TOWNE, CHARLES HANSON. "The Kindly Howells." Touchstone, 7
        (Jul 1920), 280-282. Tribute.
            Reminiscence of a personal conversation and the encourage-
        ment Howells gave to a young writer. "'Be faithful to the
        best that is in you,' he said to me, ' and you will have
        nothing to fear.'"

2148   "William Dean Howells / March 1, 1837-May 11, 1920." North
        American Review, 212 (Jul 1920), 1-16. Rpt. from Harper's
        Weekly, 56 (9 Mar 1912), II, pp. 27-34. See item 1877.
            A list of Howells' contributions to the North American
        Review and a portrait (front piece) are added.

2149   TARKINGTON, BOOTH. "Mr. Howells." Harper's, 141 (Aug 1920),
        346-350. Tribute. Rpt. with revisions and additions as
        Introd., The Rise of Silas Lapham, Centenary ed. (Boston:
        Houghton Mifflin, 1937), pp. v-xv; and Riverside Litera-
        ture Series of the same title (Boston: Houghton Mifflin,
        [c. 1937]), pp. xiii-xxi.
            Howells "revolutionized his country's best taste in
        'creative literature'; he destroyed the tawdry gew-gawed
        idols and lifted up in their place honest standards not
        fringed with tinsel" (p. 349). Although the names of
        Howells and James are popularly linked, the artists stand
        apart. Howells and his "perfect English" are less subject
        to imitation than is James. Positioned between James and
        Twain, Howells united them with himself into "a noble tri-
        umvirate." Tarkington notes his early contacts with
        Howells--at a dinner, and as local courier during the Mid-
        western lecture tour.

2150   "Books in Brief." Nation, 111 (28 Aug 1920), 251. Brief re-
        view of The Great Modern American Stories.
            "If editing can be as nearly classical as writing, this
        collection may have to be called a classic."

2151   QUINN, ARTHUR HOBSON. "The Art of William Dean Howells."
        Century, 100 (Sep 1920), 675-681. Critical estimate.
            Subtitled, "A study of the literary characteristics of
        the man who for many years was generally acknowledged as

(QUINN, ARTHUR HOBSON)
the leader of American letters." Quinn concludes, "It
was not satire alone...that secured Howells his audience.
It was his really deep insight into certain phases of
human character, his careful study of human emotions, of
human purposes and motives, his kindly, tolerant attitude
toward mankind, the probability of his events and characters, and the art with which his plot, slight as it often
is, works out logically and inevitably to the destined
end." Full-page portrait (p. [674]).

2152   ROOD, HENRY. "William Dean Howells / Some Notes of a Literary Acquaintance." Ladies' Home Journal, 37 (Sep 1920),
42, 154, 157. Informal essay.
An abundance of anecdotal reminiscence, with a substantial review of Howells as a literary business man, and a
judgment: "From the very first Mr. Howells stood for
something--something far above money, something far more
precious than mere popularity... --literary tradition,
literary integrity, literary art." Portrait (p. 42).

2153   COOKE, DELMAR GROSS. "The Humanity of William Dean Howells."
Texas Review, 6 (Oct 1920), 6-25. Critical estimate.
"He will inevitably be established in the critical
consciousness as a literary leader, as a social historian,
and as an unrivalled technician"--as one who pointed direction during a period of artistic evolution. But he
belongs to the past. His unique importance relates to
"the humanity of his motives."

2154   "Fiction." A. L. A. Booklist, 17 (Oct 1920), 33. Very brief
review of The Great Modern American Stories.
"A fascinating collection" with a "delightful introduction." One finds here the stories he looks for.

2155   PHELPS, WILLIAM LYON. "William Dean Howells." Yale Review,
n.s. 10 (Oct 1920), 99-109. Informal essay. Incorporated
in Howells, James, Bryant, and Other Essays (New York:
Macmillan, 1924), pp. 156-180.
"It is as a novelist that Howells will be remembered.
He set up a department-store of literature, where the
visitor could buy anything from a song to a sermon; but
much of the stock is sure to remain on the shelves. I
have never met anybody who could quote a line of his
poetry; and his essays in literary criticism are perish-
able freight" (p. 100).

1920

2156   BLACK, ALEXANDER. "A Suppressed Howells Novel." <u>New York Times Book Review and Magazine</u>, 3 Oct 1920, p. 1. Major review of <u>The Vacation of the Kelwyns</u>.
    It is "a delightful example of Mr. Howells's method and (every creation being a form of confession) a vivid revelation of the man himself." One "cannot read of the Kelwyns without feeling that there is no other right way in which they could be described." Howells was "as native as Whitman." Although his wide sympathies extended beyond national boundaries, "at his desk he was always an American."

2157   ROURKE, CONSTANCE MAYFIELD. "The American Short Story." <u>Freeman</u>, 2 (6 Oct 1920), 91. Full review of <u>The Great Modern American Stories</u>.
    "This book is more than an assemblage; it is a unity; and the stories, many of them familiar, gain immensely by their aggregation." The anthology "has something of the perfection of a classic; it may indeed be the summary of a period."

2158   "The Book Table." <u>Outlook</u>, 126 (20 Oct 1920), 333-334. Brief notice of <u>The Vacation of the Kelwyns</u>.
    "A finely wrought out presentation of American life and character."

2159   VAN DOREN, CARL. "Howells His Own Censor." <u>New York Evening Post Literary Review</u>, 23 Oct 1920, p. 3. Full review of <u>The Vacation of the Kelwyns</u>.
    The Kelwyns are "victims of the subtlety of life." The novel does not hold together and does not make enough of the basic situation. "Something or other obscures [Howells'] interpretation of the problem." Van Doren contrasts this novel with the sharpness of Howells' earlier <u>Private Theatricals</u>.

2160   "Briefer Mention." <u>Dial</u>, 69 (Nov 1920), 547. Very brief mention of <u>The Great Modern American Stories</u>.
    Catholicity of selection.

2161   No Entry

2162   "New Books." <u>Catholic World</u>, 122 (Nov 1920), 270-271. Review of <u>The Great Modern American Stories</u>.
    "Mr. Howells' omissions are indeed decidedly more striking than his selections." The publishers' "blurb" claiming that the volume will become standard "illustrates the triumph of hope over critical judgment."

2163   V[AN] D[OREN], C[ARL]. "An Elder America." <u>Nation</u>, 111
        (3 Nov 1920), 510-511. Review of <u>The Vacation of the</u>
        <u>Kelwyns</u> (and Edith Wharton's <u>The Age of Innocence</u>).
          Howells' novel "is more than farce and timid hesitancy";
        it is a document upon the pastoral seventies.

2164   "Fiction." <u>A. L. A. Booklist</u>, 17 (Dec 1920), 116. Very brief
        review of <u>The Vacation of the Kelwyns</u>.
          "New England rural life of the eighteen-seventies por-
        trayed with a quiet fidelity will lure those who appreci-
        ate finished artistry rather than those who want plot
        thrills. For complete collections."

2165   BOYNTON, H. W. "Book Reviews / New England Revisited."
        <u>Weekly Review</u>, 3 (1 Dec 1920), pp. 534-535. Full review
        of <u>The Vacation of the Kelwyns</u>.
          "The whole affair [the mating of the Kelwyn niece] has
        the effect, at least, of something altogether casual and
        artless. The action is no more dramatic than Rollo's ad-
        venture with the wood-pile." Only the "faultless voice"
        of Howells could have told the story so well.

2166   "New Novels / <u>The Vacation of the Kelwyns</u>." <u>Times Literary</u>
        <u>Supplement</u>, 9 Dec 1920, p. 829. Full review.
          "It is really interesting to me that a novelist of this
        true and distinguished talent, at the end of the long span
        of his career, had still the freshness and the good faith
        to tell a simple story with simplicity."

Index to Identified Authors

(by item number)